A TEXT BOOK OF

PROJECT MANAGEMENT AND ENGINEERING ECONOMICS

For
SEMESTER – II
THIRD YEAR DEGREE COURSE IN CIVIL ENGINEERING

As Per New Revised Syllabus of Savitribai Phule Pune University

(2012 Pattern)

Mrs. S. V. PATASKAR
M. E. (Civil)
Head, Deptt. of Civil Engineering
D. Y. Patil College of Engineering
Akurdi, Pune 44

Prof. N. S. MUJUMDAR
M.E. (Civil)
Director, N.M.V. Polytechnic and NMIT Engineering College,
Talegoan Dabhade
Formerly Head of Civil Engineering Department,
Government College of Engineering,
Aurangabad

Project Mgt. and Engg. Eco. (TE Civil Sem - II, PU) ISBN 978-93-5164-352-4
First Edition : November 2014
© **Authors**

The text of this publication, or any part thereof, should not be reproduced or transmitted in any form or stored in any computer storage system or device for distribution including photocopy, recording, taping or information retrieval system or reproduced on any disc, tape, perforated media or other information storage device etc., without the written permission of Authors with whom the rights are reserved. Breach of this condition is liable for legal action.

Every effort has been made to avoid errors or omissions in this publication. In spite of this, errors may have crept in. Any mistake, error or discrepancy so noted and shall be brought to our notice shall be taken care of in the next edition. It is notified that neither the publisher nor the authors or seller shall be responsible for any damage or loss of action to any one, of any kind, in any manner, therefrom.

Published By :
NIRALI PRAKASHAN
Abhyudaya Pragati, 1312, Shivaji Nagar,
Off J.M. Road, PUNE – 411005
Tel - (020) 25512336/37/39, Fax - (020) 25511379
Email : niralipune@pragationline.com

Printed By :
Repro India Ltd.,
Mumbai.

DISTRIBUTION CENTRES
PUNE

Nirali Prakashan
119, Budhwar Peth, Jogeshwari Mandir Lane
Pune 411002, Maharashtra
Tel : (020) 2445 2044, 66022708, Fax : (020) 2445 1538
Email : bookorder@pragationline.com

Nirali Prakashan
S. No. 28/25, Dhyari,
Near Pari Company, Pune 411041
Tel : (022) 24690204 Fax : (020) 24690316
Email : dhyari@pragationline.com
bookorder@pragationline.com

MUMBAI
Nirali Prakashan
385, S.V.P. Road, Rasdhara Co-op. Hsg. Society Ltd.,
Girgaum, Mumbai 400004, Maharashtra
Tel : (022) 2385 6339 / 2386 9976, Fax : (022) 2386 9976
Email : niralimumbai@pragationline.com

DISTRIBUTION BRANCHES

NAGPUR
Pratibha Book Distributors
Above Maratha Mandir, Shop No. 3, First Floor,
Rani Jhanshi Square, Sitabuldi, Nagpur 440012,
Maharashtra, Tel : (0712) 254 7129

JALGAON
Nirali Prakashan
34, V. V. Golani Market, Navi Peth, Jalgaon 425001,
Maharashtra, Tel : (0257) 222 0395
Mob : 94234 91860

BENGALURU
Pragati Book House
House No. 1, Sanjeevappa Lane, Avenue Road Cross,
Opp. Rice Church, Bengaluru – 560002.
Tel : (080) 64513344, 64513355,
Mob : 9880582331, 9845021552
Email:bharatsavla@yahoo.com

KOLHAPUR
Nirali Prakashan
New Mahadvar Road,
Kedar Plaza, 1st Floor Opp. IDBI Bank
Kolhapur 416 012, Maharashtra. Mob : 9855046155

CHENNAI
Pragati Books
9/1, Montieth Road, Behind Taas Mahal, Egmore,
Chennai 600008 Tamil Nadu, Tel : (044) 6518 3535,
Mob : 94440 01782 / 98450 21552 / 98805 82331, Email : bharatsavla@yahoo.com

RETAIL OUTLETS
PUNE

Pragati Book Centre
157, Budhwar Peth, Opp. Ratan Talkies,
Pune 411002, Maharashtra
Tel : (020) 2445 8887 / 6602 2707, Fax : (020) 2445 8887

Pragati Book Centre
676/B, Budhwar Peth, Opp. Jogeshwari Mandir,
Pune 411002, Maharashtra
Tel : (020) 6601 7784 / 6602 0855

Pragati Book Centre
Amber Chamber, 28/A, Budhwar Peth,
Appa Balwant Chowk, Pune : 411002, Maharashtra,
Tel : (020) 20240335 / 66281669
Email : pbcpune@pragationline.com

PBC Book Sellers and Stationers
152, Budhwar Peth, Pune 411002, Maharashtra
Tel : (020) 2445 2254 / 6609 2463

MUMBAI
Pragati Book Corner
Indira Niwas, 111 - A, Bhavani Shankar Road, Dadar (W), Mumbai 400028, Maharashtra
Tel : (022) 2422 3526 / 6662 5254, Email : pbcmumbai@pragationline.com

www.pragationline.com info@pragationline.com

PREFACE

We are very glad to present you the book on **'Project Management and Engineering Economics'** which is strictly written as per the New Revised Syllabus of Savitribai Phule Pune University for the Students of Third Year Degree Course in Civil Engineering (2012) Pattern.

With the tremendous growth of construction sector, more and more manpower is required in all branches of Civil Engineering. Truly speaking, large population is a boon to India and not a curse. But one has to remember that we have to take efforts to mould technicians and engineers according to our requirement. More and more practical expertise should be provided to aspiring engineers so that they can stand in large competitions. Management has become a key word which controls the cost, time and monitors quality. With the uniqueness of construction field, study of Project Management and related techniques are very important to Civil Engineers.

At the same time, basics of Economics are very important to learn. This will help the students to understand how the money flows, what are the effects of one organisation on other, what are the relations between crude oil process and value of rupee, what is balance sheet, what is working capital, what is depreciation, what is annuity, etc. Economics is a branch of science which is very much attached to our day to life. It is a very interesting subject and we appreciate University of Pune to include it alongwith Project Management.

We have made an effort to include the basics of **Project Management and Engineering Economics** in this single book. Our primary aim is to develop and present the subject matter in concise and easily understandable manner to meet the requirements.

We express our sincere thanks to Shri. Dineshbhai Furia, Shri. Jigneshbhai Furia and Shri M. P. Munde and Staff of Nirali Prakashan Namely Mrs. Deepa Lachake, Mrs. Neeta Kulkarni, Mrs. Ulka Chavan, Mrs. Roshan Khan for publishing this book in time. We expect that the book will be well received by the students and teachers of Civil Engineering.

Suggestions and constructive criticism so also errors, omissions or misprints, if any brought to the notice of the authors will be thankfully acknowledged and shall be incorporated in the forthcoming editions.

Pune

Prof. Mrs. S.V. Pataskar
(svpataskar@gmail.com)
Prof. N.S. Mujumdar

SYLLABUS

Unit I : Introduction to Project Management (8 Hours)

Importance, objectives and functions of management, Principles of Management, Categories of project, Project Failure, Project life cycle Concept and Cost Components, Project Management Book of Knowledge {PMBOK}, Different Domain Areas, Project management Institute and Certified Project Management Professionals (PMP) Importance of organizational Structure in Management- Authority / Responsibility Relation.

Unit II : Project Planning and Scheduling (8 Hours)

WBS – Work Breakdown Structure, Gantt/Bar chart and its limitations Network Planning, Network Analysis , CPM Activity on Arrow (A.O.A.), Critical path and type of floats ,
Precedence network analysis (A.O.N.) P. E. R.

Unit III : Project Monitoring and Control (8 Hours)

Resource Allocation – Resource Smoothening and levelling, Network Crashing, Time – Cost, Resource optimization, Project Monitoring Methods, Updating and Earned Value Analysis Introduction to use of Project Management Softwares, MS Project / Primavera, Case study on housing project scheduling for a small project with minimum 25 activities.

Unit IV : Project Economics (8 Hours)

Introduction to project economics - Definition, principles, Importance in construction Industry, Difference between Cost, Value, Price , Rent, Simple and compound interest, Profit, Annuities, Demand, Demand schedule, law of demand, demand curve, elasticity of demand, supply, supply schedule, supply curve, elasticity of supply Equilibrium, Equilibrium price, Equilibrium amount, factors affecting price determination. Law of Diminishing Marginal Utility, Law of substitution, Concept of Cost of Capital, Time value of money, Sources of Project Finances – concepts of Debt Capital and Equity Capital. Types of Capital – Fixed and working. Equity shares and debenture capital.

Unit V : Project Resources and Safety Aspects (8 hours)

Objectives of Materials management – Primary and secondary Material Procurement Procedures - material requirement- raising of indents, receipts, Inspection, storage, delivery, record keeping – Use of Excel sheets, ERP software ,Inventory control- ABC analysis, EOQ, Introduction to Equipment Management – Fleet Management, productivity studies, Equipment down time, sizing - matching, Construction Safety norms – measures and precautions, implementation of safety programs

Unit VI - Project Appraisal (8 hours)

Types of Appraisals such as political, social, environmental, techno - legal, financial and Economical, Criteria for project selection - benefit - cost analysis, NPV, IRR, Pay-back period, Break Even analysis [Fundamental and Application Component, Study of Project Feasibility report and Detailed Project Report (DPR), Role of Project Management Consultants – pre tender and Post tender.

CONTENTS

Unit 1 : Introduction to Project Management		**1.1-1.34**
1.1	Management	1.1
1.2	Definition of Management	1.2
1.3	Importance of Management	1.3
1.4	Characteristics of Management	1.3
1.5	Functions of Management	1.4
1.6	Managerial Objectives	1.6
1.7	Evaluation of Scientific Management	1.7
	1.7.1 Scientific Management	1.7
	1.7.2 Basic Approach of Scientific Management	1.8
1.8	Definition of Project	1.11
	1.8.1 Project Management (PMBOK)	1.12
1.9	Categories of Projects	1.13
	1.9.1 Introduction	1.13
	1.9.2 Project Categories	1.14
1.10	Stages in Project	1.14
1.11	Project Life Cycle	1.16
	1.11.1 Advantages of Project Life Cycle	1.18
	1.11.2 Project Life Cycle Phases	1.18
1.12	Organisation	1.19
	1.12.1 Importance of Organisation	1.19
	1.12.2 Characteristics of Organisation	1.20
	1.12.3 Principles of Organisation	1.20
	1.12.4 Key General Management Skills	1.21
1.13	Authority	1.22
	1.13.1 Delegation of Authority	1.23
1.14	Types of Organisation	1.24
1.15	Matrix Structure	1.29
1.16	Project Management Institutes	1.30
•	**Important Points**	**1.32**
•	**Questions**	**1.33**
Unit 2 : Project Planning and Scheduling		**2.1-2.68**
2.1	Introduction	2.1
2.2	Historical Review of Management Techniques	2.1
2.3	Project and Its Objectives	2.3
2.4	Project Planning	2.4
2.5	Scheduling	2.5
2.6	Controlling	2.5
	2.6.1 Decision Making – A Key in Project Management	2.6
2.7	Methods of Planning	2.7

2.8	Work Breakdown Structure	2.7
	2.8.1 Advantages of Work Breakdown Structure	2.9
2.9	Bar Chart	2.9
	2.9.1 Salient Features of Bar Chart	2.11
	2.9.2 Remedial Measures for Removal of Shortcomings of Bar Chart	2.12
	2.9.3 Comparison of Project Progress with the Schedule and Review	2.13
	2.9.4 Inter-Relationship of Activities	2.15
2.10	Introduction to Network	2.16
	2.10.1 Objectives of Network Planning and Scheduling	2.17
	2.10.2 Development of Network from Bar Chart	2.17
	2.10.3 Basics of Network	2.18
	2.10.4 Types of Network	2.18
	2.10.5 Characteristics of Projects Amenable to Network Planning	2.19
2.11	Types of CPM Network	2.20
	2.11.1 CPM Method of Project Planning	2.20
2.12	Terminology in Network	2.22
	2.12.1 Different Types of Activities and Their Inter-Relationship	2.23
2.13	Framing Network for a Project	2.27
	2.13.1 Rules for Framing Network	2.28
	2.13.2 Shapes of Network Diagram	2.31
	2.13.3 Numbering of Events	2.31
2.14	Time Estimates	2.34
	2.14.1 Event Times	2.35
	2.14.2 Forward Pass	2.35
	2.14.3 Backward Pass	2.36
	2.14.4 Activity Times	2.36
	2.14.5 Floats	2.39
2.15	PERT	2.50
	2.15.1 Programme Evaluation and Review Technique (PERT)	2.50
	2.15.2 Extension of PERT	2.53
	2.15.3 Successful Application of PERT	2.53
	2.15.4 Comparison of CPM And PERT	2.56
•	**Important Questions**	**2.57**
•	**Questions**	**2.57**
Unit 3 : Project Monitoring And Control		**3.1 - 3.40**
3.1	Introduction	3.1
3.2	Project Cost	3.2
	3.2.1 Introduction	3.2
	3.2.2 Direct Cost	3.2

		3.2.3 Indirect Cost	3.3
3.3	Cost Slope for Direct Cost		3.4
3.4	Crashing of Network for Cost Optimisation		3.5
3.5	Updating		3.14
		3.5.1 Introduction	3.14
		3.5.2 Necessity of Updating	3.14
		3.5.3 When to Do Updating	3.15
		3.5.4 Procedure of Updating	3.16
3.6	Frequency and the Time of Updating		3.19
3.7	Resource Allocation		3.20
		3.7.1 Representing the Resources	3.21
		3.7.2 Histogram	3.22
		3.7.3 Resources Smoothening	3.24
		3.7.4 Resource Levelling	3.26
3.8	Cost Control		3.26
		3.8.1 Purposes of Cost Control	3.27
		3.8.2 Stages at Which Cost Control is Effected	3.27
		3.8.3 Classification of Cost Control System	3.27
3.9	Project Time Control		3.28
3.10	Line of Balance Technique		3.29
		3.10.1 How to Draw LOB?	3.29
		3.10.2 Advantages of LOB Technique	3.31
		3.10.3 Limitations of LOB Technique	3.31
•	**Important Points**		**3.31**
•	**Questions**		**3.31**
Unit 4 : Project Economics			**4.1-4.40**
4.1	Introduction		4.1
4.2	Importance of Economy in Construction Industry		4.1
4.3	India : Construction Industry and Economy		4.3
4.4	Definition of Economics		4.4
4.5	Types of Economy		4.4
4.6	Laws of Economics		4.4
4.7	Definitions of Some Importance Terms		4.5
		4.7.1 Cost and Price	4.6
4.8	Law of Diminishing Utility		4.6
4.9	Law of Substitution		4.8
4.10	Demand and Supply		4.9
4.11	Determination of Market Price		4.11
4.12	Types of Demand		4.12

4.13	Demand Curve	4.13
	4.13.1 Law of Demand	4.14
4.14	Supply Curve	4.14
	4.14.1 Law of Supply	4.14
	4.14.2 Equilibrium Price	4.15
4.15	Elasticity of Supply	4.16
4.16	Price Determination	4.17
4.17	Indifference Curve Analysis	4.20
4.18	Price Line or Budget Line	4.22
4.19	Consumers Equilibrium or Maximum Satisfaction	4.23
4.20	Income Effect	4.24
4.21	Substitution Effect	4.25
4.22	Elasticity of Demand	4.26
4.23	Types of Elasticity	4.28
4.24	Cost of Capital	4.31
4.25	Time Value of Money	4.32
	4.25.1 Interest	4.32
4.26	Sources of Project Finance	4.34
	4.26.1 Equity Finance	4.34
	4.26.2 Debt Finance	4.34
	4.26.3 Advantages of Debt Compared To Equity	4.35
	4.26.4 Disadvantages of Debt Compared To Equity	4.35
	4.26.5 Equity Shares	4.36
	4.26.6 Debenture Capital	4.37
•	**Important Points**	**4.37**
•	**Questions**	**4.37**
•	**University Questions**	**4.38**
Unit 5 : Project Resources and Safety Aspects		**5.1-5.98**
5.1	Introduction	5.1
	5.1.1 Materials Management	5.1
	5.1.2 Objectives	5.2
5.2	Functions of Material Manager	5.3
	5.2.1 Qualities of a Material Manager	5.3
5.3	Material Planning and Programming	5.4
	5.3.1 Functions in Material Management	5.5
	5.3.2 Purchasing	5.5
	5.3.3 Method of Purchasing	5.7
	5.3.4 Procurement of Materials	5.7
	5.3.5 Material Handling and Control	5.8

5.4	Functions of Material Manager	5.10
	5.4.1 Economical Uses of Materials	5.11
5.5	Requirement of Construction Materials and Phasing	5.11
	5.5.1 Some Important Points Related to Material Management	5.12
	5.5.2 Indent, Storing of Material and Issue	5.13
	5.5.3 Organisation of Purchase Department	5.16
5.6	Inventory	5.18
5.7	Inventory Management	5.19
	5.7.1 The Objectives of Inventory Control	5.20
	5.7.2 Steps in Inventory Control	5.22
5.8	Economical Order Quantity	5.21
	5.8.1 Inventory Costs (Indirect Cost)	5.21
5.9	Safety Stock	5.32
5.10	Lead Time	5.32
	5.10.1 Parts of Lead Time	5.33
5.11	Inventory Models	5.34
	5.11.1 Introduction	5.34
	5.11.2 Willson's Model	5.34
	5.11.3 Replenishment Model	5.35
	5.11.4 Two Bin Model	5.36
5.12	ABC Analysis	5.37
5.13	Avoiding Misuse and Wastage	5.46
5.14	Fleet Management	5.47
	5.14.1 Introduction	5.47
	5.14.2 Aspects of Fleet Management	5.47
5.15	Productivity Studies	5.55
	5.15.1 Types of Productivity	5.56
	5.15.2 Overall Equipment Effectiveness (OEE)	5.57
5.16	Down Time	5.58
5.17	Selection of Equipments	5.59
5.18	Sizing and Matching of Equipment	5.61
5.19	Safety Consciousness	5.62
5.20	Accidents	5.63
	5.20.1 Accident Control	5.63
	5.20.2 Conceptions Regarding Accident	5.63
	5.20.3 Basic Factors for Occurrence Of Accidents	5.64
	5.20.4 Causes of Accidents	5.64
	5.20.5 Types Of Accidents	5.65

5.21 Economic Aspects of Accidents	5.65
5.21.1 Costs Associated with Accidents	5.65
5.21.2 Direct Costs of an Accidents	5.66
5.21.3 Indirect Costs of an Accidents	5.66
5.22 Nature and Extent of Accidents	5.66
5.23 Causes and Precautions	5.67
5.24 Accident Proneness	5.69
5.25 Prevention of Accident	5.70
5.26 Importance of Safety Training On Construction Site	5.71
5.27 Safety Programme	5.72
5.27.1 Guidelines Related to Building Construction	5.72
5.27.2 The Principle Hazards	5.73
5.27.3 Competent Person	5.75
5.27.4 Safe Working Conditions	5.75
5.27.5 Scaffolding	5.76
5.27.6 Inspections and Maintenance Of Scaffolds	5.76
5.27.7 Excavations	5.77
5.27.8 Other Precautions	5.78
5.27.9 Lifting Appliances and Lifting Gear	5.78
5.27.10 Roof Work and Working at Heights	5.79
5.27.11 Work Above Ground	5.80
5.27.12 Inspection and Maintenance	5.82
5.27.13 Moveable Access Equipment	5.82
5.27.14 Ladders	5.83
5.28 Work Below Ground	5.84
5.29 Construction of Tunnels	5.85
5.30 Safety Programme For a National Highway Project	5.85
5.31 Management of The Demolition Process	5.86
5.31.1 Pre-Demolition Survey	5.86
5.32 Personal Protective Equipments	5.86
5.32.1 Categories Of PPE	5.88
5.32.2 PPE For Head Protection	5.88
5.32.3 PPE For Eye Protection	5.88
5.32.4 PPE For Hand And Arm Protection	5.89
5.32.5 PPE For Foot And Legs Protection	5.89
5.32.6 Safety Belts And Harness	5.90
5.32.7 PPE For Ear Protection	5.90
5.3.8 PPE For Respiratory Protection	5.90
• **Important Points**	**5.93**
• **Questions**	**5.93**
• **University Questions**	**5.94**

Unit 6 : Project Appraisal		**6.1–6.30**
6.1	Phases In Development Of Project	6.1
6.2	Project Appraisal	6.2
	6.2.1 Social Appraisal	6.3
	6.2.2 Environmental Appraisal	6.4
	6.2.3 Technical Appraisal	6.7
	6.2.4 Financial Appraisal	6.7
	6.2.5 Economical Analysis	6.8
	6.2.6 Technological Appraisal	6.9
6.3	Methods Of Framing Appraisals	6.9
	6.3.1 Technical Appraisal	6.9
	6.3.2 Financial And Economical Appraisal	6.10
6.4	Criteria for project - Capital Budgeting	6.11
	6.4.1 Payback Period	6.12
	6.4.2 Accounting Rate Of Return (ARR) Method	6.13
	6.4.3 Net Present Value Method	6.14
	6.4.4 Internal Rate Of Return Method	6.17
	6.4.5 Benefit Cost Ratio	6.19
	6.4.6 Break Even Analysis	6.19
6.5	Detailed Project Report (DPR)	6.21
	6.5.1 Contents Of DPR	6.21
6.6	Project Feasibility Report	6.24
	6.6.1 Feasibility Study Report Contains	6.24
6.7	Role of Project Management Consultant	6.25
	6.7.1 Definition of Project Management Consultant	6.25
	6.7.2 Preconstruction Stage Responsibilities	6.25
	6.7.3 Responsibilities In Construction Phase	6.26
	6.7.4 Post Construction Responsibilities	6.26
•	**Important Points**	**6.30**
•	**University Questions**	**6.30**
•	**University Question Papers**	**P.1-P.14**
	(May 2011 to November 2014)	

Unit - I
INTRODUCTION TO PROJECT MANAGEMENT

1.1 MANAGEMENT

Management in reality is both art as well as science. It is oldest of Art because it was practiced even in the olden days and it is as old as human civilization and human history. Management is youngest of science as it is still under the stage of development. As the environment of business becomes more dynamic, competition increases, business grows in size, area and volume and the science of management will also change in leaps and bounds. The art of management and the science of management are complementary to each other. Management was developed as a practical art but importance of science of management has increased only recently. Science of management is well developed though not as perfect as physics or chemistry because science of management deals with human beings. Thus, it is a social science and it inexact and suffers from certain limitations.

- **Management : As an Art**

Management is an oldest art. The success of management lies in application of its principles and technologies to various aspects and problem in organisation. The basic definition of management proves it by saying that "Management is an Art of getting things done from others".

In an organisation the goals and objectives are to be achieved and for that the manager has to decide the task, plan the future, analyze the situation, co-ordinate resources, control and evaluate the functions. All this needs the fine art of management which comes only after practice and being in constant touch with the situation. Knowledge acquired by the manager is not sufficient but how the art of management is applied by the manager is more important. Thus, it is an art where manager uses all his skill to get result, just like a painter or musician or a sportsman who try to achieve their goals.

- **Management : As a Science**

Management as a science was recognized only in the later part of nineteenth century but since then the progress and advancement has been rapid in this area. Management is a science because the subject of management has become well organized and a systematic body of knowledge just any other subject of physical science. It can be learnt and taught in well organized manner. Just like any other subject of science, management also has certain principles which are developed over a period of time through observation and experiments. Physical Science has universal application. Similarly, subject of management has universal applications. They are not restricted or partial for a particular country or organisation. The subject of management has capacity to produce same results irrespective of the development of the country or organisation.

- **Management : As a Profession**

Management satisfies many of the conditions of profession. Management has a well defined body of knowledge. There are many management education bodies who undertake the responsibility to educate young graduates to enable them to take up management as a profession or career. In the modern business word, there has been a great demand for the professional managers.

1.2 DEFINITION OF MANAGEMENT

The term management is defined by various management thinkers differently.

Drucker

The first definition of management is that 'it is an economic organ of industrial society'. It means taking action to make the desired result.

Terry

'Management is a distinct process consisting of planning, organising, actuating, controlling performance to determine and accomplish the objectives by the use of people and resources'.

Appley

'Management is a development of people and not the direction of the things. It is the selection, the training, the supervision and the development of people'.

Koontz and O'Donnel

'Management is an art of getting things through and with people in formally organized groups'.

Henry Fayol

'To manage is to forecast, to plan, to organize, to command, to co-ordinate and to control'.

F.W. Taylor

'Management is knowledge exactly what is to be done and seeing how it is to be done in the best and the cheapest way'.

Oliver Sheldon

'Management is the function in an industry concerned in the execution of policy with the limits set up by administration and the employment organisation for the particular objects before it'.

1.3 IMPORTANCE OF MANAGEMENT

- Truly speaking, no enterprise can survive without management, even if it possesses huge money, excellent machinery and expert man-power, because without management, it will be all confusion and no body will know what to do and when to do.
- Management which guides and controls the activities of man-power for the optimum utilization of company resources, such that Five M's (Men, Material, Money Machines, Methods).
- Management creates a vital, dynamic and life giving force to the enterprise.
- Management co-ordinates activities of different departments in an enterprise and establishes team-spirit among the persons.
- Management provides new ideas and vision to the organisation to do better.
- Management tackles business problems and provides a tool for the best way of doing things.
- Management only can meet the challenge of change.
- Management provides stability to the enterprise by changing and modifying the resource in accordance with the changing environment of the society.

1.4 CHARACTERISTICS OF MANAGEMENT

- Management is goal oriented. It achieves the organisational goals through co-ordination of the efforts of the personnel.
- Management works as catalyst to produce good using labour, materials and capital.
- Management is a distinct process comprising of functions such as planning, organising, staffing, directing and controlling.
- Management represents a system of authority a hierarchy of command and control. Managers at different levels possess varying degrees of authority.
- Management is a unifying force. It integrates human and other resources to achieve the desired objective.
- Management harmonizes the individual's goals with the organisational goals to minimize conflicts in the organisation.
- Management is a multi-disciplinary subject.
- Management is universal in character. The principal and techniques of management are equally applicable in all engineering fields.

1.5 FUNCTIONS OF MANAGEMENT

Management has following important functions :
- Forecasting
- Planning
- Staffing
- Organising
- Directing
- Co-ordinating
- Controlling
- Decision making

1. Forecasting : Forecasting is necessarily preliminary to planning. Forecasting estimates the future scope of work. Forecasting begins with cost of project, finance available, method of payment, profit, rate of interest, government subsidy and environmental concern. Many manufacturing firms produce their material in advance to meet the future demand.

Following are the Important Advantages of Forecasting :
- Overproduction and short supply of raw material can be avoided if there is proper production policy.
- Accurate forecasting can reduce the cost of production.
- It gives proper control over inventory.
- It sets the sales target.
- It gives clear idea for future financial requirements in advance.
- It gives an idea about expansion of existing unit.
- It helps to plan the long-term financial requirement.

2. Planning : It is a process by which a manager anticipates the future and discovers alternative courses of action open to him. Planning is a rational, economical, systematic way of making decisions today, which will affect the future. Without proper planning, the activities of enterprises may become confused, haphazard and infective. Prior planning is very essential for utilizing the available facilities (men, material, money, machines and methods etc.) to the best of advantages. Now-a-day's computer and software based on CPM and PERT such as MS- Project and Primavera is used for planning of construction project.

The main functions of the management are to plan and to take correct decisions. This important activity covers the following sub-activities :
- To determine the Company's objectives.
- To formulate correct polices.

- To prepare cost and performance standards and includes them in the company's budget.
- To prepare short-range plans and to measure the achievements of the company.

3. Organising : Organising is the process by which the structure and allocation of jobs is determined. Organising involves calculating activities, its grouping, organising people, materials, jobs, time etc. and establishing a framework in which responsibilities are defined and authorities are laid down. There are two types of organisations viz,
- Formal organisation
- Informal organisation

4. Staffing : It is the process by which managers select, train, promote and retire their subordinates. Staffing is a continuous process. It involves the developing and placing of qualified people in the various jobs in the organisation.

5. Directing : It is the process by which actual performance of subordinates is guided towards common goals of the company. Directing involves following function such as
(a) Leadership
(b) Communication
(c) Motivation
(d) Supervision

(a) Leadership : Leadership is the quality of behaviour of a person, where by they inspire confidence and trust in their subordinates, get maximum co-operation from them and guide their activities in organized effort. Leadership is more important than personal ability and skill.

(b) Communication : Communication is a process by which ideas are transmitted, received and understood by others for the purpose of effecting desired result. Verbal, written order, reports, instruction, slides are the various types of Communication.

(c) Motivation : Motivation means inspiring the subordinates to the work or to achieve company objectives effectively and efficiently.

(d) Supervision : Supervision is an important function of directing which measures whether the work is going on in proper sequence, quantity and quality.

6. Co-ordinating : Co-ordinating means achieving harmony of individual effort towards the accomplishment of company objective. Co-ordination involves making plans that co-ordinate the activities of subordinates, regulate their activities on the job and regulate their communications.

7. Controlling : It is the process which measure current performance and guide it towards some predetermined goal. Controlling is necessary to insure that orders are not misunderstood, rules are not violated and objectives have not been unknowingly shifted. Control means control of person and other things such as time, quality, speed and project cost etc. It is a continue process which measures the progress of operation.

8. Decision Making : Decision making is the process by which a course of action is consciously chosen from available alternatives for the purpose of achieving desired result. An outstanding quality of a successful manager is his ability to make sound and logical decisions. Following are important decisions, which the manager of an organisation is supposed to take.
- Marketing decision
- Cost price decision
- Capital investment decisions

1.6 MANAGERIAL OBJECTIVES

Managerial Objectives

Managerial objectives may be defined as 'the intended goals which prescribe scope and suggest direction to the efforts of a manager'.

Management objectives should be,
- Clearly defined and communicated,
- Reasonably attainable,
- Based upon the overall organisational goals,
- Containment of expenditure within budget and time.

Managerial objective may be classified as
- General objectives
- Specific objectives

General Objectives

General objectives contains following terms
- Nature of project
- Continuous supply of capital
- Growth of company
- Increase in work
- Economic objective such as profit, Low cost production

Environmental Objective
- Social objective
- Human objective
- Time scale

Specific Objectives

Specific objectives contains following terms
- Nature of work to be done.
- Types of project to be selected.
- Market standing (local, national, international).
- Product and service diversification if any.

1.7 EVALUATION OF SCIENTIFIC MANAGEMENT

The origin of management can be traced back to the days when man started living in groups. History reveals that strong men organized the masses into groups and become their leader. Management is looked from the leadership point of view which is essential to co-ordinate the efforts of group members in order to arrange the necessaries.

1.7.1 Scientific Management

The early decades of this century witnessed the emergence of Scientific Management. This school of thought attempted to introduce a rational, systematic approach to work and to the management work.

- In his early writings F.W. Taylor referred to his idea as task management. In 1910 Louis Brandeis coined the word Scientific Management.
- F.W. Taylor got recognition as the father of Scientific Management, he wrote a book on the principle of Management in the year 1911.
- The primary emphasis of scientific management was on planning, standardizing and improving human effort at the operative level in order to maximize output with minimum input.
- Taylor believed that managing should be based on objective assessment of facts, on measurement and not on guess work.
- Scientific Management is the result of applying scientific knowledge and the scientific methods to the various aspects of management and the problem that arise from them.
- Taylor thought that by maximizing the productive efficiency of each worker, scientific management would also maximize the earnings of the employees and employers.
- Scientific management could be summarized as :
  - Science, not rule of thumb,
  - Harmony, not disorder,
  - Co-operation, not individualism,
  - Maximum output, in place of restricted output, and
  - The development of each worker to his greatest efficiency and prosperity.

1.7.2 Basic Approach of Scientific Management

Following are the important points while going for scientific management :

- Analyse work scientifically. Investigate all aspect of work on a scientific basis rather than using rules of thumb.
- Provide specific guidelines for worker performance.
- Develop one best way of doing a job.
- Select workers best suited to perform the specific tasks.

- Train and develop each workman in the most efficient method for doing the job. Divide the work so that workmen and management share almost equally in the daily performance of each task; workers do their jobs as per the standards laid down and Management does planning and makes sure that all aspects are ready at the right time so that the resultant efficiency is high.
- Achieve support and co-operation from workmen by arranging conditions, services, guidance and by giving them greater economic rewards which in turn are obtained through increased efficiency and productivity.

The main aims of management should be :
- Standard method,
- Adopt best implements and working conditions, and
- Obtain co-operation from workmen.

Contribution of F.W. Taylor

Fredrick Winslow Taylor is known as the founder of Scientific Management. Taylor laid the foundation for modern scientific management between 1880 and 1890.

He began his carrier in 1871 as an apprentice machinist and turner at the Cramp shipyard at Philadelphia, U.S.A. After three years he joined the Midvale Steel Works as a machine shop worker. By dint of his hard labour, he progressed rapidly to become machinist, gang boss, foreman and finally Chief Engineer in 1884. He served Company till 1889. To satisfy his hunger for technical know-how, Taylor joined the Stevens Institute and obtained the Master Degree in Engineering. Then he joined the Bethlehem Steel Company, where he served from 1898 to 1901. During his carrier as machinist and foreman, Taylor saw much disorder and wastage of human and other resources at work-places. The workers did not produce more than one third of a day's work. The workmen did not want the management to know how much work they could do. Because they feared that wages would be cut. Moreover, the management did not have any idea about the capacity of the workers and further, management did not want to pay more to workers. Taylor tried to work out some system whereby the interest of management and the workers might be the same.

Other Contributions of Taylor as Follows

- Taylor developed the principle of breaking a task into element for the same timing.
- He is remembered as 'Father of Scientific Management' for his 'Principles of Scientific Management'.
- He kept himself involved in exploring the causes of inefficiency and labour difficulties in the industry. Through time studies he experimented the way to recognize losses in efficiency in industrial operations.
- Taylor introduced operation of various of costing systems.

- Taylor paid maximum attention towards time studies and he established work standards.
- Taylor developed Functional Organisation in which one foreman was made in-charge for each function.
- Another concept connected with the name of Taylor is 'A Fair Day's Task'.
- In 1903, he presented the important paper on 'Shop management'.
- In 1906, he published an article 'On the art of cutting metals'.
- Taylor evolved certain principles such as investigating work on scientific basis, selecting best worker etc.
- Taylor suggested a Wages Incentive Scheme known as 'Taylor's Differential Piece Rate Plan'.

F.W. Taylor's Principles of Scientific Management
- Separation of planning and doing function.
- Function foremanship.
- Work Planning.
- Scientific selection and training.
- Time study.
- Motion study.
- Incentives.
- Standardization of tools and equipments.
- Production planning and control.
- Co-operation between management and workers.

This last principle is so important that if there is no co-operation between management and workers then all the other principle fail.

Taylor's Scientific Management suffered from criticism by American workers and trade union leaders and social thinkers. Their criticism mainly emphasized following points.
- Average worker being treated as a machine.
- Taylor's Functional foremanship implied specialization which resulted in repetitive and monotonous jobs causing dis-satisfaction among workers.
- Taylor concentrated mainly on production side of any unit. i.e. shop floor thereby neglecting administrative wing.

Contributions of Henri Fayol

Henri Fayol, the father of Principle of Management was born in 1841 in France and graduated as a Mining Engineer in 1860 from the National School of Mining at St. Etienne. In 1860, he joined the famous French Combine in the mining and metallurgical field. Fayol analyzed the process of management as he had observed it first-hand. His conclusion was that all the work done in business enterprises can be divided into six groups.

- Technical activities
- Commercial activities
- Financial activities
- Security activities
- Accounting activities
- Managerial activities

Fayol believed that if any kind of business was to operate successfully, these six functions had to be performed. If any one was neglected, the enterprise would suffer accordingly.

- Fayol devoted most of his attention to the managerial activities. In doing so he enunciated certain principles which hold ground to this day.
- The principles laid down by him were

1. Division of work	8. Authority and responsibility.
2. Discipline	9. Unity of command
3. Units of direction	10. Subordination of individual to general interest
4. Remuneration	11. Centralization of authority
5. Scalar chain	12. Order
6. Equity of treatment	13. Stability
7. Initiative	14. Espirt de corps

- Fayol also spelt out function of management. The present pattern of management functions follows broadly the lines set by him. The functions of Manager enumerated by him were :
  - Forecasting and planning
  - Organising
  - Command
  - Co-ordination, and
  - Control
- In addition to his over-all concept of management, Fayol signaled out and described with clarity and understanding - principles of the unity of command and direction.
- Fayol emphasized the importance of non-functional incentives.

Fayol's Fourteen Principles of Management

1. **Division of Labour :** This helps in specialization. Each job should be assigned to a specialist of the job which increases efficiency.
2. **Authority and Responsibility :** Both the things should go hand in hand. Manager is held responsible for getting the task done with the right or authority to give orders and instructions.
3. **Discipline :** It implies the members of organisation to respect the rules, regulation and agreement between organisation and its employees.

4. **Unity of Command :** All employees must receive orders and instructions from one source only, other- wise that will lead the problem of control.
5. **Unity of Direction :** Each group of activity having the same objective must have one head and one plan.
6. **Subordination of Individual Interest to the Common Interest :** The interest of individual employees should not take prime importance over the interest of organisation as a whole.
7. **Remuneration :** The compensation for the services rendered should be fair and must provide maximum satisfaction to both employees and employer.
8. **Centralization :** There should be one central point to exercise overall direction control of all the activities. Managers should retain final responsibility of decision making but subordinates should also be given enough authority to do their jobs properly.
9. **Scalar Chain :** It is the chain of superiors ranging from ultimate authority to the lowest level of organisation. An employee must communicate to his next superior.
10. **Order** : Order alone can create an efficient management. Disorder leads to confusion. Material and people in the organisation should be in the right place at right time.
11. **Equity :** Kindness and justice should be exercised by management while dealing with the subordinates. This will maintain loyalty and support of workers towards organisation.
12. **Stability of Tenure :** A high employee's turnover rate disturbs the efficient functioning of the organisation. Minimum employee turnover/ job security to employees promotes organisational efficiency as employees can contribute more to the organisation.
13. **Initiative :** Subordinates should be given opportunity to show their imagination and curiosity while completing their assignments, their plans. This may lead to some creativity by subordinates.
14. **Esprit de Corps :** This means 'unity is strength'. The whole organisation should function as a team and every member of the organisation should work at his best to achieve organisational goals and objectives.

1.8 DEFINITIONS OF PROJECT

The definition of project as given by many experts are given below
(1) Oxford Dictionary
"A project is an individual or collaborative enterprise that is carefully planned to achieve a particular aim."
(2) International Project Management Association (IPMA)
"A project is a time and cost constrained operation to realize a set of defined deliverables (the scope to fulfill the projects objectives) up to quality standards and requirements."
(3) Association of Project Management (APM)
"Project is a unique, transient endeavour undertaken to achieve a desired outcome."

(4) Project Management Association of Japan (PMAJ)

"A project refers to a value creation undertaking based on a specific, which is completed in a given or agreed time frame and under constraints, including resources and external circumstances."

(5) ISO 10000 : 2003

"Project is a unique process consisting of a set of co-ordinated and controlled activities with start and finish dates, undertaken to achieve an objective conforming to specific requirements including constraints of time, cost and resources."

(6) British Standard Institute (BS 6079–1)

"Project is a unique set of co-ordinated activities, with defined starting and finishing points, undertaken by an individual or organization to meet specific objectives with defined schedule, cost and performance parameters."

(7) Australian Institute of Project Management (AIPM)

"A project is a temporary endeavour undertaken to create a unique product, service or result in order to achieve an outcome."

(8) J. Rodney Turner

"A project is a temporary organization to which resources are assigned to do work to deliver beneficial changes."

1.8.1 Project Management [PMBOK]

Project Management Body of Knowledge (PMBOK) book presents collection of knowledge in the field of project management which is applicable to all professionals associated with this field. PMBOK defines Project as "A temporary endeavour undertaken to create a unique product or service."

Temporary

- Which has a definite beginning and a definite end.
- "End" when projects objective are reached or when projects objectives can not met or when need for the project no longer exist.
- Project can be of smaller duration or longer duration.

Unique

- Means doing something that has not been done before.
- "Unique" because each project has different owner, different design, different location, different locations and so on.

One of the characteristics of project is its "Progressiveness" which means "proceeding in steps; continuing steadily by increment." Also, project is elaborated names "worked out with care and detail; developed thoroughly."

When the project starts, the term "Project Management" helps to achieve the objectives.

The characteristics of project management are as follows :

- It is the application of knowledge, skills, tools and techniques of project activities to meet project requirements.
- It is accomplished through the use of processes such as : initiating, planning, executing, controlling and closing.
- Many of the processes within project management are iterative in nature.

1.9 CATEGORIES OF PROJECTS

1.9.1 Introduction

As per the new industrial policy resolution 1956, the Government has accepted the policy of socialistic pattern of society and accordingly industries were divided into following categories.

Schedule A :

These were industries which were to be exclusively under the control and regulation of the Government. Some of them are :

- Arms and Ammunition
- Atomic Energy
- Iron and Steel
- Heavy Machine and Plant
- Heavy Electrical Plant
- Minerals
- Railways and Roads
- Aircraft and Air Transport
- Mineral Oils
- Post and Telegraph
- Irrigation

Schedule B :

These were industries on which there would be Government Control and were to be progressively owned by Government, some of them are :

- Fertilizer
- Automobiles
- Synthetic rubber
- Road and Water Transport
- Ferrow alloys.

State had more prominent role in the setting up and running of these industries which had to be run on business lines. Rest of the industries were open for private sector.

However, with the industrial revolution and with the pressure from the world community and institutions like World Bank supporting the different state and other project, there has been a revolutionary change in the Government Policy and many fields of industries which were run by the Government have been opened to private sector.

1.9.2 Project Categories

In general projects categorized based on the following criterias :

Size

- **Minor Projects :** Repair and maintenance, Very small constructions, e.g. Construction of Bungalow.
- **Medium Projects :** Medium construction. e.g. Construction of housing, small industrial shades.
- **Major Projects :** Large construction projection e.g. Infrastructure projects.

Types of Ownership

- Government projects
- Private projects.
- Public private partnerships.

Types of Applications

- Commercial : For example hotels, banks, IT sectors.
- Residential.
- Industrial.
- Infrastructure.

Based on Risk Involves

- High risk.
- Medium risk.
- Low risk.

1.10 STAGES IN PROJECT

The different steps in any project can be summarized as below :

1. Identification Stage

Identification of product which can satisfy the consumers' requirements and also the manufacturers' requirements. The idea of launching a new product should be well conceived.

2. Pre-Selection Stage

(a) **Preliminary Investigation and Thorough Study :** Clear and definite shape has to be given to conceived idea. The practicability of the product has to be tested, working model may be framed.

(b) **Market Survey :** It is very necessary that before the project is launched, a market survey has to be carried out to ascertain the demand for the product. This could be judged in the beginning by introducing the product on small scale and finding out the results about the demand. Possibility of prevailing competition should be given due consideration.

(c) **Clarity About the Objective :** This should be very clear. The ultimate aim is to sell the goods which are manufactured and to earn the profit. Estimation of profit, investment and cost of operation, outline of manufacturing process, description of the project and the probable risk and any other problems arising should be given due consideration in pre-selection stage.

3. **Feasibility Report**

Thorough analysis has to be made about the proposed project and a feasibility report has to be prepared. This is a self-containted project scheme prepared on the basis of the

- Market analysis
- Technical analysis
- Financial analysis including Break Even Analysis
- Social profitability analysis.

4. **Administrative Work**

This includes obtaining permission from the Government and other authorities regarding starting of the project. A self-contained project report will have to be submitted to the different authorities for the same and after completing the different formalities, permission may be obtained for starting of the new venture.

5. **Production Planning**

This step will consist of the following :

- Product Planning and Process Planning
- Plant Layout
- Material Management which includes Purchase and Stores Management
- Production Planning and Control
- Inspection and Quality Control
- Marketing
- Evaluation of Financial Analysis.

Flow chart of a Simple Production System is given in Fig. 1.1.

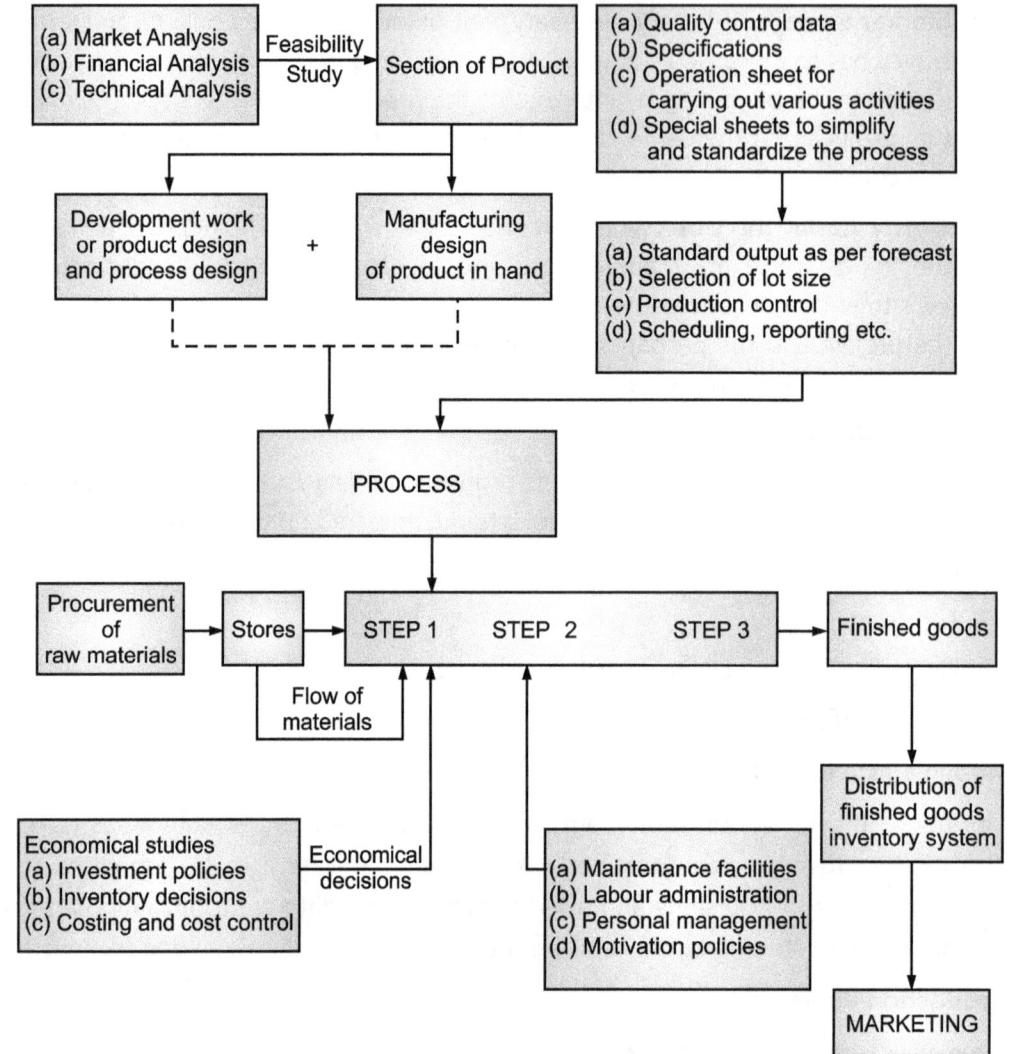

Fig. 1.1 : Flow chart of a simple production system

1.11 PROJECT LIFE CYCLE

A project is bounded by various phases from project conception through project execution to project completion. These phases differ from project to project. Broadly, the phases can be given as project planning, project scheduling and project controlling. Planning and scheduling take place before commencement of the project while controlling is a continuous process after the project starts.

The project life cycle is represented as a line graph with the level of effort (usually measured in manhours) plotted against time. The typical life cycle profile shows the level of effort starting from a low base, building up slowly to a peak, then declining to completion and termination.

Following is the project life cycle of a housing project.

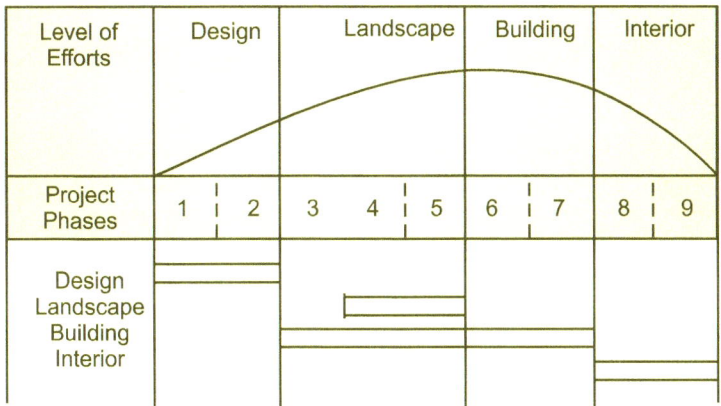

Fig. 1.2 : Project life cycle

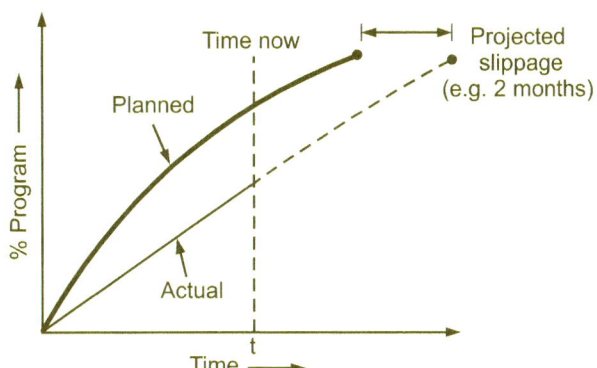

Fig. 1.3 : Planned and actual life cycle curve

The housing project is subdivided into four phases as Design, Landscape, Building and Interior. As shown in the above figure, the level of efforts is maximum in building phase before declining during interior phase. It is overlapping to some extent with landscape phase. Design phase is slowly gaining momentum as it is the initial phase.

In the above method, we have considered the planned progress of the project. When the project starts, the planned progress can be compared with the actual progress estimating the project slippage (or additional duration required).

The planned life cycle curve can be plotted by taking time on x-axis and percentage progress on y-axis. While constraints and sequence remain the same, time duration changes depending upon the quantity of work.

At point t, the percentage progress is compared with the planned (thick line). Depending upon the amount of work remaining, projected completion of work is calculated. The slippage is found out (e.g. 2 months) as shown in Fig. 1.3.

1.11.1 Advantages of Project Life Cycle

1. This curve is used for progress review and control the slippage.
2. On this curve, the project performance is shown very clearly and in a very simple manner.

Following is the Project Life Cycle (PLC) for different parameters on site.

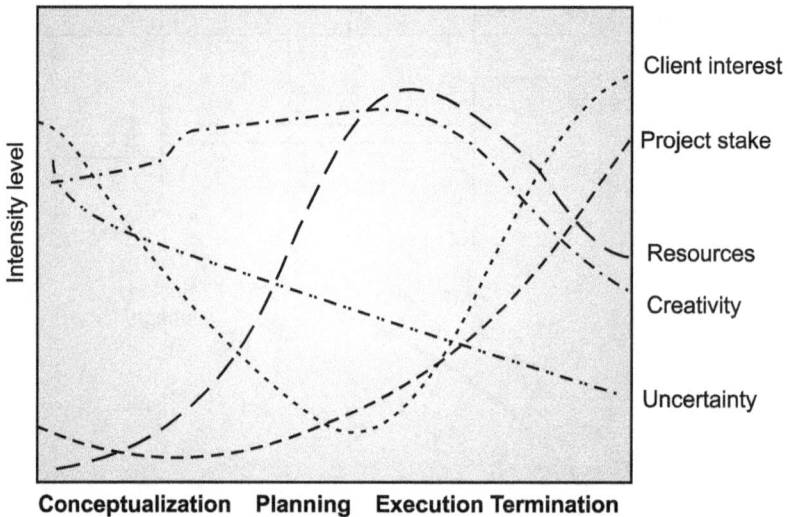

Fig. 1.4 : Project life cycle depending upon various parameters

Project Life Cycle for Resources is discussed earlier. From client's point of view, he is keen at the conceptualization and termination stage. He is least bothered about how the execution is taking place. Project stake goes on increasing as the project approaches completion. The creativity is required at conceptualization, planning and execution stage for minimizing the cost, maximizing quality and benefits. Least creativity is required at termination stage. In the initial phases of project, uncertainty level is high from duration, expenses and resources point of view. In the termination stage, as activities are also less, the uncertainty is very low.

1.11.2 From PMBOK

A project comprises of various project phases to improve management control which are termed as "Project life cycle". Each project phase is marked by completion of one or more deliverables which are tangible and verifiable.

Project life cycle adopted specially for construction consists of the following phases :

- Feasibility : Project formulation, feasibility studies and strategy design and approval. A go/no-go decision is made at the end of this phase.
- Planning and Design : Base design, cost and schedule, contract terms are let at the end of this phase.

- Construction : Manufacturing, delivery, civil works, installation and testing. The facility is substantially complete at the end of this phase.
- Turnover and start-up-final testing and maintenance. The facility is in full operation at the end of this phase.

1.12 ORGANISATION

An organisation is a group of person working together to achieve an establishment goal. It is the relationship which exists between people taking part in a group activity. It defines the responsibilities and authority of individuals in relation to men, materials, money and machinery which constitute the resources of an organisation. An organisation is needed because a manager at any level can effectively manage the functions of only a limited number of persons working directly under him. The setting up of suitable organisation for various civil engineering works is all the more necessary because the construction industry is a competitive field of endeavors which is susceptible to many risks, variable labour conditions and diverse construction problem. The importance of organisation is given below.

1.12.1 Importance of Organisation

- Sound Organisation can contribute greatly to the continuity and success of the enterprise.
- Facilitates Administration : A properly designed and balanced organisation facilitates both management and operation of the enterprise; inadequate organisation may not only discourage but actually preclude effective administration.
- Facilitates growth and diversification : Sound organisation permits organisational elaboration.
- The organisation structure can profoundly affect the people of the enterprise. Proper organisation facilitates the effective use of the manpower.
- Optimum use of resource : Sound organisation structure permits use of technical and human resources. The organisation can introduce latest technological improvement.
- Stimulates creativity : Sound organisation stimulates independent, creative thinking and initiative by providing well defined areas of work with broad latitude of the development of new and improved ways of doing things.
- A sound organisation leads to specialization.
- A sound organisation minimizes corruption and inefficiencies.
- A sound organisation does not generate confusion

- A sound organisation decrease wastages and expenditure.
- A sound organisation facilitates the training and managerial development of personnel.

1.12.2 Characteristics of Organisation

The Characteristics or essential features of an organisation are given below :

- Organisation is a group of people, small or large.
- The group works under an executive leadership.
- Organisation is a tool of management.
- It leads to division of work and responsibilities.
- Organisation defines and fixes the duties and responsibilities of employees.
- Organisation is a step towards the achievement of established goals.
- It establishes a relationship between authority and responsibility and controls the effort of the group.

1.12.3 Principles of Organisation

Common principles of organisation are given below :

- Considerable of objective.
- Relationship of basic components of the organisation.
- Principle Balance between responsibility and authority.
- Span of control.
- Dividing and grouping work.
- Effective delegation.
- Principle of Communication.
- Line and staff relationship.
- Balance, stability and flexibility.

1. **Considerable of Objective :** The objectives of the enterprise have an important bearing on the organisation structure, only those objectives should be taken up and accomplished for which there is real need in the organisation such as action may be taken to increase speed, production, quality, profit etc.

2. **Relationship of Basic Components of the Organisation :** Objective as decide above determines the work to be performed and the type of work dictates the selection of personal and physical facilities.

3. **Responsibility and Authority :** Responsibility means accountability. It may be considered as the obligation of a subordinate to his boss to do a work given to him.

Authority means right and power to act.

The responsibilities and authority should go hand in hand. One without other leads to demotivation and chaos.

4. **Span of Control :** Span of control or span of management refers to the number of subordinates that report to an executive or the number of subordinates that an executive can supervise directly.

5. **Dividing and Grouping Work**

    Dividing : Divisionalisation provides a broader perspective, a greater sense of responsibility on the part of the personnel and more clear-cut control over profits.

    Grouping : The process of grouping is essential for specialization and co-ordination.

6. **Effective Delegation :** Effective delegation is said to be existing when an executive instead of doing all the thinking for the unit himself, passes down to his subordinates any task on which they can take decisions themselves and perform it efficiently and effectively.

7. **Communication :** Communication means transmitting instructions and information within the organisation and to all those are affected Communication serves as a linking process by which parts of an organisation are tied together. Good Communication is essential if all employees are to know what to do in order to achieve the goals of the organisation.

8. **Line and Staff function :** All the activities of an organisation are divided in to two groups (i) Line function (ii) Staff function.
    - Line functions are those which contribute directly and vitally to the objectives of an organisation.
    - Staff functions are those that aid the line or are auxiliary to line functions.

9. **Balance, Stability and Flexibility :** All the units of organisation should be balanced. Also organisational stability refers to the capacity to withstand the losses of key personnel without serious loss to the effectiveness of the organisation in performing its work.

1.12.4 Key General Management Skills (PMBOK)

The important skills that a project manager possess, essentially consist as following :

(1) Leading

It includes, (a) developing vision and strategies, (b) Communicating the vision to all concerned, (c) Motivating and inspiring people.

(2) Communicating

It involves exchange of information which should be clear, unambiguous complete and received in its entirely, understood correctly. There are various dimensions of communication such as written and oral, internal and external, formal and informal, vertical and horizontal.

(3) Negotiating

It involves conferring with others to come to terms with them to reach an agreement. Negotiations occur around many issues, at many times and at many levels of the project.

(4) Problem Solving

It involves problem definition (to distinguish between causes and symptoms) and decision making (to analyse problems to identify viable solutions and then making a choice between them.) "Right" decision should be made at "Right" time.

(5) Influencing the Organisation

It means the ability to "get things done" by the mechanics of power and politics taken in a positive sense.

1.13 AUTHORITY

Authority

Different people interpret authority in different ways. In the legal sense, authority means the right of the person to take an action.

The following are the types of Authority :

Technical Authority : It means recognition of person's opinion in certain specialized field.

Ultimate Authority : It deals with the original source from which the person derives the right to take certain action.

Administrative Authority : It means the right to act the company in the specified areas. Administrator should be clear as to what rights are associated with the task that is to be delegated.

Operational Authority : It is the permission given to the subordinates to do certain jobs.

- Authority means right and power to act.
- Authority is the right to make decisions direct the work of others and gives orders. It is a right to direct, act and control.
- The authority is the rightful legal power to request subordinates to do a certain thing or to refrain from doing that, and if he does not follow these instructions the manager is in a position, if needed, to take disciplinary action, even to discharge the subordinate. Without authority, only anarchy and chaos would result.

Rational – Legal Authority : The authority which is defined legally.

Traditional Authority : It is the authority which comes through traditions. People are emotionally attached to this authority.

Charismatic Authority : This is the authority due to influence of some leaders on the public.

Characteristic of Authority :

- Authority is given by the Institution and is therefore, legal or legitimate.

- Authority is not endless or unlimited.
- Authority should invariably be in writing, through in small organisations, it may be verbal.
- Authority must be commensurate with responsibility.
- Authority may be centralized or de-centralized.
- Authority is given to the position and not to the position holder.

1.13.1 Delegation of Authority

- Delegation may be defined as 'the entrustment of responsibility and authority to another and the creation of accountability for performance'.
- Delegation may be defined as 'dividing his load and sharing his responsibilities with others'.
- Delegation of Authority merely means 'the granting of authority to subordinates to accomplish a particular assignment while operating within prescribed limits and standards established'.

Delegation is important because it is both the gauge and the means of a manager's accomplishment. Once a man's job grows beyond his personal capacity, his success lies in his ability to multiply himself through other people.

The Essential Element of Delegation

- Assignment of work to another for performance.
- Grant of authority to be exercised.
- Creation of an obligation or accountability on the part of the person accepting the delegation to perform in terms of the standards established.

Principles of Delegation of Authority

- Parity between authority and responsibility.
- Responsibility in terms of results.
- Principle of Unity of Command.
- Delegation of responsibility.
- Overlapping of responsibilities.
- Free flow of information.
- Delegated authority.

Problems of Delegation of Authority

Problem in Delegation of Authority is classified under the following heads.

On the part of management / executive

- Felling of perfection.
- Lack of ability to direction.
- Lack of confidence in subordinate.
- Fear of being exposed.
- Absence of controls.
- Conservative attitude.
- Desire of dominance.

On the part of the subordinate

- Dependence on boss.
- Fear of criticism.
- Lack of self-confidence.
- Overburdened with work.
- Lack of proper facilities.
- Lack of incentives.

On the part of the organisation

The process of delegation of authority may suffer due to some internal organisational problems such as :

- Defective organisation structure and non-clarity of authority-responsibility relationships.
- Defective and inadequate planning and policy formulation.
- Lack of unity of command.
- Lack of effective control mechanism in the organisation.

1.14 TYPES OF ORGANISATION

The structure of one industrial organisation differs from that of another organisation and it depends upon following.

- Size of the organisation,
- Nature of the product being manufactured,
- Complexity of the problems being faced

Common Types of Organisation

- Line, Military or Scalar Organisation
- Functional Organisation
- Line and Staff Organisation

(a) Line, Military or Scalar Organisation : It was called military organisation because it resembled to old military organisation. It is the simplest form of organisation structure. Line organisation is based upon authority and responsibility rather than on the nature and kind of operation or activities. Line organisation is direct and people at different levels know to whom they are accountable.

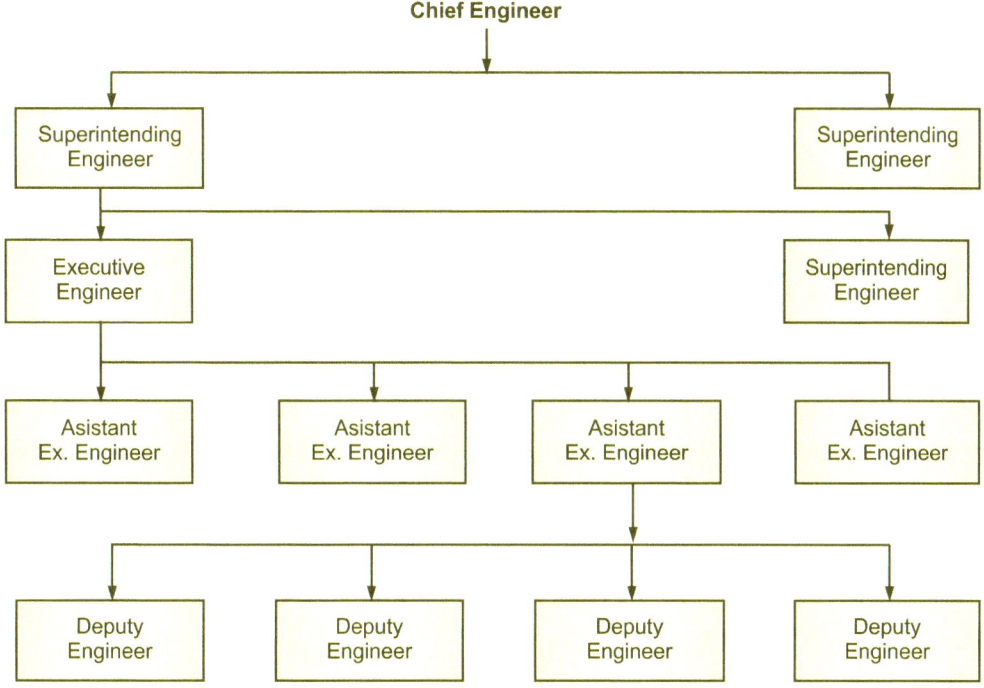

Fig. 1.5 : Line, military or scalar organisation

This type of organisational structure is followed in most government departments and autonomous engineering organisations. (Structure is given above).

Advantages of Line, Military or Scalar Organisation

- It is simplest and easy to understand.
- It makes clear division of authority.
- It encourage speedy action.
- It is flexible, easy to expand and contract.
- It fixes responsibility on an individual therefore it is strong in discipline.
- It is capable of developing the all round executive at the higher levels of authority.

Disadvantages of Line, Military or Scalar Organisation

- Speculation is not considered in this type of organisation.
- It overloads a few key executives.

- It is limited to very small concerns.
- It encourages dictatorial way of working.
- For controlling work high supervision is required.

Application of Line, Military or Scalar Organisation

- All types of small firm.
- Automatic and continuous process industries such as construction company, sugar factory, paper mill etc.

(b) Functional Organisation : F.W. Taylor suggested functional organisation because it was difficult to find all round person qualified to work at middle management levels in the line organisation. The basic functional organisation is specialization. In such an organisation, work is carried out on a functional basis and each functional is carried out by a specialist. According to Taylor the ideal situation in such an organisation would be when each person performs a specified function only. This removes the staff personnel from his assisting capacity and gives him authority and responsibility for supervision and administration.

The idea behind this type of organisation is to divide the work in such a manner that each person has to perform a minimum number of functions and is fully responsible for those aspects of work. All similar and related work is grouped under one person. In order to perform his function effectively, a person has to report to several superiors for different phases or aspects of the work. Thus, a subordinate anywhere in the organisation will be commanded directly by a number of superiors, each with authority in his own field.

Advantages of Functional Organisation

- In Functional Organisation one person or department is responsible for one function therefore he / they can perform his their duties in a better manner.
- Functional Organisation makes use of specialists to give expert advice to worker
- Functional Organisation relives line executives of routine, specialized decisions.
- It reduces wastages, time and increase profit.
- By using Functional Organisation quality of work is improved.

Disadvantages of Functional Organisation

- Co-ordination of the efforts of various functions is difficult.
- Discipline is difficult to maintain by using this type of organisation.
- Fixing of responsibility is very difficult in case something goes wrong.
- Workers are not given opportunity to make use of their ingenuity, initiative and drive.
- All round executives cannot be developed.
- In functional organisation maintain an industrial relationship is more complex.

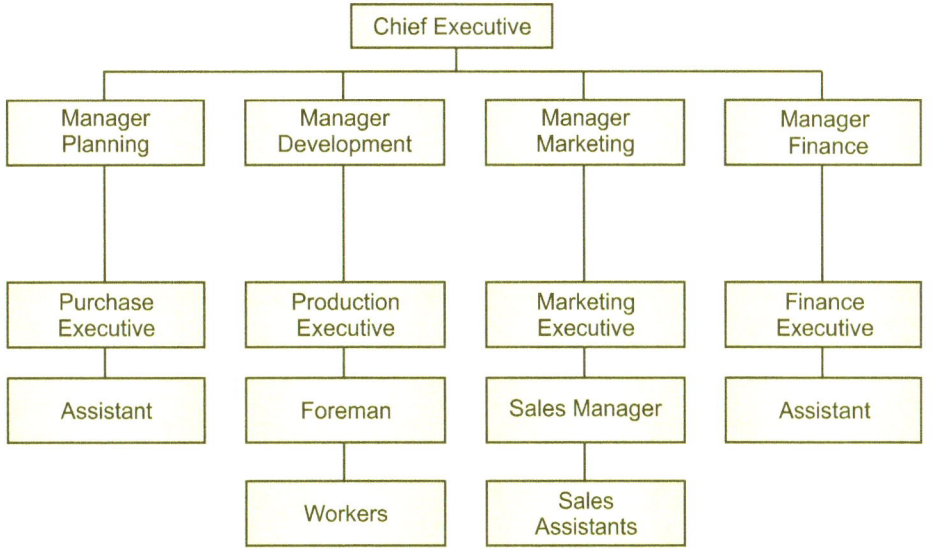

Fig. 1.6 : Structure of functional organisation

Application of Functional Organisation

Due to large disadvantages it is not used in construction industry but modified form is used in same most modern and advanced concerns.

(c) Line and Functional Organisation : Line organisation is unsuitable for large and complex projects, where the key men need to be assisted by specialists in different fields. The individuals who constitute the staff in an organisation are experts, who have no line authority but whose function is largely advisory. This type of organisation comes into existence because line authority cannot assume direct responsibilities for all functions such as research, design, planning, scheduling and recording of performance etc. All these activities are performed by staff, while the line authority maintains discipline and stability in an organisation. The authority by which the staff performs its advisory functions is delegated by the 'line' and their advice is generally accepted keeping in view their experience and expertise.

Advantages of Line and Functional Organisation

- Staff executive take advices of experts.
- Less wastages of material, money and man power.
- There is no confusion as exist in functional organisation.
- Quality of work is improved.
- More attention is given on work.

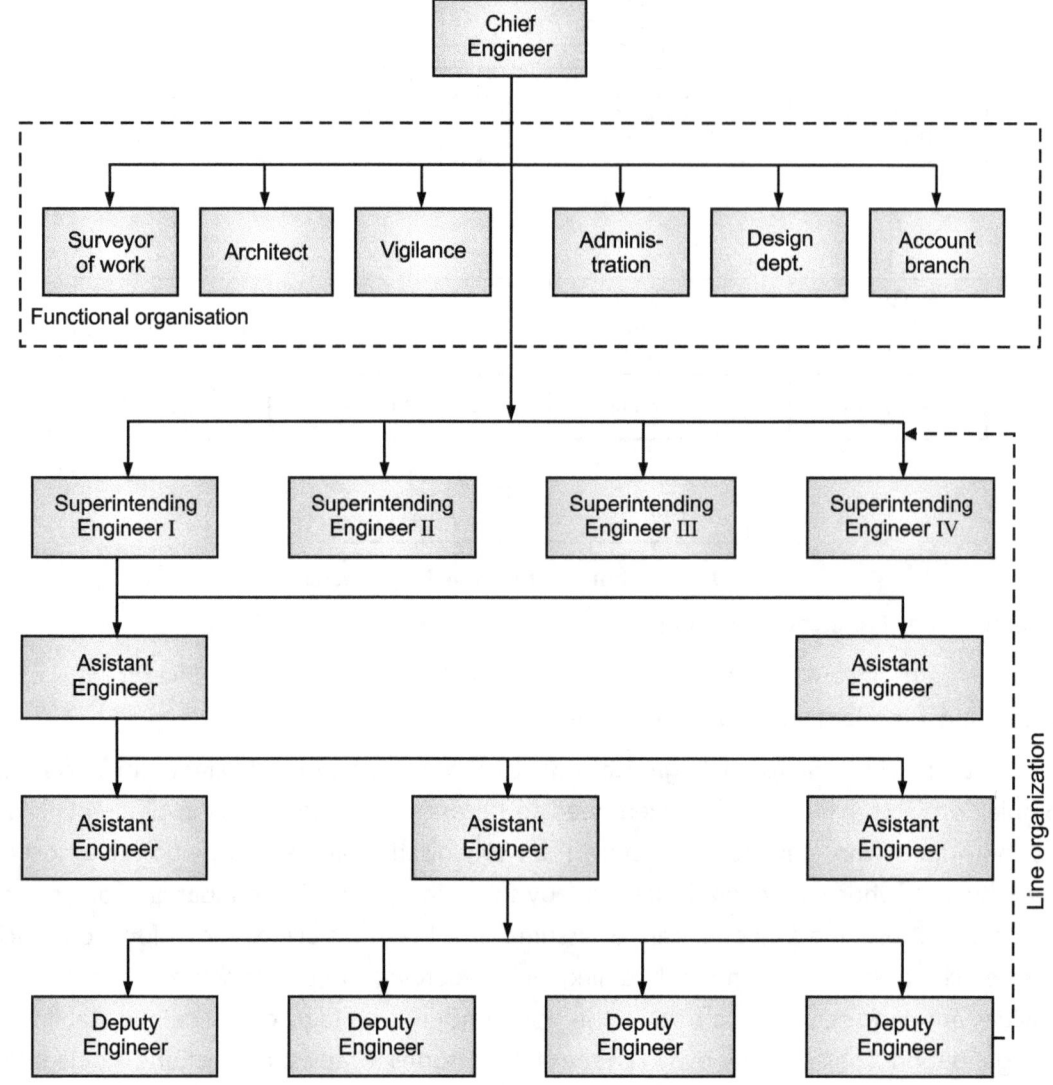

Fig. 1.7 : Line and functional organization

Disadvantages of Line and Staff Organisation

- Product/consultancy cost will increase because of high salaries of staff executives.
- Line and staff organisation may get confusion in case functions are not clear.
- In this type of organisation staff may lose their initiative, drive and ingenuity.

Application of Line and Staff Organisation

Line and staff organisation is very common among the medium and large company/consultancy/project.

1.15 MATRIX STRUCTURE

Matrix structure offers a flexible and adaptive means of providing temporary project assignments. It combines some of the advantages of project organisations with those of functional organisation. It is the organisation system of Burns and Stalker wherein an organisation is required that can meet changing and unstable conditions. It is used in situations where organisational changes have to be made in order to cope up with different situations and conditions including unfamiliar problems. Fig. 1.8 illustrates the general principles of a matrix organisation. In this organisation, the functional groups take their place in line below the chief executive or a general manager in the same manner as is in functional organisation.

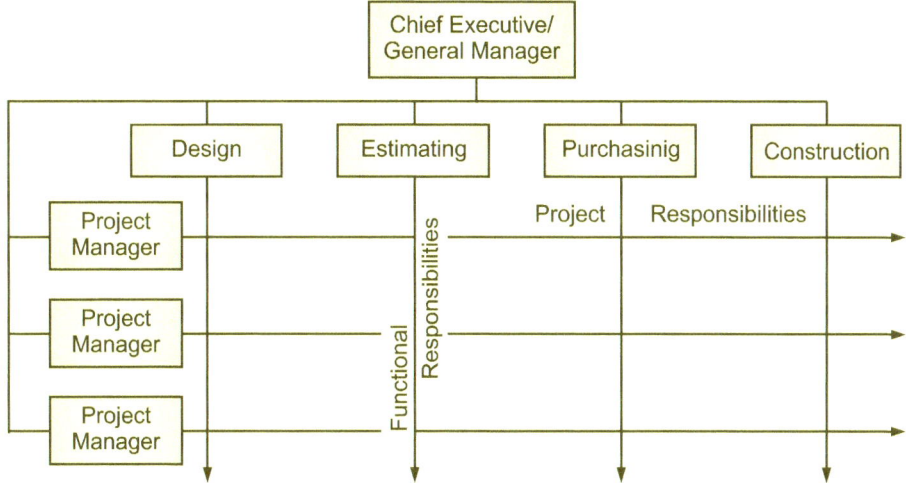

Fig. 1.8

Each functional head can, therefore, ensure the excellence of his own specialisation and in particular its technological advance. As is demonstrated in the figure the vertical responsibilities are functional while the horizontal responsibilities lie with the individual project groups. It will be the responsibility of a project manager to obtain the appropriate contribution and expertise needed from each function for his own project even though individuals are permanently assigned to functional departments and are responsible to the departmental heads.

An important aspect of such an organisation concerns the technical interchange which can take place between projects as a result of experience gained by different personnel. It has been observed that a matrix organisation tends to result in greater utilisation of technical personnel; career progression can take place for an individual within a functional department or through project management. It is also useful in situations where an organisation has to handle such projects where there is a combination of small and large projects. In fact, in such type of organisation there is somewhat merging of functional organisation and project organisation. It permits better planning, flexibility and service.

A disadvantage of matrix management occurs as a result of apparently divided responsibility of personnel as between the project manager and the functional head. Conflict can occur. Similarly it is easy for a project manager to blame a functional department for schedule delays and cost overuns.

Matrix organisation is useful in various industries such as Electronics, Banking, Advertising etc. where there is real need of functional department.

Modified Matrix Structure

As the organisation grows, it is difficult to control over all project managers and functional manager₹ To avoid this difficulty, a separate Director (Project) is appointed. He controls all projects managers and reports to General Manager directly.

The Director (Projects) evaluates all projects under his control to see if they are in tune with the overall objectives of organisation. The modified structure of Matrix type of organisation is as follows :

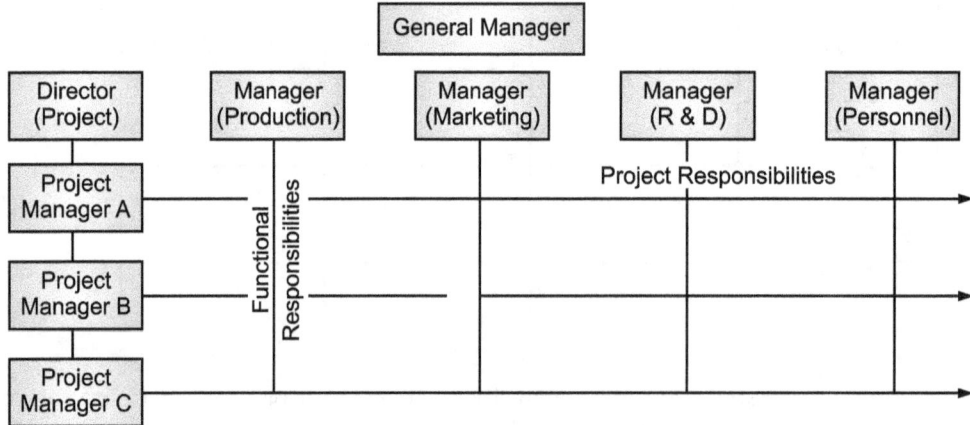

Fig. 1.9

1.16 PROJECT MANAGEMENT INSTITUTES

Various project management institutes are working at National and International levels and contributing a lot towards development of project management. A brief overview of some of the institutes as follows :

(1) International Project Management Association (IPMA)

Founded in 1965, IPMA is the world's first project management association with more than 55 member associations. IPMA actively promotes competence in Project Management for individuals, project teams, businesses, organizations and government agencies around the world. Following goals are adopted to increase the recognition and effectiveness of project management profession :

- Certify project managers in a wide range of specific roles.
- Seek to highlight, improve and increase the behavioural and contextual competencies of all project and programme stakeholders.
- Recognise and award excellent and successful project teams, research projects and individual.
- Assess and certify the PM maturity of entire organization.
- Support basic and advanced PM education and learning.
- Acknowledge and further develop the performance competence of emerging young professionals.
- Offer distinctive and useful project management publications.

(2) Association of Project Management (APM)

Association for project management is a registered charity in United Kingdom which aims to develop and promote the professional disciplines of Project Management and Programme Management through a programme called "5 Dimensions of Professionalism". The APM Business Management System (BMS) is the management frame work within which APM operates. The APM is the certification body in the UK for the IPMA.

(3) Construction Industry Council (CIC)

It is the representative body for the professional bodies, research organizations and specialist business associations in the construction industry in UK. CIC works with a mission to serve society by

(a) promoting quality and sustainability in the built environment,
(b) giving leadership to the construction industry, encouraging unity of purpose, collaboration, continuous improvement and career development
(c) adding value and emphasis to the work of members.

CIC allows memberships in three categories as (i) Full members, (ii) Associate members, (iii) Honorary affiliate membership.

(4) Project Management Association of Japan (PMAJ)

PMAJ is established with an urgent need to train personnel who carries out Project Management in a practical manner and to keep the Japanese industries at par with their U.S. and European counterparts. For this purpose, to carry out promotion and distribution related activities for the project and program management a standard guidebook called "P2M" is prepared. It is the abbreviation for "Project and Program Management for Enterprise Innovation" and can be used by students, business people, managers and professional. It enlarges the scope of project and program management from conventional focus on work front to the overall organization including general management level.

(5) Society of Project Managers Singapore (SPM)

It is an amalgam of learning society and a professional body which acts as a vehicle for advancing the development of project management. The objectives are stated in brief as follows :

- To promote and develop profession and project management.
- To promote and propagate sound managerial, technical and commercial practices relating to project management.
- To stipulate training and experience requirements.

(6) Global Alliance for Project Performance Standards (GAPPS)

GAPPS is an alliance of government, private industry, professional associations and training/academic institutes working together to develop globally applicable project management competency based standards, frameworks and mapping. It also facilitate mutual recognition and transferability of project management qualifications. The aim of GAPPS is to provide global project management community with information that is freely available for use by businesses, academic institutions, professional associations and government standards and qualifications bodies globally.

(7) Australian Institute of Project Management (AIPM)

AIPM is the premier body of project management in Australia that represent a federation of over 50 national project management associations from around the world. Institutes role is to improve the knowledge, skills and competence of project managers and related project personnel, all of whom play a key role in the achievement of business objectives.

Web Sites Referred

For the above topics are follows : Students are required to refer these websites and get more information about these institutes :

- International Project Management Association (IPMA) ipma.ch/
- Association for Project Management : www.apm.org.uk
- Construction industry Council : www.cic.org.uk/
- Project Management Association of Japan : www.pmaj.org.jp
- Society of Project Managers Singapore : www.sprojm.org.sg
- Global Alliance for Project Performance Standards : www.globalpmstandards.org
- Australian Institute of Project Management : www.aipm.com.au

IMPORTANT POINTS

- Definition of Management by various management thinkers.
- Importance of Management and its characteristics.
- Different functions of management for smooth functioning of site.

- F.W. Taylor's concept of scientific management, his contribution points and principles of scientific management.
- Fayol's 14 principles of management.
- Different categories of project as per governments policy for socialistic pattern.
- Different stages in project with points.
- Concept of organisation, importance of organisation and characteristics of organisation.
- Common principles of organisation.
- Different types of authority and its characteristics.
- Concept of delegation, its principles and problems.
- Types of organisation and its types with advantages and disadvantages.
- Project structure, its importance, advantages and limitations of it.
- Project planning, its steps, concept of scheduling and controlling.
- Different network techniques for project planning, bar chart, CPM, PERT, TOPS, GERT.
- Concept of CPM and PERT in project planning and comparison of CPM and PERT.
- Salient feature of Bar Chart i.e. Advantages of bar chart, limitations of bar chart and remedial measures for removal of shortcomings of bar chart.

QUESTIONS

1. Write short notes on
   - (i) Project life cycle phases.
   - (j) Merits and Demerits of Matrix Structures. =
   - (g) Importance of Project Management in Construction Industry
   - (f) Categories of Project.
2. Discuss the merits and demerits of matrix structure.
3. Explain the following principles of Management
   - (i) Division of work.
   - (ii) Decentralisation of authority.
   - (iii) Unity of direction.
4. What is project ? Explain the concept of project.
5. What is meant by 'Project Life Cycle' ? Explain the 'Planning and Organising phase' of project life cycle.
6. Differentiate between public sector and private sector.
7. Explain characteristics and principles of organization.
8. Explain, what is a Matrix Structure ?

9. Explain the Evolution of Scientific Management.
10. Explain Line and Staff Organization w.r.t. its merits and demerits.
11. Define : Project, Management
12. What is the importance of management?
13. Give characteristics of management?
14. Describe each function of management of brief.
15. What is PMBOK?
16. What are different categories of project?
17. What are different stages in a project?
18. What do you mean by Project Life Cycle? What are different phases considered?
19. What do you mean by organization? Explain principles of management in brief.
20. What is meant by Authority? also state the meaning of delegation of authority.
21. What are the different Project Management Institutes established in the world? Explain importance of each.

Unit - II

PROJECT PLANNING AND SCHEDULING

2.1 INTRODUCTION

Planning is the most important part of management processes. Without proper planning, successful completion of any project or running of any organization will not be possible. The objective of planning is to complete the project in a better manner in proper time and to make logical decisions which will help to understand the complexity of situation in execution in a better way. In construction management, the work must be completed in a fixed predecided duration at previously estimated cost. The analytical methods of planning include system analysis, operation research, system engineering and the like. However, in very simple language, the planning of any project includes

1. What to do ?
2. When to do ?
3. How to do ?
4. Who will do ?
5. Where to do ?

The planning, therefore, deals with execution of any project after it has been decided to undertake the same. Any project consists of different activities which will have inter-dependence. A system is a sequence of arrangement of different activities of work considering their interdependence.

Planning is proper sequencing of these activities. Proper scheduling of the different activities before commencement of the work and controlling the operations in a systematic manner is the heart of planning. Early era of scientific management and planning may be pointed to introduction of Gantt charts. This may be said to be beginning of scientific project management technique. This method of scheduling was developed by Henry Gantt sometime in 1899. Modern techniques of management include Critical Path Method (CPM) and Project Evaluation and Review Technique (PERT). These techniques aid the managers in planning, scheduling and control of large and complex projects wherein there may be different constraints on various resources.

2.2 HISTORICAL REVIEW OF MANAGEMENT TECHNIQUES

Historical construction projects were undertaken in ancient Egyptian and Roman Empires. The projects were architectural brilliance. Very little is known about the planning of these monumental projects, the scheduling and controlling during construction. It took nearly nineteenth century for the planners to think of work and time relationship through graphical representation. Credit goes to W. Taylor sometime in 19th century for establishing graphically work-time relationship in construction management.

However, the popularisation of this graphical representation on scientific basis was made by Henry L. Gantt and Fedric. This may be said to be commencement of work scheduling on scientific basis. The present day bar chart is modification of the Gantt chart which is an excellent and very easy representation of different activities in any project. With different limitations of this bar chart regarding interdependence of activities and resource limitations, different other methods of scheduling like 'line on balance', 'mile stone' and 'curves' were some developments over the Gantt chart. But their use was limited and were not of much help in controlling and hence served only as a preliminary method of scheduling. To suit with the complex problems in construction or any other project and different rapidly changing methods in construction, it was very necessary that the scheduling methods should have built-in provisions for showing clearcut inter-relationship of different activities, scope for decision making with due consideration for the shortening of the time to do so. This evolved the new techniques like CPM and PERT. Many other forms of this techique such as Graphic Evaluation and Review Technique (GERT), Resource Allocation and Manpower Planning System (RAMP'S) etc. have been evolved and have also become popular.

Since ancient period when gigantic construction projects have been completed and today also they are in existence, there must have been some management techniques used. Management must be an age-old science which must have been applied to simple and complex problems and everyday problems to long duration projects. Without being put into words and in books, this science must have been in use for many thousands of years. It may be that the ancient day-to-day problems were simpler and very big projects were a few. Also the persons involved were also handful in number as such they used to follow their own techniques based upon previous experience, their innovative ideas and process of contemplation. However, after the industrial revolution, there was tremendous growth in the complex problems related to development of industries, small as well as large and especially development of factory system. It also led to big construction project needed for big industries, steel, cement etc. and even small industries for consumer goods. With the advent of industrial revolution, the population in the urban areas went on increase in geometrical proportion and this also lead to construction of big complexes and construction projects for Government and other public establishments. This also needed projects for public amenities and completion of such complex projects and even simple projects in comparatively small duration economically was a challenge. Proper management was the only tool to face this situation and with the completion of such complex project, the methodology used and the experience was shared and was studied. This systematic study, probably, became science of management. The importance of this science was evident when it was being studied and used. Later on scientific analysis and studies were conducted and this science was based on firm principles and different aspects were further studied in details and scientific technology was evolved on different aspects. This led to modern science of Project Planning and Management and its different aspects such as :

- Project Planning
- Project Management Techniques
- Organisation
- Material Management
- Work Study
- Financial Management
- Safety Engineering
- Personnel Management
- Management Information System (MIS)
- Communication in Management
- Maintenance and Replacement Studies
- Industrial Budgeting and Cost Analysis
- Marketing Management
- Forms of Industrial Enterprises
- Plant Layout
- Production Planning and Control
- Production System Analysis Techniques.

2.3 PROJECT AND ITS OBJECTIVES

A project is composed of different jobs, tasks, functions or activities which are related to each other. The job has some objectives so that completion of all these related jobs or tasks successfully will lead to completion of the project and the objective of the project is fulfilled. Any project has to commence at a specific moment and will be finished when all the related jobs are completed. For working and completion of any project, basic things required are

1. Material resources including raw material and machinery, and
2. Manpower resources.

Availability of both of the above is absolutely necessary for successful completion of the project. However, availability, quality and proper use of human resources is most important determinant factor in completion of the project and thereby accomplishing the project objectives. In project planning, technology and management both are very important. The technology considers the recent innovations in using the material and working of processes while the management deals with the manpower resources and its critical use in handling materials and processes. It is, therefore, necessary that the rapid accumulation of scientific techniques and innovations should match the corresponding improvement in the sphere of human group relation and this can be achieved through proper management. Management is necessary to increase the productivity using technological innovations and critical use of the manpower resources available.

Any project will have following objectives

- The project should be completed at a minimum capital investment i.e. the project should be economical.
- The project should be completed within as minimum time period as possible.
- It should be completed with the critical use of the available manpower.

Project Management is the process of achieving the above three objectives in completion of the project. This involves planning before the project commences and also planning during the execution of the project. The phases of planning before commencement of the project are

1. Project Planning and
2. Project Scheduling.

The phase of planning during the execution involves Project Controlling.

This phase involves recognising the different difficulties encountered during the execution and to overcome these difficulties by applying suitable measures so that the execution confirms to the pre-execution schedule and the pre-execution phases.

2.4 PROJECT PLANNING

The first of the precommencement phases of the project is planning. Planning consists of the following steps :

1. Defining clearly the objective of the project.
2. Dividing the project into different independent tasks or unit jobs for completion of the project.
3. Determination of total requirement of different types of material for completion of the unit jobs.
4. Determination of machinery needed.
5. Determination of needed manpower.

6. Preparing estimates of cost of different tasks.
7. Determination of duration of completion of different unit jobs or tasks.
8. Decide on a plan.

The above steps are absolutely necessary for successful completion of the project. This planning is important as it will decide the direction of the implementation, help in preparing framework of jobs and will be able to reveal the possible breaks. It will also be useful in setting some performance standard. The starting point of planning in many projects is available resources. Sometimes this becomes a problem which has to be solved in planning phase before proceeding to the next phase which is scheduling for the project.

2.5 SCHEDULING

Scheduling is the sequencing of different independent tasks with their time relationship with reference to each other. With the available manpower and other resources, the time duration for each individual task will have to be determined. Alternatively, the required resources will have to be planned if the duration of the individual task is to be fixed if there is any constrain for the same. However, normally the available resources will decide the duration of the task. With this step completed, the sequencing of the different operations or activities will have to be decided and according to the duration of activities the allocation of available resources will have to be decided. Scheduling forms a very important phase of the project and especially in this phase attention will be needed to those resources whose availability is limited as they will be imposing a constrain in the project. Skilled technical manpower and the capital investments are the two important limitations of the resources. Scheduling is very important part of the project planning as it deals with inter-relationship between the individual tasks and realistic estimates of the duration of the same in commensurating with the available resources. Allocation of the available resources to the different concurrent activities will also decide the duration of the different activities and it will have to be given due consideration that concurrent activities are simultaneously taken up with allocation of resources and the project is not delayed because of undue delay of any of the activities.

2.6 CONTROLLING

The planning and scheduling form the two important steps before the actual project commences. The controlling phase starts after the project starts and is undertaken during the conduct of the different project operations, activities or tasks. As far as possible, it is necessary to see that the project performs as per the predecided schedule. But because of the different difficulties faced during the operation due to different unavoidable reasons, it may not be possible to adhere to the schedule. It is, therefore, necessary at different stages of the operation of the project to review the difference between predetermined schedule and the actual performance. This will be effective to determine the precise effect of the deviation of the actual performance from the schedule. It will also be necessary to review, to replan and to reschedule so that the deviations are compensated and the project is completed, as far as possible in the predecided duration.

Project control can, therefore, be defined as 'a formal mechanism in determining the deviations in actual performance compared to the basic plan and predetermined schedule and to determine the precise effect of the deviation with respect to the duration of completion of the project so that, if necessary the project can be replanned and rescheduled to compensate for the deviation for completion of the project in the predetermined duration.

The different steps in accomplishing controlling can be summarized as below :

- Establishing standards and targets in terms of the time for completion of different phases of the project.
- Actual measure of performance compared to the set down target and standard at the end of different stages.
- To identify the deviations from the standards in terms of time and other measures.
- To suggest and select the correcting measures. This will consist of problem of identifying the bottle necks and the different drawbacks and shortcomings in terms of resources, decision making, organising the needed correction especially in terms of resources. This will include the skills necessary for the decision maker. In fact, the controlling of any project consists of
    1. Time control
    2. Cost control and
    3. Quality control.

2.6.1 Decision Making – A Key in Project Management.

In all the phases of project planning, decision making is most important. It will be necessary to make right decisions at all the stages of management which include planning, organising, staffing, scheduling and controlling.

The decisions to be taken will depend upon the available resources at any stage and should lead to the goal to be achieved. The success or failure of the project will depend upon the decisions taken by the management at different stages.

Even though the decision mainly depends upon the available resources, it is very necessary at each stage to identify the central problem and find out the different alternatives to solve the same. It is also necessary to analyse the different alternatives and considering the short falls and strength of different alternatives, final decision will have to be made.

2.7 METHODS OF PLANNING

It is not very easy to manage complex projects and also research and development projects which may have certain uncertainties. It is, therefore, very necessary to plan the project properly, prepare work schedules and control the project-accordingly while in execution. It will be necessary to see that the project is completed as far as possible in the estimated duration and at the estimated cost and achieve its technical performance objectives. For this, it is necessary that improved modern techniques of management be employed from the conception of the project and also at any intermediate stage. These modern improved techniques in any form consist of the following :

- Defining clearly the work to be performed, with the help of work breakdown structure.
- Developing more realistic schedule and cost estimates based on available resources to perform the work.
- Determining the optimum use of available resources to achieve the best in terms of time, cost and technical performance objectives.
- Identifying areas which may develop potential delays and cost overruns in time so that corrective measures and action can be taken in time.

The modern techniques to achieve above objectives of project management are as below :

- Bar chart and its modifications.
- Network diagram and its modifications.

2.8 WORK BREAKDOWN STRUCTURE

The most important function of management is **"Planning"** which involves listing of activities, finding logic and interdependence and assigning the durations to each activity. As the project grows larger, number of tasks increases and it becomes necessary to break them into smaller manageable units called as "**activities**" which can be easily supervised and estimated. Hence, this method is called as *work breakdown structure*. This method is used by project managers to simplify the project execution.

The general steps which are followed in the process of work breakdown structure are as follows :

- A team of project managers and Subject Matter Experts (SME) who are involved in the project, is formed.
- Breaking down the tasks is started from the end product in its entirely and work downwards to increasing levels of detail. This is usually can be the title of the project e.g. Construction of Bungalow at Lonavala. (Bungalow at Lonavala)
- Define the main deliverables i.e. the main components of the projects end product e.g. substructure, superstructure, landscaping etc.

- This step defines the 'main branches' of the project.

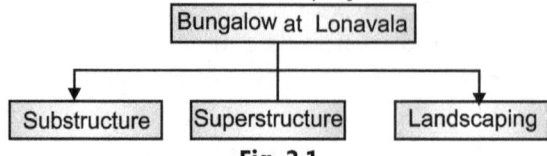

Fig. 2.1

- These 'main branches' are again broken down into their subcomponents using as many sub-branches as needed until manageable 'activities' are defined. These need not be sub-divided further.

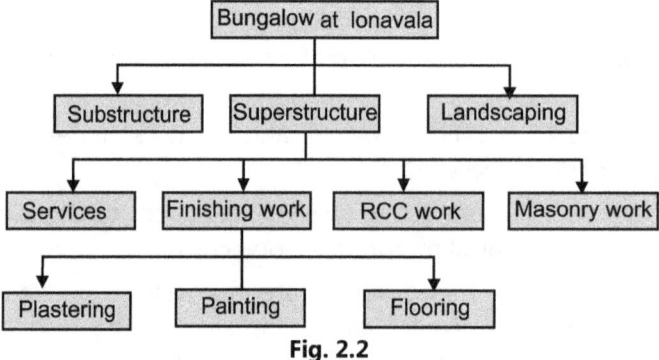

Fig. 2.2

- A detailed "WBS" is as shown in the following Fig.

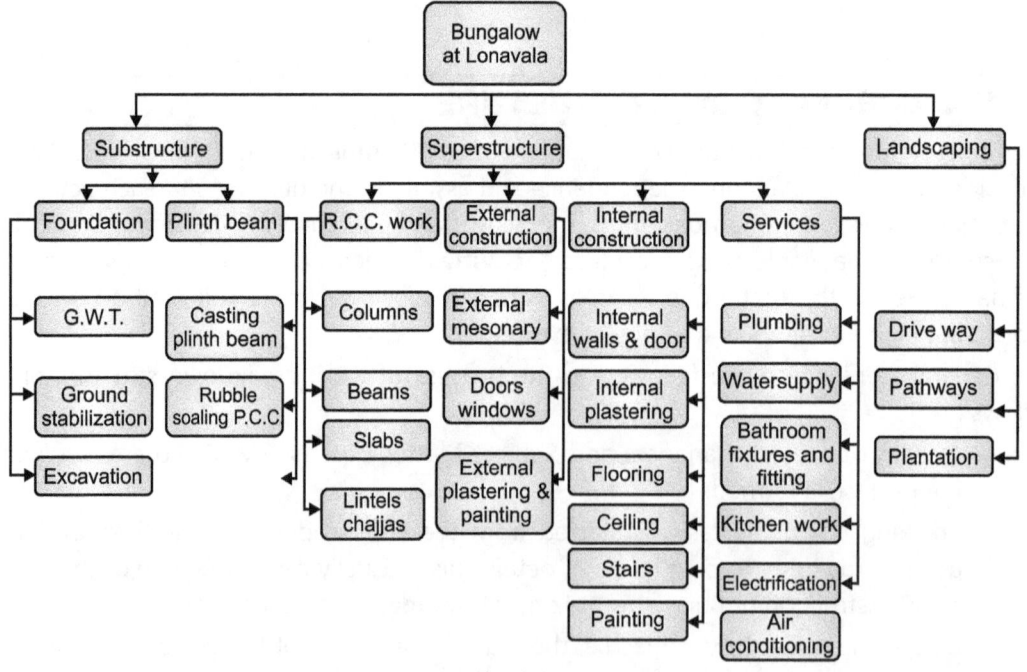

Fig. 2.3

- There are no hard and fast rules that are to be followed while break-down the tasks. One has to rely on his experience, type of project and the management style followed for the project. Generally, 8/80 rule is used, which says, no task should be smaller than 8 hours of work (i.e. 1 day approx.) and should not be larger than 80 hours of work (i.e. 10 days approximately)

2.8.1 Advantages of Work Breakdown Structure

- It assigns accurate responsibilities to the project team.
- WBS indicates project mile stones and control points.
- It also helps to estimate cost, time and risk.
- WBS defines the project scope so that the stakeholders can have a better understanding of the same.
- It provides the foundation for planning, resource allocation and scheduling.
- It gives us the information of necessary work that is distribute between elements of the project, distribution of cost and budget between different elements of the project, division of larger elements into smaller ones.

WBS can also be represented on a list as shown below

Project : Construction of Bunglow at Lonavala

- 1.0 Structure
- 1.1 Foundation
    - 1.1.1 Excavation
    - 1.1.2 Ground Stabilisation
    - 1.1.3 Construction of Footing
- 1.2 Plinth beam
    - 1.2.1 Casting of plinth beam
    - 1.2.2 Rubble soling
    - 1.2.3 PCC
- 2.0 Superstructure
- 2.1 RCC work
    - 2.1.1 Columns
    - 2.1.2 Beams
    - 2.1.3 Slabs
    - 2.1.4 Intel Chaijass

2.9 BAR CHART

A project, whatsoever, complex can be easily divided into number of well-defined manageable jobs or units called activities. These activities have to be performed in a definite sequence for successful completion of the project. These different activities consume resources and take time for their completion. Bar chart developed by A. Gantt was the first introduction of scientific management technique for project controlling. It was an improved method of planning and controlling than the available method of production of ordinance factories introduced and developed by Henry L. Gantt for U.S. Army sometime around 1900.

This simple method consisted of preparation of a chart which displayed different activities by horizontal bars representing the schedule of different activities. The duration of the different activities were represented by the horizontal length of the bars. This pictorial representation of scheduling was probably one of the earliest methods of scheduling on some rational basis and therefore, was named after the innovator as Gantt's chart or more popularly as Bar chart as the different activities were represented by horizontal rectangular bars. The different activities of any project or the horizontal bars were represented on Y-axis against the duration of respective activities on X-axis. Horizontal lines of duration on X-axis are plotted to scales whereas on the Y-axis the activities are represented as to suit the representation of pictorial view and are arbitrary. Each bar represents one specific unit job or activity to be performed and the beginning and the end of each bar represent the time of commencement and completion of the activity on the horizontal time scale. Hence, the length of the bar represents the time of completion of that activity as indicated earlier.

These bar charts can be explained with the help of following examples

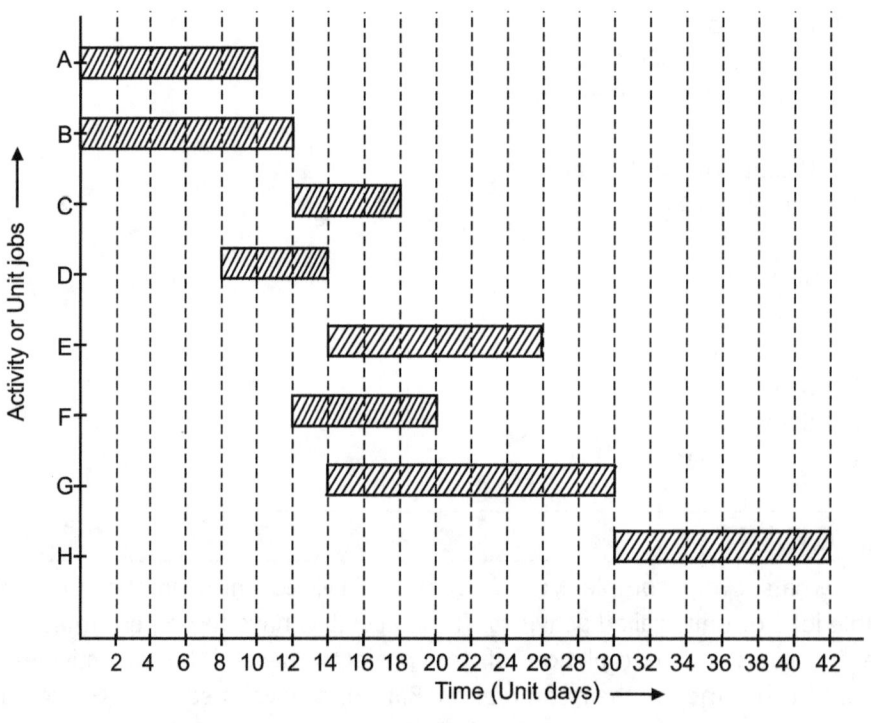

Fig. 2.4

Bar Chart 1

A Gantt chart is shown in Fig. 2.4. A project consisting of 8 different activities A, B, C, D, E, F, G, H is represented in the Fig. 2.4. The duration of the activities are 10, 12, 6, 6, 16, 8, 16, 12 days respectively.

These activities are analysed and sequence of the activities are decided using work break down structure. The analysis is given below :

1. Activities A activities D and G are completed.
2. End of activity H is completion of the project.

The above analysis of the different activities can be tabulated as shown below :

Sr. No.	Name of Activity	Duration in Days	Preceding Activity	Succeeding Activity	Remark
1	A	10	NIL		
2	B	12	NIL		
3	C	6	B		
4	D	6	NIL	E	8 days after A and B have commenced
5	E	12	D		
6	F	8	A		
7	G	16	A, D		
8	H	12	D, G		

After this tabulation the bar chart is prepared as shown below. For any activity if there is any preceding activity, the succeeding activity should start at the same instant, the preceding activity is completed so that the project is completed in minimum period. However, if there is no preceding activity, such activities can start simultaneously but the resources should be taken into consideration.

2.9.1 Salient Features of Bar Chart

Advantages of Bar Chart

- It is very simple and easy method of scheduling.
- Each activity is shown separately. Actual progress of work can be easily compared with the proposed schedule. Hence, modifications can be carried out easily if required.
- Interdependence of the different activities can be represented to a limited extent.

- Achievements on a particular date in progress can be easily represented.
- Cumulative progress can be represented on bar chart.
- It can represent possible delays.

Limitations of Bar Chart
- Interdependence of the various activities cannot be shown absolute clearly and sequence of activities is not clear.
- By itself it does not indicate the progress of the project and hence cannot be used for effective controlling.
- It cannot represent and reflect tolerance and uncertainties in time estimation for various activities.
- It does not give optimum duration of the project.
- Different alternatives cannot be evaluated from bar chart.
- It is not possible to locate critical activities.
- In some the projects there are activities wherein estimation of time required for completion of these activities cannot be precisely determined. This is so in case of projects involving research or development projects or projects like space vehicle launching and the like. In case of such projects the bar chart may not be useful as there may be frequent rescheduling in case of many activities because of change in time of completion of such activities. It is not possible to incorporate such rescheduling flexibility in the bar chart and hence bar charts are not useful in research and development or innovative projects.
- Bar chart diagrams, though very simple to construct and understand, are useful only in case of small-size conventional projects in which number of activities are limited and time duration of completion of them are definite. These bar charts are, therefore, used in construction and manufacturing projects wherein the time estimation can be made with fair degree of accuracy.
- Along with research and development projects, bar charts are not normally used in case of complicated projects involving multifarious activities large in number which are interdependent even though their time estimation may be finite.

2.9.2 Remedial Measures for Removal of Shortcomings of Bar Chart

Lack of Degree of Details

Too many activities cannot be separately shown on the bar chart as it may become clumsy. Hence, different small activities are coupled into major activities and such major tasks are only represented in the bar chart. Hence, in big projects where there are too many activities, representation on bar chart is difficult and hence bar chart cannot be used for big projects. A particular activity is shown by a single bar, the subactivities cannot be separated out and hence effective control over the activities is not possible and cannot be achieved.

One example of such major activity involving different subactivities may be cited. In the project of renovation of a workshop, a major activity may be replacement of old machine by a new one.

This activity in a bar chart may be represented by a single bar. But this activity involves the following different subactivities :

- Ordering a new machine.
- Getting delivery of new machine.
- Incorporating power and other changes for fixing new machine.
- Removing old machine.
- Installation of new machine.
- Testing new machine.
- Disposal of old machine.

A separate bar chart as given below may be prepared for this single activity.

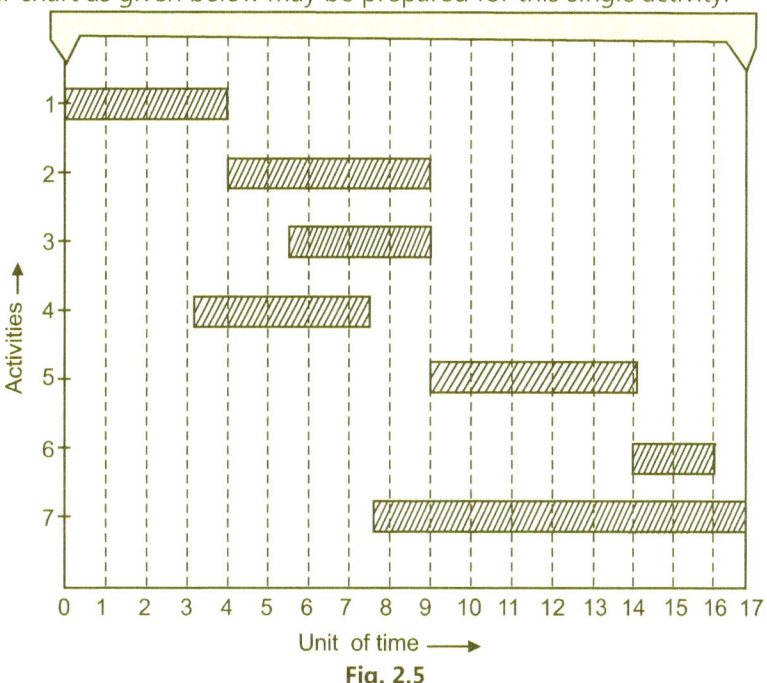

Fig. 2.5

2.9.3 Comparison of Project Progress with the Schedule and Review

As the bar chart itself duly represents the schedule, it cannot show the progress of work and hence it is not a useful device in control of the project. It is absolutely necessary that the actual progress of the work has to be compared with the schedule at specific instances of time so that if necessary some rescheduling can be thought of. The remaining activities may be rescheduled suitably if the actual progress differs much from the designed progress. The actual progress of work at a particular instant of time can be depicted on the existing bar chart prepared prior to the start of the project representing the proposed schedule. The progress of different activities can be shown on this bar chart by hatched lines on the top half of the bar rectangle representing the same activity or in short the bar chart of actual progress is superimposed on the bar chart of the proposed schedule and can be shown by different colours. Fig. 2.6 represents a bar chart with 4 activities. The proposed progress and actual progress is compared after completion of 11th week of the project. The actual progress of each activity at the end of 11th week is represented on half the width of the same activity by hatching.

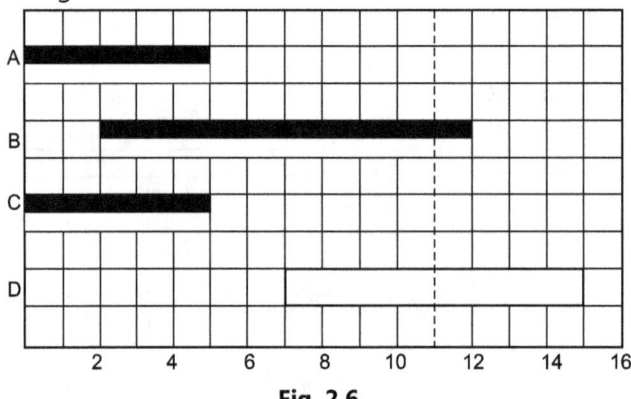

Fig. 2.6

The following table gives the complete information regarding the comparison of proposed progress with actual progress.

Sr. No.	Activity	Proposed Duration in Weeks	Proposed Progress after 11th Week	Actual Progress after 11th Week	Comparison
1.	A	7	7 weeks work completed	5 weeks work completed	2 weeks lagging
2.	B	11	9 weeks work completed	10 weeks work completed	1 week ahead of schedule
3.	C	5	5 weeks work completed	5 weeks work completed	As per schedule
4.	D	8	4 weeks work completed	Nil, not started	4 weeks lagging

Activity A is 2 weeks behind the schedule. Activity D is succeeding activity of A. Hence its start is 4 weeks lagging and the actual work is also lagging by 4 weeks, hence the project is likely to be completed behind the schedule by 4 + 4 = 8 weeks even though the progress of activity B is 1 week ahead of the schedule and activity C is as per schedule.

2.9.4 Inter-relationship of Activities

In any project some activities are inter-dependent i.e. a particular activity can commence only after some other activity is completed. Such activities whose start and end depend upon each other, have to be represented serially in bar chart as their interdependence is clearly established. However, many other activities can run simultaneously or are cocurrent activities and as such they are shown by bars over same time scale. This concurrency cannot be clearly depicted as it is not very clear whether these activities, though concurrent, start simultaneously or there is only some overlap of time. As such the overlap cannot represent the degree of concurrency and the inter-relationship cannot be clearly represented in bar chart. These activities which are shown by the overlapping bars on time scale may be completely independent or may have some interdependency. However, this cannot be represented on bar chart or the parallel bars cannot give any information about independency or interdependency of these concurrent activities.

This will be clear from the example of project of canal construction which includes layout, excavation and lining.

The different activities are

A   Layout of the canal on proposed central line according to the section – 6 weeks

B   Excavation for canal – 12 weeks

C   Lining of canal – 12 weeks

Activity C is succeeding activity of B which is further a succeeding activity of A. Independently, the different events would take durations as given above. If all the activities would be undertaken serially, the project would take 31 weeks for completion. However, since work in the project is in linear extension, it could be divided in sections and for each section all the above three activities can be undertaken serially and the bar chart would be as shown below after staggering the activities.

Activity B is started 2 weeks after commencement of activity A. After completion of activity A, 9 weeks work of activity B is left. Similarly activity C has 4 weeks work left after completion of activity B. Now, if due to some difficulties, the time of completion of activity A is delayed by 2 or 3 weeks, what effect it will make on the succeeding activities B and C ?

How will these activities be affected ? This cannot be clearly depicted in the bar chart and inter-dependence of the different activities cannot be clearly indicated in the bar chart or can be revealed from the bar chart.

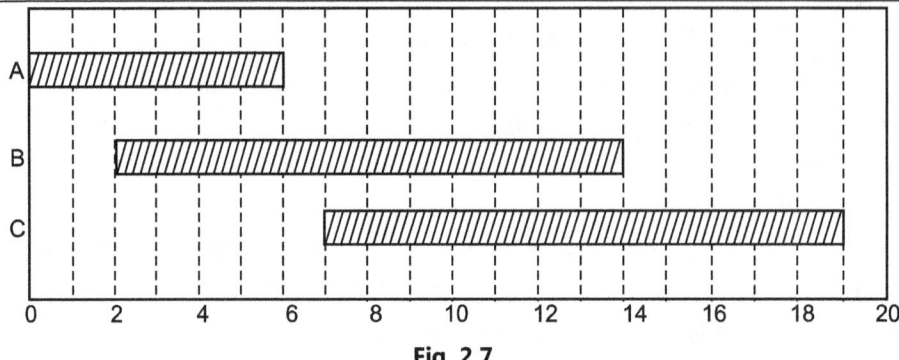

Fig. 2.7

However, by modifying the bar chart, this difficulty can be overcome. Each activity in the bar chart can be suitably divided into different equal sections so that all the three activities can be taken up sequentially for these sections. This is represented in Fig. 2.8.

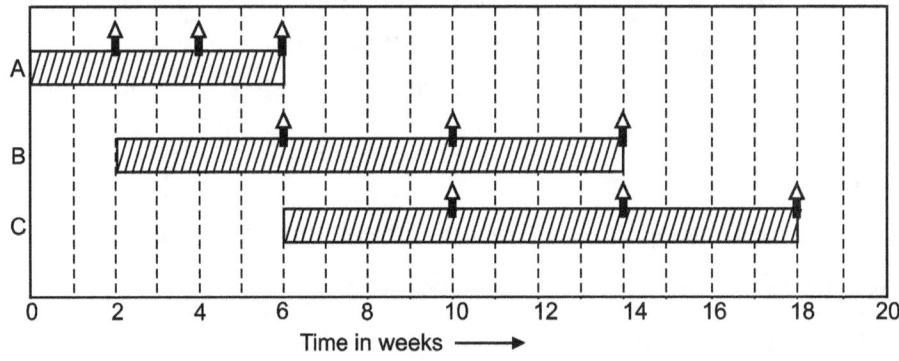

Fig. 2.8

Each activity is divided in three sections. For activity A each section will require 2 weeks for completion, for activity B each section will require 4 weeks for completion and for activity C each section will require 4 weeks for completion. With this modification, effect of delay in work of activity A can be very easily contemplated on next activity B or that of delay in activity B can be easily found out on activity C. With this, control measures necessary can be easily worked out so that the project may not be unnecessarily delayed.

2.10 INTRODUCTION TO NETWORK

The necessity of better planning and scheduling has increased due to increasing complexity of the extent of project.

The method of planning and rescheduling in case of complex large projects should enable the management to view the whole project and if necessary the management should be able to review and reschedule the project during the process of execution. The network technique is one of the most modern tools of project management which enables the planners to View at a glance, Review and Reschedule.

This network planning and scheduling technique developed sometime in 1940 in western countries is used extensively now in planning of complex projects and controlling the execution of various activities and operation in the projects. The main advantages of this network technique are simplicity, flexibility and necessary overall control on the work. This technique is a useful tool for management of a project.

To determine the date of completion of any Civil Engineering project, or a Mechanical Engineering Project an Electrical Engineering Project, it is not only enough to prepare an estimate of cost of the project but most important is the planning of various operations or activities involved, time required for the completion of all these activities and the knowledge of inter-relationship and interdependency of each activity is also essential. The total time required for the completion of the project depends upon the time required for the different activities and on their interdependence. Network planning and scheduling technique is the study of all such activities, their inter-relationship and interdependency.

2.10.1 Objectives of Network Planning and Scheduling

It is necessary for successful completion of any project that schedules and objectives of the different operations involved should be defined in a project with reference to the targets to be achieved taking into account all the problems which may creep in at the time of planning stage or during the execution of the project. Network planning and scheduling requires efficient integrated management. The main objectives can be summarized as below :

- There should be a detailed integrated planning of the different unit jobs or activities involved.
- Realistic schedules should be developed.
- Exercising effective control : There should be periodical checking and evaluation of the progress of work in comparison with the planned schedule.
- The effect of current progress of work on the time of completion of project. This review may need some remedial action and if necessary reschedule with the necessary changes in the allocation of resources.
- There should be optimum utilisation of scarce resources, time and money.

The above objectives can be achieved by proper planning, analysing and scheduling and controlling. Network Technique is the tool towards the objective.

2.10.2 Development of Network from Bar Chart

To overcome the limitation of bar chart for not showing the interdependence of activities clearly, a modification is done in which arrows are used. Consider an example in which activity (1) is the starting activity, (2) and (3) Starts only after completion of activity (1), Activity (4) can not start before completion of activities (2) and (3).

This can be shown with the help of arrows as below

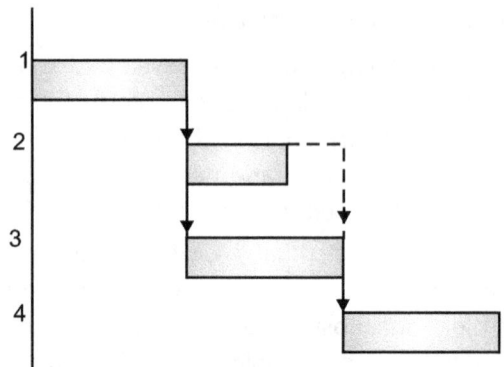

Fig. 2.9

If the bars are represented as a node, the same bar chart can be shown as a network using arrows and circles as below :

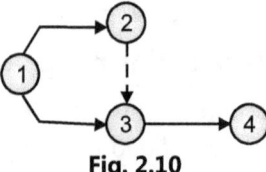

Fig. 2.10

2.10.3 Basics of Network

Network technique is one of the modern methods of project management. Any complex project can always be broken down into a number of distinct, well-defined jobs or tasks. These different tasks when completed successfully end into completion of the project. These unit tasks are called "Activities." The beginning and end of any, such unit job or activity is an important point in the network and is called an "event." Thus, activity is a unit job or task which flows between two successive events. A project, therefore, can be said to consist of different events which mark the beginning or end of different activities and the network is a flow diagram which connects the different events logically and sequentially through different activities. The network diagram is graphical representation of the different events or activities which should be completed in a sequential manner for the successful completion of the project. The event being either beginning or end of a unit job, is only a point and hence is represented by a circle. It does not consume any time or any resource and only indicates either beginning or end of an activity. The activity on the other hand is a unit job or task end of which is an event.

2.10.4 Types of Network

Networks are of two types :
    (1) Critical Path Method (CPM)
    (2) Programme Evaluation and Review Technique (PERT)

The CPM network is activity oriented whereas the PERT network is event oriented depending upon the importance of the activities and events in those methods. Fundamentally, the CPM and PERT networks are the two techniques of project management which are used in planning, scheduling and controlling the different operations involved in the project. The basic theory and the method of graphical representation of the network in both the above methods are same.

2.10.5 Characteristics of Projects Amenable to Network Planning

A project which has to be analysed by network planning either by CPM or PERT should have following characteristics.

- It should be possible that the project can be broken down into clearly recognisable distinct unit tasks or operations so that the sequential completion of all such unit jobs will end in completion of the project. Such unit jobs or tasks are named as activities. They consume time and resources.
- These different recognisable unit jobs or activities should have definite point of commencement and a definite point of conclusion. All the activities into which a project is divided should have a definite start and should have a definite end which can be distinctly recognised. This commencement or conclusion of any activity which can be defined precisely is called as *event*. which is a definite accomplishment in the project.
- For completion of the project, the different events must occur in some definite sequence which is decided by logic. This logic is decided by technological sequence in which the different events should occur so as to complete the project, which are derived by "work breakdown structure."

Thus, the basic elements of the project network are

- Activities or definite unit jobs or tasks.
- Events : Definite accomplishment in the project.

It is very clear that the activities and events are securely connected with each other. Start and end of any activity is a definite accomplishment in the project and therefore, marks an event. Any two sequential events can occur only if the unit job or activity between them is completed. So that the connection between two successive events is an activity. An event is represented by a circle or a square and an activity by a arrow joining two successive events.

Critical Path Method (CPM)

Any project consists of clearly recognisable unit jobs or operations which are called activities which consume time and resources. Commencement or completion of any activity is a definite point which is termed as event : One or More activities may commence simultaneously and may emerge from a single event whereas in the similar manner one, two or many activities may end simultaneously i.e. merge to a single event. After the project is broken down in different activities, their sequence is decided. An activity is represented by an arrow and all the activities are represented sequentially by arrows which form a CPM network. In this network, the junction between the different activities represent different events.

CPM network is generally used for such project in which it is possible to make fairly accurate estimate for the time duration required for the different activities constituting the project. Knowing the resources necessary for completion of different activities, cost estimates for the different activities can also be made to a fair degree of accuracy and hence with this knowledge, it is possible to make a very accurate estimate for the duration of completion of the project and also the estimated cost of the project. It is obvious that such information can be accurately collected from similar type of projects already executed and hence CPM networks are generally used for repetitive type of projects and have been effectively used for construction projects whatsoever complex. However, in case of research and innovative development projects, the duration of the different activities, as well as resources needed cannot be precisely decided and hence for such projects the CPM network cannot be used. Where duration of the different activities cannot be precisely decided, an optimistic, normal and pessimistic duration may be decided and most probable time for completion of the activities is decided. As such in repetitive type of projects, stress is on completion of activities and hence CPM networks are activity oriented. In research or innovative development projects, the stress is on events and in such projects which are event oriented 'Project Evaluation and Review Technique' (PERT) is used.

2.11 TYPES OF CPM NETWORK

2.11.1 CPM Method of Project Planning

CPM Method of Project Planning involves identification of specific activities, their time of completion i.e. duration and their interrelationship. In general, there are two types of networks used. They are

- Activity On Arrow (AOA) type of arrow diagramming.
- Activity On Node (AON) type of precedence diagramming.

1. Activity On Arrow Type Network

As said earlier the events are shown by numbers in geometrical figure like circle or square and the activity shown and by an arrow. The head and the tail of an arrow represent event. The event is a point and it does not consume any time. The event is also called as *Node* or *connector*. The activity is represented by letters like A or B or C or D ... etc. They are also represented by pair of numbers as 1 – 2, 2 – 3, 3 – 4 etc. In activity 1 – 2, the points 1 and 2 are the two nodes of the activity. Out of the two nodes, 1 is a 'From' node and 2 is a 'To' node and the From node must be a lower number than To node. In this way, the direction of activity arrow is clearly established. The project is divided into different activities, inter-relationship between the activities and the sequence is decided and the CPM diagram is prepared.

Fig. 2.11 shows construction of network by Activity On Arrow method (AOA).

Activity Symbol	Activity Description	Inter Dependancy	Duration in Days
A	Study of plan layout	Start Activity	1
B	Clearance of site	Follows A	1
C	Earthwork in Excavation	Follows B	6
D	Laying of foundation concrete	Follows C	5
E	Procurement of Bricks	Constant after B	3
F	Brick work	Follows D and E	10

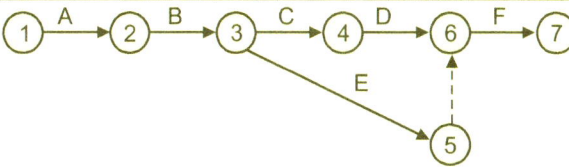

Fig. 2.11

2. Activity On Node Type Network

The problem in Activity On Arrow type or AOA network is necessity of Dummy activities for maintaining the logic and the right sequence in the network. This increases the length of the tables, enlarges the network graph and takes time for calculation work and increase the complexity of the network for large and complex projects. Another type of network is the Activity On Node diagram or precidence diagram which overcomes the problem of AOA network.

In AON network diagram, the activities are represented by boxes and arrows, and are used for designating the inter-relationship between the activities. The AON diagram is simpler to prepare and is easier to explain. It presents a clearer picture of the project as compared to AOA diagram. The AON diagram for the same problem (used for AOA) is represented in Fig. 2.14.

Both methods have their own advocates. The principal under both the methods should be understood. But the A – O – A method was first developed and is very widely used. Further, the use of numbers for events in A – O – A method has made it amenable to programming on computer and the Dummy activities used make the logic more clear. Hence A – O – A or Activity on Arrow method is more popularly used in CPM.

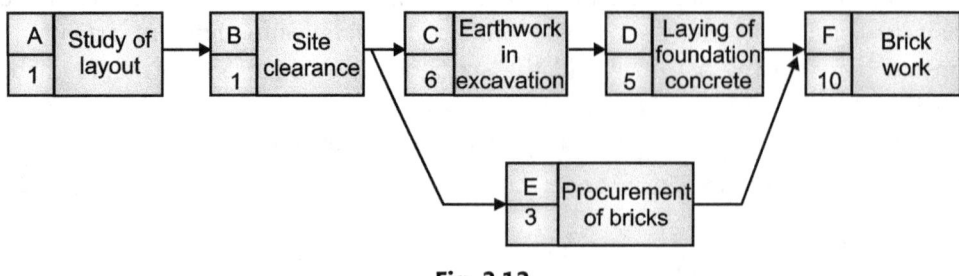

Fig. 2.12

2.12 TERMINOLOGYIES IN NETWORK

1. Event and Activity

Event is well-defined point or stage or accomplishment of the project. An event is that particular instant of time at which some specific part of a plan has been or is to be achieved. It is, therefore, the commencement or completion of an activity. Specifically, it is a definable specific accomplishment in a project plan which is recognisable at a particular instant of time. It should be definitely distinguishable as a specific point in time and should be readily understood by all those who are concerned with the project. It does not consume time or resources.

Activity is a specific job or unit task in any project and event is start or end of the activity. In construction project, excavation for foundation is an activity whereas starting of excavation for foundation is an event.

Activity	Event
1. Location of site.	(a) Site located.
2. Excavation for foundation.	(b) Commencement of excavation for foundation.
	(c) Completion of excavation for foundation.
3. Installation of new machinery.	(d) New machinery installed.
4. Laying of sewer pipeline.	(e) Sewer pipeline laid.

2. Representation of Event

An event is a well-defined point in a project and hence is represented by a node. The shape used to represent the node may be

(i) circular, (ii) square, (iii) rectangle, (iv) oval shape or (v) any other regular geometrical figure such as triangles. However, generally a circle has been chosen to represent the nodes.

Events are numbered for their identification and these numbers are written inside the geometrical figure representing the node.

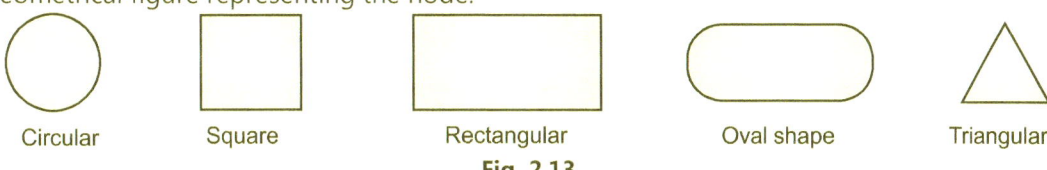

| Circular | Square | Rectangular | Oval shape | Triangular |

Fig. 2.13

3. Activity

It is the actual performance of a task or a unit job. It is a recognisable part or item or operation of the project. It, therefore, consumes time and resources in the form of manpower, material, use of machinery or any other facility. It is a positive specific tangible and meaningful effort having a proper description understandable by all concerned with the project.

4. Representation of Activity

Activities are represented by simple arrows in network diagram. The arrow runs from left to right generally so that the tail is towards left and the arrow head is towards right. The tail of the arrow represents the start of the activity and arrow head represents the end of the activity. However, the length of the arrow neither represents the magnitude of the work completed in the activity nor time required for completion of that activity. The length of the arrow is chosen to suit the convenience of drafting and proper representation of the complete network in the available space for drawing.

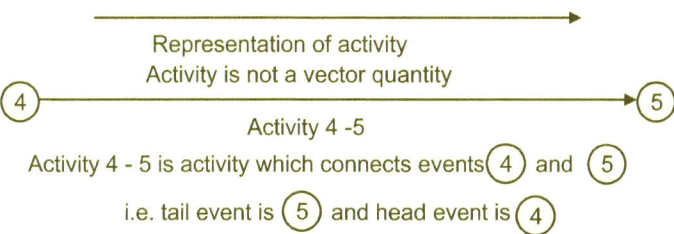

Representation of activity
Activity is not a vector quantity

Activity 4 -5

Activity 4 - 5 is activity which connects events 4 and 5

i.e. tail event is 5 and head event is 4

Activities can be identified with the use of English alphabets such as above activity is A.

    Activity A – Excavation of earth work
    Activity B – Foundation concrete
    Activity C – Construction of brick work in foundation and plinth
    Activity D – Laying of D P C
    Activity E – Brickwork in superstructure

2.12.1 Different Types of Activities and Their Inter-Relationship

A project is broken into different types of unit tasks or activities. Depending upon their interdependency, some activities are to be taken serially whereas some of the activities can be undertaken simultaneously which are subsequently called as predecessor Activities and Successor Activities.

Depending upon their way of occurrence, the different activities can be termed as below :

Parallel Activities

Activities which can be undertaken and completed simultaneously and independently to each other are called parallel activities.

Serial Activities

Those activities which are performed immediately one after the another are called serial activities. They are dependent on each other and cannot be performed independently.

Predecessor Activities

Activity or number of activities which are necessary to be performed before a particular activity is undertaken, they are called predecessor activities. Unless these predecessor activities are completed, the next activity cannot commence.

Successor Activities

Any activity or activities which immediately begin after the performance of predecessor activities are termed as successor activities to those predecessor activities.

In Fig. 2.13,

C and E are parallel activities, D and E are also parallel activities.

A and B are serial activities.

A is predecessor activity of activity B.

B is predecessor activity of activities C and E.

B is successor activity of activity A.

C and E are successor activities of activity B.

F is successor activity of activities D and E.

Dummy Activity or Dummy

Dummy is a device to identify a dependence amongst the activities. It is not performance of any actual job or task and hence does not consume any time or resources. It is necessary to maintain the logic and uniqueness of the different activities in the project and serves as a connecting link for the control purposes. Dummy is, therefore, an activity without any actual job to be performed. To differentiate the same from other performing activities, the Dummy Activity is represented by a dashed arrow. It is identified in the same way as other activities but the dashed arrow clearly represents that it is a dummy activity. With the help of dummy activity, logical sequence is maintained and confusion is avoided. Dummy serves the grammatical purpose as well as logical purpose.

Grammatical Purpose of Dummy

It will be illustrated with following example. Two persons are to leave place A and to go to place B. The first person uses a scooter and second uses a car. Event (1) is leave A whereas event (2) is reach B. This cannot be properly represented for the two persons as the diagram would be as shown below

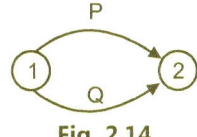

Fig. 2.14

Activity P – Person with scooter going from A to B. (Activity 1 – 2)
Activity Q – Person with car going from A to B. (Activity 1 – 2)

With this type of representation, uniqueness of the identification is lost as Activity P and Activity Q though different, are represented and treated like one single activity. (1-2) This inconvenience leads to mistake and has to be solved suitably for which dummy activity is used. To avoid the said confusion, Dummy activity is introduced as shown below

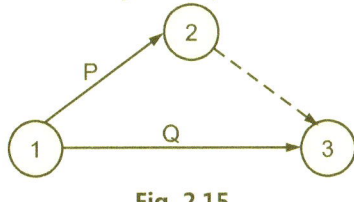

Fig. 2.15

Event (1) – Leave A
Events (2) and (3) – Reach B

The two activities P and Q are represented as below

Activity P – represented as 1 – 2
Activity Q – represented as 1 – 3

Since Activity 2 – 3 is a dummy activity practically event (2) and event (3) are same i.e. reach B. But to represent that activities A and B are different, a dummy activity 2 – 3 is introduced so that activity P or 1 – 2 represents activity that person with scooter is moving from A to B and activity Q or 1 – 3 represents activity that person with car is moving from A to B. Activity 2 – 3 is dummy activity for first person with scooter. The same can also be represented meaningfully as below

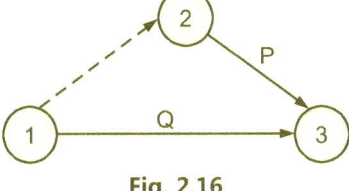

Fig. 2.16

Events (1) and (2) – Leave A
Event (3) – Reach B
Activity 1 – 2 is Dummy activity.
Activity P is 2 – 3 activity for person with scooter.
Activity Q is 1 – 3 activity for person with car.
Activity 1 – 2 is Dummy activity for first person.

However, it should be noted that dummy activities should be provided only if it is necessary. Provision of redundent dummy in the network may lead to confusion. Hence in initial stages, dummy activities may be introduced liberally which can further be removed by careful inspection of the network wherever such dummy activities are unnecessary.

Examples of dummy provided in initial stage and then dummy removed in the final network are as below :

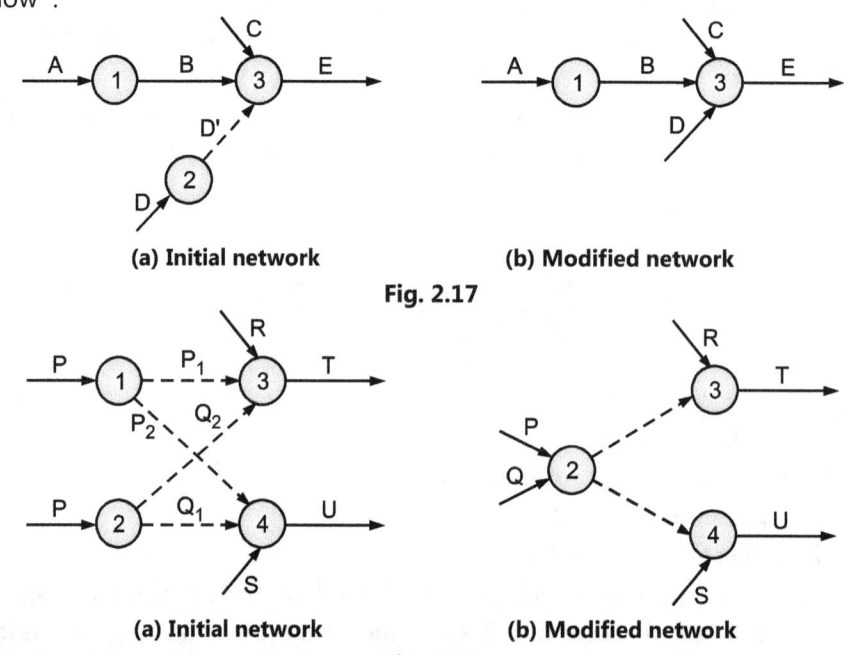

Example 2.1 : Convert the following Activity On Node (AON) Network into Activity On Arrow (AOA) Network.

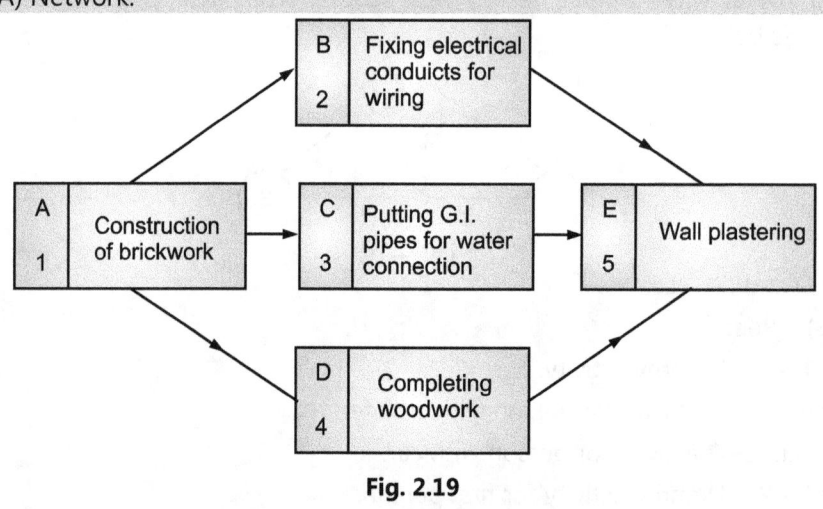

Fig. 2.19

Solution :

Activity 1 – 2 : Construction of Brickwork.
Activity 2 – 3 : Fixing Electrical Conduits.
Activity 2 – 4 : Fixing GI pipes for water connections.
Activity 2 – 5 : Completing woodwork in doors and windows.
Activity 5 – 6 : Plastering the brickwork.

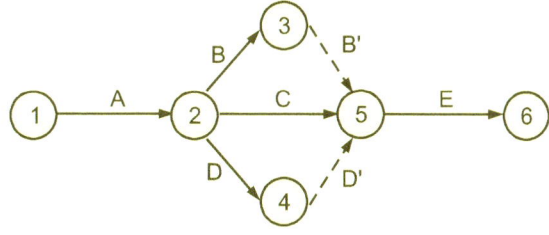

Fig. 2.20

2.13 FRAMING NETWORK FOR A PROJECT

The different steps in framing the network for any project can be summarized as below :

1. **Objective :** The project objective is the specific achievement which must be very clear, specific and well-defined. It is a complete task to be accomplished which is to be achieved by completing the different unit jobs sequentially.

    Examples : 1. Erection of a statue in a public place.
    2. Replacement of an old machinery by a new one.
    3. Construction of a residential building.

2. **Breakdown of the Project into Different Unit Tasks or Activities :** The complete project is the sequential accomplishment of different unit jobs. Therefore, by careful thinking the whole project should be broken down into simple unit jobs or activities with the help of work Breakdown Structure, where specific and the sequential accomplishment will make the project complete and the objective is achieved. The commencement and completion of these specific activities will be the different events in the completion of the project and they are the specific stepwise achievements of the project.

3. **Sequencing :** After breaking down the project into different activities, an analysis is to be made about the sequencing of the events and activities. This will lead to interrelationship between the different events and also activities. A clearcut picture should be worked regarding the predecessor events and the successor events and

also predecessor activities, succeeding activities, parallel activities. A table may be prepared showing the inter-relation between the events. Such a table may also be prepared showing relation between the activities.

4. **Drawing of Network :** With above information ready and knowing the rules of framing the network, one can start locating the events sequentially starting with the first event on the left hand end and the proceeding towards right and locating the different events sequentially. Thus, starting from the first event, which is commencement of the project, one will be able to reach the last event which is completion of the project. The different unit jobs or activities will be arrows joining the successive events. Thus, the network for the project can be completed.

5. **Checking the Network :** After the network is completed, it has to be checked for the contents, sequence and sense. In content it is to be checked that all the necessary unit jobs are incorporated and no job or activity is missing. It should also be seen that logic and grammer of the network is maintained and network correctly represents the sequence. If necessary, for maintaining the sequence, dummy activities are used but there should not be redundant dummy activities and any error such as looping, or cycles and dangling. After checking the network if any such mistakes or errors are found they are removed suitably and network is corrected and redrawn. After the final network is drawn, the events are numbered using Fulkerson's Rule. It should be noted that number of activities may be equal to or more than the number of events. In good network, $\dfrac{\text{No. of Activities}}{\text{No. of events}}$ should be between 1 to 1.6.

2.13.1 Rules for Framing Network

While framing network, following rules should be borne in mind

- Initial event is starting of the project. Hence, the different activities will emerge from this initial node. Hence, there is always a single initial node in network. (Fig. 2.21).

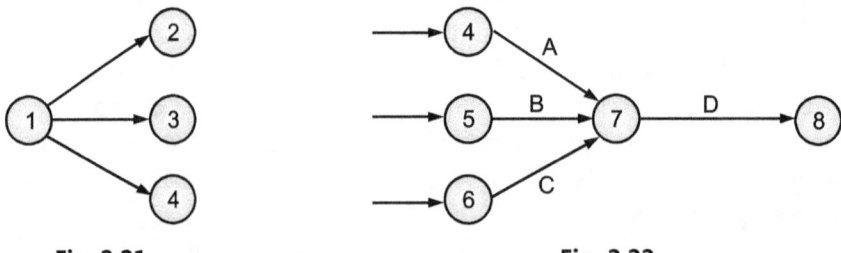

Fig. 2.21   Fig. 2.22

- An event cannot be said to have occurred unless all the activities merging in that event are completed. Event (7) can be said to have occurred when all the activities A, B, C are completed. (Fig. 2.22)

- No event depends for its occurrence on the occurrence of any succeeding event. This means that there cannot be any path in the network looping back from a succeeding event to a preceding event. Such a situation is known as **"Looping"** which should not occur anywhere in the network.

In Fig. 2.23 there is looping from event (5) to event (2) through event (4).

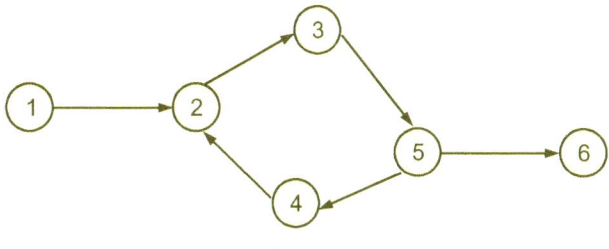

Fig. 2.23

If such a situation occurs, the logic underlying the diagram must be re-examined and the inter-relationship between the activities may be properly decided.

- No activity can start unless the tail event has occurred. In Fig. 2.22, activity D cannot commence unless event (7) has occurred.

- There should not be dead end loop for any activity except the final event node which is completion of the project. If there is any other dead end in the network that is called **"Dangling."** There should not be any dangling in the network. This dangling situation can be corrected with the use of dummy.

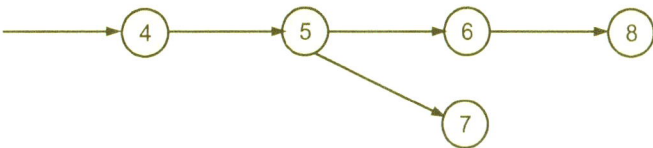

Fig. 2.24 : Dangling

Activity 5 – 7 is a dangling activity. It cannot remain separate from other activities before project concludes. This can therefore be connected to some other activity in the project by a dummy activity. (Fig. 2.25).

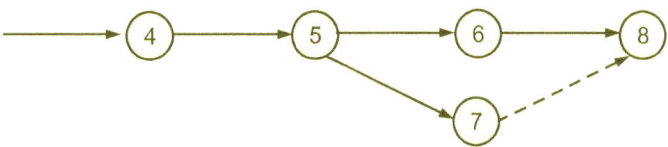

Fig. 2.25

- Any activity in the project should be represented by a single arrow and each arrow should represent a singular activity and hence the number of arrows must be equal to number of activities.

- Dummy activities should properly represent the interdependency and constraints between the different events.
- Logic of the network be maintained. Initial event is start of the project which is shown at the left hand end and final event is project concluding which is shown at the right hand side. Hence, the activity arrow heads will point towards progress of the project i.e. from left to right.
- This leads to usual practice that the line flows from left to right.
- Arrow representing activities are not vectors and hence their length does not indicate the duration of any activity to any scale. Length is chosen to suit the drafting requirements.
- As far as possible straight lines are used for arrows representing the activities, curved arrows are avoided.
- Orientation of angles between the arrows representing the different activities does not lead to any specific information and is chosen to suit the drafting convenience and proper use of the available space.

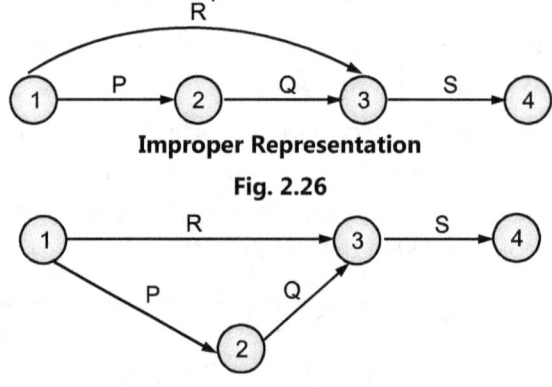

Improper Representation
Fig. 2.26

Proper Representation
Fig. 2.27

- Activity arrows, as far as possible, should not cross. But if the interdepen-dency of the activity demands the same and crossing is unavoidable, the activity arrow should be broken to bridge over the other.

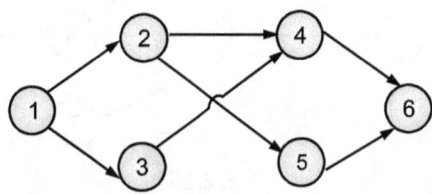

Fig. 2.28

- Head events have always higher numbers than the tail events.

2.13.2 Shapes of Network Diagram

Normally, with the above cited guidelines, the network shape is angular where activity arrows are horizontal and making some acute angle with horizontal. However, network diagram can also be drawn in rectangular shape where activity arrows are either horizontal and vertical.

However, to maintain the logic and the requisite flow of the progress of activities, these horizontal and vertical arrows are required to be given a right angle turn. Such a type of rectangular network is quite compact but may sometimes become little clumsy. The angular type of network shows natural flow from left to right and is easy to understand.

Fig. 2.29 represents the above two networks.

Network technique is a flow diagram consisting of events and activities which must be accomplished in a planned sequence representing the interdependency and inter-relationship between the different activities and events in the project. In the network diagram activities, dummy activities and events that constitute the project are represented with the help of three symbols which have been already discussed.

Activity is represented by arrow   ---→

Dummy activity represented by broken arrow   ---→

Event is represented by circle :   ◯

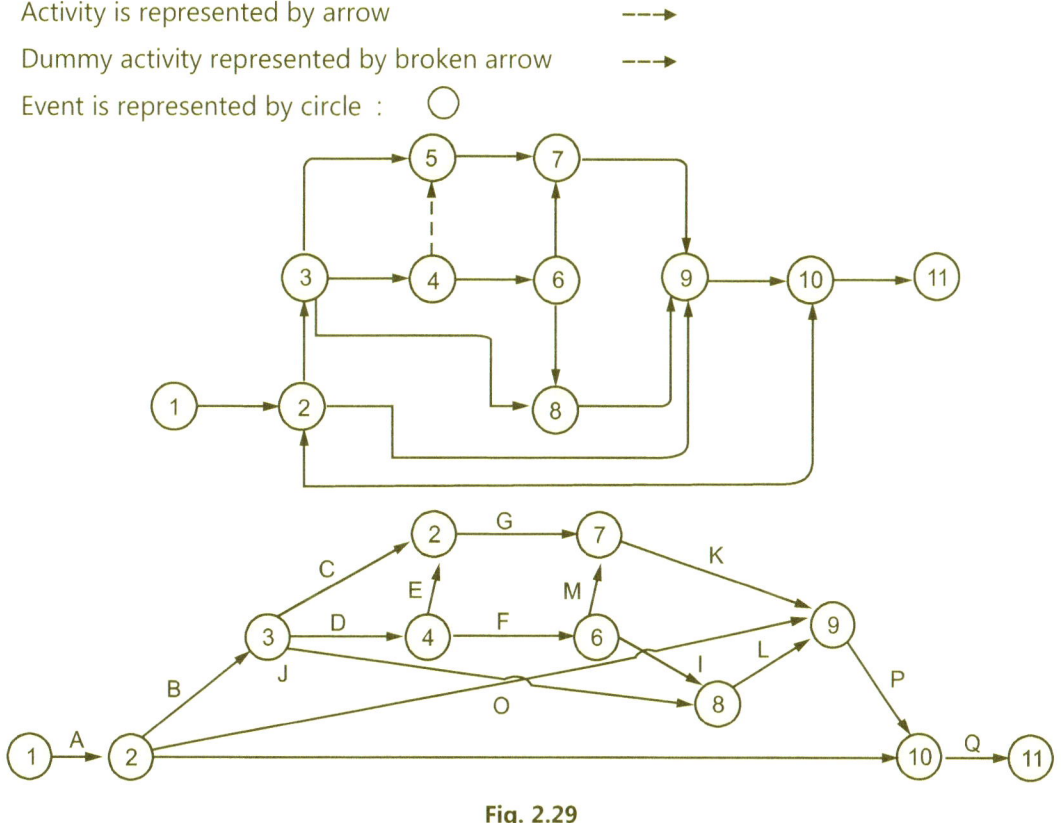

Fig. 2.29

2.13.3 Numbering of Events

In network diagram, events are numbered so that they can be identified. Different activities joining the events or nodes are identified with alphabets or with the event numbers at the tail and head of the activity. In numbering events, **'Fulkerson's Rule'** is followed.

1. The single initial event which is starting point of the project is numbered 1.
2. Initial event is head event for different activities. The head of arrows will lead to different other events which can be numbered serially 2, 3, 4 ......
3. These new events will be head events for further activities in the project. The head events of these activities will be numbered serially.
4. The process will continue till the last event which is completion of the project.
5. In this process all the events will be numbered serially. It is to be remembered that the head event will have a lower number than the head event.
6. In bigger network extensive modifications may be necessary and some additional activities or events may be required to be introduced in this modification. This will, therefore, need renumbering of events. This will be avoided by numbering events serially with numbers 10, 20, 30 ...... etc. in place of serial numbers 1, 2, 3, ... so that in case some events are required to be added they can be suitably numbered in between the predecessor and successor events. This method of numbering events is called Fulkerson's method.

Example 2.2 : Using Fulkerson's method, number the events in the network shown below

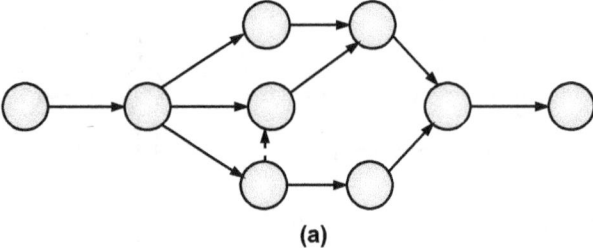

(a)

Solution :

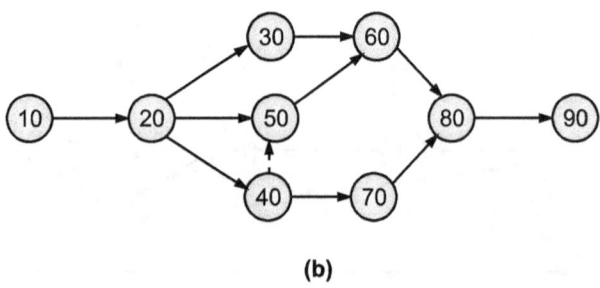

(b)

Fig. 2.30

Example 2.3 : Draw a network diagram for project laying a drainage pipeline.

Solution : The project can be broken into different activities and events as shown below

Activities : A - Layout (10 – 20)
B - Excavation for trenches (20 – 40)
C - Procurement of pipes (10 – 30)
D - Pipe laying in excavated trenches (40 – 50)
E - Pipe testing (50 – 60)
F - Refilling of trenches (60 – 70)

Events : A - Start of the project
1 - Starting layout
2 - Layout completed, excavation started
3 - Procurement of pipe started
4 - Pipes procured
5 - Excavation completed, Pipe laying started
6 - Pipe laying ended testing of pipes started
7 - Pipe testing started earth filling started
8 - Earth filling completed

Event	Predecessor Event	Successor Event
Start of layout	–	Layout completed
Start of Excavation	Layout completed	Excavation completed
Procurement of pipe started	–	Procurement of pipe completed
Pipe laying started	Excavation completed, pipe procured	Pipe laying completed.
Pipe testing started	Pipe laying completed	Pipe testing completed.
Refilling started	Pipe testing completed	Refilling of trench ends.

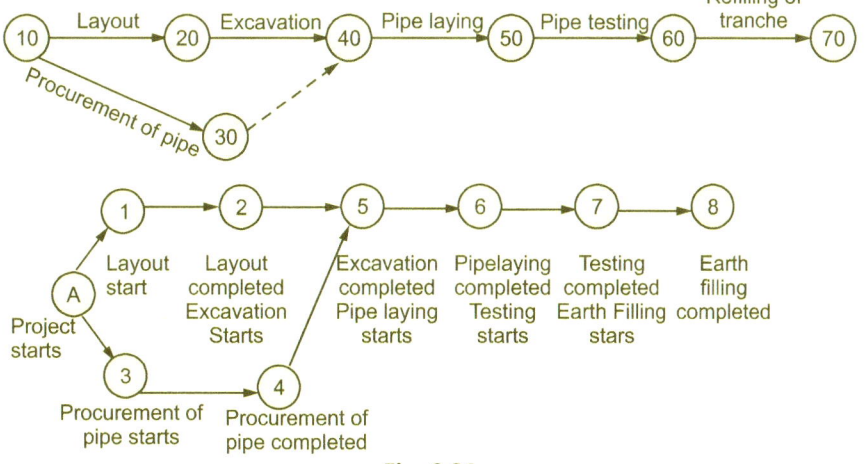

Fig. 2.31

Example 2.4 : Draw the network for the activities and events shown in the table given below

Activity	Events / Nodes		Duration in Days	Activity Inter-relationship		
	I Node	J Node		Preceeding	Succeeding	Parallel
A	10	20	3	–	B, C	–
B	20	30	3	A	D, E	C
C	20	40	4	A	F	B
D	30	40	0	B	F	E
E	30	50	6	B	G	D
F	40	50	2	D, C	G	–
G	50	60	4	E, F	–	–

Solution :

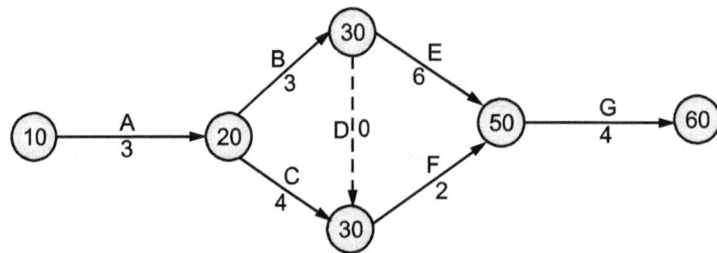

Fig. 2.32

Activities are denoted by Letters A, B, C ... and also by the tail node and head node. The tail nodes and head nodes are in general denoted by I nodes and J nodes. The duration of the activity is shown below the activity arrow and identification of the activity above the arrow. Duration of an activity is the estimated time required to complete the activity.

2.14 TIME ESTIMATES

The time duration used for different activities is any convenient unit consistent throughout the network. The unit is usually either days or weeks. For estimating time duration, a normal work crue depending upon the type of the work and experience is assumed. Generally in CPM the duration of the different activities in the project are deterministic and can be estimated fairly precisely. Depending upon the duration of different activities, the project duration will be decided.

2.14.1 Event Times

For each event two type of times are expressed depending upon occurrence of that event. Earliest Occurrence Time (EOT) of any event is the time wherein all the activities emerging to the event are completed in the least period possible. This is computed by adding the duration of all the activities along an activity path leading to that event. If more than one activity path is leading to that event, then the maximum of earliest occurrence time of the different activity paths is taken as Earliest Event Occurrence time and is denoted by T_E.

$$\text{EOT for an event} = \text{EOT of preceding event} + \text{Duration of activity}$$
$$EOT_j = EOT_i + t_{ij}$$
or
$$T_E^j = T_E^i + t_{ij}$$

Similarly, Latest Occurrence Time (LOT) for any event is the maximum time for completion of any event without causing any delay in completion of the project. This time is computed by subtracting the duration of all activities along the activity path from the concluding event to the event in question. If more than one event is emerging out, then the latest occurrence time is least of the time calculated from different activity paths.

$$LOT_i = LOT_j - t_{ij} \quad \text{i.e.} \quad T_L^i - T_L^j = t_{ij}$$

EOT for an event = EOT of preceding event + Duration of leading activity.
LOT for an event = LOT of following event − Duration of leaving activity.

In case more than one activities are leading to an event, EOT is taken maximum of all leading paths. Whilst LOT is taken minimum of all activity paths leaving the node. EOT is calculated by forward pass method and LOT is calculated by backward pass method.

2.14.2 Forward Pass

The minimum or expected duration of any project is the earliest occurrence time of the last event. Hence, to find out the duration of the project, one has to find out EOT of last event in the network of the project. This is done by calculating the EOT for each event of the network by forward pass method till the last event is reached. In case of merge events, EOT is calculated by all the possible paths and the maximum of values of EOT calculated from different paths is considered EOT for that event. This will give the duration of the project.

$$EOT_{(j)} = EOT_{(i)} + t_{ij}$$

Where, $EOT_{(j)}$ = Earliest occurrence time of jth event i.e. succeeding event
$EOT_{(i)}$ = Earliest occurrence time of ith event i.e. preceeding event.
$t_{(ij)}$ = duration of activity i – j i.e. intervening activity

The first event in the network occurs at zero time and with this basis the EOT of all the subsequent events and project duration can be calculated. This is the minimum period in which the project can be completed.

2.14.3 Backward Pass

Normally, the earliest event occurrence time of last event is the project duration and the same is taken as the latest event occurrence time of the last event. However, if there is any imposed duration for the project that is taken as the latest event occurrence time for the last event. Assuming this latest event occurrence time of the last event, sequentially the latest event occurrence time for successive predecessor events can be calculated. The latest event occurrence time for any event in the network is the latest allowable event occurrence time for the succeeding event minus the duration of intervening activity.

$$LOT_{(i)} = LOT_{(j)} - t_{ij} \quad \text{i.e.} \quad T_L^i = T_L^j - t_{ij}$$

where, $LOT_{(i)}$ = Latest event occurrence time of ith event i.e. preceding event

$LOT_{(j)}$ = Latest event occurrence time of jth event i.e. succeeding event

$t_{(ij)}$ = duration of activity (i – j) i.e. intervening activity.

In case there are more than one bursting activities originating from event i, the $LOT_{(i)}$ is calculated by all possible paths and whichever is minimum is taken as the LOT for that event. Thus, starting from the last event, LOT of all the events can be calculated and this will lead to finding LOT of first event as zero. This will help in finding the allowable delay in occurrence of different events without affecting the overall duration of the project. The allowable delay in occurrence of any event is the difference between the LOT and EOT for the event. This allowable delay is the slack period of the event.

2.14.4 Activity Times

For the different activities there is a time of start and time of finish.

For forward pass,

Activity finish time = Activity start time + Duration

and for backward pass,

Activity start time = Activity finish time – Duration

For the different activities, following times are calculated :

EST – Earliest Start Time

EFT – Earliest Finish Time

LST – Latest Start Time

LFT – Latest Finish Time

EST and EFT are the time of earliest start and earliest finish respectively of any activity without changing the sequence of the activities in the network.

Similarly, LST and LFT are the time of latest start and latest finish respectively without delaying the project duration without changing the sequence of the activities in the network.

An activity can start only after the tail event has occurred.

Hence, Earliest Start Time of any activity is the Earliest Occurrence Time of Tail Event of the activity.

∴ EST of an activity = EOT of tail event

EFT of any activity = EST of that activity + Duration

Similarly, an activity must conclude before the time of occurrence of head event.

Hence the Latest finish time of any activity is the Latest Event Occurrence time of head event of the activity.

LFT of an activity = LOT of head event

LST of an activity = LFT of the activity – Duration

The above terminologies can be very well explained with the help of following network.

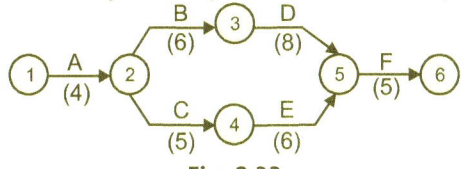

Fig. 2.33

Explanation of this network is
- Activity A is the starting activity.
- Activities D and E ends the project.
- Activities B and C emerges from A.
- Activity D will start only after completion at activity B.
- Activity E is the succeeding activity of C.
- Activity F starts only after completion of activity D and E.

The duration of each activity is shown below the arrow and the activity name.

Now, let us calculate EST, EFT, LST and LFT using forward and backward pass. The nomenclature which we will be using is as follows

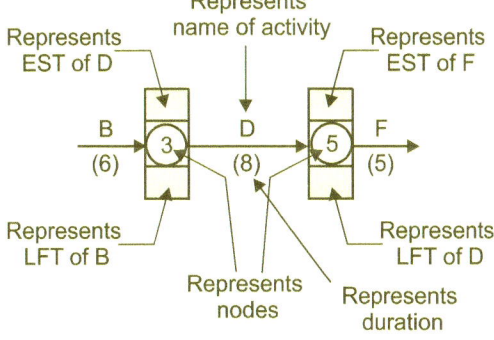

Fig. 2.34

Forward Pass

In this, we will move from left to right.

(1) The project starts at 0th time i.e. starting time on first day.

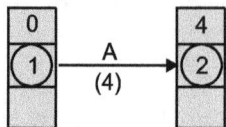

Fig. 2.35

∴ Activity will start earliest at 0th day.

∴   EST of A = 0

As activity A has EST = 0, it will finish earliest at 0 + 4 = 4 days.

i.e. EST of A+ duration of A. This is called as Earliest Finish Time (EFT) of A.

(2)

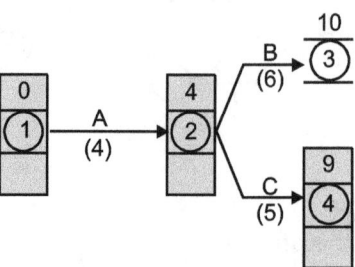

Fig. 2.36

As 'A' finishes at 4th day, activities B and C will start on 4th day. Hence EST for B and C both is '4'.

∴ $(EFT)_B$ = $(EST)_B$ + duration of B
                               = 4 + 6 = 10

Similarly, $(EFT)_C$ = $(EST)_C$ + duration of C
                               = 4 + 5 = 9

(3)

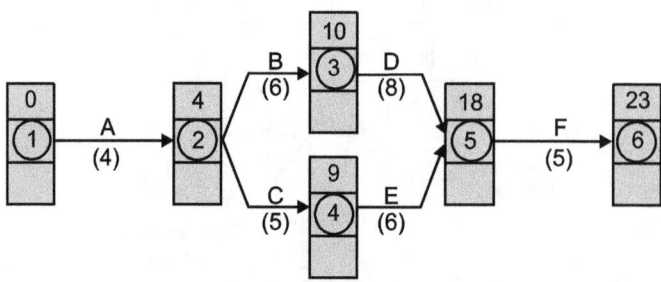

Fig. 2.37

Activity D will start after completion of activity B which is EFT of B. Similarly, activity E will start after completion of activity C which is EFT of C.

∴ EST of D = 10

EST of E = 9

∴ EFT of D = (10 + 8) = 18

And EFT of E = (9 + 6) = 15

Now, as per the logic of the network, activity F will start only after completion of both the preceeding activities D and E i.e. 18 days which is the "highest" of both the EFTs.

∴ EST of F is 18 which gives EFT of F as (18 + 5) = 23 days. This is the total project duration.

Backward Pass

In backward pass, we will calculate the time estimates from right to left. Duration of project is 23 days which means the activity F should be finished latest by 23 days.

∴ LFT of F is 23 days, hence it has to start latest by (23 – 5) = 18 days, which is LST of F.

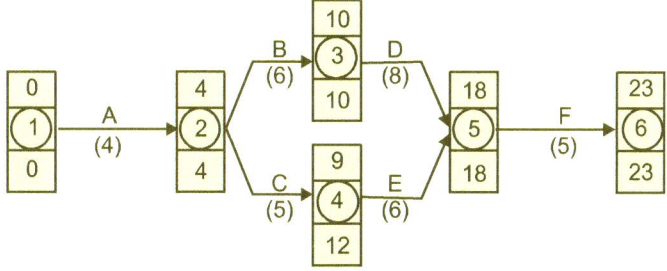

Fig. 2.38

LST of F as 18 indicates that, activities D and E should be finished latest by 18.

∴ LST of D = lFT of E = 18 as these are parallel activities

∴ LST of D = (18 – 8) = 10 and LST of E = (18 – 6) = 12.

Similarly, LST's and LFT's of all remaining activities are calculated as under

LFT of B = 10   ∴ LST of B = (10 – 6) = 4
LFT of C = 12   ∴ LST of C = (12 – 5) = 7

In the backward pass, we have to consider the minimum time of all for calculating LFT of A. i.e. 4. ∴ LFT of A = 4, LST of A = (4 – 4) = 0

2.14.5 Floats

As there can be allowable delay or slack in case of events without affecting the duration of the project, similarly there can be some allowable delay in completion of any activity and measure of such delay is called *Float*.

It is a measure of time by which an activity may be delayed without affecting the logic of the project or the total duration of the project. There are four types of floats with different identification. They are Total Float (TF), Free Float (FF), Interfering Float (IF) and Independent Float (F_{ind}).

Total Float

'It is the time by which a particular activity can be delayed without causing any effect on the duration of the project'. It is, therefore, the difference between the maximum time available for any activity and its duration. The maximum time available for any activity without causing delay to the project is difference of its Latest Finish Time and the Earliest Start Time.

Hence, Total Float = (LFT − EST) − Duration

∴ TF = (LFT − Duration) − EST

= LST − EST

= (LST + Duration) − (EST + Duration)

= LFT − EFT

∴ TF = LST − EST

= LFT − EFT

It can also be pointed out,

Total Float = (LOT of head event − EOT of tail event) − Duration of activity.

Free Float

'It is the amount of time by which the commencement of any activity may be delayed without any effect or interference on the start of the next activity'. If there has to be no effect on the subsequent activity, the time of earliest occurrence of the head event of the activity must be maintained. Hence, free float is the difference between EOT of the head event and EFT of the activity so that if the start of the activity is delayed by this duration, it will get just completed before EOT of the head event.

FF = EOT of head event − EFT of the activity

= EST of the following activity − EFT of the activity

Hence, free float of any activity i − j is the difference between its earliest finish time and the earliest start time of the succeeding activity.

FF = EOT of Head Event − EOT of Tail Event − Duration of Activity

= EOT of Head Event − (EOT of Tail + Duration of Activity)

Hence FF = EOT of Head Event − EFT of Activity

Free float is that portion of positive total float that can be used by an activity without affecting the earliest start time of succeeding activity.

The concept of free float is based on the possibility that all activities start at their EST and all the events occur at their earliest time.

Interfering Float

It is the slack of head event. It is equal to difference of LOT and EOT of the head event and is also difference of Total Float and Free Float.

$$IF = TF - FF$$

Interfering float is the potential downstream interference of any activity. If the full interfering float is made, subsequent activities become critical and if it is exceeded the total duration of the project will increase and the project will be delayed.

Independent Float

It is the excess time that is available if the preceeding activity ends as late as possible and the succeeding activity starts as early as possible. The independent float is defined as the excess of minimum available time over the required activity duration.

Minimum available time for any activity

$$= \text{EOT of Head Event} - \text{LOT of Tail Event}$$

$\therefore \quad F_{ind} = \text{EOT of Head Event} - \text{LOT of Tail Event} - \text{Duration of the Activity}$

$= \text{EOT of Head Event} - \text{EST of Activity} + \text{EST of Activity} - \text{LOT of tail event} - \text{Duration of Activity}$

$= \text{EOT of Head Event} - (\text{EST of Activity} + \text{Duration of Activity}) - (\text{LOT of tail event} - \text{EST of Activity})$

$= (\text{EOT of Head Event} - \text{EFT of Activity}) - (\text{LOT of Tail Event} - \text{EOT of Tail Event})$

$= \text{Free float} - \text{Slack of Tail Event}$

$\therefore \quad \text{Independent Float} = \text{Free Float} - \text{Slack of Tail Event}$

If tail event is i^{th} event and head event is j^{th} event and the activity is denoted by $i - j$,

$T_L^j = \text{LOT of } j^{th} \text{ event}$

$T_E^j = \text{EOT of } j^{th} \text{ event}$

$T_L^i = \text{LOT of } i^{th} \text{ event}$

$T_E^i = \text{EOT of } i^{th} \text{ event}$

$t_{ij} = \text{Duration of Activity}$

Total Float of an activity is the excess of maximum available time for activity over activity duration

$\therefore \quad TF = \left(T_L^j - T_E^j\right) - t_{ij}$

$= \text{LFT} - \text{EFT of the activity} = \text{LST} - \text{EST of the activity}$

Free Float of an activity is the excess of available time over the activity duration when all the activities start at their earliest start line.

$$\therefore \quad FF = \left(T_E^j - T_E^i\right) - t_{ij}$$
$$= \text{EST of following activity} - \text{EFT of the activity}$$
$$= \text{EOT of head event} - \text{EFT of the activity}$$

Independent Float of an activity is the excess of minimum available time over the activity duration.

$$\therefore \quad F_{ind} = \left(T_E^j - T_L^i\right) - t_{ij}$$
$$= \left(T_E^j - T_E^i + T_E^i - T_L^i\right) - t_{ij}$$
$$= \left(T_E^j - T_E^i\right) - t_{ij} - \left(T_L^i - T_E^j\right) = \text{Free Float} - \text{Slack of tail event}$$

Interfering Float of an activity is the difference between the Total Float and Free Float. It is equal to slack of head event.

$$IF = TF - FF = T_L^j - T_E^j = \text{Head event slack}$$

The above floats are represented diagrammatically in Fig. 2.39.

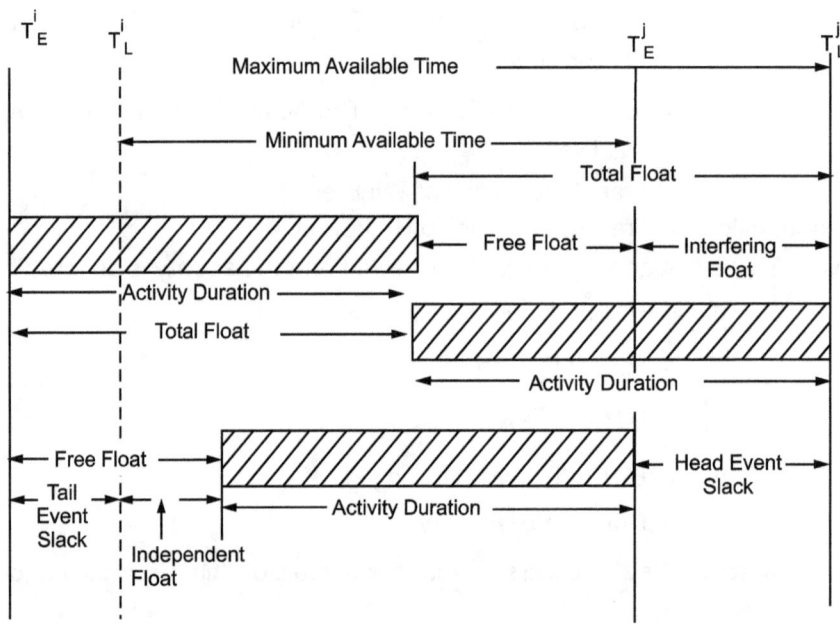

Fig. 2.39

Floats are used in scheduling to show where flexibility exists. This flexibility is meaningful and can be made use for large one time projects such as construction of a highway or dam or developing a new missile or launching a satellite. Out of the four floats, only two of them namely, total float and free float are of practical use. Total float is most useful since it is difference of maximum available time for any activity and its duration. There may be three possibilities regarding total float.

- It may have a negative value if the maximum available time is less than activity duration.
- It may have zero value if the maximum available time is equal to activity duration.
- It may have positive value if the maximum available time is greater than activity duration.

When the float is negative, such activities are most important and they demand special attention and special action. Such activities are termed as "Super Critical Activities." The activities where float is zero, they are called "Critical Activities." They demand good attention and no freedom of action can be taken with such activities as it may result in delay of the project. The activities with positive float are "Subcritical Activities" and hence some freedom in terms of delay may be possible with such activities. They demand normal action.

Negative float indicates that the activity duration is more than maximum available time in the project which is little abnormal situation and attempt may be made for compressing the duration by rearranging the resources or arranging additional resources to bring the negative float to positive or at least to zero. Critical path is one which joins the critical activities for which float is zero. These critical activities control the project duration. Any delay in the execution of critical activity than the scheduled duration will extent the project duration by the same time slab. Critical path starts from the initial event and passes through all such events where there is no slack and ends in the last event. In order to identify the critical path, float concept provides the necessary and sufficient conditions for activities to be critical. It may be possible that some activities joining event with zero slack may not be found critical with float concept. It should also be noted that there can be more than one critical path in the network.

The activity times and floats for the previous example are tabulated as under

Activity	Duration	EST	EFT	LST	LFT	TF	FF	Int F	Ind F
A	4	0	4	0	4	0	0	0	0
B	6	4	10	4	10	0	0	0	0
C	5	4	9	7	12	3	0	3	0
D	8	10	18	10	18	0	0	0	0
E	6	9	15	12	18	3	3	0	0
F	5	18	23	18	23	0	0	0	0

The activities which are having Total Float (TF) = 0 are termed as critical activities. Hence, as per the above table, activities A, B, D and F are critical activities. If we join these activities, we get a continuous path which is termed as critical path and total duration of the project is 23 days. The network with critical path will be shown as below

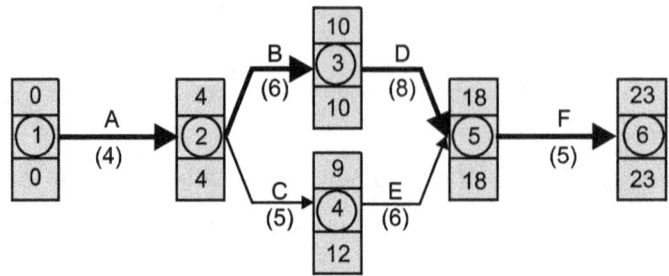

Fig. 2.40

Example 2.5 : Draw an AOA network diagram and find critical path, total duration of project and all floats.

Activity	Duration in Days	Preceeding Activities	Succeeding Activities
A	3	–	C, D, F
B	10	–	E, H
C	4	A	E, H
D	6	A	G
E	4	B, C	G
F	6	A	J
G	8	D, E	I
H	2	B, C	I
I	6	G, H	K
J	8	F	K
K	8	J, I	–

Solution : The network is drawn as given below

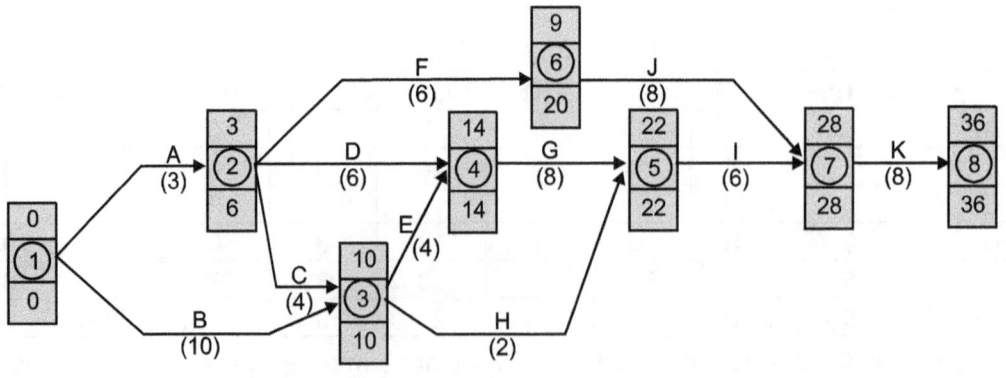

Fig. 2.41

Activity	Duration	EST	EFT	LST	LFT	TF	FF	Int F	Ind F
A	3	0	3	3	6	3	0	3	0
B	10	0	10	0	10	0	0	0	0
C	4	3	7	6	10	3	3	0	0
D	6	3	9	8	14	5	5	0	2
E	4	10	14	10	14	0	0	0	0
F	6	3	19	14	20	11	0	11	−3
G	8	14	22	14	22	0	0	0	0
H	2	10	12	20	22	10	10	0	10
I	6	22	28	22	28	0	0	0	0
J	8	9	17	20	28	11	11	0	0
K	8	28	36	28	36	0	0	0	0

Example 2.6 : Analyse the work of construction of a Steel Rolling Mill and construct a CPM Network for the same. Calculate the project duration after marking the critical path. Also calculate the Total Float and Free Float.

Solution : The work of erection of a steel mill on analysis can be divided into different independent jobs as shown below. The estimated duration of completion of these activities is also indicated in table below. The duration of each activity has been estimated by proper analysis and with experience of duration of similar activities undertaken in earlier projects. The correlation and sequence of different activities is properly studied and if necessary dummy activities are introduced to maintain proper flow and sequence of work.

The details of preparing the network and calculation of floats will comprise of the following steps

Step 1 : Table of inter-relation between different activities.

Step 2 : Preparation of network with the help of above table.

Step 3 : Calculation of EST and EFT of different activities by Forward Pass Method.

Step 4 : Calculation of LFT and LST of different activities by Backward Pass Method.

Step 5 : Marking the Critical Path.

Step 6 : Calculation of Project Duration.

Step 7 : Calculation of Total Float and Free Float.

All the above are worked out in tabular form

Sr. No.	Description of Job or the Activity	Activity Symbol	Estimated Duration in Weeks
1.	Preliminary Investigation	A	5
2.	Design of Building	B	10
3.	Preparation of specifications of machinery and equipment	C	4
4.	Procuring Machinery and Equipment	D	32
5.	Construction of Building Foundation	E	12
6.	Construction of Machinery Foundation	F	7
7.	Construction of Building Superstructure	G	14
8.	Laying underground pipes, conduits and other anciliary utility	H	4
9.	Installation of Machinery and Equipment	I	18
10.	Installation of Electrical Driving Unit	J	12
11.	Installation of Wiring and Control Equipment	K	10
12.	Final Checking and Testing	L	9
13.	Clearing site	M	2

Step 1 :

Sr. No.	Activity	Duration	Preceding Activity	Succeeding Activity	Remarks
1.	A	5	–	B, C	Starting Activity
2.	B	10	A	E, F, H	
3.	C	4	A	D	
4.	D	32	C	J, I	
5.	E	12	B	G	
6.	F	7	B	J, I	
7.	G	14	E	L	
8.	H	4	B	R	
9.	I	18	D, F	K	
10.	J	12	D, F	P	
11.	K	10	I, P	L	
12.	L	9	K, G, R	M	
13.	M	2	L	–	End Activity
14.	P (Dummy)	00	J	K	Dummy
15.	R (Dummy)	00	H	L	Dummy

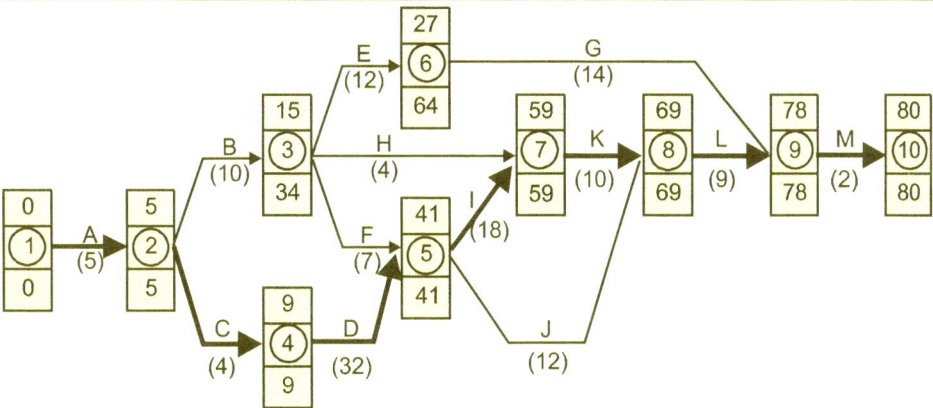

Fig. 2.42

Total duration of project : 80 days.

Activity	Duration	EST	EFT	LST	LFT	TF	FF	Remarks
A	5	0	5	0	5	0	0	Critical
B	10	5	15	24	34	19	0	
C	4	5	9	5	9	0	0	Critical
D	32	9	41	9	41	0	0	Critical
E	12	15	27	52	64	37	0	
F	7	15	22	34	41	19	19	
G	14	27	41	64	78	37	37	
H	4	15	19	55	59	40	40	
I	18	41	59	41	59	0	0	Critical
J	12	41	53	57	69	16	16	
K	10	59	69	59	69	0	0	Critical
L	9	69	78	69	78	0	0	Critical
M	2	78	80	80	80	0	0	Critical

Critical path : A-C-D-I-K-L-M

Example 2.7 : Work out the project duration and indicate the critical path. Also calculate the interfering float.

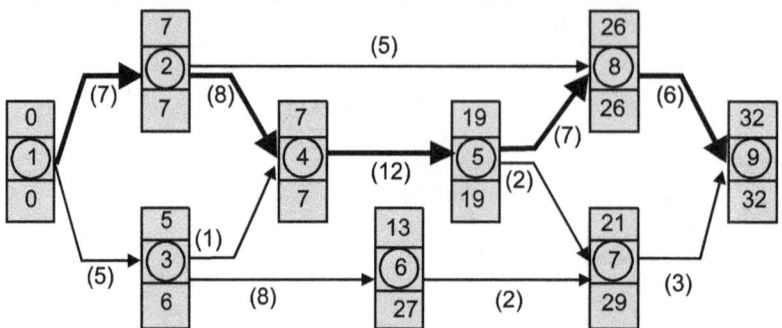

Fig. 2.43

Project Duration = 32 days

Activity	Duration	EST	EFT	LST	LFT	TF	FF
1-2	07	0	7	0	7	0	0
1-3	05	0	5	1	6	1	0
2-4	00	7	7	7	7	0	0
3-4	01	5	6	6	7	1	1
2-8	05	7	12	21	26	14	14
3-6	08	5	13	19	27	14	0
4-5	12	7	19	7	19	0	0
5-8	07	19	26	19	26	0	0
5-7	02	19	21	27	29	8	0
6-7	02	13	15	27	29	14	6
8-9	06	26	32	26	32	0	0
7-9	03	21	24	29	32	7	8

Example 2.8 : For construction of a small residential block, prepare the network and calculate the duration of the project by CPM.

Solution : The project is broken into different unit jobs or activities and depending upon the resources available, the activity duration is decided.

Table is prepared for the different activities with the predecessor and successor activity as shown below

Sr. No.	Activity	Description	Duration in Weeks	Preceding Activity	Succeeding Activity
1.	A	Excavation, Foundation, Plinth, Masonry and DPC	3	–	C
2.	B	BB work in superstructure including fixing door and window frames, casting lintels, shelves	4	C, D	K, J, G
3.	C	R.C.C. work in beams and slab	4	A	B
4.	D	Preparation of door, window frames and panels	2	–	B
5.	E	Inside Plaster in CM 1 : 5	3	J	F
6.	F	Marble Mosaic tile flooring	2	E	I
7.	G	Outside Plaster in CM 1 : 5	3	B	I
8.	H	Distempering inside and outside & oil painting to doors & windows	2	I	–
9.	I	Fixing doors and window panels	2	F, G	H
10.	J	Providing water supply and sanitary fittings	3	B	E
11.	K	Providing electrical wiring and fittings (concealed)	4	B	–

L, M, N and P are dummy activities.

The network diagram is as shown below in Fig. 2.44.

The critical path and duration of the project is determined as shown in Table below.

Solution :

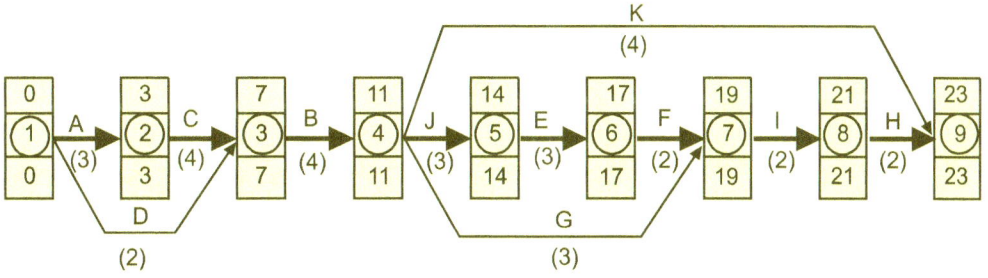

Fig. 2.44

Activity	Duration (Weeks)	EST	EFT	LST	LFT	TF
A	3	0	3	0	3	0
B	4	7	11	7	11	0
C	4	3	7	3	7	0
D	2	0	2	5	7	5
E	3	14	17	14	17	0
F	2	17	19	17	19	0
G	3	11	14	16	19	5
H	2	21	23	21	23	0
I	2	19	21	19	21	0
J	3	11	14	11	14	0
K	4	11	15	19	23	8

Total duration of project = 23 weeks.

Critical path A – C- B – J – E – F – I – H

2.15 PERT

2.15.1 Programme Evaluation and Review Technique (PERT)

This method was developed for U.S. Navey Special Project Office for Polaris Missile Programme. The Lockhead Missile System Division along with management consultant firm Booz, Allen and Hamilton developed this programme for evaluating the feasibility of existing schedule for reporting the progress.

As discussed above, the PERT emphasises events which is start or completion of an activity and commencement of further activities. The method of development network for CPM and PERT are to some extent identical but the basic difference is, for CPM, since the time duration of activities are fairly accurately known, the emphasis is on activities whereas in PERT since probabilistic time duration for the different activities are evolved the network has to be event oriented as the point where a specific part of programme is achieved or activity completed is important.

Basically there is not much difference between CPM and PERT. In place of activities in CPM, the PERT consists of number of events arranged in sequential order joined by arrows. The most important part of PERT is selection of specifically identifiable events which are planned to accrue in the completion of the project.

The sequential arrangement of these events will, of course, depend upon inter-dependency in the similar manner as interdependence of activities is decided in CPM. The most important job is estimation of duration of moving from one event to next event throughout the project wherein uncertainties are involved. Hence, the probabilistic duration of completion of events is considered in PERT. Rest of the procedure of forming network and analysis, highlighting the critical activities in CPM and critical events in PERT, is same. Since PERT depends on probabilistic duration of occurrence of events, it is used for such project where the management cannot be guided by past experience. PERT network is, therefore, suitable for non-repetitive or once-through projects which are research or innovative form.

Three Time Estimates in PERT

Due to uncertainty of the project, three times estimates are made as follows :

1. **Optimistic Time (t_o) :** 'It is the shortest possible time in which activity can be completed when everything goes smoothly'. No provisions are made for delays or setbacks.

2. **Pessimistic Time (t_p) :** 'This is the longest time the activity takes if everything goes wrong'. Major hurdles like labour strikes or natural calamities are excluded from this time.

3. **The Most Likely Time Estimate (t_m) :** 'This is the time required by the activity under normal circumstances'. It assumes that things are going in normal ways, a few setbacks, no excitements and no dramatic breakthroughs.

The beta distribution of PERT time estimates is as given below :

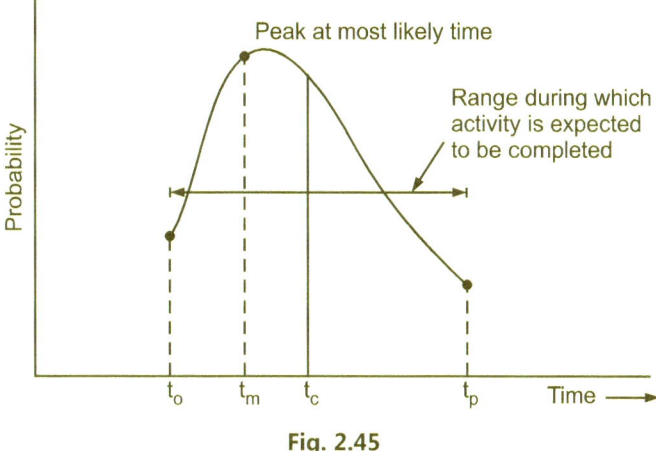

Fig. 2.45

The expected time $\quad t_e = \dfrac{(t_o + 4t_m + t_p)}{6}$

Standard Deviation

'It is the statistical measure of the uncertainty being the spread of distribution curve about the mean value'.

$$\therefore \quad S.D. = \sigma = \frac{(t_p - t_o)}{6}$$

Variance (V)

'It is a function of difference between t_p and t_o'. If $(t_p - t_o)$ is small, there is certainty of meeting the schedule. But if it is large, there are less chances of meeting the time schedule.

$$\therefore \quad V = \sigma^2 = \frac{(t_p - t_o)^2}{6^2}$$

Using the standard deviation, the probability of meeting scheduled event time is calculated as follows

$$Z = \frac{\text{Scheduled date} - \text{Expected data}}{\sqrt{\text{Variance of evetns involved}}}$$

For corresponding values of Z, the probability can be read from standard normal distribution as follows :

Z	Probability	Z	Probability
2.8	0.997	– 0.2	0.421
2.6	0.995	– 0.4	0.345
2.4	0.992	– 0.6	0.274
2.2	0.986	– 0.8	0.212
2.0	0.977	– 1.0	0.159
1.8	0.964	– 1.2	0.115
1.6	0.945	– 1.4	0.085
1.4	0.919	– 1.6	0.055
1.2	0.885	– 1.8	0.036
1.0	0.841	– 2.0	0.023
0.8	0.788	– 2.2	0.014
0.6	0.726	– 2.4	0.008
0.4	0.655	– 2.6	0.005
0.2	0.579	– 2.8	0.003
0.0	0.500		

PERT consist of the following steps :
- Project is broken down in events.
- Events are arranged in logical sequence.
- Network is drawn and events are numbered.
- Using three time estimates, expected time is calculated.
- Standard deviation and variance is calculated.
- Network is marked with expected time of each event, and forward and backward pass is made as in CPM.
- Critical path is marked on network and project duration is found out.
- The probability of completing the project on due date is calculated.

2.15.2 Extension of PERT

There are three major developments in the use of PERT. They are as follows :
1. Introduction of possibility of realisation of an activity in PERT.
2. Use of PERT in mass production.
3. Auto PERT.
    When the PERT network for a complex project is found to be complicated, the analysis of network becomes very difficult and time consuming. In order to eliminate such situation a possible method has been devised for automatically producing a type of standard network in the computer. This innovation is named 'AUTO PERT'. This was first time used by Shell Chemical Co. of U.S.A. under the guidance of G. Mechenzie who is the father of this technique.
4. GERT means Graphical Evolution and Review Technique. It is the latest tool in the hands of the management. This not only deals with the uncertainties in the completion time of the activities but also deals with the probability of realisation of the activity itself. This approach combines the concept of PERT type of network with flow graph concept. Application of GERT has been made in the following fields.
    - Space vehicle count down analysis.
    - Manufacture of semiconductor material analysis.

However, this latest technique is yet to become popular in the industry.

2.15.3 Successful Application of PERT

For successful use of PERT technique the following conditions are necessary :
1. **Support of Top Management :** It is absolutely necessary that there must be whole hearted support to the use of this technique. The top management should understand the potentials and also the limitations of PERT that it can provide encouragement in use of PERT in planning stage of innovative projects. With unwillingness on the part of top management it is worthless to spend time and effort in use of PERT.
2. **Publicity :** Proper publicity is made throughout the organisation and all the persons involved in the programme should be informed well in advance about the use of

PERT for the project. All the managerial and supervisory personnel should know about the launching of PERT which will help in creating the necessary involvement of all concerned in the use of this tool and will create necessary climate in the organisation.

3. **Team Effort and Co-ordination :** The nature of PERT calls for a co-ordinated effort by all the departments involved in the plan. It is very necessary that the project manager should provide leadership and take all the concerned heads of the department into confidence so that best co-ordination is available from them.

4. **Training :** A thorough training is must for all concerned who are actively associated with the planning and execution of the project. There should be proper training which may take sometime for developing the necessary skills to work on the network at the time of planning and execution.

5. **Abuses :** PERT is a planning technique as well as an information system, as such there should not be mistakes in preparing the extensive reports on progress. This may defeat the basic purpose of planning mechanism. Time estimates are likely to give longer duration to be on safer side which may also defeat the purpose of PERT. There is no trouble with this if new activities take more time than the average time estimations. This may be counterbalanced for catching up subsequent events as there is bound to be some flexibility.

6. **Use of Computers :** In complex projects of very long duration the activities may increase to a large extent. If the number exceeds even 200, it will not be possible to handle the project without the use of computer However, small projects can be handled even without any use of computer. But the use of computers may make the work handy and easier.

Example 2.9 : Following is the data for a small project having 10 activities. Draw PERT diagram. Find t_e, σ, variance. What will be the probability of completing the project in (i) 35 days, (ii) 40 days.

Activity	t_o	t_m	t_p
1 – 2	3	8	13
1 – 3	2	5	8
2 – 4	3	8	7
2 – 5	4	7	10
3 – 5	2	3	10
4 – 6	7	9	11
5 – 7	4	6	8
6 – 8	6	9	12
6 – 7	5	7	9
7 – 8	2	5	14

Solution : 1. Draw the network

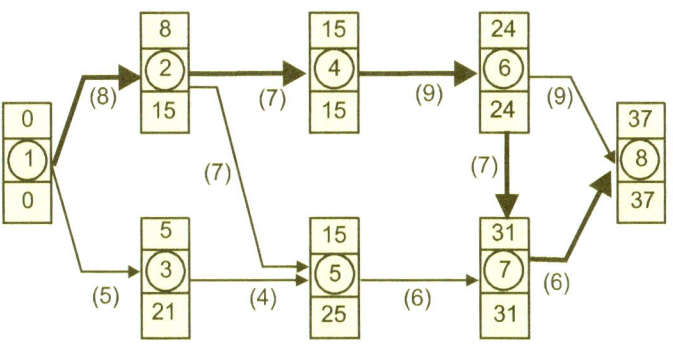

Fig. 2.46

Calculation of various parameters are as follows :

Activity	t_o	t_m	t_p	t_e	σ	V
1 – 2	3	8	13	8	1.67	2.78
1 – 3	2	5	8	5	1.00	1.00
2 – 4	3	8	7	7	0.67	0.44
2 – 5	4	7	10	7	1.00	1.00
3 – 5	2	3	10	4	1.33	1.47
4 – 6	7	9	11	9	0.67	0.44
5 – 7	4	6	8	6	0.67	0.44
6 – 8	6	9	12	9	1.00	1.00
6 – 7	5	7	9	7	0.67	0.44
7 – 8	2	5	14	6	2.00	4.00

Critical path : 1 – 2 – 4 – 6 – 7 – 8

Duration : 37 days

Sum of variance along critical path

1 – 2 – 4 – 6 – 7 – 8 = 2.78 + 0.44 + 0.44 + 0.44 + 4 = 81

Standard deviation = σ = $\sqrt{\text{Variance of the project}}$

= $\sqrt{8.1}$ = 2.846

Probability of completing the project

(i) $$Z = \frac{\text{Scheduled date} - \text{Expected date}}{\sqrt{\text{Variance of events involved}}}$$

$$Z = \frac{(35-37)}{2.846} = -0.7027$$

Probability corresponding to Z from the table of standard normal distribution
$$= 0.243 \text{ i.e. } 24.3\%$$

(ii) $$Z = \frac{(40-37)}{2.846} = 1.05$$

Probability corresponding to Z from the table of standard normal distribution
$$= 0.852 \text{ i.e. } 85.2\%$$

2.15.4 Comparison of CPM and PERT

Though the method of framing the network and location of critical operations or unit jobs and events are similar, the CPM is an activity oriented network system and the PERT is an event oriented network system. In both the systems, unit jobs i.e. activities and points of start or completion of unit jobs i.e. events are used in framing of the network diagram. The method of representation of the activities by arrows and events by circles is also similar. However, in CPM emphasis is given on activities as their duration period can be precisely decided while in PERT the emphasis is on events as point where a particular unit job is completed is important. The methodology of preparation and analysis of network is mostly similar and utilises the same logic. Though many things are common, the points of difference in the above two systems of network can be summarized as below

- CPM is activity oriented and PERT is event oriented.
- In CPM, the time estimates i.e. duration of completion of different activities can be decided with fair degree of accuracy whereas the time of completion of different events cannot be precisely decided in PERT.
- CPM is used for repetitive type of projects wheras PERT is used for research or innovative type of project.
- In CPM, cost estimates for the different activities can be precisely arrived at. By varying the resources the duration of completion of the project can be changed. As such the cost optimisation is possible in CPM. In CPM, cost may not be proportional to the time and hence cost optimisation is given prime importance in CPM. In PERT, on the other hand since duration cannot be specified precisely,

- the cost goes on increasing as the duration of the project increases and to some extent the cost is directly proportional to the duration. To minimise the cost, therefore, it is necessary to pay attention to minimise the duration of the project.
- In projects where cost is controlling factor, CPM is used and in projects where time is controlling factor, PERT is used.
- CPM is used for deterministic projects whereas PERT is used for probabilistic projects. Where long developed well-seasoned components and stable technology is used, CPM is always preferred. In such projects any changes made during the execution can be easily incorporated in CPM network. In case of projects where extreme degree of uncertainty rules in deciding the event durations, PERT has to be used. In such projects, control over time overweighs the control over the cost.
- PERT is therefore, frequently used for Research and innovative development projects wherein uncertainties reign time required for different events and eventually in completion of the project.

IMPORTANT POINTS

- Framing a network for a project and following rules for framing network.
- Framing of network with different steps.
- Concepts of floats in networking, its different types.
- Three time estimates in PERT.

QUESTIONS

1. Explain the two important methods of project planning in brief and bring out the difference between the two.
2. Explain salient features of CPM and PERT and the circumstances in which each is used.
3. What do you understand by Bar chart ? With suitable example, describe the process of construction of Gantt's chart.
4. What are different strong points and shortcomings of a Gantt's chart ?
5. How the different shortcomings of bar chart can be removed ?
6. How milestone chart differ from a bar chart ? How it overcomes some of the shortcomings of bar chart ?
7. Give out the advantages and limitations of milestone chart.

8. Differentiate between CPM, PERT, Bar chart and Mile stone chart.
9. Draw the bar chart for a project with 8 different activities as shown below and calculate the total time of completion.

Sr. No.	Name of Activity	Duration in Days	Preceding Activity	Succeeding Activity	Remark
1	A	3	–	C, D	
2	B	5	–	–	
3	C	3	A	E* G	
4	D	5	A	F	
5	E	8	C*	H	*Cannot start unless 60% work of C is completed.
6	F	5	D		
7	G	6	C		
8	H	5	E		Last Activity

If there is increase of 3 days in the time of completion of activity A, calculate the corresponding delay in completion of the project.

10. What do you understand by Event and Activity ?
11. What is AOA network and AON network ? Explain with suitable examples.
12. Differentiate between CPM and PERT network. Explain where each is used.
13. What are different types of events ? Explain with examples.
14. Describe the different types of activities in a network and explain the use of dummy activity.
15. What are difficulties in logic in the network ? Explain looping and dangling.
16. What are the different rules to be observed in framing of network ?
17. A project consists of 6 events and inter-relationship between them is as shown below. Draw the network.

Event	Predecessor Event
(1)	–
(2)	(1)
(3)	(2)
(4)	(2)
(5)	(3) (4)
(6)	(5)

18. Write about characteristics of CPM and PERT networks.

19. Inter-relationship between the different activities in a project is as shown below. Draw the network and find the critical path.

Activity	Predecessor Activity	Successor Activity	Duration
A	–	B, C	6
B	A	E, H	8
C	A	D	9
D	C	I, J	4
F	B	I, J	3
G	E	L	6
H	B	R	10
I	D, F	I, J	8
J	D, F	P	1
K	I, P	L	2
M	L	–	4
R	H	L	6
P	J	K	5

20. What do you understand by CPM and PERT ? Give the points common to both and also the points of differentiation.

21. Compare CPM and PERT.

22. Explain the procedure of construction of CPM network with example of erection of statue of a national leader in a square of a city.

23. Define the following

    (i) Optimistic time (ii) Most likely time (iii) Pessimistic time (iv) Expected mean time

24. Differentiate between the following terms

    (i) Activity and Event

    (ii) Dummy activity and Critical activity

    (iii) Total float and Free float

    (iv) Looping and Dangling.

25. Define the following

    (i) Earliest Event Occurrence Time and Latest Event Occurrence Time.

    (ii) Latest Start Time and Latest Finish Time of an Activity.

    (iii) Slack of an Event and Independent Float for an Activity.

26. Define Free Float and bring out its importance. How is it determined ?

27. How is probability of completion of a project in given definite period is determined ?

28. Different activities and their duration for construction of a residential building is given below. Frame the network and work out the period of completion of project. Mark Critical Path.

Name of Activity	Description	Duration in Weeks
A	Select plot for construction	2
B	Selection of Architect	2
C	Purchase of Plot	3
D	Preparation of Plan and Estimate	2
E	Approval of plan from local authority	2
F	Preparation of material requirement	4
G	Place order for different materials	1
H	Obtain timber for shutters	3
I	Obtain glass	1
J	Obtain door window frames	3
K	Obtain building materials (bricks, cement, aggregate)	2
L	Obtain marble mozaic tiles	2
M	Clear site	1
N	Give layout	1
O	Construction of foundation concrete	1
P	Constrution of plinth and DPC	2
Q	Construction of superstructure till lintels	2
R	Casting of lintels	2
S	Construction of superstructure above lintel till slab	2
T	Construction of RCC roof including beams and slab	2
U	Preparation of timber shutters	1
V	Fitting of shutters	1
W	Construction of tile flooring	2
X	Inside and Outside plaster	1
Y	Obtaining pipe and sanitary fittings	1
Z	Obtaining Electrical fittings	1
A'	Fixing water supply and sanitary fittings	1
B'	Fixing electrical fittings	1
C'	Interior decoration	3
D'	Clean up	1

29. Different activities in construction of a small culvert with 2 spans are listed below with their period duration. Prepare a CPM network and construction schedule starting from 1st day of next month. Find out the period of completion of the project.

Activity Identi-fication	Name of Activity	Duration Days
A	Excavation for abutments	4
B	Procurement of sand, cement and aggregate	3
C	Excavation for piers	2
D	Foundation concrete of abutments	2
E	Curing of PCC of abutments	2
F	Foundation concrete for pier	1
G	Curing of PCC for pier	2
H	Excavation for wing walls	2
I	Foundation concrete for wing walls	2
J	Curing of PCC for wing walls	2
K	Procurement of Rubble	4
L	UCR masonry of first abutment	3
M	UCR masonry for second abutment	3
N	UCR masonry for pier	3
O	UCR masonry for wing wall for first abutment	2
P	UCR masonry for second abutment	2
Q	Earth filling for first wing wall	4
R	Earth filling for second wing wall	4
S	Rolling of Earth filling	4
T	Formwork of Deck slab	6
U	Procuring steel	4
V	Placing reinforcement	4
W	Concreting Deck slab	2
X	Curing Deck slab	21
Y	Procuring and fixing hand rails	6
Z	W.B.M. and Surfacing	7

30. Fig. 2.47 shows the network for a construction project. The three different time estimates for each activity are marked. Determine the critical path and probability of completion of the project in 80 days.

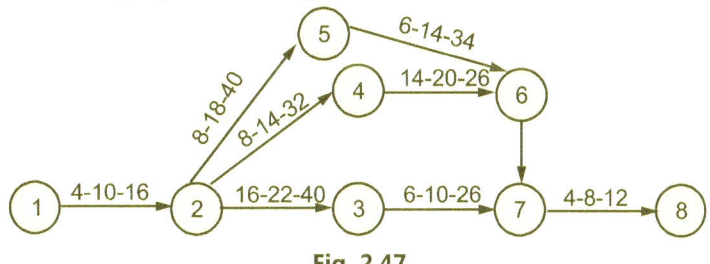

Fig. 2.47

31. Justify the importance of planning and network technique in Civil Engineering works.
32. What do you understand by CPM and PERT ? Give the points common to both and also the points of differentiation.
33. Compare CPM and PERT.
34. Define the following
    (i) Optimistic time
    (ii) Most likely time
    (iii) Pessimistic time
    (iv) Expected mean time
35. How is probability of completion of a project in given definite period is determined ?
    (a) Draw the network for the following data. Show the critical path. Also find the expected project duration of the project.

Activity	Estimated Duration in Days		
	Optimistic Time (t_o)	Most likely Time (t_m)	Pessimistic Time (t_p)
1 – 2	2	5	8
1 – 3	3	87	7
1 – 4	3	8	13
2 – 4	2	3	10
2 – 5	4	7	10
3 – 6	4	6	8
4 – 6	7	9	11
5 – 7	6	9	12
6 – 7	2	5	14
6 – 8	5	7	9
7 – 8	4	6	8
8 – 9	8	10	12

(b) Explain Three times estimates in PERT.

36. (a) For small construction project, the time estimates of different activities are given below

Activity	Estimated Duration in Days		
	Optimistic	Most Likely	Pessimistic
1 – 2	4	10	22
2 – 3	2	5	8
2 – 4	4	7	16
2 – 5	4	7	10
3 – 5	4	7	22
4 – 5	5	8	17
5 – 6	6	9	18

Draw the network and determine the critical path and expected minimum duration.

(b) What are the different points on which site documentation depends.

(c) What is PERT ? Explain its applications.

37. Explain 'super critical' and 'sub-critical' activities.

38. What are predecessor activities, successor activities, concurrent activities and zero-time activities ? Explain giving a suitable example.

39. The table below gives activities and their durations.

Activity	Duration (Days)
1 – 2	5
2 – 3	5
2 – 4	9
2 – 5	11
3 – 5	7
4 – 5	0
5 – 6	8
6 – 7	6
6 – 8	15
7 – 8	12

(i) Draw a network and calculate project duration and highlight the critical path by heavy ruling line.

(ii) Calculate EST, EFT, LST, LFT for the activities.

(iii) Calculate Total float, Free float, Independent float and Interference float for the activities.

40. Write a note on 'Gantt Chart and its limitations'.

41. Write short notes on

    (a) Tools and Techniques of Project Management.

    (b) Gantt chart and its limitations.

    (c) Total float, Free float, Interference float and Independent float.

    (d) Network Analysis.

    (e) Critical, Subcritical and Super Critical activities.

    (f) EST, EFT, LST, LFT and TF.

42. Listed below are the activities of a project along with dependence.

    (i) Draw a network and calculate total project duration and highlight the critical path.

    (ii) Calculate EST, EFT, LST, LFT and Total Float for the activities.

Activity	Duration (Days)
1 – 2	8
2 – 3	12
2 – 4	12
3 – 5	0
4 – 5	0
3 – 6	16
5 – 7	20
4 – 8	12
6 – 9	16
7 – 9	10
8 – 9	16

43. Differentiate between CPM and PERT.

44. What do you mean by Dummy activity ? What is the use of providing dummy activity in a network ?

45. What are the basic tools and techniques of project management ? Explain in brief.

46. Explain Critical, Sub-critical and Super Critical activities.

47. Describe the procedure for preparing CPM network for any construction project in Civil Engineering.
48. What are predecessor activities, Successor activities, Concurrent activities and Zero-time activities ?
49. (a) What do you mean by dummy activity ? What is the use of providing a dummy activity in a network ?
    (b) What possible errors of logic do you predict while drawing a network ? Describe these with neat sketches.
50. Compare Bar chart and CPM on the following points
    (i) Activity dependence
    (ii) Resource allocation
    (iii) Interpretation and ease in reading
    (iv) Time control
51. Enlist six different factors affecting duration of an activity.
52. The following constraints are given for the activities of a project.
    (i) 'G' follows 'F' but precedes 'H'.
    (ii) 'G' follows 'D' but precedes 'J'.
    (iii) 'M' follows 'H' but precedes 'L'.
    (iv) 'K' follows 'A' but precedes 'L'.
    (v) 'F' follows 'A'.
    'A' and 'D' are starting activities. J and L are terminal activities. The duration of the activities are in weeks.
    A = 3, H = 3, F = 2, L = 2, G = 1, M = 4, D = 6, K = 5, J = 7.
    (a) Draw a network, compute project duration and show critical path.
    (b) Tabulate the statement showing therein EST, EFT, LST, LFT and TF of each activity.
    (c) Also calculate Free Float, Independent Float and Interference Float of each activity.
53. (a) Define 'Updating' and explain in detail with the help of one example.
    (b) What are logical errors in case of CPM ? Draw sketches to illustrate your answer.
54. Listed below are the activities of a project along with their respective duration and dependence. Sketch the network diagram showing critical path by heavy rule line and find the project duration.
    Also prepare a mathematical table showing EST, EFT, LST, LFT, Total float for activity in a project alongwith critical and non-critical activities of a network you have drawn.

Preceding activities	Activity	Duration (Days)	Following Activity
–	A	9	K, G, H, J
–	B	6	E, F
–	C	11	K
–	D	5	–
B	E	3	K, G, H, J
B	F	5	K
A, E	G	3	L
A, E	H	6	M
A, E	J	3	–
A, C, E, F	K	4	–
G	L	10	M
L, H	M	3	–

55. (a) What are logical errors in case of CPM? Draw sketches to illustrate your answer.
    (b) Define
       (i) Interfering floats
       (ii) Independent float

56. Listed below are the activities of a project along with their durations.

Activity (i – j)	Duration (Weeks)
1 – 2	6
1 – 3	5
2 – 4	10
3 – 4	3
3 – 5	4
4 – 5	6
4 – 6	2
5 – 6	9

    (i) Draw AOA network and calculate the total project duration. Highlight the critical path.
    (ii) Calculate EST, EFT, LST, LFT, Total Float, Free float and Independent Float.

57. (a) The activities of a small project can be described by the following relationships.
       (i) A, B and C can start simultaneously.
       (ii) A and B precede D.
       (iii) B precedes E, F and H.

(iv) F and C precede G.
(v) E and H precede I and J.
(vi) C, D, F and J precede K.
(vii) K precedes L.
(viii) I, G and L are terminal activities of the project.

Draw a network diagram for the project.

58. How does PERT differ from CPM, State the areas where PERT can be applied and its limitations.

59. Draw the network with the help of following information.

Activity	A	B	C	D	E	F	G	H	J	X	Y
Duration	10	12	16	18	9	15	12	16	19	5	8
Preceding Activity	–	–	–	A	A, B	C	A	DEF	G	J, H	J, H

(a) Draw the neat network.
(b) Show critical activities and critical path with the help of table.
(c) Find the total duration of project.

60. State the differences between AOA and AON.

61. The following table gives the time estimates of the various activities of a project

Activity i – j	Duration in Weeks		
	t_o	t_m	t_p
1 – 2	1	2	3
2 – 3	3	6	9
2 – 4	2	4	6
3 – 5	4	6	9
4 – 6	4	6	8
5 – 6	0	0	0
5 – 7	3	4	5
6 – 7	2	5	9

(i) Draw the project network and find the total project duration.
(ii) Calculate the variance along with critical path.
(iii) What is the probability that the project will be completed in the estimated time ?

62. (a) Compare Gantt chart with CPM network.
(b) Explain with sketches, the various relationships in a Precedence Network.

63. A project has the following time schedule

Activity (i – j)	Duration (Weeks)
1 – 2	3
1 – 3	4
1 – 4	14
2 – 4	2
2 – 6	5
3 – 5	4
3 – 6	6
4 – 6	1
5 – 6	1

(i) Draw AOA network and calculate the total project duration. Highlight the critical path.

(ii) Calculate EST, EFT, LST, LFT, total float and free float.

64. Give definitions of following with suitable example of each

(i) Dummy activity, (ii) Critical activity,
(iii) Critical path, (iv) Concurrent activity,
(v) Preceding activity, (vi) Succeeding activity.

65. Show following logic with the help of AOA network.

(i) Activity C depends on A and B.

(ii) Activity P depends on C and D but activity Q depends on C only.

(iii) Activity C cannot be started before completion of activities Y and X whereas D depends on X and Z.

(iv) Activity S must not start before Q gets completed. Activity X depends on S but will start only after 3 days after completion of S.

(v) Activities M and N depends on Q, P and O.

UNIT III
PROJECT MONITORING AND CONTROL

3.1 INTRODUCTION

The duration of a project or for that matter duration of a activity is related to cost. In general, time is related to cost in performance of any job. In using CPM, one of the objectives is to develop optimum time-cost relationship so that the project can be scheduled in a way so as to complete the same at the minimum cost without any undue delay in completion of the project. Network technique is used to bring improvement in planning, scheduling, controlling, at the same time directing all above objectives. Hence, planning techniques should be used to arrive at a feasible and desirable time-cost relationship so as to complete the project at the total minimum cost.

All clients always have monetary limitations and the investments are of primary concern for all the programmes. For any project the earliest possible and practicable date of completion is of great importance. The financial resources should be made available during the various time periods throughout the development of any programme. Without availability of the funds in time, there will not be orderly progress and the completion of the project may be delayed. In this context, the modern methods of planning like CPM system are useful.

Upon completion of the network each activity must be studied with respect to its duration and the cost. In most of the projects, approximately 30% of the activities are found to be critical and remaining 70% of the activities have some float. The policy of every organisation and every owner is to reduce the duration of the project so that the utilisation of the project may be started before the schedule and time saved may be utilised gainfully. The overall project duration can be reduced by reducing the time period for the critical activities which control project duration. It would be useless to pay attention to non-critical activities and spend extra resources to expedite them.

There are two ways of reducing the duration of critical activities.

They are :
   (1) By increasing and employing more resources so that the activity duration is reduced.
   (2) By relaxing technical specifications of the activity.

However, it is not the aim and objective that the project duration be reduced at the cost of the quality and therefore, the only way of reducing the project duration is by utilising and developing more resources of all the critical activities. Of course, there is a limit for reduction of completion time of any activity irrespective of availability of all possible resources and hence there is a range of time duration for completion of any activity and for completion of the project depending upon the available resources.

Larger the duration of the project, lesser is the cost and reduction in the period of completion will increase the cost. It is, therefore, necessary to strike golden mean between the cost and the duration and optimum duration is the one which will give most economical total cost of the project.

3.2 PROJECT COST

3.2.1 Introduction

For any project two types of costs are involved. They are
1. Direct cost
2. Indirect cost

Direct cost is the cost spent or accomplished for that particular activity or project whereas the indirect cost is related to control or direction of that work, financial overheads, losses if any and the like. The total cost can, therefore, be divided as below

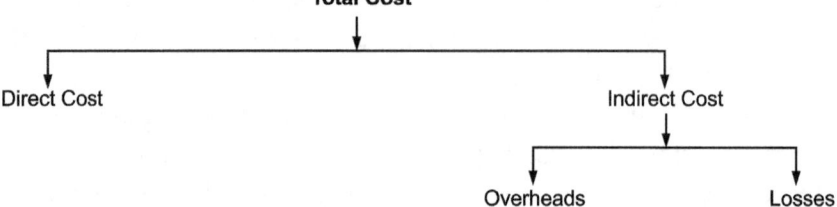

3.2.2 Direct Cost

It is the expenditure which is charged to the specific activity and can be identified to be so. It consists of direct investment made for the completion of that activity or the project in terms of material, labour and the equipment.

Material required for any activity will not change, hence the direct cost on materials will remain unaltered.

However, if more equipment and labour are employed, it reduces the duration of activity upto a certain minimum. Hence, less the duration, more is the direct cost and the graph of variation of direct cost against duration is as shown in Fig. 3.1.

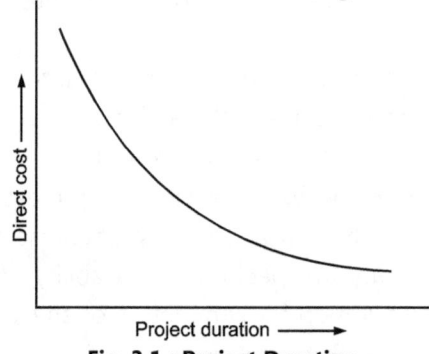

Fig. 3.1 : Project Duration

3.2.3 Indirect Cost

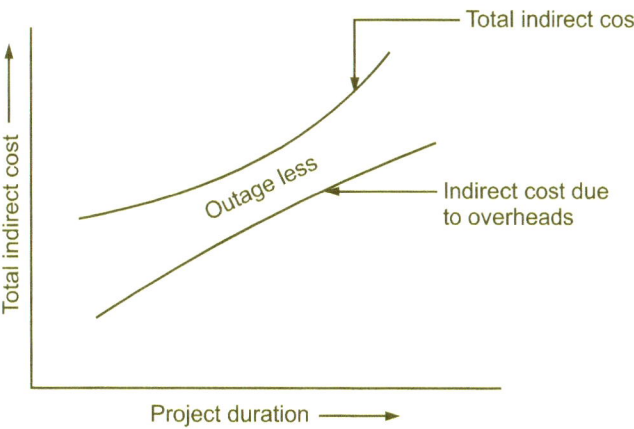

Fig. 3.2

Indirect costs on a project are those expenditures which are related to control and direct the project. It consists of overheads such as supervision charges, office establishments, electricity charges indirect labour and material, loss of revenue, lost profit, penalty etc. Indirect costs are those expenditure which cannot be appropriated or clearly allocated to any individual activity of the project but are assessed as a whole. This indirect cost is directly proportional to the time and, therefore, rises with duration. Considering only overhead and supervision, the indirect cost is represented by a straight line with a slope equal to daily overheads. But if the loss in profits and the other charges such as penalty etc. are added which are termed as an outage loss, the indirect cost graph may become curved as shown in Fig. 3.3.

Generally for any project, presuming there are no outage losses, the indirect cost variation is taken to be straight line only. With the available resources, the duration of the different activities represented in the network are the normal durations. However, if the resources are increased, activities can be completed in minimum possible period. This is known as 'crashing of the activity' and the cost associated is known as 'crash cost'. Thus, by crashing different critical activities, the project can be completed in minimum possible duration and the associated total cost which is sum of direct and indirect cost is the crash cost. Crash duration is, therefore, the minimum duration and the crash cost is the maximum cost of the project.

The total cost at the normal duration is the normal cost but this normal cost is not the minimum cost of the project. The optimum cost of the project is the minimum cost as represented on the total cost curve and the duration corresponding to this optimum cost is called *the* optimum duration of the project. It can be seen from the total cost curve that the total cost of the project goes on increasing on either side i.e. whether the duration is increased or decreased the total cost of the project increases. This will be clear from Fig. 3.3.

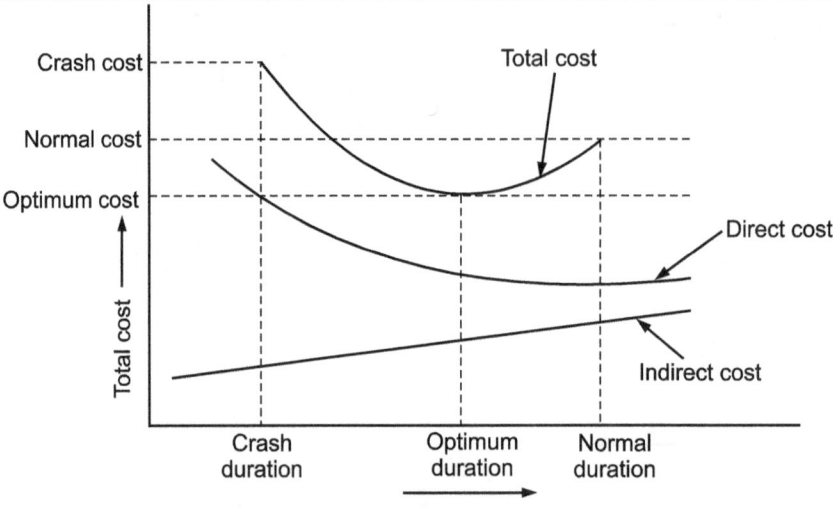

Fig. 3.3

If the network analysis indicates that the project duration and the project completion date do not match and duration has to be reduced, following alternatives are considered

1. Examine the estimated duration of different activities and study the possibility whether the estimated duration may be reduced without any extra cost.
2. The logic of the network and interdependency of the different activities to be examined to check where some of the interdependent and sequential activities may be converted into independent and concurrent activities.
3. Examine whether some of the critical activities may be crashed by utilising extra resources involving extra costs.

3.3 COST SLOPE FOR DIRECT COST

The direct cost curve can be approximated by a straight line. The slope of the line represents additional cost to be incorporated to reduce the duration of the network by each day. Depending upon the flatness of the curve, a single straight line or number of broken straight lines can be used for this approximation. The cost slope is the slope of the cost curve approximated as a straight line.

$$\text{Cost slope} = \text{Slope of straight line AB}$$
$$= \frac{C_s - C_n}{t_n - t_c}$$

where, C_s = Crash cost

t_c = Crash duration of activity

C_n = Normal Cost

t_n = Normal duration of activity

That critical activity with minimum cost slope is crashed first until other parallel activities are non-critical.

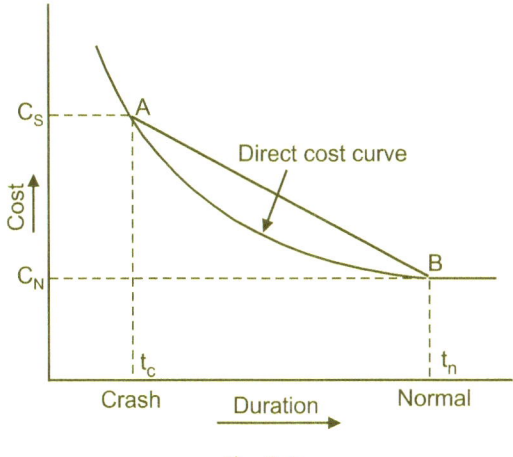

Fig. 3.4

3.4 CRASHING OF NETWORK FOR COST OPTIMISATION

As seen in the previous section, to decrease the schedule duration of the project, the duration of critical activities or crashing the critical activities is done. This may cause increase in the cost beyond the optimum limit. Crashing any activity is completing the activity in the minimum possible time limit.

However crashing of the project can be carried for the following objectives :

- For finding the minimum duration of the project and the corresponding cost of the project.
- For optimisation of the project i.e. for finding optimum duration and optimum cost of the project.
- For finding the extra cost of reducing the project duration by a particular duration.

It may be possible that while crashing the activities, some activities which are non-critical may become critical. However, for reducing the project duration, the focus is directed on the critical activities as critical path decides the project duration. Let us, understand the procedure of crashing of network by solving following example.

Example 3.1 : Frame the CPM network for the data given in the table below

Also find

1. Critical path and Normal duration of the project.
2. Calculate the normal cost and optimum cost. Assume the total cost of the project ₹ 11,000 and indirect cost ₹ 300/- per day. Calculate the optimum duration.

Activity	Events		Duration (Days)		Slope of Cost Curve in ₹/Day
	Preceding	Succeeding	Normal	Crash	
A	10	30	7	3	100
B	10	20	9	7	60
C	30	50	4	1	150
D	20	50	5	3	250
E	20	40	3	1	20
F	50	60	6	4	332
G	40	60	2	1	1,000

Solution : Step I : The network as shown below

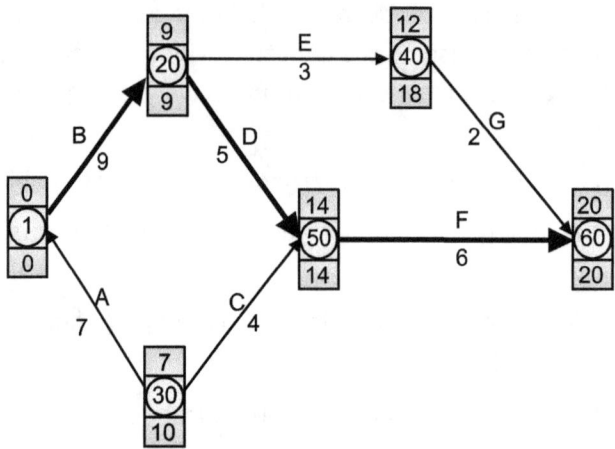

Fig. 3.5

Step 2 : The EST and LFT for the different events are calculated by the forward pass and the backward pass methods and are indicated near the events. The critical path is 10–20–50–60 and the critical activities are B, D and F. (Refer Table 3.1)

Table 3.1

Sr. No.	Activity	Duration	EST	EFT	LST	LFT	TF	Crash Slope	Remarks
1.	A	7	0	7	3	10	3	100	
2.	B	9	0	9	0	9	0	60	Critical
3.	C	4	7	11	10	14	3	150	
4.	D	5	9	14	9	14	0	250	Critical
5.	E	3	9	12	15	18	6	20	
6.	F	6	14	20	14	20	0	332	Critical
7.	G	2	12	14	18	20	6	1000	

Hence, the normal duration – 20 days; Normal cost = ₹ 11,000/-

Step 3 : Transfer the network as a squared network to understand the concurrency of activities and the float available with non-critical activities.

Remember the following points while drawing squared network :
  (a) The critical path is drawn as a straight line starting from 0 to normal duration (critical path B-D-F).
  (b) All the nodes on critical path are shown on it (nodes (10), (20), (50) and (60).
  (c) Non critical paths are shown above or below the critical path.
  (d) All the activities are starting at its EST. Activities A and C spans between nodes (10) and (50). Total duration of activities A and C is 11 days while the duration between nodes (10) to (50) is 14 days.

Therefore, Total float = 3 days.

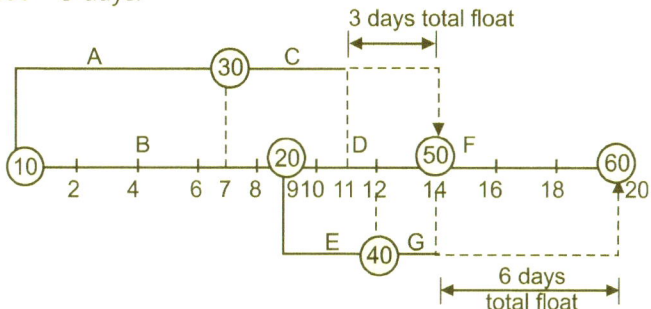

Fig. 3.6

Similarly, total duration of activities between nodes (20) and (60) is 11 days while that of activities E and G is 5 days. Therefore, total float = 6 days.

It is very important to note that total float is a 'shared float' i.e. this float is shared between the serial activities between two nodes. i.e. Activities A and C have total float as 3 days, if Activity A uses float on 1 day, C will have remaining float as 2 days and so on. Similarly, total float of 6 days is shared between E and G.

Step 4 : Crashing of activities will start by compressing the critical activity with minimum crash slope. i.e. by increasing the total cost at minimal for each day's crashing.

Therefore Out of B, D and F activities, activity B will be crashed since it has minimum cost slope i.e. ₹ 60/- days. Now, once we have decided that activity B is to be crashed, the next question is "by How many days?"

To answer this questions, study the squared diagram carefully. If we crash activity B by 2 days (from 9 days normal duration to 7 days crash duration), the float available for A and C will be come 1 day (3 days − 2 days). This ensures that activities A and C do not become critical activities.

∴ Crash activity B by 2 days (its duration becomes 7 days).

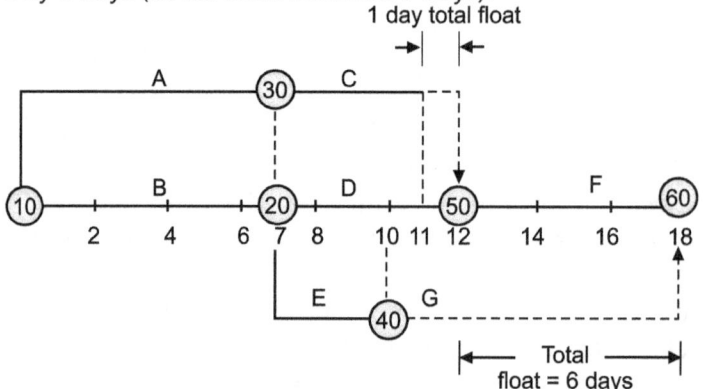

Fig. 3.7

Note that total float for activities E and G are 6 days as before.

∴ (Duration) = 18 days
(Cost)$_1$ = 11000 + 2 (crash slope of activity B)
= ₹ 11,120/-

Step 5 : As activity B can not be compressed further, the critical activity with next higher cost slope is D, which can be crashed by 2 days. Activity D is a Concurrent activity with A, C (1 day TF) and E, G (6 days TF). As TF for A, C is only 1 day, we can crash activity D by only 1 day though activity D can be crashed by 1 more day. Activities A and C will also become crticial then this can be shown as follows :

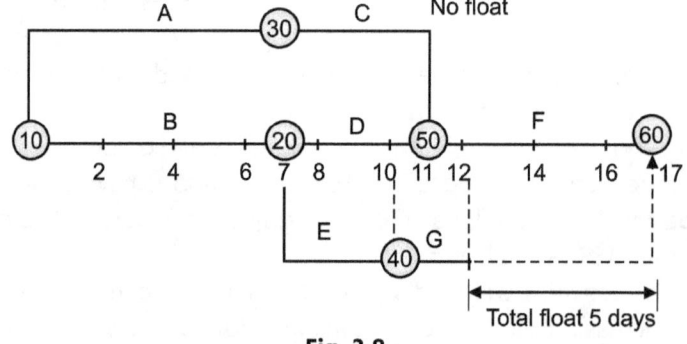

Fig. 3.8

Total Float = 5 days
∴ (Duration)₂ = 17 days
(cost)₂ = ₹ 11,120 + 250
= (vii) Demand 11,370/-

Step 6 : Now if we want to compress activity D, it is to be crashed along with A and C as they are parallel to D and critical. Hence, the options available are

(a) Crash activities D and A (by 1 day) ⇒ Crash slope = 250 + 100 = 350

(b) Crash activities D and C (by 1 day) ⇒ Crash slope = 250 + 150 = 400

(c) Crash activity F by 2 day ⇒ Crash slope = 332.

Minimum cost slope out of the above options is considered.

∴ Crash activity F by 2 days.

∴ (Duration)₃ = 15 days
(Cost)₃ = ₹ 11370 + ₹ 332 × 2
= ₹ 12,034/-

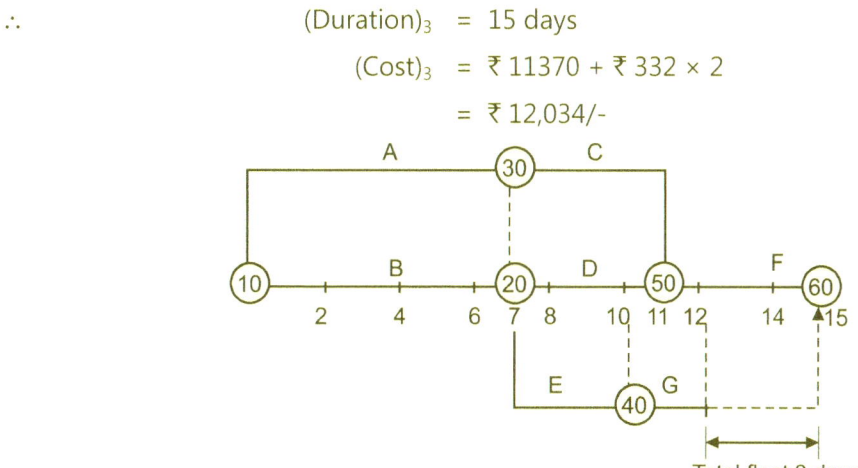

Fig. 3.9

Step 7 : Now, at present the scenario is

(a) Critical activity B is completely crashed.

(b) Activity F is completely crashed.

(c) Activity D can be crashed by 1 more day. But as it is parallel with A and C any one activity which gives minimum cost slope is to be crashed along with D.

(d) Activities E and G are non-critical activities and hence they will not play any role in crashing. Considering the minimum crash slope (₹ 350 per day) A from the previous step, the squared network after crashing D and A by 1 day will become.

∴ (duration)₄ = 14 days
(cos)₄ = ₹ 12,034 + ₹ 350
= ₹ 12,384/-

This ends the crashing steps as critical activities B, D and F are completely crashed and can not be crashed further. This is called as "All crash solution."

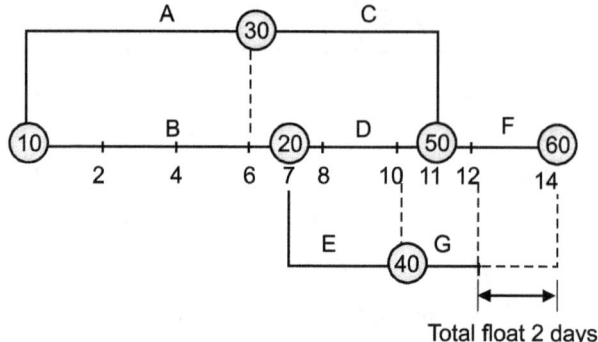

Fig. 3.10

Summary of all the steps along with indirect cost and total cost is as follows :

Duration	20	18	17	15	14
Direct Cost	11,000	11,120	11,370	12,034	12,384
Indirect Cost	6,000	5,400	5,100	4,500	4,200
Total Cost	17,000	16,520	16,470	16,534	16,584

Minimum Cost = ₹ 16,470/-

And Optimum Duration = 17 days

Hence, the solution of this crashing problem is,
- Crash activity B by 2 days.
- Crash activity D by 1 day.

Example 3.2 : For the network shown in Fig. 3.11 the data about the cost is given in the table. The indirect cost of the project is ₹ 3,000 per week. Determine the optimum cost and optimum duration.

Activity	Normal Duration in week (t_n)	Crash Duration in week (t_s)	Normal Cost C_n	Crash Cost C_s
10 – 20	12	6	14,000	29,000
10 – 30	16	10	8,000	17,000
20 – 30	8	2	12,000	18,000
20 – 40	10	6	16,000	30,000
30 – 40	10	6	10,000	22,000

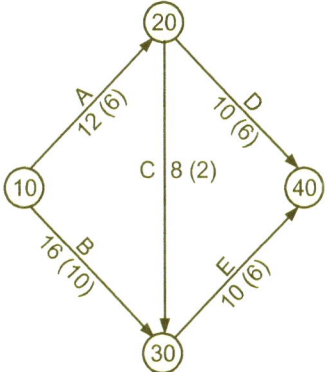

Fig. 3.11

Solution : The EST and LFT of different activities are calculated and critical activities are noted. Cost slopes of different activities are also calculated.

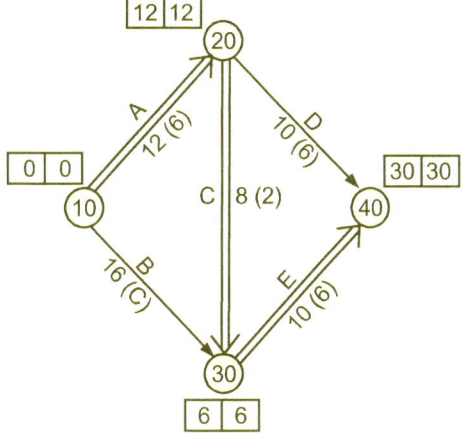

Critical events are 10, 20, 30, 40 and

Critical path 10 – 20 – 30 – 40

Critical Activities are A, C and E

Fig. 3.12

Indirect cost is ₹ 3,000/- per week. All the activities have cost slope less than the indirect cost. Hence, crashing of any activity may reduce the total cost. However, the reduction in duration will be achieved only in crashing the critical activities. Skipping the detailed description as done in the previous example, the step by step crashing of network is given on below

Activity	Normal Duration (week)	Crash Duration (week)	Normal Cost (C_n)	Crash Cost (C_s)	Cost Slope $\dfrac{C_s - C_n}{t_n - t_s}$ ₹/week	Remark
A	12	6	14,000	29,000	2,500	Critical
B	16	10	8,000	17,000	1,500	–
C	8	2	12,000	18,000	1,500	Critical
D	10	6	16,000	30,000	3,500	–
E	10	6	10,000	22,000	2,000	Critical

Step 1 : The squared of Network for the different durations are as below. The total cost for the different durations are as per table given below. The optimum duration, as found from the table and the graphs, is 22 weeks.

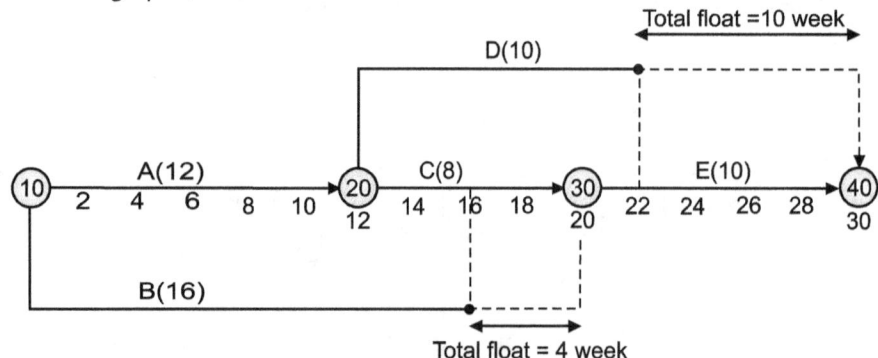

Schedule No. 1

Fig. 3.13

$(Duration)_1$ = 30 weeks

$(Cost)_1$ = Sum of costs of all activities

= ₹ 60,000/-

Step 2 : Crash activity C by 4 weeks so that activity B will critical.

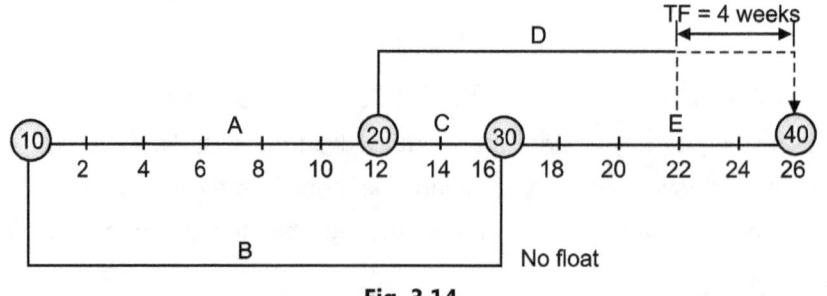

Fig. 3.14

$$(\text{duaration})_2 = 26 \text{ weeks}$$
$$(\text{cost})_2 = ₹ 60{,}000 + 4 \times 1500$$
$$= ₹ 66{,}000/\text{-}$$

Step 3 : As activity B is also become critical activity, alternatives available are as follows
(a) Crash activities A and B by 6 weeks $\Rightarrow$ crash slope = 4,000/-
(b) Crash activities C and B by 2 weeks $\Rightarrow$ crash slope = 3,000/-
(c) Crash activity E by 4 weeks $\Rightarrow$ crash slope = 2,000/-

The alternative with minimum rash slope is considered i.e. crash activity E by 4 weeks.
Therefore, the squared network will become,

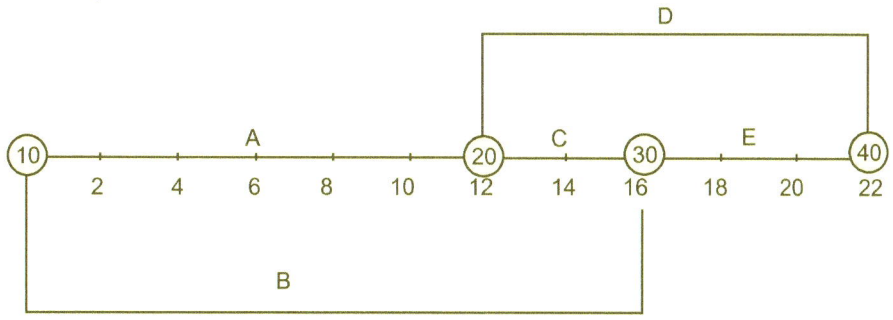

Fig. 3.15

$$(\text{Duration})_3 = 22 \text{ weeks}$$
$$(\text{Cost})_3 = ₹ 66{,}000 + 2000 \times 4$$
$$= ₹ 74{,}000/\text{-}$$

Step 4 : Now the whole network is critical in which following scenario is existing
   (a) Activity E is completely crashed.
   (b) Activity C can be crashed by 2 weeks further along with activity B and D $\Rightarrow$ crash slope = 6500/-
   (c) Activity A and B can be crashed simultaneously for 6 weeks $\Rightarrow$ crash slope 4,000/-.
   The maximum crash slope is ₹ 4,000/- per day. Hence, activities A and B can be crashed by 6 weeks and the network will be,

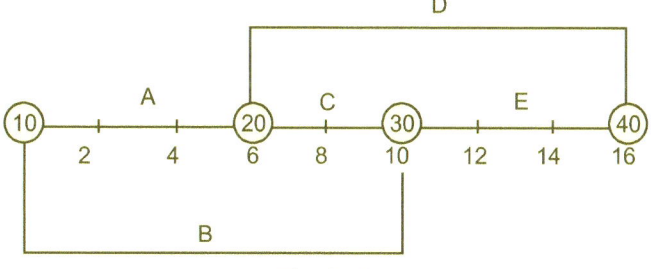

Fig. 3.16

$(\text{duration})_4 = 16$ weeks

$(\text{cost})_4 = ₹\,74{,}000 + 6 \times 4{,}000$

$= ₹\,98{,}000/-$

Step 5 : As activities E and B are completely crashed, further compressing the network is not possible. Hence, it is the all crash solution. Let us calculate the total cost by adding indirect cost as follows :

Duration	30	26	22	16
Direct Cost	60,000	66,000	74,000	98,000
Indirect Cost	90,000	78,000	66,000	48,000
Total Cost	1,50,000	1,44,000	1,40,000	1,46,000

Minimum Cost = ₹ 1,40,000/-

And Optimum Duration = 22 days

Hence the solution of this problem is

(1) Crash activity C by 4 weeks.

(2) Crash activity E by 4 weeks.

3.5 UPDATING

3.5.1 Introduction

The important use of the Network diagram occurs during actual implementation of the project. After the start of the execution, control over the progress is to be exercised. It should be examined at regular interval whether the progress in implementation of the project is as per schedule or otherwise. The actual achievements have to be compared with the planned progress so that any variation may be corrected at that stage only. Thus, during execution of the project, controlling is essential which is complementary to the planning. The control monitor phase is therefore, a continuous phase to see whether the project implementation is as per the schedule and if not, to take corrective steps to bring it back to the planned schedule. This, therefore, requires a flow of information from the persons involved in implementation to the designers and planners through a suitably designed reporting system. This upward flow of information is analysed and the implementation or progress of the project is brought up-to-date with necessary corrective measures.

3.5.2 Necessity of Updating

During the process of implementation of the project according to the network, one may come across one or more of the following situations upon analysing the upward flow informal.

- Some or all the activities are progressing as per the schedule and the plan is being implemented up-to-date.
- Some or all the activities are ahead of the planned schedule.
- Some or all the activities are behind the schedule.

It is seldom that one meets with the situations 1 or 2 above in which case there need no change in the schedule or for updating the network. But in most of the cases the actual implementation is found to be behind the schedule due to the unavoidable difficulties or overestimation in activity duration. If planned network diagram does not conform to the actual progress, the network diagram has to be revised so that the delay is met with. This process is continued till the date is compensated and the project is completed in the planned period or on the date of completion decided at the planning stage. This, therefore, necessitates reconstruction of the network for the remaining part of the work and the complete network diagram has to be revised and redrawn. This process is known as *'updating'*. It may be necessary to reduce the duration of activity wherever possible. This can be done either by logical change or compression of duration of activity period i.e. by crashing the activities which are in progress or which are yet to begin. The critical activities are examined that will reduce the activity duration and later on the period of completion of the project. However, while compressing the activities their cost-time relationship may be taken into consideration so that with the reduction in duration the cost is not increased disproportionately.

3.5.3 When to do Updating

As already stated earlier, CPM has its utility in planning stage as well as in implementation stage. With the preparation of the network and detailed original plan and schedule from the network, about 60 per cent utility may be supposed to be achieved and remaining 40 per cent utility has to be utilised at the implementation stage to see where one stands on a particular date in the progress of the implementation. If this monitoring with the CPM is not done at definite intervals it may result in situation which are :

- Early activities take more time than estimated. Late finishing of critical activities may delay the project whereas non-critical activities consume most of the total float available making all the later activities to be critical or near critical.
- Slippage in schedule continues till close to the end of the project and is detected as the tail activities are reached. This provides a situation where few alternatives remain open to the management to make an attempt to exercise any control and to bring the project back to the schedule.

Therefore, it is very necessary that the actual progress achieved during implementation be compared with the planned schedule and if necessary due corrective steps be taken to bring the progress back to schedule if it is lacking. Updating is therefore, a process of incorporating changes that have occurred or are anticipated in the network plan with respect of time and logic so that the delay caused, if any till the date, is compensated in the implementation of the remaining part of the project. It necessitates replanning and rescheduling to suit the changed conditions. This process of replanning and rescheduling is based on the knowledge received during the implementation, the resources available and the information about overall situation and the results obtained till date about the part of the project completed. There are no hard and fast rules regarding the frequency of updating. Depending upon the working period, the progress achieved and overall situation about the difficulties met with, it is upto the person incharge to decide the frequency of updating. For a big work which is running in three shifts updating weekly or even sometimes daily may be required as a large quantity of work is completed during that period whereas there may not be any necessity of updating monthly. In general project updating in later stages may be more frequent than in early stages as changes if any can be easily incorporated at early stages. However, in general the situations which necessitates immediate updating may be given below

- Each time where there is change in the scope of work.
- When non-critical activities have consumed the available float completely.
- If there are non-avoidable difficulties and delays which result in major set back on critical activities.

3.5.4 Procedure of Updating

The information necessary for updating the project at any stage will be as below

- Original network and calculation chart.
- Stage at which updating is done i.e. point in the time of updating.
- Position of execution of the project at that stage i.e. Activities completed and time required for the activities in progress for completion.
- Any new information and knowledge about the activities yet to commence which may affect their duration.
- Change in logic if any.
- New activity in the remaining part of project to be introduced if any and its logic.

The information received may be summarised in a tabular form given below. The duration of time of completion of the activities which are in progress and which are yet to start may be suitably revised in the light of the experience gained and additional information and knowledge received during the execution.

Table for updating network

Activity	Position on the Day of Update and Duration for Completion		
	Completed	In Progress	Yet to commence

The information is superimposed on the original network and new network is framed. For the events which have occurred the Earliest event occurrence time is taken as zero and for the activities which are completed the duration is taken as zero. For the activities which are in progress and those which are yet to begin, new estimated duration is entered and on this basis the Earliest Occurrence Time and Latest Occurrence Time of the events are calculated. Thus, the new period of completion of the project or rescheduled date of completion may be decided and the project lying behind the schedule may be brought back to the schedule. The updating cycle is as shown below :

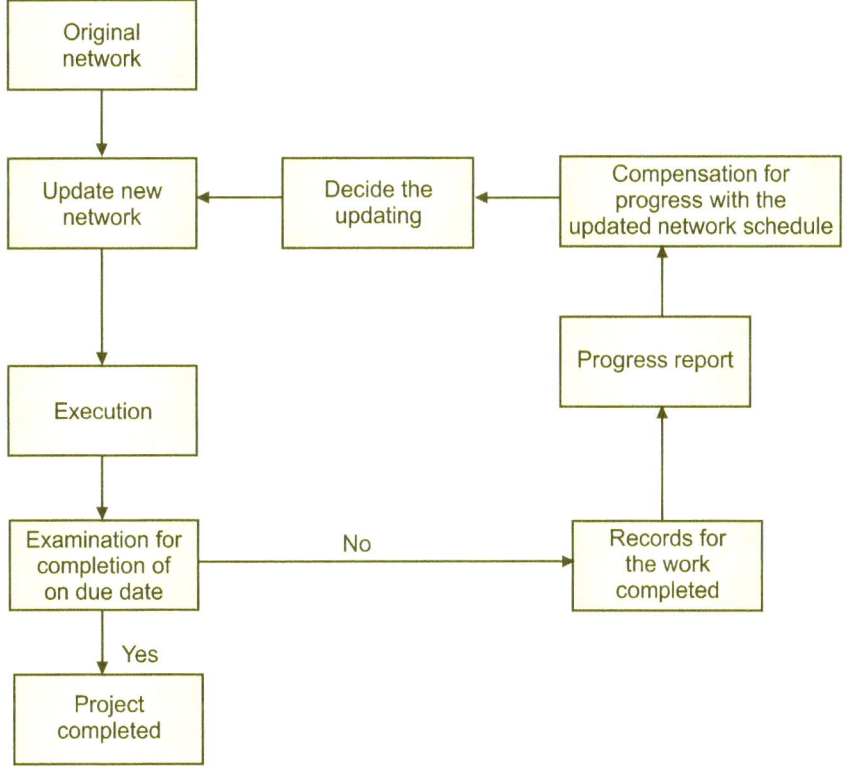

Fig. 3.17

Example 3.3 : The table shows different activities in a project, their duration and the position of the project at the end of 24 days from commencement. Mark the original critical path after drawing the network, update the network and calculate the time of completion.

Activity	Preceding Activity	Succeeding Activity	Duration	Position at the end of 24 days			
				Position	Time taken for activity	Additional Time for completion	Duration Needed
A	–	F	10	Completed	20	–	–
B	–	D	16	Not started	–	20	20
C	–	E	20	Completed	16	–	–
D	B	I	12	Not started	–	–	18
E	C	F	6	Completed	6	–	–
F	A, E	G, H, J	14	In progress	2	12	–
G	F	I	6	Completed	–	–	6
H	F	K	8	Incomplete	–	–	8
I	D, G	–	10	Not started	–	–	10
J	F	–	12	Not started	–	–	20
K	H	–	10	Not started	–	–	10

Solution :

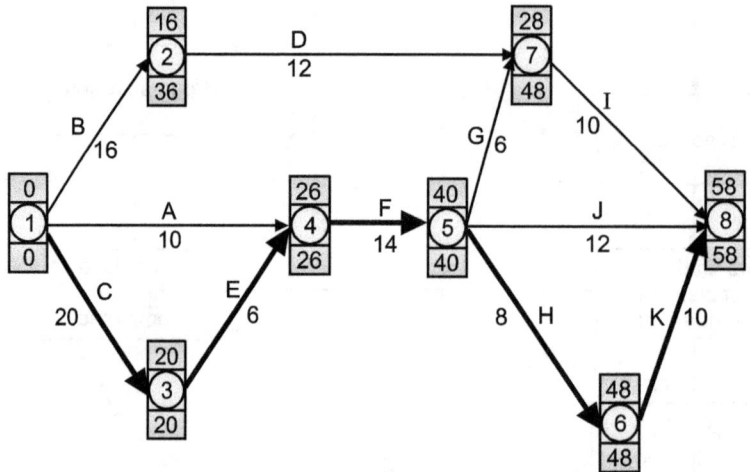

Fig. 3.18

Note that activity J will required more time than scheduled.

Original network and the EST and LFT of different events is as shown above and the critical path is C, E, F, H, K or 1 – 3, 3 – 4, 4 – 5, 5 – 6, 6 – 8. The updated network can now be drawn as shown below :

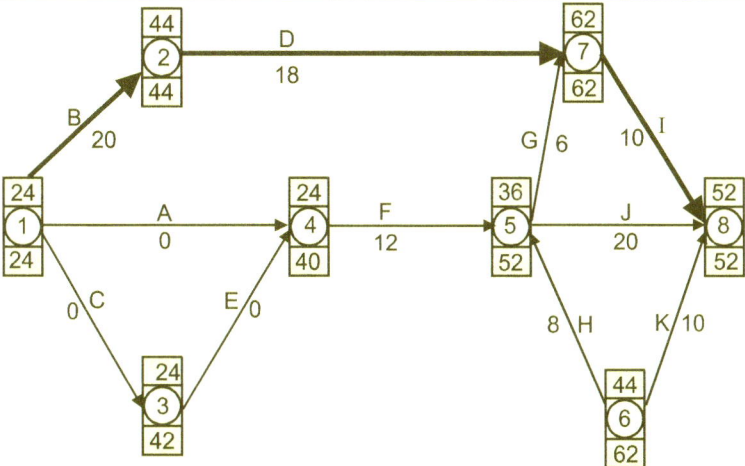

Fig. 3.19

For the events which are yet to occur, the EST is 24 days and for the activities which have been completed the duration is 0. Hence, for event (1) and (3) EST is 24 days and for activities A, C and E duration is zero. The network calculations are completed in usual manner. The critical path is now 1-2-7-8 and now for the updated network the time of completion of project is 72 days in place of 58 days.

3.6 FREQUENCY AND THE TIME OF UPDATING

After the implementation, project starts the actual progress which has to be compared with the planned schedule of progress and when it is found that the actual progress lags behind by considerable period, updating will have to be done. However, the following points will have to be kept in mind while deciding the time of updating :

- For the project of shorter duration frequent comparison between the actual progress and the planned progress will have to be made and this may lead to frequent updating.
- For the project of larger duration in the early stages the updating may not be required frequently. However, as the project is progressing towards completion and as the time of completion is continuously decreasing it will be necessary to check the actual progress with the planned one or previously updated network and frequent updating may be necessary compared with the frequency of updating in the early stages of the project. As the project approaches completion it behaves like a project of shorter duration.
- With the knowledge and information received in the part execution of the project if there is found to be a major change in the duration of any activity then updating will be necessary. If the activity happens to be critical, increase in duration will increase

the total duration of the project and hence remedial measures will have to be taken to see that the project will be completed on the date. However, decrease in the duration of critical activity may allow certain changes to be incorporated.

3.7 RESOURCE ALLOCATION

For actual implementation of the project, different resources are required. They include men, material, machines, money and also space without which, implementation of any project cannot commence.

'Men' include planners, designers, specialist personnel, supervisory staff at senior level and at the work site and skilled and unskilled labour. Machinery includes different kinds of equipment for different activities. Out of all above resources except the money and material, all other can be repetitively used. It is presumed that all the resources are available as and when required. Also duration of different activities is derived assuming a particular amount of the resources in the form of men and machinery is available.

However, it is not so due to following reasons :

- Many activities run concurrently and it may be possible that the total man power needed for concurrently running the activities may not be available.
- There may be limitation of the space available and hence the available resources will have to be used.
- At the planning level, if particular attention is not paid to the availability of manpower, the needed manpower at some level of the project may exceed the demand at other levels which is not desirable.
- Large fluctuations in the demand of resources not only create problems in execution but may delay the project completion and may result in additional cost when the demanded additional resources are not made available as and when needed. It is therefore, necessary that the alternative ways of using the available resources be so decided that the available manpower, machinery and space i.e. limited resources are allocated carefully on the different activities at different phases of implementation and the demand of the different resources is somewhat uniform during the complete duration of the project. This will obtain best outcome and profits from all the resources.

3.7.1 Representing the Resources

The resources, especially incase of manpower, are limited and it is necessary that the person incharge of execution or the manager has to prepare a resource analysis report which may enable him to put to best use at his hand. There will be peaks and valleys in the form of required resources and the manager can try to level out these with the help of resource analysis report. The requirement of a particular type of resource e.g. mason or carpenter or unskilled labour over the complete period has to be known. A graph is plotted for the requirement of resource against the period of requirement and this is known as 'Resource Usage Profile' or in general in the language of statistics a 'histogram'. The histogram will reveal the non-uniform demand over the project duration very clearly. The manager has a definite availability of this resource and he has to plan the requirement of the resource over different periods of execution of the project. He has therefore the following information and alternatives.

- The total requirement of resources over its duration as given by Histogram.
- If the available resources are insufficient, it will result in delay in completion of the project. He has to decide the best allocation of available resources over the entire period of project so that the completion period of the project is extended by minimum duration.
- If the project has to be completed in a fixed period, how best can the available resources be utilised to achieve the goal.

In the above situation it is necessary to have proper resource scheduling to achieve any one of the following objectives

- If project duration is fixed, to level or smoothen the resource demand in such a manner that peaks and valleys in the demand are avoided as far as possible by suitably spacing the different activities and uniform amount/quantity of the resource. Thus, the required uniform resource in the form of manpower or any other is made available. It is presumed that unlimited resource is available. This is 'resource smottening. '
- If the availability of the resources is fixed the same should be so judiciously used so as to complete the project in minimum possible duration. This is 'Resources allocation' and is necessary when a particular type of resource is in scarcity or is limited.

3.7.2 Histogram

Consider the network shown for a project as given below :

Example 3.4 : The Early Start Time (EST) and Latest Start Time (LST) of each event is shown on the network. The critical path 1-2-3-6-10-11-12 is marked. Requirements of skilled labour (mason) and the unskilled labour as envisaged at the time of Network framing comensurating with the duration of the activities are given in the table. The duration of the project is 40 days.

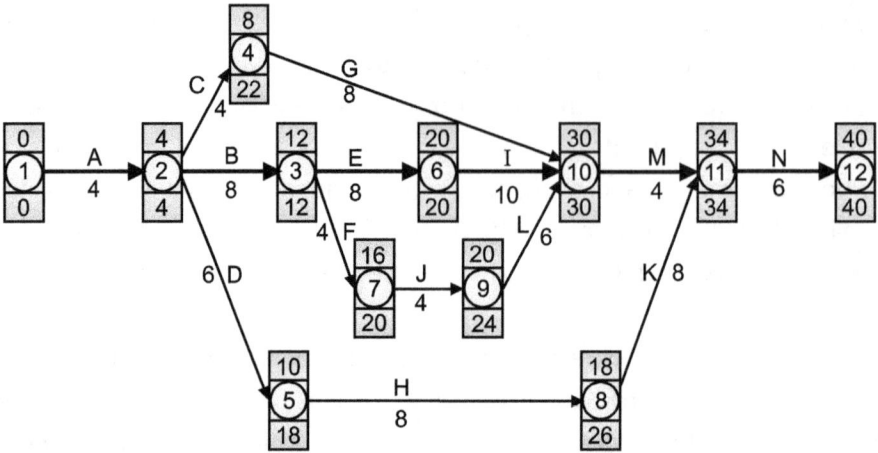

Fig. 3.20

Activity	A	B	C	D	E	F	G	H	I	J	K	L	M	N
Duration (Days)	4	8	4	6	8	4	8	8	10	4	8	6	4	6
Requirement of Mason (M)	2	6	2	4	6	6	10	4	2	2	2	–	2	2
Requirement of Labourers (L)	4	4	6	4	6	4	6	4	6	4	4	8	2	4

The time scaled diagram for the network is as shown below. In plotting this diagram it is planned that all the activities commence its EST. The critical activities will govern the period of completion of the project and hence shown along the horizontal line.

Mason	2	2	12	12	20	20	26	26	12	10	4	4	2	2	2	2	2	2	2
Labour	4	4	14	14	14	14	20	20	14	14	18	18	14	6	6	2	2	4	4	4

The histogram shows wide variations in the requirement of masons and labours over the entire period of the project. The peak requirement is 26 masons and 20 labours and the minimum or valley requirement is 2 masons and 2 labour It is obvious that if 26 masons and 20 labours are employed throughout the project to satisfy the peak demand, they would sit idle during the period of minimum demand and the proposal would be highly uneconomic increasing the project cost enormously and unnecessarily.

The solution may be employing minimum amount of masons and labourers on permanent basis and employing the needed additional masons and labourers as and when required by the peak demand. Practically, however this is risky as not only skilled workers like mason but sometimes even unskilled labourer are also not available on temporary basis without any continuous employment. Hence, proper planning will have to be done so that masons and labourers or any such resource is utilised in a more or less uniform manner and such number be employed on permanent basis till the project is completed. As already indicated this situation is dealt with in two different manners that is either by 'resources smootherning' or by 'resource levelling'.

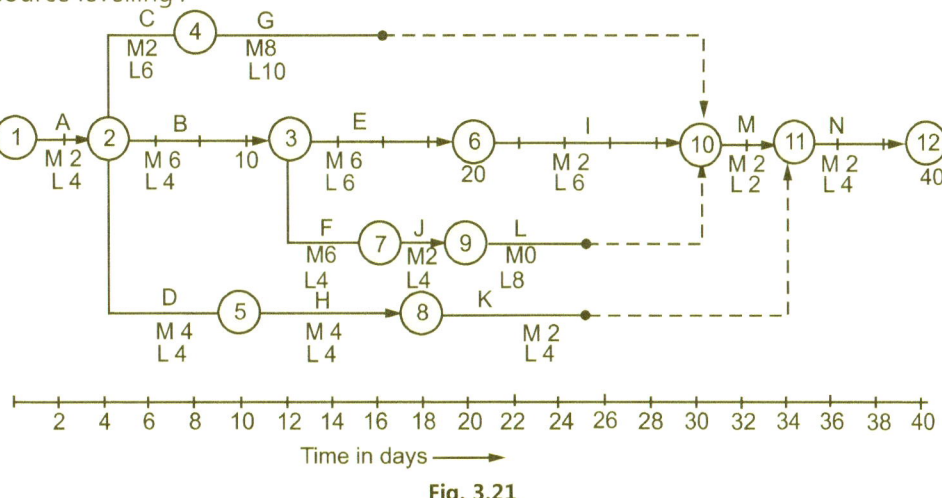

Fig. 3.21

This is employing a set of skilled and unskilled workers for complete period of the project so as to see that the project is completed in its fixed duration. This is also known as *resource smoothening.* Other approach is to utilise the available resources uniformly and to reschedule the activities so that the peak demand is reduced to availability. Here the emphasis is on the proper and uniform use of available resources even at the cost of increase in the duration of the project. This is known as *resources levelling.*

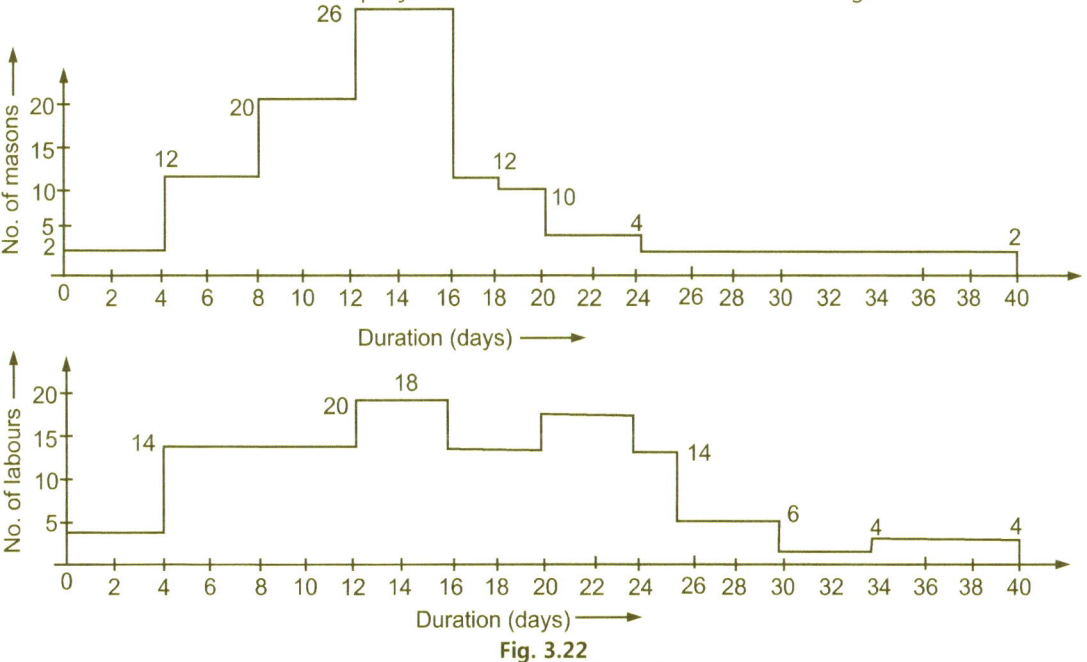

Fig. 3.22

3.7.3 Resources Smoothening

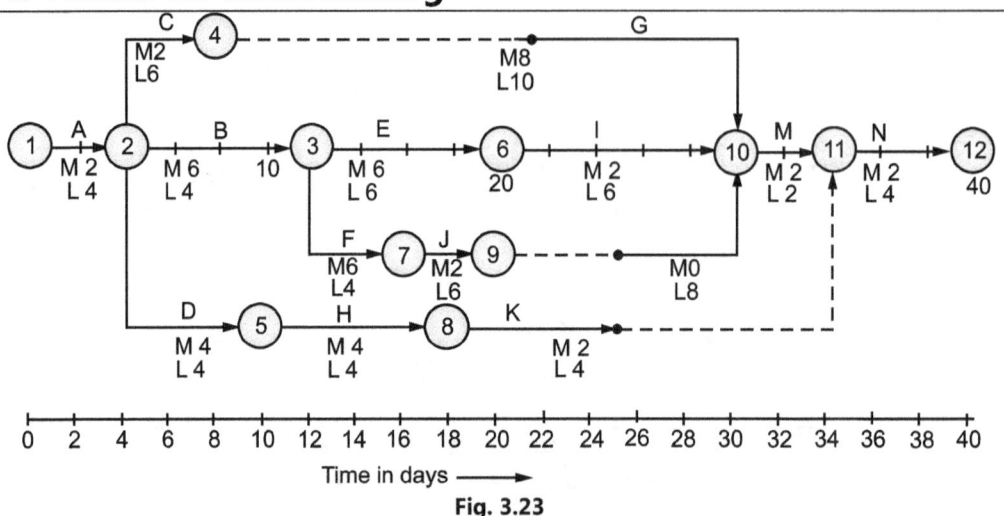

Fig. 3.23

Constrain in this approach is completion period of the project and resources to be uniform as far as possible or for a continuous period of time. Since time period of the project is to be maintained, the critical activities should not be disturbed and the requirement of resources for these activities should be met with. The additional resources which are needed for the concurrent non-critical activities now can be varied by shifting these activities to the period where requirement of critical activities is reduced. This can be done by utilising the floats of the non-critical activities by shifting them suitably. This is illustrated by using the data of Example 3.4. From the network it could be seen that non-critical activities have floats as shown below :

Activity	2 – 4	2 – 5	3 – 7	4 – 10	5 – 8	7 – 9	8 – 11	9 – 10
Float (Days)	14	8	4	14	8	4	8	4

Some of these activities can be suitably shifted utilising the float so that they are concurrent with the critical activities requiring less resources and somewhat uniform requirement is met with. This will have to be done with two or three trials and the best of the these will have to be adopted. In the above problem it is seen that the requirement of mason between day 12 to day 16 is maximum.

The activity 4 – 10 which is shown in the fig. from 8th day to 16th day be shifted to the period of 23rd day to 30th day so that the requirement of mason is reduced from 20 to 10 and 26 to 16 in the period of 8 to 12 and 12 to 16 days and the requirement of mason from 23rd to 24th day is increased from 4 to 14 and that from 25th to 30th day from 2 to 12. This will also reduce the labour requirement as shown in the Fig. 3.24. Additional labour requirement can further be reduced by shifting the activity 9 – 10 by utilising its float of 4 days. With these changes the time scale diagram, requirement of masons and labours and the histogram is as shown below in Fig. 3.24.

Mason	2	2	12	12	10	10	16	16	10	8	4	14	10	10	10	10	2	2	2	2
Labour	4	4	14	14	8	8	14	14	10	10	10	16	18	14	14	14	2	4	4	4

The below example shows the peak demand for mason is reduced from 26 to 16 and that for the labours are is reduced from 20 to 18 but with more uniform spread over for a long time of the project duration.

Different trials may give still better results and following this procedure it is always possible to smoothen the resources without affecting the duration of the project.

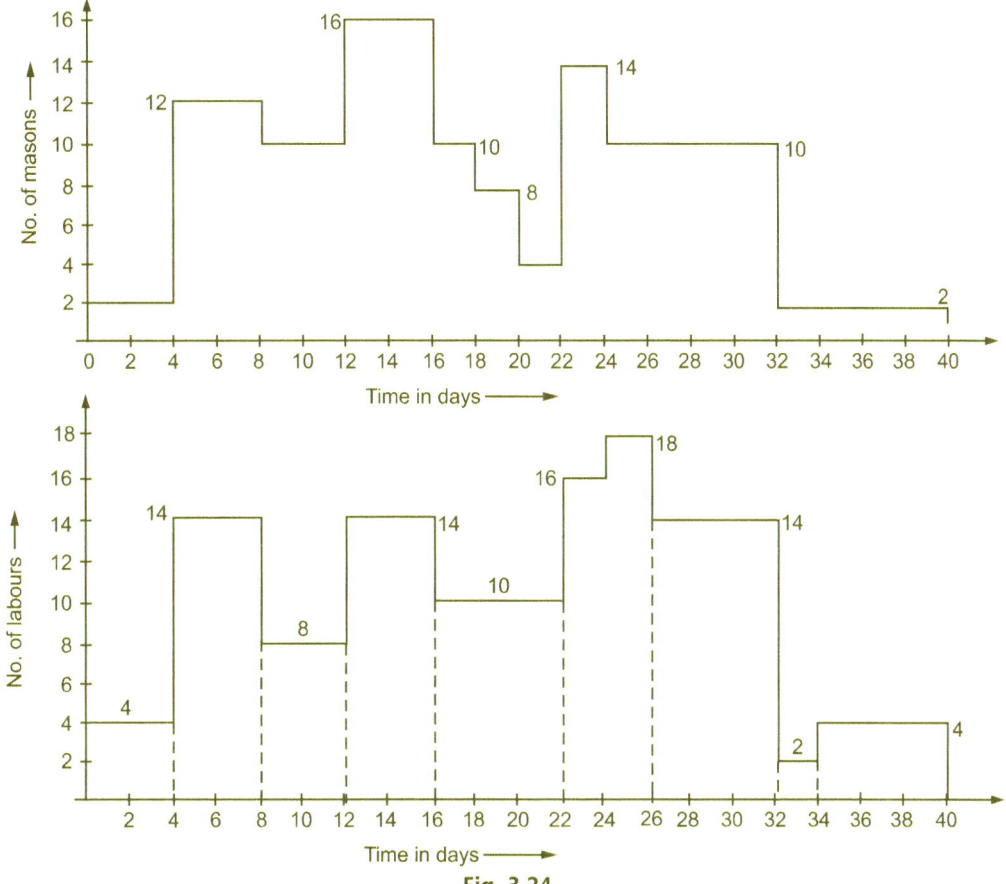

Fig. 3.24

3.7.4 Resource Levelling

In this, there is limited availability of resources. However, normally the available resources should not be less than the maximum number or quantity required for any activity of the project. Therefore, the activity requiring maximum resources dictates the method and along with execution of such activity which ever concurrent activities would be executed, they will be utilising limited resources. Since the requirement of skilled labour, say carpenter, is more and the availability is less, the rescheduling will have to be effected. In this rescheduling, non-critical activities are shifted suitably utilising the available floats. However, even with such shifting the demand for resources may exceed the availability and in that case even the critical activities also cannot be completed in their duration and hence the duration will have to be increased to suit the availability of the resources. This will therefore, result in increase in the duration of the project. But the available resources being the constraint on the project there is no other way than to accept this delay in completion of the project. As such where the completion date is not to be conformed strictly or where there is not likely to be major loss because of some delay in completion of the project and there is availability of limited resources, resource levelling will have to be adopted.

In Example 3.4 the maximum requirement of mason of activity 4 – 10 is 10 masons and maximum requirement of labour of activity 9 – 10 is 8 labour. As such the number of masons and labours available should not be less than 10 and 8 respectively. But even if 10 masons and 8 labours are available as it is seen from the revised histogram that this availability is insufficient even after rescheduling the non-critical activities by using available floats duration of activities to be executed will have to be increased accordingly. Where the requirement of mason is more than 10 and labour more than 8. If the critical activities fall in this process the project duration will be unavoidably increased. Resource levelling is also a process of trial and mathematical complexity is involved in complex projects having many activities. No technique have been evolved as yet to give a optimum solution to such resource levelling problems and a straight forward solution cannot be obtained. It is only by trial, one can come to a conclusion to the problem of resource levelling. Mathematically, it is not possible to arrive at a unique solution of minimising the maximum required resources for the project. Manager's experience in such problems will only help in bringing out an acceptable and practicable solution for resource levelling.

3.8 COST CONTROL

'Cost control is the process of controlling the expenditure on a construction project at all stages from its inception through its development and design, till the execution and final payment'. It is a process to maximise the benefits or profit from the limited finance available.

3.8.1 Purposes of Cost Control

- It provides data of the total expenditure of the work at any instance at a regular time interval. Hence, the contractor can find his profit and loss by comparing the completed work and work ahead and the expenditure involved.
- In the process of cost control, focus can be made on the area of inefficient functioning and measures can be taken to reduce the cost by controlling the expenses. Cost control data indicates the day-to-day cost incurred on various items

of work and gives immediate warning to the site engineers when expenditures exceeds the estimated costs. Also, if two similar jobs constructed by the same method, shows differences in unit costs, it can be result of varying degree of efficiency of workers or due to mismanagement on the site. Corrective actions can be taken to put the work again at the same speed.

- Cost control data of a work provides feedback to the estimator for updating the knowledge of output data of men and machines. The unit rates of cost for various items of works can be worked out after the completion of a job and these would help in preparing realistic estimates for other works for which the contractor may like to tender.

3.8.2 Stages At Which Cost Control is Effected

1. **At the Design Stage :** The cost control is dependent to some extent on the design and specifications. Among the various alternatives of designs, only those are considered which are most economical as well as consistent with the requirements. The specifications which add benefits without increasing the cost are chosen. Local materials should be specified as they reduce the cost of transportation.
2. **At the Construction Stage :** Construction cost consists of expenditures on (1) labour, (2) materials, (3) machinery and equipment, and (4) overheads. Out of these four, substantial economy can be achieved in labour and machinery in which the wastage of man-hours can be more. Machinery to be used on site should get fully utilised otherwise its cost/use increases. Also the labour intensive jobs are time consuming and unsuitable for jobs required to be completed within a limited time.

3.8.3 Classification of Cost Control System

The type of cost control system used should not be too costly such that it consumes more expenditure than the cost saved by using it. Hence depending upon the various types and sizes of works, cost control system must be selected. The selection of a cost control system depends on the following factors :

- Type and nature of work.
- Detailing of the various operations recorded.
- Whether the system is quick and simple ?

Depending on the requirements, following are the types of cost control system

1. **Overall Profit or Loss :** The contractor waits till the work is over and then compares the money he receives for the work with the amount he has spend on it. Such a system is useful only in very small contracts of short duration. In fact, it is hardly a method of control as the information it produces can only be used to avoid similar mistakes in later contracts.
2. **Profit or Loss with Reference to Part Payment :** The contractor is paid for the portion of work completed by him at regular intervals. The costs incurred by

contractor and the payments received can be compared to know the profit and loss position for that part of the work. But this does not take into account all the items of work done and the unused materials on site. It also does not provide break-up of the cost figures and hence does not point to the area needing attention for cost saving.

3. **Unit Costing :** The rate of cost of each item of work is calculated by dividing the expenditure on the item by the quantity of work done. By comparing the rate of cost with the rates in the cost estimates, the efficiency of work can be assessed. It gives the items which need attention. But it does not indicate clearly whether the poor performance of labour, material or machinery which caused the increase in cost.

4. **Comparison with Standard Cost :** In this method, the cost record consists of details of the rate of cost of labour, materials and machinery. These are then compared with the rates of those items known as 'cost standards' as worked out when estimating cost. It is hence possible to pinpoint the area in which there is inefficiency and scope for improvement. This is a costly method as great amount of details are involved.

3.9 PROJECT TIME CONTROL

Project time control is a continuous process starting from the project planning upto project completion. The project is to be controlled in order to complete the job within or before the stipulated time period. Steps in project time control can be given as follows :

1. **In the Planning Stage**
    - The scope of the work should be finalised and the requirements of the owner are to be clearly understood by the consultant and the contractor.
    - All the activities are to be planned according to their sequence and requirement of resources. If the sources required for the overlapping activities are the same, more numbers are to be provided so that there will not be idle time left for men and machinery.
    - The quantities for each item of work should be calculated exactly so that at the time of construction, chances of shortage of materials are minimised.
    - Priorities are to be given to the critical activities and no delays are allowed for them. To achieve expected results, the planning for the critical activities is done keeping in mind all the requirements, probable difficulties and provision of finance.
    - Planning for the materials and its orders is to be done carefully keeping in mind the lead time required for each order. The rates of the materials are to be decided with the supplier before the orders are placed and care is to be taken to avoid any kind of misunderstanding.
    - Check lists for each item of work is to be made in advance and it is to be followed scrupulously.

2. In the Execution Stage

- Safety stock is to be maintained on the site so that there is no time wasted for want of material.
- A monitoring cell is to be formed that will look after the progress of the work. Any delays are to be rectified quickly to avoid any increase in the project duration.
- Techniques such as Crashing of activities are to be used to minimize the project duration.

3.10 LINE OF BALANCE TECHNIQUE (LOB)

Many construction projects like construction of roads, laying of pipelines or multistorieyed projects contain repetitive activities either horizontally or vertically. E.g. Road construction, involves activities such as preparation of sub-base, preparation of base course, laying of bitumin, compaction etc. These activites span along the length of road. Similarly, for multistoreyed construction, activities like concreting of columns, beams and slab,s brickwork, plastering, tiling, plumbing, painting etc go on repeating at each floor. For such kind of activities an effective technique of 'line of balance' (LOB) is used. It is a 3 dimensional technique of planning i.e. it shows duration, activities and the place of work or length of project or stages of the project.

The LOB technique assumes that the rate of production for an activity is uniform. It is a graphical presentation in which time is plotted on horizontal axis and units or stages of an activity on the vertical axis. The production rate of an activity on the slope of the production line and is expressed in terms of units per time.

3.10.1 How to Draw LOB ?

Let us, take an example of construction of multistoried building in which repetitive activities are involved

Step 1 : The starting step involves plotting of project duration on x-axis and no. of floors on y-axis. The Fig. shows total duration as 32 weeks for 5 floors. It is to be noted that the LOB starts after the plinth level is constructed which is not a repeating activity i.e. a unique activity. (Show Fig. 3.25 for step 1).

Step 2 : The duration of each activity are estimated by normal techniques. E.g. activity 'A' takes 12 weeks to complete for all floors. This means the production rate is 2.4 weeks per floor. It is indicated as shown below. (Show the Fig. 3.26 for step 2).

Step 3 : Now consider activity B with the production rate as one week per floor. It will start when activity 'A' ends on each floor. It is shown as below (Shown in Fig. 3.27 for step 3).

This will be continued for the entire project for other activities. As it is seen from the above Fig. 3.27, there are breaks for activity B at each floor. These breaks or gaps means the crew for 'B' is waiting for some time at each floor and starts as soon as activity A completes on that floor.

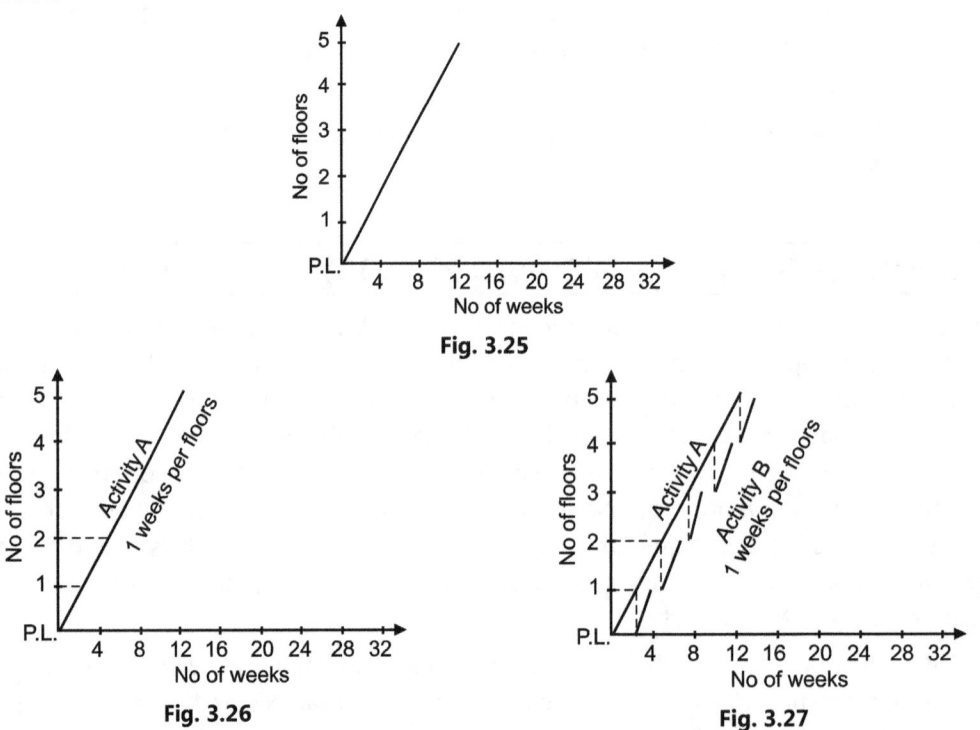

Fig. 3.25

Fig. 3.26

Fig. 3.27

This indicates loss of production and idle manpower for activity B at each floor i.e. avoid this situation, the same activities are represented as below :

The time buffer of week is kept when activity A ends for 5th floor. Working in a reverse way, it activity B has to be completed. 1 week after end of activity A i.e. 13th week, it should start at (13 – 5) = 8th week (rate of production of B is 1 week per floor).

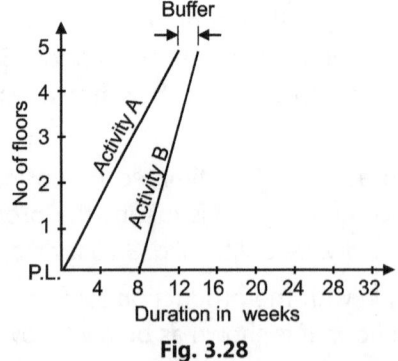

Fig. 3.28

The buffer provides an margin of error and ensures that one activity does not interfere (intersect) with another activity. It is also to be noted that the activities never intersect with each other. The buffer is estimated by the experience of the construction manager and considering the risks, difficulties and probable delays that may occur. The process of drawing LOB is repeated for all activities. The buffers are placed at end or start of activities and are named as 'End Buffer' or 'Start Buffer' respectively. The complete LOB can be shown as adjacent.

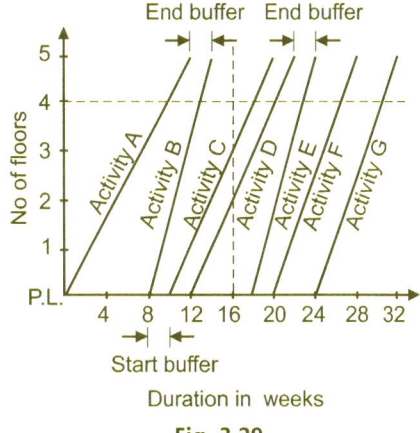

Fig. 3.29

3.10.2 Advantages of LOB Technique

- It's a graphical representation in 3 dimensions i.e. duration, activity and place of work.
- It gives the progress of work at each place of work. E.g. in the above Fig., it indicates the activities which are taking place on 4th floor at different time. Also, on 16th week, it tells us that activities A and B are completed and activities C and D are running. It even gives us the percentage of activity completed.
- It can be effectively used for projects involving repetitive activities.

3.10.3 Disadvantages of LOB Technique

- It is difficult to recognize the time and space dependencies between the activities.
- It is also difficult to deal with resource and milestone constraints.
- Sometimes, non-linear and discrete activities come across the project which can not be shown on LOB.
- Critical activities can not be shown on LOB.
- Flowless softwares are not available which uses LOB effectively.

IMPORTANT POINTS

Project costs with its two types Direct cost and Indirect cost.

- Concept of cost slope for direct cost.
- Concept of crashing of network for cost optimization.
- Concept of updating with its necessity procedure.
- Frequency and the time of updating.

PROJECT MGT. & ENGG. ECO. (TE CIVIL SEM. II – PU)   PROJECT MONITORING AND CONTROL

QUESTIONS

1. Differentiate between direct cost and indirect cost. What do you understand by outage losses ?
2. What is cost slope and how is it determined ?
3. How is optimum duration and optimum cost of a project determined ?
4. Details of a project consisting of 6 activities are as given below :

Activity	1 – 2	1 – 3	2 – 3	3 – 4	2 – 5	4 – 6
Normal Time weeks	2	7	6	4	2	8
Crash Time weeks	1	5	4	3	1	6
Normal cost ₹	3,000	2,400	4,800	800	8,000	3,000
Crash cost ₹	3,400	4,000	6,000	1,200	8,400	5,000

   (a) Draw the network and identify critical path.

   (b) Calculate the project duration and associated cost if the indirect cost is ₹ 800 per week.

   (c) If the project duration is to be reduced by 1 week how best this could be done and what is the associated cost.

   (d) Calculate the optimum duration and the optimum cost.

5. What do you understand by updating ? Explain its necessity.
6. What information is necessary for updating the project during execution ? How is frequency of updating decided ?
7. Update the network given below after 20 days of execution.

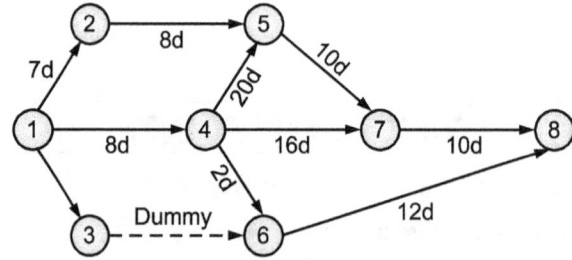

Fig. 3.30

After 20th day of execution the position of activities are as given below

Activity	1 – 2	1 – 3	1 – 4	2 – 5	3 – 6	4 – 5	4 – 6	5 – 7	6 – 7	7 – 8
Position	Completed	Completed	Completed	Not started	In progress	Progress	Not started	Not started	Not started	Not started
Remarks	As per schedule	As per schedule	As per schedule	As per schedule	1	6	As per schedule	To be compressed by 4 days	As per schedule	As per schedule

8. Discuss the problem of resource allocation in brief with different methods of solving.

9. What is resource smoothening and resource levelling ? Differentiate with examples.

10. Illustrate the method of resource smoothening with the help of example.

11. Explain the procedure of controlling the cost is detail.

12. Differentiate various cost control systems and explain each in brief.

13. Manpower requirement for various activities of a project are as follows :

Activity	Duration (Days)	Resource (Men)/Day
1 – 2	5	10
2 – 3	5	5
2 – 4	6	10
3 – 5	5	6
4 – 5	10	4
5 – 6	6	10

(i) Draw a network and calculate project duration. Show critical path.

(ii) Draw EST squared network and calculate EFR and IFR for EST solution.

(iii) Draw LST squared network and calculate EFR and IFR for LST solution.

14. Following data pertains to a small project.

Activity	1 – 2	1 – 3	2 – 3	3 – 5	3 – 4	5 – 6	6 – 7	4 – 7
Duration (Days)	7	9	4	13	10	8	9	16

(i) Draw a network, calculate project duration and critical path.

(ii) At the end of 13th day, review was taken which indicates.

    (a) Activity 1 – 2, 1 – 3 and 2 – 3 completed.

    (b) Activity 3 – 4 progressing for 2 days and needs 10 more days.

    (c) Re-assessment of activity 6 – 7, observed that it can be completed within 8 days.

Draw UPDATED NETWORK and calculate project duration and show critical path.

15. What do you mean by cost control ? Write importance and purpose of cost control.

16. Following table pertains to a small project work, indirect cost of which is ₹ 250 per day.

Activity	Normal		Crash	
	Duration (Weeks)	Cost (₹)	Duration (Weeks)	Cost (₹)
1 – 2	7	6,000	5	6,400
2 – 3	9	10,000	5	11,200
2 – 4	8	5,500	4	6,100
3 – 6	10	6,500	7	7,700
4 – 6	4	7,000	3	7,100
6 – 7	0	–	0	–
6 – 8	2	4,000	2	4,000
7 – 8	5	8,000	3	9,000

(i) Draw network and highlight critical path.

(ii) Calculate Normal project duration and cost of the project.

(iii) Calculate optimum duration and optimum cost of the project by stage by state compression.

(iv) Draw 'optimum duration' squared network of the project.

17. The manpower requirements for the various activities of a project are as given below :

Activity	Duration in days	Restraints	Resource (Men/Day)
A	4	Starting activity	5
B	5	Starting activity	8
C	6	C follows A	3
D	2	D follows B	6
E	2	E follows C & D	9
F	4	F follows C & D	7
G	1	G follows E	5
H	2	H follows F	4
I	4	I follows G & F	2
J	2	J follows I	9

(i) Draw a network and find out project duration and show critical path.

(ii) Draw EST squared network and calculate EFR & IFR for EST solution.

(iii) Draw Histogram for EST solution.

18. What are the objects of Resource allocation ?

19. The following table gives the cost duration data for the various activities of a small construction project.

Activity	Normal		Crash	
	Duration (Weeks)	Cost (₹)	Duration (Weeks)	Cost (₹)
1 – 2	6	7000	3	14500
1 – 3	8	4000	5	8500
2 – 3	4	6000	1	9000
2 – 4	5	8000	3	15000
3 – 4	5	5000	3	11000

The Indirect cost of the project is ₹ 3000/- week.

(i) Draw network and find critical path. Calculate normal project duration.

(ii) Draw EST squared network for normal durations.

(iii) Draw EST squared network at optimum stage.

Determine optimum duration of the project and corresponding minimum cost.

(iv) Draw EST squared network at all crash solution stage. Calculate duration and corresponding cost.

20. The following table gives the cost duration data for various activities of construction project.

Activity	Normal Duration (Weeks)	Normal Cost (₹)	Crash Duration (Weeks)	Crash Cost (₹)
1 – 2	4	2000	3	2600
2 – 3	7	4000	5	7000
2 – 4	6	4500	5	6000
2 – 5	7	1500	6	2300
3 – 6	6	3000	4	4000
4 – 6	4	6000	3	8000
5 – 6	3	1000	2	1150
6 – 7	2	900	1	1600

The Indirect cost is ₹ 1000/week.

(a) Draw network and calculate project duration and show critical path by heavy ruling line.
(b) Draw EST squared network.
(c) Calculate normal project duration and normal project cost.
(d) Calculate optimum project duration and optimum project cost.
(e) Draw EST squared network at optimum stage.

21. (a) Manpower requirement for various activities of a project are as follows

Activity	Duration (Days)	No. of Carpenters
1 – 2	7	12
2 – 3	7	7
2 – 4	8	12
2 – 5	7	8
3 – 5	12	8
4 – 5	8	6
5 – 6	9	6

(i) Draw a network and calculate project duration. Show critical path by heavy ruling line.
(ii) Draw EST squared Network and prepare Resource accumulation table and Calculate EFR and IFR.
(iii) Draw Histogram for EST network.

(b) Explain Resource levelling and Resource smoothing with suitable example.

22. The following are the manpower requirements for each activity in the project.

Activity	Duration (Day)	Manpower Required
1 – 2	4	6
2 – 3	6	6
2 – 4	6	6
3 – 5	0	0
4 – 5	0	0
3 – 6	8	2
5 – 7	10	6
4 – 8	6	4
6 – 9	8	2
7 – 9	10	6
8 – 9	8	4

Draw the squared network and find out EST and LST solution and EFR and IFR.

23. The following table gives the cost duration data for various activities of construction project.

The Indirect cost is ₹ 80/- per day.

(a) Draw network and calculate project duration and show critical path by heavy ruling line.
(b) Draw EST squared network.
(c) Calculate normal project duration and normal project cost.
(d) Calculate optimum project duration and optimum project cost.
(e) Draw EST squared network at optimum stage.

Activity	Normal Duration (Weeks)	Normal Cost (₹)	Crash Duration (Weeks)	Crash Cost (₹)
1 – 2	2	1000	2	1000
1 – 3	7	500	3	900
2 – 3	6	300	3	420
2 – 4	5	200	4	250
3 – 4	0	0	0	0
3 – 5	9	600	4	900
4 – 6	11	600	6	1000
5 – 6	6	700	3	910

24. Cost and Schedule data for small project are given below. The indirect cost is ₹ 1000/- day.

(i) Draw normal duration network and calculate project duration.

(ii) Carryout stage by stage network compression and find out optimum duration and optimum cost.

Activity	Normal		Crash	
	Duration in Days	Cost in ₹	Duration in Days	Cost in ₹
0 – 1	2	500	1	1000
1 – 2	4	400	3	1000
1 – 3	4	250	3	870
1 – 4	3	550	2	1050
2 – 8	4	700	2	2100
3 – 5	7	650	4	1550
3 – 8	2	620	1	1820
4 – 6	5	520	3	2600
5 – 7	2	470	1	1570
6 – 9	5	390	5	390
7 – 8	2	430	1	480
8 – 9	3	530	2	630
9 – 10	2	570	2	570

25. Following table shows the cost-duration data for a small construction project. Indirect cost for the project is ₹ 300 per week.
   (i) Draw the network, find the normal project duration and the corresponding project cost.
   (ii) If all activities are crashed, what will be the project duration and corresponding cost ?
   (iii) Find the optimum duration and minimum project cost.

Activity i – j	Normal		Crash	
	Duration (Weeks)	Cost (₹)	Duration (Weeks)	Cost (₹)
1 – 2	6	1400	4	1900
1 – 3	8	2000	5	2800
2 – 3	4	1100	2	1500
2 – 4	3	800	2	1400
3 – 4	Dummy	–	–	–
3 – 5	6	900	3	1600
4 – 6	10	2500	6	3500
5 – 6	3	500	2	800

26. Explain the conditions under which updating is carried out.
27. What are the objectives of Resource Levelling ? Explain the procedure of carrying out resource leveling.
28. List factors affecting man-power planning.
29. Find the optimum solution for the following network

Activity	Succeeding Activity	Normal Duration	Crash Duration	Crash Cost (in ₹)	Normal Cost (in ₹)
A	B, C	8	8	500	500
B	D, E	4	3	1000	750
C	I	4	3	800	500
D	G	3	3	750	750
E	F	6	4	1500	800
F	H	9	6	2500	1600
G	–	5	4	500	400
H	–	7	5	800	600
I	f	8	5	3000	1500

The indirect cost of each activity is given as ₹ 150/- per day.

(a) Find the duration and normal cost of the project, (b) Find all crash solution.

(c) Find the optimum solution.

30. Explain the steps for quality control for construction of substructure.
31. Explain the terms – Rescheduling and Updating. Also write the procedure for updating of network.
32. Explain Resource Levelling and Resource Smoothening by giving suitable example.
33. Explain the procedure of carrying out Resource Levelling.
34. Discuss the procedure for step by step network compression.
35. Explain the following terms with example : (i) Direct cost of an activity, (ii) Indirect cost of an activity, (iii) Crash cost of an activity, (iv) Normal cost of an activity
36. What are the objectives of Resource Scheduling ?
37. Draw the following network.

Activity	Succeeded by	Duration (Days)	Resources
A	C, D	3	4
B	E	2	6
C	G	1	3
D	E	6	6
E	F, H	4	6
F	G	5	8
G	I, J	3	5
H	K	8	5
I	L	5	4
J	M	6	2
K	M	9	1
L	–	3	2
M	–	3	2

(i) Find the critical path and duration.

(ii) Carry out resource smoothening.

(iii) Carry out resource leveling. (Solve the example by drawing time scale graph of the network).

38. Explain the concept of line of balance in detail.

39. What are the applications of LOB technique.

UNIT IV

PROJECT ECONOMICS

4.1 INTRODUCTION (May 2011)

The term economics touches every field whether it is engineering or day to day working. How many times do we afford to go to a five star hotel for dinner ? How much we can save every year ?

Why do petrol prices rise every year ? On what factors do my increments or promotion depend ? Is there any relation exist between price of crude oil to rise in price of gold ? What is the relation between NSE and BSE index ? How the earthquake in Japan may rise the prices of goods in India ? What are the factors that makes the dollar and pound strongest ? Answers to all these questions can be found by studying economics.

In short, Economics is the study of flow of finance right from production to consumption of goods or services. *It is the study of how the society decides what, how and for whom to produce.*

It is a science that studies human behaviour which aims at meeting maximum objectives of an individual with the help of scarce means. Economics is also an art as well as science that studies those activities of social, real and normal human beings, which are related to worth.

4.2 IMPORTANCE OF ECONOMY IN CONSTRUCTION INDUSTRY (Nov./Dec.-11, 12, May 11, 12)

Construction activities touch every aspect of economy. Following pi chart shows the employment created by construction industry as compared to others. (the figures are taken as tentative. It may vary from country to country).

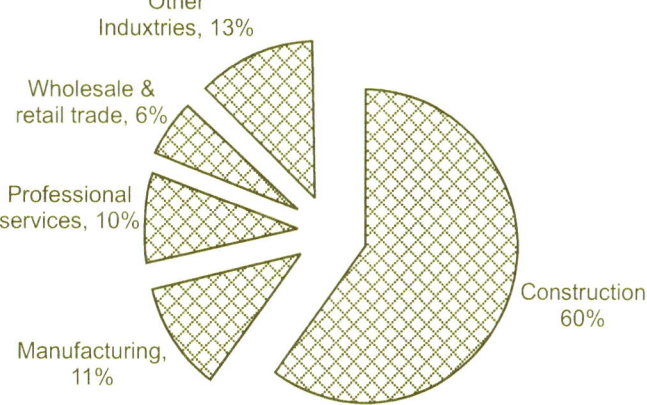

Fig. 4.1 : Contribution of construction industry in economy

With the increasing demand of infrastructure, construction industry is flourishing. Consider any industry, may be day by day service sector or manufacturing unit, one need to invest in construction by one or the other way.

The share of construction industry in overall development of economy is as follows :

Construction industry gives employment to millions of workers, directly or indirectly. Following Fig. 4.2 shows, how construction influences other industries and overall economic development directly or indirectly.

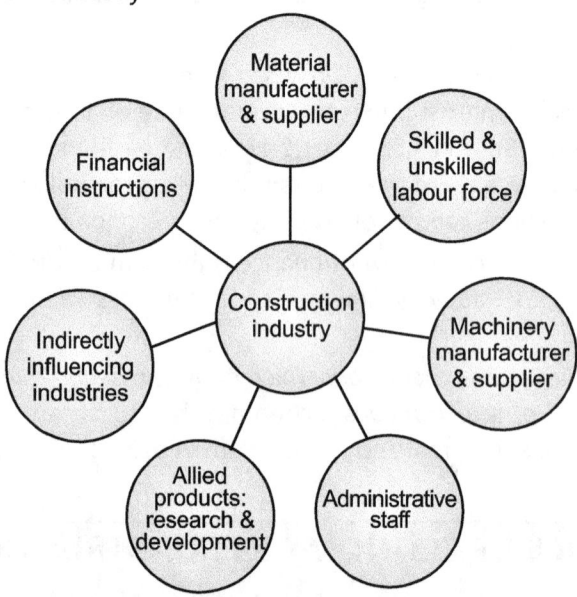

Fig. 4.2

Consider a project, e.g. construction of multistoried buildings. The direct businesses associated with it are :

- Material manufacturer and suppliers such as cement, steel, sand, admixtures, tiles, plumbing, electrical, air conditioning, paints, glass, plywood and many more.
- The requirement of skilled and unskilled labours is huge. It attracts large population and provides daily wages to them.
- Machineries like cranes, mixers, transit mixers, vibrators, trolleys, lifts, concrete pumps etc. are required for faster work. So the manufacturing industries get business.
- Large administrative staff is required on site and off site to maintain the organisations. These are indirectly influencing the economy.
- The other allied products such as green building materials, low cost materials, alternate techniques to reduce expenses and increase quality etc. are a need of time. Many nations are investing huge amount in it. The direct and indirect staff required for this also to be counted.

For these large projects, financial backing is given by many institutions on long term basis. This keeps the money circulating and increasing the GDP of nation. Construction also affects the other industries indirectly. Tourism is one of the best example of it. If the infrastructure is good, tourism flourishes in that area. We can also say that for growing tourism, infrastructure development like roads, water supply, hotel industry is a must. By looking at these reasons and many more, one can say that now-a-days, construction is the vital factor that affects the economy.

4.3 INDIA : CONSTRUCTION INDUSTRY AND ECONOMY

Infrastructure Industry in India has been experiencing rapid growth in its different sectors with the development of urbanization and increasing involvement of foreign investments in this field. Infrastructure development and maintenance is a major input to economic development and sustained growth to Indian Economy. Nearly all of the infrastructure sectors present excellent opportunities, with roads and highways, ports and airports, railways and power standing out as particular bright spots, with staggering sums of investment planned. As India is progressing, construction industry is playing a vital role in nations GDP. To highlight the importance of construction industry in the development of Indian economy, following facts are to be considered:

- India is currently the second fastest-growing economy in the World. The Indian construction industry has been playing a vital role in overall economic development of the country, growing at over 20% Compound Annual Growth Rate over the past 5 years and contributing 8% to GDP.
- As opportunities in the sector continue to come to the fore, foreign direct investment has been moving upwards. The real estate and construction sectors received FDI of $216.53 million in the first half of the current fiscal year.
- The construction industry is one of the largest employment generators currently employing around 33 million people representing 14% of work force. While the Indian economy grew by 5% in FY13 as compared to 6.2% in FY12, the construction industry grew by 5.9% in FY13 against 5.6% in FY12.
- India is expected to emerge as the world's third largest construction market by 2020.
- In the last decade, "the country has witnessed a tremendous housing boom and over the span of five years, from 2012 to 2016, the real estate sector is expected to account for 43% of the construction spend in India. This segment is forecast to achieve a CAGR of 13.6% during this period.
- Market for real estate construction segment in India is likely to aggregate to approximately US$ 380 billion over the five year period, 2012 to 2016.

All these sectors contribute in the development of and strengthening of the national economy and hence it is very essential to learn the economics which is the backbone of Nations.

4.4 DEFINITION OF ECONOMICS (May 12)

With this introduction to the economy related to construction, let us study Economics further. Let us start with definition of Economics.

- **By A. Marshall :** It is the study of mankind in the ordinary business of life; it examines that part of individual and social action which is most closely connected with the attainment and with the use of material requisites of well being.
- **By L. Robbins :** Economics is a science which studies human behaviour as a relationship between ends and scarce means which have alternative uses.
- **By J. M. Keynes :** It is the study of the administration of scarce resources and of the determinants of income and employment.

In short, Economics can be defined as 'a social science concerned with the proper uses and allocation of resources for the achievement and maintenance of growth with stability'.

4.5 TYPES OF ECONOMY

1. **Micro-Economy :** It offers a detailed treatment of individual decisions about particular commodities. i.e. the study of household's decision whether he prefers bungalow to flat and the developer's decision whether to construct a bungalow scheme or apartment.
2. **Macro-Economy :** It emphasizes the interaction in the economy as a whole. It treats all the goods as 'consumer goods' and study the interaction between household's decision and developer's decision.
3. **Command Economy :** It is a society/market where the government makes all decisions about production and consumption.
4. **Free Economy :** It is a society/market where Government do not intervene.
5. **Mixed Economy :** It is a society/market where Government and private sector interact in solving economic problems. Our country, India is following mixed economy.

4.6 LAWS OF ECONOMICS

- The consumer gets maximum satisfaction of the goods or services for which he is paying.
- Man is sensible to balance marginal cost and marginal money gains.
- All the theories are based on the behaviour of an average man. i.e. their actions cannot be reduced to scientific laws.
- The theories are based on the things such as taste, price, fashion, price of substitute goods and income of the society. The effect of changes on the demand and supply can be studied by changing any one of these and **keeping other things constant.**

4.7 DEFINITIONS OF SOME IMPORTANT TERMS

(May 11, 12, Nov./Dec.12)

- *Market* is a set of arrangements by which buyers and sellers are in contact to exchange goods and services.
- Markets in which Government do not intervene is called as *Free market*.
- When all decisions about the production and consumption are taken by Government, the economy is called as *command economy*.
- *A mixed economy* allows the interaction of Government as well as private sectors.
- *Gross investment* is the money used for production of new capital goods and improvement in existing goods.
- *Net investment* is the gross investment minus the depreciation of the existing capital stock.
- *Assets* are what the firm owns.
- *Liabilities* are what the firms owes.
- *Physical capital* is the machinery, equipment and buildings used in producing future wealth.
- A firms *revenue* is the amount it earns by selling goods or services in a given period such as a year.
- *Wealth* is the addition of capital and land.
- *Goods* are the physical commodities such as steel, cars, mangoes etc.
- *Price* is the amount of money given in exchange for a commodity or service.
- *Costs* are the expenses incurred by the firm in producing goods and services during the period of manufacturing.
- *Profits* are the excess of revenues over costs.
- *Value* of a commodity is decided by its utility and one's sentiments and expresses the power of purchasing other goods.
- *Money* is anything that has general acceptance and passes freely from hand to hand as a medium of exchange.
- *Inventory* is the goods held in stock by the firm for the production processing to manufacture new goods.
- *Want* is the desire that can be fulfilled and supported by the ability and willingness to satisfy it.
- *Services* are the activities such as theatres or teaching which can be consumed or enjoyed at the instant they are produced.
- *Utility* is the capacity of a commodity to satisfy human wants and depends upon the intensity of the want which it satisfies. It is the amount of satisfaction derived from a commodity or service at a particular time.

4.7.1 Cost and Price

We have seen the definition of cost, price and value. Let us elaborate more on cost and price.

Cost : Total cost of an industrial enterprises is given as :

Total Cost = Factory Cost + Selling Overhead + Distribution Overhead + Administration Overhead

where, the factory cost is given as :

Factory Cost = Prime Cost + Factory Overhead
= (Direct material cost + Direct labour cost + Direct expenses) + Factory overhead

Price : Price = Total Cost ± Profit or Loss

Hence, the cost and price are related with the help of the following chart.

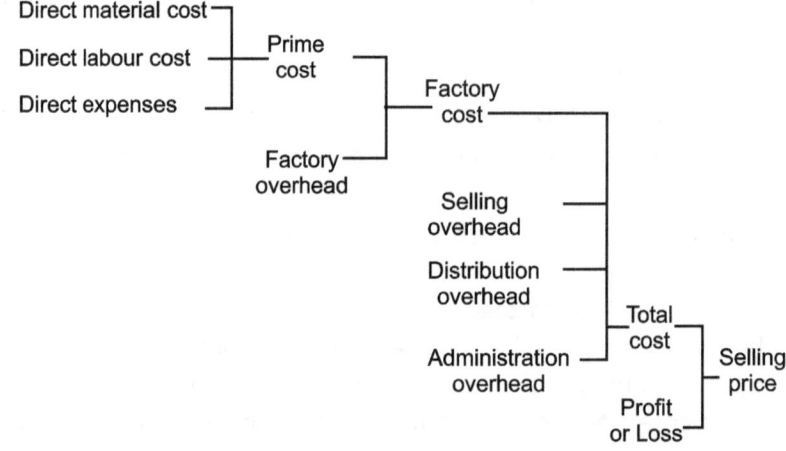

Fig. 4.3

4.8 LAW OF DIMINISHING UTILITY (May 11, 12, Nov./Dec. 11, 12)

Law of Diminishing Utility

The law is stated by Marshall as 'the additional benefit which a person derives from a given increase in his stock of a thing diminishes with every increase in stock that he already has'.

Definition of Marginal Utility

Marginal utility can be defined as 'the change in the total utility resulting from a one unit change in consumption of a commodity per unit time'.

A person who is purchasing the commodity will constantly weighing it against the price he is giving for it. He will continue till the marginal utility equals the price. For example : he will buy a mango for ₹ 10. but if he wants to buy two mangoes, he will not pay ₹ 20, but will try to bargain on ₹ 18 only. Thus, the marginal utility for the second mango will be ₹ 8 and not 10. Thus, we can also define marginal utility as the addition made to the total utility by the consumption of last unit considered just worth while.

Consider one more example of a person having only one shirt that gives him maximum utilization. As the number of shirts goes on increasing, the utility from each additional shirt goes on decreasing. This can be depicted with the help of the following representative Fig.

Table 4.1

Units (shirts)	Marginal Utility (additional units of satisfaction)	Total Utility (units of satisfaction)
1	30	30
2	26	56
3	20	76
4	14	90
5	7	97
6	0	97
7	− 11	86
8	− 25	61

The same can also be applied to the number of bread slices that a man eats.

The Table 4.1 can be represented with the help of histogram as follows :

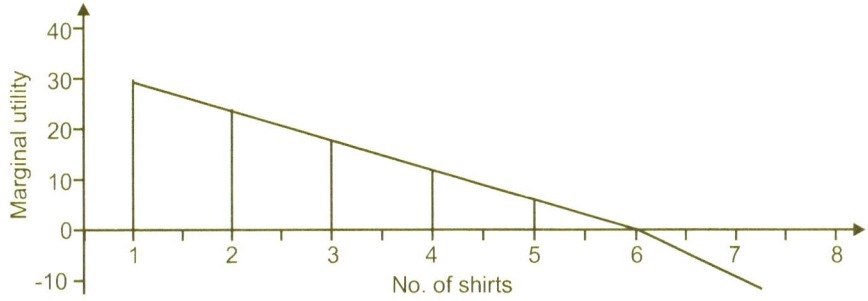

Fig. 4.4 : Diminishing marginal utility

The marginal utility as shown in the above figure goes on reducing as shown in Fig. 4.4. The reason for this decrease is that the consumer gets satisfied with the consumption of more and more commodity; his wants get satisfied and does not wish further. Another reason is; the same commodities are imperfect substitutes for each other. The utility would have increased by use of another commodity.

Assumptions of the Law

- The commodity should be taken in suitable units. e.g. The water for drinking for a thirsty man should be measured in glass as the unit and not mere spoonful.

- The consumption of the commodity should be done at the same time. The foods taken at 10 a.m. and at 2 p.m. have the same utility.
- The taste of the consumer remains the same.
- Consumer is an average man without having a strong desire for the commodity and not a miser.
- Income of the consumer should remain the same.
- There is no change in fashion.

The law does not hold good for the collection of rare goods and for money but holds good for all types of satisfaction whether good or bad.

4.9 LAW OF SUBSTITUTION

At the time of purchasing a commodity, we are continuously weighing in our mind a little more or little less of it. It means we are balancing the marginal utility of commodity and money. For Example : while purchasing one dozen of banana, if the unit price of it seems to be high, then we may think of less number of bananas or the bananas of small size and less price. Similarly in the reverse way, if the price per dozen is less, we may think of purchasing another fruit which will match our budget. Thus, we are continuously substituting one commodity with another with money as a bridge and aiming at maximum satisfaction. This principle is called as **Law of Substitution** or **Law of Economy of Expenditure** or **Law of Indifference** or **Law of Maximum Satisfaction.**

The law of substitution can also be stated with the help of the following graph. Consider a customer who is having ₹ 10 to spend on items A and B. He spends ₹ 6 on item A and ₹ 4 on item B which is giving him maximum satisfaction. It means that the marginal utilities for both the items are equal. Now, consider that he spends ₹ 7 on item A and ₹ 3 on item B, the marginal utilities becomes unequal.

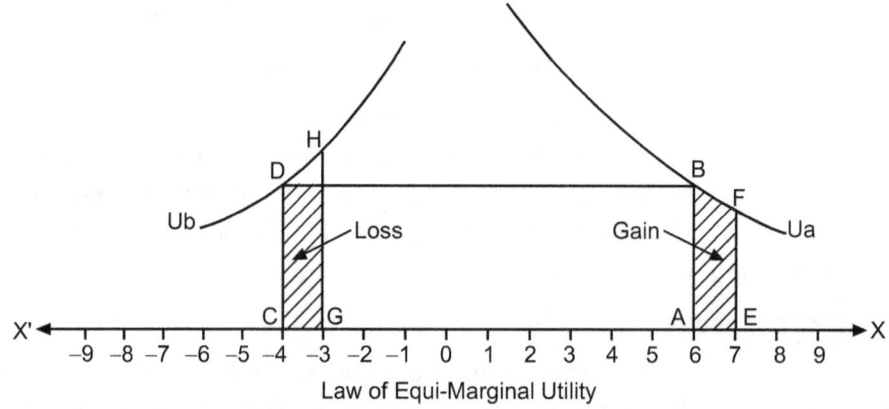

Fig. 4.5 : Law of equi-marginal utility

The gain in utility of A, represented by area AEFB is less than the loss in utility of B represented by the area CGHD. As a result, the marginal utility becomes unequal giving less satisfaction to him.

Limitations of the Law
- The comparison between the expected satisfaction with the given amount of money is not always possible, since most of the expenditures by the consumers are governed by their habits. So, the law of substitution may not hold good for small purchases but may be proved in case of big expenditures.
- The consumer may not be aware of the substitute goods that give him more satisfaction.
- People do not like to change their habits or customs and hence for many goods a little substitution takes place.
- The law is not applicable to the goods that can not be divisible into small bits to enable the consumer to equalize the marginal utilities.
- The law does not hold good for the goods which are free as the consumer does not have to pay for it.

Applications of the Law
- The law is applicable to the consumption of limited resources. The expenditures can be rearranged to get maximum satisfaction.
- It is also applicable to the production in deciding the most economical combinations of the factors of production by equalizing the marginal utilities. For Example : if marginal productivity of labour is greater than that of capital, then labour can be substituted for the capital to maximize the profit.
- At the time of exchange of one thing to another, the substitution takes place for the goods having equal marginal utility.
- The law can be applicable very well in case of determination of price of scarce resources. We substitute less scarce goods by more scarce goods thus making price down.
- The law is applicable to the distribution of national dividend among various agents of production such as rent, wages, interest and profits.
- The law finds its application in case of public expenditure by the Government to maximize the benefits from public expenditures.

4.10 DEMAND AND SUPPLY

Demand and Its Meaning
Consider a begger who needs to have a piece of bread. Now, consider a clerk working in a bank who wants one TV set in his house. These needs and wants do not make a demand, but when a person is willing to pay for his desire, the desire is changed to Demand.

Definition of Demand

Thus, the demand can be defined as "The various quantities of a given commodity or service which consumers would buy in one market in a given period of time at various incomes or at various prices of related goods" or

"Demand is the quantity of a good, buyers wish to purchase at each conceivable price"

Definition of Supply

"Supply is the quantity of a good; sellers wish to sell at each conceivable price".

Example 4.1 : Consider an example of chocolates demanded and supplied at varying prices. The demand and supply is changing depending upon price as shown below.

Table 4.2

Unit price (₹/no.)	Demand (millions/year)	Supply (millions/year)
0.00	200	0
0.10	160	0
0.20	120	40
0.30	80	80
0.40	40	120
0.50	0	160
0.60	0	200
0.70	0	240

The first column is the different prices of a chocolate and the second column denotes the probable demand of it. Third column indicates the number that the sellers want to supply.

Even if the chocolates are free of cost, there is a limited demand depending upon the age and taste of the consumers. Also they become bore for eating the chocolates. As the price increases, demand starts decreasing and it becomes zero when the price exceeds ₹ 0.4/- this is also because the consumers may think its marginal utility as zero for more price. Similarly, the seller does not wish to sell them free of cost or with a very low price such as ₹ 0.1/- which is not going to add to his profit. The quantity supplied goes on increasing with the increase in the price. Also, as the demand is more than the supply, the seller will quickly run out of stock, realizing that he should have charged more price. At some intermediate price, the quantity demanded just equals the quantity supplied which is called as *equilibrium price*. So, ₹ 0.3/- is the equilibrium price. If the price of the chocolate is more than ₹ 0.3/-, there is excess supply and the sellers get frustrated. Similarly, for higher prices i.e. for price of ₹ 0.5/-

per chocolate, nobody wish to buy the chocolate. To recoup the money spent on the production, the seller will cut down the price to clear the stock. The process of cutting the prices will continue until price is ₹ 0.3/- per chocolate which is called as *Equilibrium price* and the quantity is called as *Equilibrium quantity*.

At any particular instant, the market price may not be the equilibrium price. If not, there will be excess demand or excess supply, depending upon the price. But these forces themselves provide the incentive to change prices towards the equilibrium price. In this sense, markets are self correcting.

4.11 DETERMINATION OF MARKET PRICE

Market prices are decided depending upon the demand and supply curve as seen above and also on the type of good, whether it is perishable or durable.

Price Determination of Perishable Goods

In case of perishable goods, like fish, milk etc., the supply is limited to the quantity available or the stock in hand for the day. Consider the demand curve DD for a given supply as shown in Fig. 4.6.

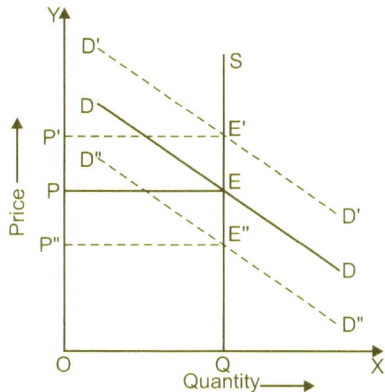

Fig. 4.6 : Market price of perishable goods

E is the point of equilibrium for the given supply and demand. If the demand increases to D'D', the equilibrium price will increase to E' as the supply remains the same. On the other hand, for a decrease of demand to D"D", the price falls to E". The quantity sold remaining the same for both the conditions.

Price Determination of Durable Goods

The supply curve is as shown in Fig. 4.7. After a certain limit the quantity remains the same as represented by QR. SQ is the stock available with the firm.

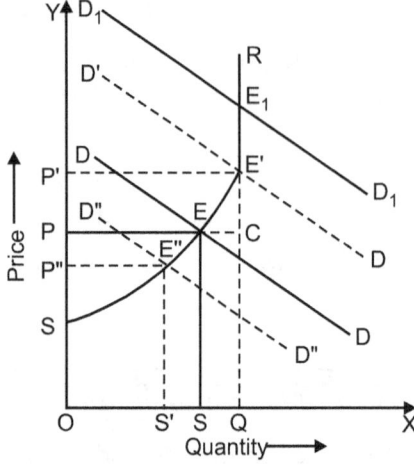

Fig. 4.7 : Market price of durable commodity

For the given price P, supply and the demand curve is DD, the equilibrium point is E. For the increase of the demand from DD to D'D', the price increase is from P to P' and the equilibrium point shifts to E' utilising all the available stock. If the demand increase still further to D_1D_1, but the supply remaining the same, only price will increase at a faster rate and the equilibrium will be point E_1 which is much higher. However, if the demand is decreased to D"D", the price will fall to OP" and the equilibrium at E".

4.12 TYPES OF DEMAND (S-11)

There are three types of Demand

1. Price demand
2. Income Demand
3. Cross Demand

1. **Price Demand :** It refers to the various quantities of a commodity or service that a consumer would purchase at a given time in a market at various hypothetical prices with other things constant. Demand of an individual consumer is called as **consumer demand** while the total demand of all consumers is called as **industry demand**. Total demand for the product of an individual firm at various prices is known as individual seller's demand.

2. **Income Demand :** Various quantities of goods and services which would be purchased by the consumer at his various levels of income is called as income demand, with other things such as taste and price remaining constant. When income of an individual increases, his purchase of high priced goods also increases and vice versa.

3. **Cross Demand :** The cross demand means the quantities of goods or services which will be purchased with reference to change in price of substitutes or complimentary goods. For example : change in the price of tea is going to affect demand for coffee.

Of all these three demands, price demand is the most commonly used. Let us study the demand curve, i.e. price demand curve in detail.

4.13 DEMAND CURVE

Consider a demand curve for an imaginary consumer.

From the Fig. 5.8 it is clear that as the price decreases, the demand increases and vice-versa. The demand curve slopes downwards in accordance with the law of diminishing marginal utility. When the price falls, more suppliers enter into the market and old purchasers may purchase more. The reasons why the people buy more when the price falls is :

- A consumer can afford to buy more because other things being cheaper, his real income increases. This is called as *income effect*.

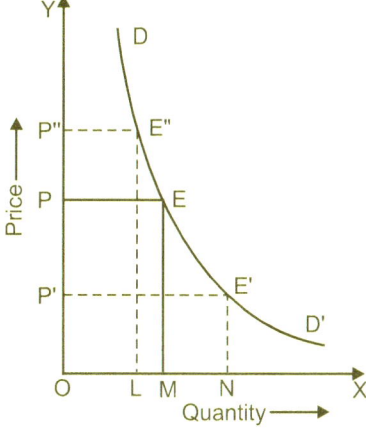

Fig. 4.8 : Demand curve

- As the good becomes cheap, it can be substituted wholly or partly by another. This is called as *substitution effect*.

    The income effect and substitution effect combines to increase the ability and willingness of the consumer to buy more.

- As the price decreases, the commodity is put to more uses and for less important works.

- By the fall in price there is a divergence between the marginal utility and price. This is rectified by buying more commodities bringing its marginal utility to the level of the price.

Exceptions to the Demand Curves

Following are the circumstances when the demand curve shows increase in demand for the price rise and vice-versa :

1. When a serious shortage is anticipated, the people get panic and buy more quantity even if the rates are high :
2. To prove the dignity, the people try to buy goods of higher price to be included in the list of distinguished personages.
3. Sometimes, people buy more at a higher price in sheer ignorance.

4.13.1 Law of Demand

The law of demand which is based on the law of diminishing marginal utility, states the relationship between increase in price and its effect on demand. It states as "A rise in the price of a commodity or service is followed by a reduction in demand, and a fall in price is followed by an increase in demand, if conditions of demand remain constant".

In other words, it can be stated as "The greater the amount to be sold, the smaller must be the price at which it is offered in order that it may find purchasers; or the amount demanded increases with a fall in price and diminishes with a rise in price".

Exceptions to the Law

1. With the change in taste or fashion, the demand may decrease though there is decrease in price.
2. If consumer's income increases, the demand for some commodities may increase though there is increase in price.
3. If the price of the substitute good decreases more than the commodity, the demand decreases. For example : if the price of coffee decreases more heavily than that of tea, people may wish to drink coffee more than tea.
4. With the discovery of substitute items, the demand may decrease inspite of decrease in the price.

4.14 SUPPLY CURVE

4.14.1 Law of Supply

Supply depends upon the price of the commodity. Thus, the Law of Supply is given as, "Other things remaining the same, as the price of a commodity rises, its supply is extended as given in Table 4.2.

The law of supply can be again elaborated with the help of previous example. For reference, the table is given below again.

At the price ₹ 0.7 per chocolates, as many as 240 million chocolates were offered to sale. But at the low price of ₹ 0.2 per chocolate, the quantity offered for sale was only 40 millions. This shows the law of supply.

The curve (in this example a straight line) is as shown below :

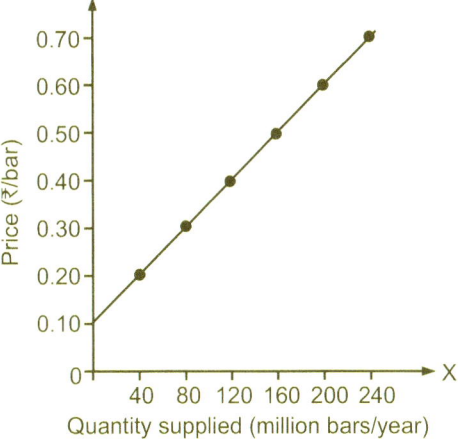

Fig. 4.9

In this diagram, the quantity supplied is shown on X-axis whereas the price is given on Y-axis. Conversely with the demand curve, the supply curve slopes upward from left to right. The price below which the seller refuses to sell is called as the **reserve price**. If the price falls too much, supply may dry up altogether.

If the price of commodity is lower than the equilibrium price, demand will be more but supply will be less and if the prices goes higher than equilibrium price, supply will increase at the cost of reduction in demand. This is how, equilibrium is maintained in the market. So we can conclude that as long as properties of a commodity remaining constant, equilibrium price is maintained in the market irrespective of the manufacturer.

4.14.2 Equilibrium Price

To find the equilibrium price, plot the demand curve DD and supply curve SS as shown in Fig. 4.10.

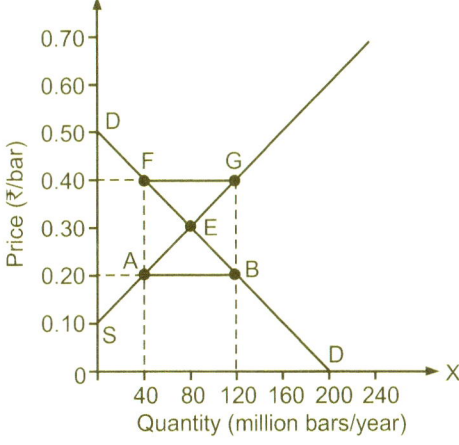

Fig. 4.10

E is the equilibrium point. At a point below E, the horizontal distance between supply curve and the demand curve at this height shows the excess demand at this price. For example : at ₹ 0.2/chocolate, the quantity supplied is 40 millions per year, the quantity demanded 120 millions per year and the distance AB represents the excess demand of 80 millions per year. Conversely at a price above the equilibrium price, there is excess supply. At ₹ 0.4/chocolate, 40 millions chocolates per year are demanded, 120 millions per year are supplied and the horizontal distance FG measures the excess supply of 80 millions chocolates per year. Hence, any quantity larger than 40 millions per year at a price of ₹ 0.40/chocolate would involve buyers in forced purchases. Similarly, when the price is ₹ 0.20, any quantity larger than 40 millions per year would involve sellers in forced sale.

Supply is the amount of the goods offered by a seller to sale at a given price. Meyer defines supply as "A schedule of the amount of good that would be offered for sale at all possible prices at any one instant of time, or during any one period of time such as a day or a week and so on, in which the conditions of supply remains the same".

4.15 ELASTICITY OF SUPPLY (Nov./Dec. 12)

'If small rise or fall in the price leads to a large decrease or increase in supply respectively, the supply is called as *elastic supply*'. On the other hand, 'if a large change, in price brings only a small change in the supply, it is called as *inelastic supply*'.

If a slight increase in price is followed by the entry of many new firms having minimum average cost equal to price and the marginal cost does not rise, the supply is said to be perfectly elastic. However, in case the increased output can be obtained only by an infinite increase in price and no new firm is attracted to the industry, the supply is inelastic. Between these two extremities, lies various degrees of Elasticity.

Measurement of Elasticity of Supply

$$\text{Price Elasticity of Supply} = \frac{\text{Proportionate change in amount supplied}}{\text{Proportionate change in price}}$$

$$E = \frac{\text{Change in amount supplied}}{\text{Amount supplied}} \div \frac{\text{Change in price}}{\text{Price}} \quad \ldots (4.1)$$

Following Fig. 4.11 gives the method used to calculate the elasticity of supply.

SS' is the supply curve. Consider three points on it A, B and C and draw tangents to the curve through these points. The tangents touches the X-axis at points E and F whereas touches the Y-axis at points D and G. The tangent through point B passes through the origin. The price elasticity of supply at a given point is measured by the distance along a tangent to the horizontal axis divided by the distance along it on the vertical axis.

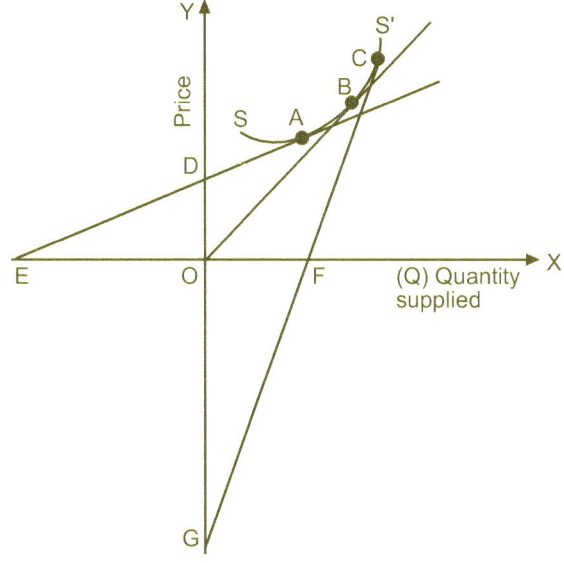

Fig. 4.11

Thus,

E_s at A is $\dfrac{AE}{AD}$ which is greater than unity since AE is greater than AD.

E_s at B is $\dfrac{BO}{OB}$ which is unity equal to one.

E_s at C is $\dfrac{CF}{CG}$ which is less than unity since CF is greater than CG.

4.16 PRICE DETERMINATION

In example 2, Market equilibrium is shown by the intersection of the demand curve DD and supply curve SS, at a price ₹ 0.3, at which 80 million chocolates per year are supplied. The Fig. 4.9 shows that there is excess supply at all prices above the equilibrium price of ₹ 0.3. Sellers react to unsold stocks by cutting prices. Only when prices are reduced to the equilibrium price, excess supply will be eliminated. The equilibrium position is shown by the point E. Conversely at prices below ₹ 0.3, there is excess demand, which bids up the price of chocolate, gradually eliminating excess demand until the equilibrium point E is reached. In equilibrium, buyers and sellers can trade as much as they wish at the equilibrium price and there is no incentive for any further price changes.

Factors Affecting the Supply Curve

1. **Technology :** A supply curve is drawn for given technology. An improvement in technology will shift the supply curve to the right since producers will be willing to supply a larger quantity than previously at each price.

2. **Input Prices :** A particular supply curve is drawn for a given level of input prices. A reduction in input prices like, lower wages, lower fuel cost etc., will induce firms to supply more output at each price, shifting the supply curve to the right. Higher input prices make production less attractive and shift the supply curve to the left.

3. **Government Regulations :** Government regulations like stringent safety regulations may increase the cost of production and thereby increase in the prices. This will shift the supply curve to the left, reducing quantity supplied at each price.

Shifts in Supply Curve

Given the above constants, a supply curve SS is drawn. (Fig. 4.12). The equilibrium is at point E for the supply quantity Q. Consider that due to the technological advancements, the goods can be produced more for the same input cost.

The supply curve get shifted from SS to S'S' as shown in Fig. 4.12. Due to this shift, the equilibrium point also shifted to the left. But note that, though the equilibrium price has increased, the quantity supplied is decreased (Q' < Q).

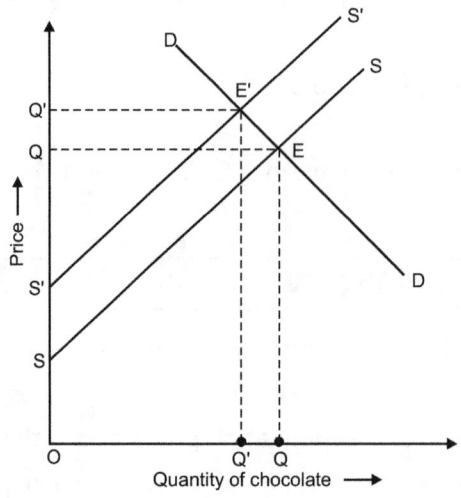

Fig. 4.12

If the supply curve shifts to the right, then the equilibrium points also shifts to the right leading to the increase in quantity supplied but decreasing the equilibrium price.

In case of free markets, the prices respond quickly to the changes in demand and supply, whereas, in case of command economy, Government intervenes for the control of the effective prices. Prices are of two types, one is the floor price (minimum price) and other is the ceiling price (maximum price). Ceiling prices are advantageous in case of goods with scarce supply, especially for the necessary food items. Otherwise the poor people suffer due to hike in price.

Consider the demand and supply curves as shown in Fig. 4.13. In normal circumstances, the equilibrium is at point E with the initial price as P_0. But due to the effect of ceiling price P_1, the equilibrium point has to be A which is below the point E. This decreases the supply of the commodity from Q_0 to Q_1.

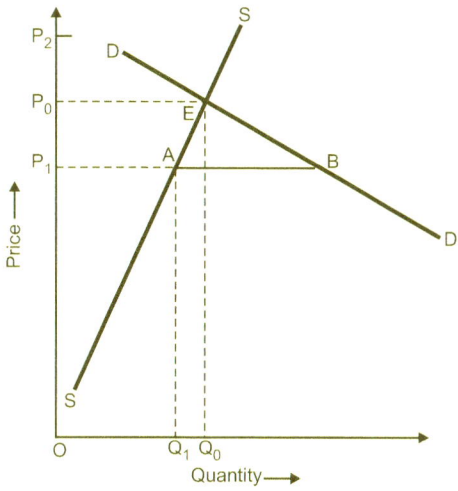

Fig. 4.13

But in this case, the excess demand is available as AB which will create a tendency among the suppliers to reserve this supply for their friends or to take bribes from the society who can afford to buy this supply. This develops the black market. Thus, price ceiling may not help the poor people. Hence, to control the black market, the ceiling prices are to be accompanied with rationing by quota organized by Government.

But, now consider another example where the Government decides some minimum wages to help the poor. (Fig. 4.14)

In the normal circumstances, the equilibrium point is at E for the Q_0 hours of employment with W_1 wage rate. If Government forces the wage rate to be minimum W_0, the hours of employment reduces from Q_0 to Q_1 that leads the excess supply CB. This results in some of the workers get benefited from the increase in wages but some will be unemployed.

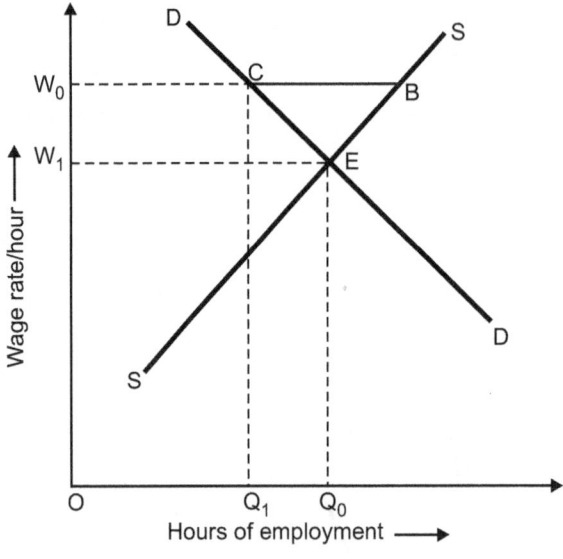

Fig. 4.14

4.17 INDIFFERENCE CURVE ANALYSIS

The various commodities required by the consumer are not on the same scale of preference. Some of them are urgent or important whereas others may not find that much necessity. The consumer ranks his desire and builds the scale of preference which is guided by the scarcity of the goods, urgency, his taste and the utility. All the time, the consumer is trying to reach the equilibrium, i.e. a position in which he gets maximum satisfaction from the money at his disposal. All the objects of his desire find place on the scale of preference depending upon the equivalence. The consumers scale of references is independent of the prices ruling in the market. He builds up scale of references from the commodities he consumes. On its basis, he knows that one combination of the goods yields him the same satisfaction as another.

On the basis of the scale of preference, we can draw the indifference curves. An indifference curve represents satisfaction of a consumer from two commodities. It is drawn on the assumption that for all possible points on an indifference curve, the total satisfaction or utility remains the same. Hence, the consumer is indifferent as to the combinations lying on an indifference curve. It is also called as *Iso-utility curve*.

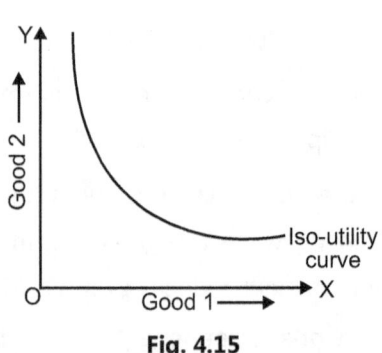

Fig. 4.15

Consider a consumer having ₹ 50/- with him and wants to buy apples and mangoes. He can have various combinations of apples and mangoes that give him the same amount of satisfaction. Thus, the indifference schedule for apples and mangoes are as follows :

Table 4.4

Combination	Apples	Mangoes
1	15	1
2	11	2
3	8	3
4	6	4
5	5	5

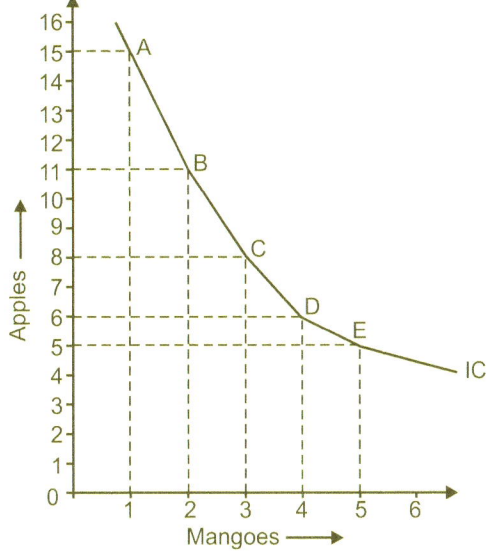

Fig. 4.16

Mangoes are measured along X-axis while apples are measured along Y-axis. For the various combinations of apples and mangoes, points are plotted as A, B, C, D and E. If we join all the points, we get the indifference curve, each point on it showing the same satisfaction or the indifference of the consumer towards the various combinations. We can draw similar indifference curves showing various combinations of apples and mangoes for various amounts to spend, which represent greater and lesser satisfaction as shown below :

In Fig. 4.17 all the points on IC_5 and IC_4 are preferred to all the points on IC_3 or IC_2 or IC_1. Indifference curve IC_1 represents a lower level of satisfaction than IC_2, IC_3, IC_4 and IC_5. It is to be noted that, we cannot say how much more utility the higher indifference curve represents. That is the aggregate utilities are rankable but not measurable.

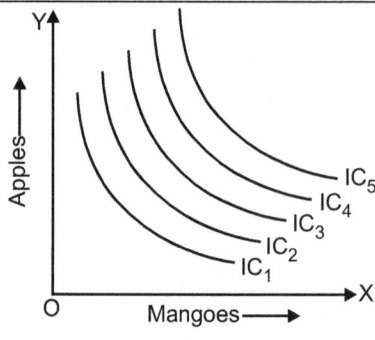

Fig. 4.17

Properties of Indifference Curve

1. **It Slopes Downwards to the Right :** It is because when the consumer decides to have more units of one of the two goods, he will have to reduce the number of the other goods, if he has to remain on the same indifference curve, i.e. if level of satisfaction is to remain the same. Looking at the Fig. 4.15, we find that when the consumer moves from point A to B, he has more mangoes than before, but the number of apples with him falls.

2. **The Curves are Non-intersecting :** The indifference curves shows higher and higher levels of satisfaction. If these are intersecting, it means that at the point of intersection of the two curves, the consumer gets equal satisfaction which is absurd.

3. **The Curves are Convex at Origin :** This is because, the marginal rates of substitution are different for different goods. If the indifference curve happened to be straight, it indirectly means that the marginal rate of substitution is equal for both the goods which is incorrect. Again, if the curve is concave at origin, it means that the marginal rate of substitution is increasing which is against the normal behaviour of the curve which has to be diminishing.

4.18 PRICE LINE OR BUDGET LINE

In an attempt to get maximum satisfaction from the available money, the consumer will try to reach the highest possible indifference curve. For example : if he is having ₹ 15 to spend for mangoes and apples and the price of apple is ₹ 1 per unit while that of mango is ₹ 1.5 per unit, then he can buy 10 mangoes and no apples(= OM) or 15 apples and no mangoes (= OA).

By joining the points A and M, we get the price line or budget line. This line shows all possible combinations of two goods that the consumer can buy if he spends the whole of his given sum of money on his purchases at the given prices.

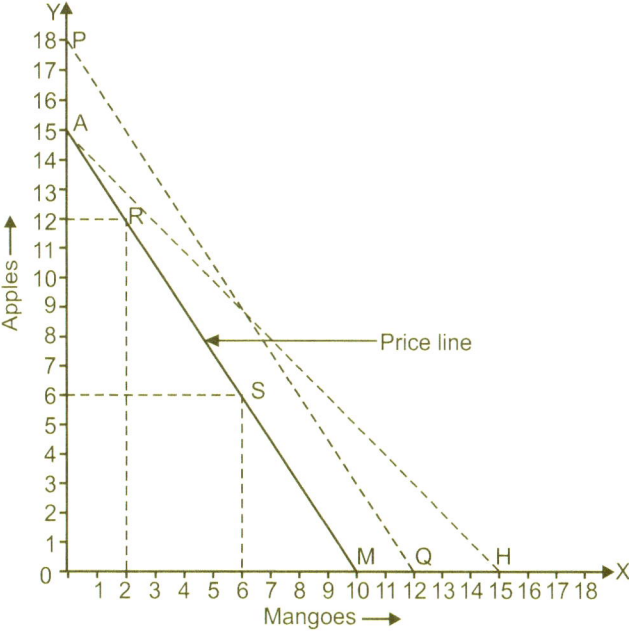

Fig. 4.18

Shifting of the Price Line

If money with the customer increases to ₹ 18, the price line will shift to PQ so that we can either buy 12 mangoes (= OQ) or 18 apples (= OP), prices of mangoes and apples remaining the same. Note that the new budget line PQ will be parallel to AM.

If the price of the mangoes falls from ₹ 1.50 to ₹ 1, keeping the budget equal to ₹ 15 and price of apple constant, the price line will shift from AM to AH. AH will not be parallel to AM as the price ratio is changed.

4.19 CONSUMERS EQUILIBRIUM OR MAXIMUM SATISFACTION

In order to explain the consumer's equilibrium the following assumptions are made :

- The consumer has indifference curves showing his scale of preferences.
- His income does not change.
- Prices of goods are fixed.
- Each unit of commodity is homogeneous and divisible.
- The consumer tries to maximize his satisfaction.

Earlier we have seen the indifference curve and the price line AM which shows all possible combinations of the two goods that are open to this consumer. Any point not lying on this price line cannot be a possible equilibrium point.

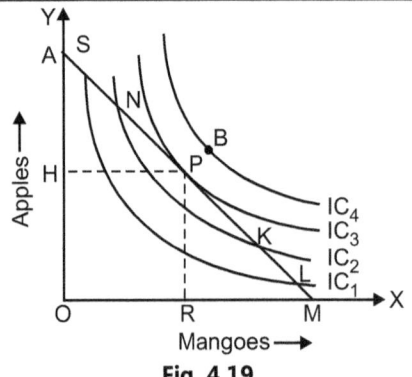

Fig. 4.19

The consumer will be in equilibrium at point P maximizing his satisfaction. This is the point where the price line is tangent to the indifference curve. So he will be buying OR mangoes and OH apples. Any combination other than point P, gives less satisfaction to the consumer.

If the consumer chooses a point say S on the curve IC_1, it gives him less satisfaction than point P. Similarly, points N, K and L gives him less satisfaction which lie on the lower indifference curves. In equilibrium at the point P, the marginal rate of substitution (MRS) of mangoes for apples is equal to the price ratio between the two goods.

$$\text{MRS of mango and apple} = \text{Price ratio} = \frac{\text{Price of mango}}{\text{Price of apple}}$$

Now, consider a point B which is on the indifference curve IC_4. As the price line cannot touch this curve, the consumer cannot go for this level of satisfaction though he desires the same.

4.20 INCOME EFFECT

Now, let us study the effect of a change in consumer's income on consumer's equilibrium, relative prices of commodities remaining the same. Obviously, as a result of change a change in income, his satisfaction will either increase or decrease, for he has larger or smaller income to spend.

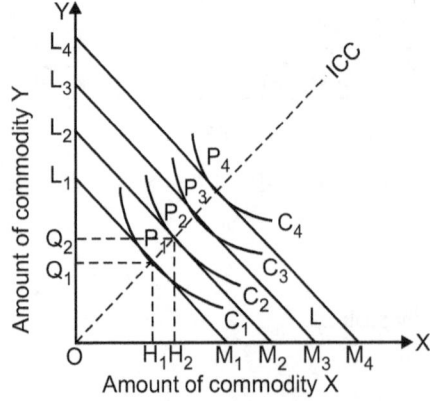

Fig. 4.20 : Income effect

The income effect is explained as shown in Fig. 4.20. Consider the initial indifference curve C_1 with the budget or price line as L_1M_1. Thus, the equilibrium point is P_1 with OH_1 quantity of commodity X and OQ_1 quantity of commodity Y.

Now, if the income of the consumer increases, the price line shifts to L_2M_2 and the new point of equilibrium is P_2. This will continue for various indifference curves and price lines and we will get various equilibrium points such as P_1, P_2, P_3 etc. If all these points are joined together, we get a line passing through all these points which is called as Income Consumption Curve (ICC).

It shows how the consumption of two goods get affected by the change in income when prices of both goods are given and constant. Most of the goods represent the shape of ICC as shown in the Fig. 4.20.

However, when the income of the consumer increases, he tries to purchase better substitute goods. As a result, the ICC tends to bend towards X or Y axis depending upon availability of the substitute goods. This is most commonly seen in case of inferior goods.

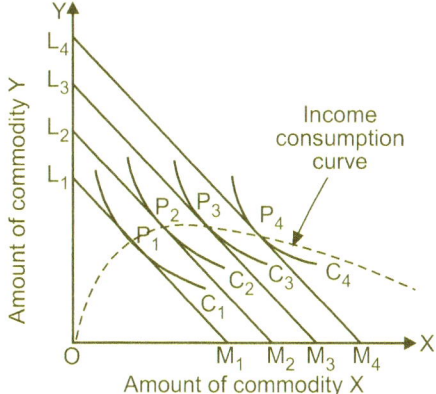

Fig. 4.21 : Income effect : Inferior good Y

4.21 SUBSTITUTION EFFECT (Nov./Dec. 12)

Keeping the income of the consumer the same, if the relative prices of the commodities are changed, the effect on the economy is called *as substitution effect*. It means the change in quantity of a good purchased which is due to the change in relative prices, money income remaining the same. The substitution effect is explained with the help of the following example :

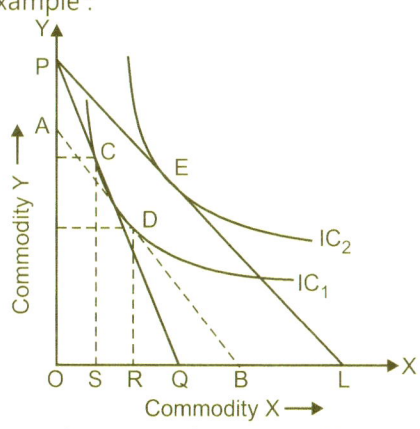

The consumer is in equilibrium at point C where the given price line PQ is tangent to indifference curve IC_1. When the price of X falls, while that of Y remaining the same, the price line will shift to PL. The consumer will now in equilibrium at point E as the line PL is tangent to IC_2. But as IC_2 is for the increase in budget, we have to find out the point of satisfaction on the curve IC_1.

Fig. 4.22 : Substitution effect

This can be done by taking a line AB parallel to PL and tangent to IC_1 as shown in Fig. 4.22. The tangent point D is now the new point of equilibrium giving the same level of satisfaction to the consumer. This shift of the equilibrium point from C to D can be explained as : When the price of good say X, falls, real income of the consumer would increase. In order to find out the change in the quantity of X purchased, due to the change in the relative price of X, the consumer's money income must be reduced by an amount so as to cancel out the gain in real income that results from price decrease. Referring the above diagram, BL or AP is the amount of money income that should be taken away from the consumer so that the gain in real income which results from the fall in the price of X is decreased. Movement from C to D on the same indifference curve IC_1 is due to the relative fall in the price of X. At point D, the consumer buys SR more of X than at C as X is now relatively cheaper. This SR is the substitution effect which involves movement from C to D.

4.22 ELASTICITY OF DEMAND (Nov./Dec. 11)

As per the law of demand, as the price of the commodity changes, the demand also changes. For some commodities, the rate of change of demand is rapid while for others it is slow. A small change in price may lead to a great change in demand (elastic demand) while for others, it is unaffected, e.g. though the price of salt increases, the quantity demanded remains the same (inelastic demand). The rate at which the demand for a commodity changes, when its price changes, is known as the **Elasticity of Demand.**

Thus,

$$\text{Elasticity of demand} = \frac{\text{Proportionate change in amount demanded}}{\text{Proportionate change in price}}$$

$$E = \frac{\text{Change in amount demanded}}{\text{Amount demanded}} \div \frac{\text{Change in price}}{\text{Price}} \quad \ldots (4.2)$$

The above method of finding the elasticity of demand is called as **proportional method.** The elasticity of demand can also be described as "The elasticity of demand in market is great or small according to the amount demanded increases much or little for a given fall in price and diminishes much or little for a given rise in price".

The elasticity of demand will be elastic, inelastic (less elastic) or having unit elasticity. There are five cases that describe the elasticity.

- Perfectly elastic (infinite elasticity)
- Perfectly inelastic (zero elasticity)
- Relatively elastic
- Relatively inelastic
- Unit elasticity

These can be shown with the help of following graphs :

Perfectly Elastic

This is a horizontal line parallel to the X-axis. It shows that even a small decrease in price can bring unlimited extension of demand.

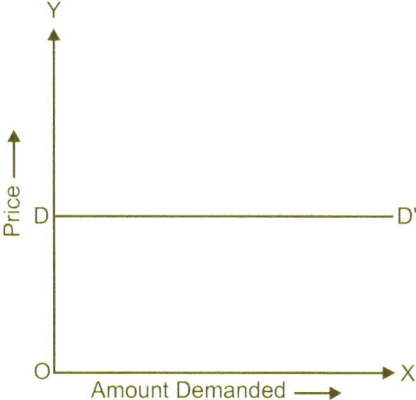

Fig. 4.23 : Infinite elasticity

Perfectly Inelastic

This is a horizontal line parallel to Y-axis indicating that even for large increase in the price, the quantity demanded remains the same. For example : though the price of salt is increased, it affects a little on the demand or consumption.

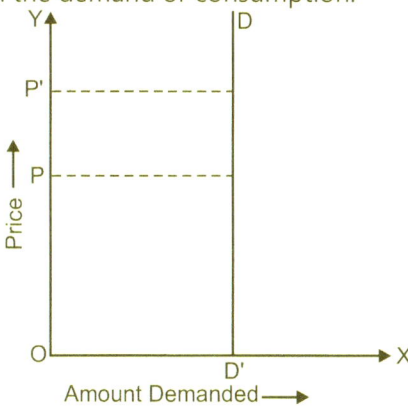

Fig. 4.24 : Zero elasticity

However it can be seen that the perfectly elastic or perfectly inelastic demands are two extremes that are seldomly seen in real life. Following two figures shows the relatively elastic and relatively inelastic demand respectively. In Fig. 4.25, the area OM'P'N', indicating the total revenue earned by the seller is less than OMPN, i.e. the total revenue earned the seller before the price change. Thus putting the values in equation 4.2, we get the elasticity less than 1 and called as inelastic demand. In Fig. 4.26, OM'P'N' is greater than area OMPN, the elasticity is greater than 1.

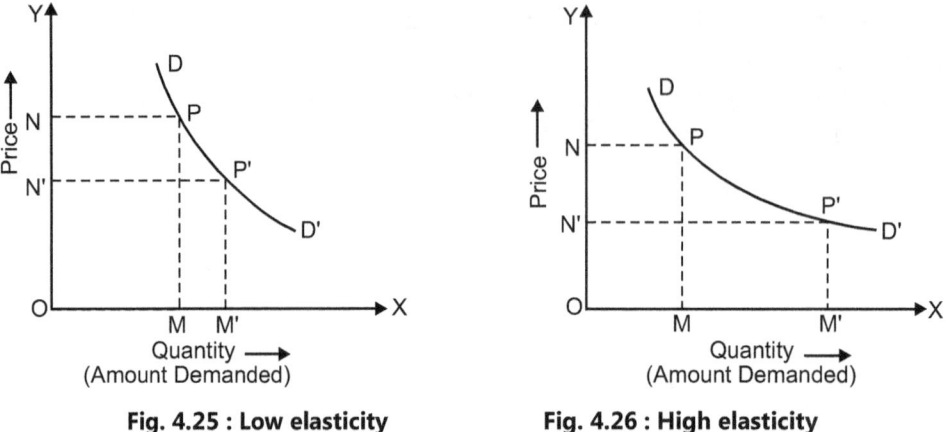

Fig. 4.25 : Low elasticity   Fig. 4.26 : High elasticity

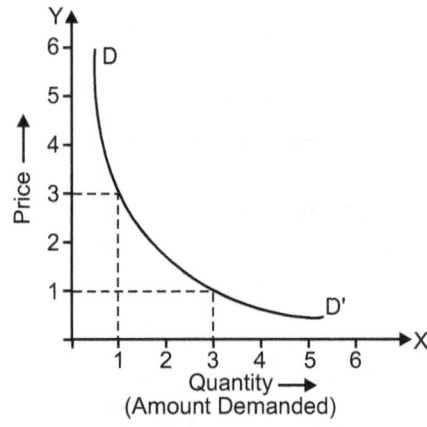

Fig. 4.27 : Unit elasticity

Now, study the graph as shown in Fig. 4.27, where it can be seen that the area of rectangles are equal and hence the elasticity is unity. Such a curve is called an equilateral or rectangular hyperbola. The demand is inelastic when the marginal utility falls rapidly, and elastic when it falls slowly.

4.23 TYPES OF ELASTICITY

1. **Price Elasticity :** It measures responsiveness of potential buyers to changes in price. It is the ratio of per centage change in quantity demanded in response to a per centage change in price. Normally, when we talk about the elasticity, we mean the price elasticity.

2. **Income Elasticity :** It is a measure of responsiveness of potential buyers to change in income. It shows how the quantity demanded will change when the income of the purchaser changes, the price of the commodity remaining the same. Thus, it can be

defined as, 'the ratio of the per centage change in the amount spent on the commodity to a per centage change in the consumers income, price of commodity remaining constant'.

Thus,

$$\text{Income Elasticity} = \frac{\text{Proportionate change in the quantity purchased}}{\text{Proportionate change in income}}$$

It is equal to unity when the proportion of income spent on a good remains the same even though income has increased. It will be greater than one when the proportion of income spent on a good increases as income increases while less than one when the proportion of income spent on a good decreases as income increases. Generally speaking, our tendency is to purchase more when the income increases unless it is an inferior good. Normally, since the income effect is positive, income elasticity of demand is also positive. It is zero when there is no change in purchase with the increase in income and it is negative when with the increase in income we purchase less as in case of inferior goods.

3. **Cross Elasticity :** Here, a change in the price of one good causes change in the demand for the another.

   Cross Elasticity of demand for X and Y

   $$= \frac{\text{Proportionate change in purchases of commodity X}}{\text{Proportionate change in purchases of commodity Y}}$$

   This type of the elasticity arises in case of substitute goods or complimentary goods. In case of complimentary goods decrease in price of X increases the demand for Y and vice versa giving positive cross elasticity while in case of substitute goods (or rival goods), increase in price of X (e.g. tea) increases the demand for Y (e.g. coffee).

Factors Determining the Price Elasticity of Demand
- Type of good whether it is a conventional and necessary good – inelastic.
- For luxury items – elastic.
- The proportion of the expenditure spent on the good with the total expenditure. If it is very small, the demand is inelastic and for more proportion, it is elastic.
- Availability of the substitutes or the complimentary goods.
- If the good has various uses, the demand for such a commodity is elastic because when it is cheap it can be used lavishly for many purposes. But when the price becomes high, its use is restricted only to the important purposes.
- For very cheap or very expensive goods, the demand is inelastic.
- The demand on the part of poor people is more sensitive to price changes as they have to fit the daily budget within very restricted income.

Measurement of Elasticity : The elasticity of demand can be found by various methods.

1. **Proportional Method :**

$$\text{Elasticity of demand} = \frac{\text{Proportionate change in amount demanded}}{\text{Proportionate change in price}}$$

$$E = \frac{\text{Change in amount demanded}}{\text{Amount demanded}} \div \frac{\text{Change in price}}{\text{Price}}$$

2. **Total Outlay Method :** This method was first used by Marshall and it is known as Marshallian method. In this method, the total expenditure on the commodity is calculated with the change in price. If with the decrease in price, the total expenditure (or total outlay) increases, the elasticity of demand is highly elastic. If with the decrease in price, the total expenditure remains the same, the elasticity of demand is unity and when the decrease in price decreases the total expenditure, the elasticity of demand is inelastic. It can be represented with the help of following table.

Table 4.5

Price	Units of Commodity Demanded	Total Expenditure	Elasticity
₹ 10	300	₹ 3000	E > 1
₹ 9	400	₹ 3600	Highly elastic
₹ 8	500	₹ 4000	
₹ 7	600	₹ 4200	E = 1
₹ 6	700	₹ 4200	Elasticity is one
₹ 5	800	₹ 4000	E < 1
₹ 4	900	₹ 3600	Low elasticity or
₹ 3	1000	₹ 3000	inelastic

3. **Geometrical Method :** This method can be used to find the elasticity of any point on demand curve. Consider a straight demand curve DD' as shown in following Fig. 4.28.

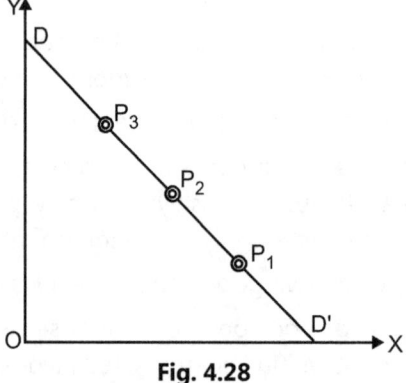

Fig. 4.28

Elasticity is represented by the fraction of distance from D to a point on the curve divided by the distance from the other end to the point. Thus elasticity for the points P_1, P_2 and P_3 are given as, $(D'P_1/DP_1)$, $(D'P_2/DP_2)$ and $(D'P_3/DP_3)$ respectively. If P is the point in the middle of the curve, its elasticity will be one. The elasticity at a lower point of the curve will be less than one and for higher point it is greater than one. This can be depicted with the help of following diagrams.

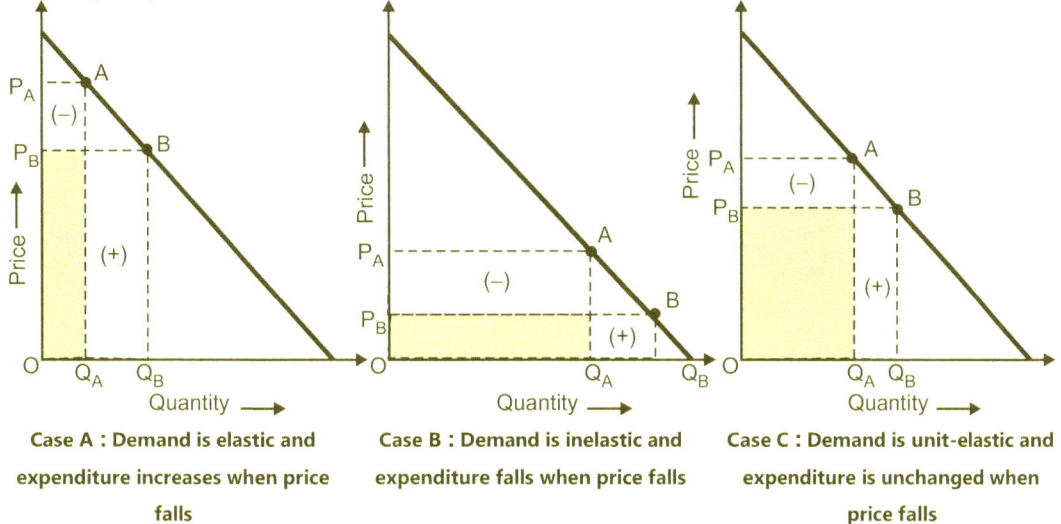

Case A : Demand is elastic and expenditure increases when price falls

Case B : Demand is inelastic and expenditure falls when price falls

Case C : Demand is unit-elastic and expenditure is unchanged when price falls

Fig. 4.29

When the price is reduced from P_A to P_B, expenditure changes from OP_AAQ_A to OP_BBQ_B. Thus, expenditure rises when demand is elastic (Case A), falls when demand is inelastic (Case B) and remains unchanged when demand is unit-elastic (Case C). Even if the demand curve is not a straight line, the above formula can be used. A tangent will, however, have to be drawn at the point on the curve where elasticity is to be measured.

4.24 COST OF CAPITAL

The rate which is used to discount a company's future cash flows to the present is known as the company's required return, or cost of capital. It also represents a hurdle rate that a company must overcome before it can generate value. It also refers to the opportunity cost of making a specific investment. It is the rate of return that could have been earned by putting the same money into a different investment with equal risk. Thus, the cost of capital is the rate of return required to persuade the investor to make a given investment.

As the name indicates, when a company raises capital from its lenders and owners, both types of investors require a return on their investment. Lenders expect to be paid interest on their loans, while owners expect a return, too. Hence, it is extensively used in the capital budgeting process to determine whether the company should take up a project or which alternative to be selected.

A stable, predictable company will have a low cost of capital, while a risky company with unpredictable cash flows will have a higher cost of capital. That means, all else equal, that the riskier company's future cash flows are worthless in present value terms, which is why stocks of stable companies often look more expensive on the surface. The cost of capital used in a DCF model can have a significant impact on the fair value, so it's important to pay attention to this estimated Fig.

Cost of capital depends on the mode of financing used – it refers to the cost of equity if the business is financed solely through equity or to the cost of debt if it is financed solely through debt. (Equity is cash in a company owned by the shareholders (shares). Debt is cash in a company that has been borrowed (bonds, Loan stocks)). Many companies use a combination of debt and equity to finance their businesses, and for such companies, their overall cost of capital is derived from a weighted average of all capital sources, widely known as the Weighted Average Cost of Capital (WACC). A company's WACC accounts for both the firm's cost of equity and its cost of debt, weighted according to the proportions of equity and debt in the company's capital structure.

The basic formula for WACC is :

(Weight of Debt)(Cost of Debt) + (Weight of Equity) (Cost of Equity)

For example, if the market value of a company's equity is $600 million and it has $400 million of debt on its balance sheet, then 60% of its capital is equity and 40% is debt. If the company's cost of equity is 10% and its cost of debt is 7%, then its WACC is :

(60% × 10%) + (40% × 7%) = 8.8%.

4.25 TIME VALUE OF MONEY (May 11, 12, Nov./Dec. 11, 12)

If the present consumption involved and output in the future is equal, then the project has not generated any surplus, the sacrifice is equal to zero. This is never true for any project. Hence as the time advances, the worth also should increase. This increase of worth is called as time value of money.

'The change in amount of money over a period of time is called Time Value of Money'.

To explain this concept, consider an example - ₹ 100 becomes ₹ 108 an year after,if the rate of interest is 8%. This indicates that value of money is increasing with the passage of time. Also, ₹ 108 an year after is equivalent to ₹ 100 today. This technique of reducing future rates of returns to present by working out the interest rate backward is known as discounting technique. The present worth of future benefits can be discounted and compared with costs involved today. The time value of money allow you the opportunity to post pone consumption and earn interest.

4.25.1 Interest

Time involves sacrifices in the present over the future. So we expect that, benefits / returns in future should be sufficient to compensate for the sacrifices in the present. This compensating factor is commonly known as "interest".

Consider an example of planting a sapling. Initially, land and labour are required for planting a tree. Its fruits will be consumed after some years. i.e. we have invested in land, labour and time. If the total supply of land and labour is given, the length of time is the only variable dimension of capital. Hence, the sacrifice is not to use the land on which the sapling is planted.

Therefore, interest has three dimensions :
- Pure time dimension – sacrifice of present consumption over future.
- Change in value of product as a function of time. i.e. old wine has more value than new one.
- Use of products for further production of goods and services.

Interest quantifies the sacrifice of present for future.

The rate of interest indicates the floor limit of the capacity of the project to earn, below which it would not be worth while to go ahead of it.

For invested money, Interest = Total amount accumulated – Original investment

For borrowed money, Interest = Present amount owed – Original loan

The original investment or loan is referred as 'Principal'.

Simple Interest

The interest which is directly proportional to the capital involved. If P is the principal or amount borrowed and F is the future sum of money paid,

$$F = P(1 + i.n)$$

Where, i is the rate of interest for n periods (usually in years)

In this method, interest is calculated on initial P only.

Compound Interest

In the above example, if the interest calculated every year is again deposited, every year the principal amount will change and the interest is compounded annually. It can be shown as follows :

Year	Principal amount	Interest	Total principal amount at year end
1	1000	100	1100
2	1100	110	1210
3	1210	121	1331
4	1331	133.1	1464.1
5	1464.1	146.41	1610.51

In short, we can state the formula as

$$F = P(1 + i)^n$$

Profit

'Profit is the payment earned by a factor of production called organized'. This organized may also be called as a manager or an owner or entrepreneur. This is the factor of production which organizes land, labour and capital, produces goods, sells them, bears risks and gets a reward for his services. The share which accrues to the organizer of business is called as profit. It is rewards for assuming final responsibility which cannot be shifted on the shoulder of any one else. Profit can be classified as :

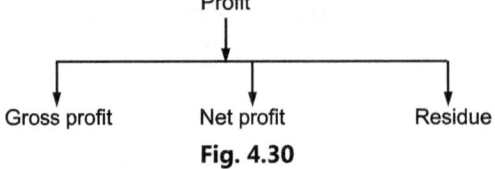

Fig. 4.30

Residue

Actual Receipts during a period- Actual payments made during that period.

Gross Profit

Residue-Imputed charge of owner's labour and capital – Tax obligations- Value of balance stock.

Net Profit

Gross Profit- Value of capital equipment added during the periods- Depreciation charge.

4.26 SOURCES OF PROJECT FINANCE

In order to expand, it is necessary for business owners to tap financial resources. Business owners can utilize a variety of financing resources, initially broken into two categories, debt and equity. "Debt" involves borrowing money to be repaid, plus interest. "Equity" involves raising money by selling interests in the company. Deciding whether to seek out equity capital or debt financing is the first step. Usually, companies trying to get equity capital are very early stage with little or no real assets. While companies on their way to a steady growth curve use debt financing.

4.26.1 Equity Finance

As the owner of a business idea, plan, or company - you hold ownership to a subjective value called equity. The equity of any type of property whether intellectual or physical is the value someone is willing to pay for it minus any liability attached to it. Once the owner and investor determine the "valuation" of the equity, the owner can then sell parts of the equity in order to raise capital. An equity capitalist is interested in picking a company that shows great potential. They are expecting that there will be significant growth due to their involvement. That could mean that the company will grow tenfold within five years.

4.26.2 Debt Finance

Conversely, raising capital through debt financing does not involve "selling" equity, but works by "borrowing" against it. Debt financing is only available to business owners who have something of value that the lender can instantly liquidate. The debt finance company does not become a partner with lenders, but they are in business to make money from their money, letting the lenders to use it for periods of time.

4.26.3 Advantages of Debt Compared to Equity

- Because the lender does not have a claim to equity in the business, debt does not dilute the owner's ownership interest in the company.
- A lender is entitled only to repayment of the agreed-upon principal of the loan plus interest, and has no direct claim on future profits of the business. If the company is successful, the owners reap a larger portion of the rewards than they would if they had sold stock in the company to investors in order to finance the growth.
- Except in the case of variable rate loans, principal and interest obligations are known amounts which can be forecasted and planned for.
- Interest on the debt can be deducted on the company's tax return, lowering the actual cost of the loan to the company.
- Raising debt capital is less complicated because the company is not required to comply with state and federal securities laws and regulations.

The company is not required to send periodic mailings to large numbers of investors, hold periodic meetings of shareholders, and seek the vote of shareholders before taking certain actions.

4.26.4 Disadvantages of Debt Compared To Equity

- Unlike equity, debt must at some point be repaid.
- Interest is a fixed cost which raises the company's break-even point. High interest costs during difficult financial periods can increase the risk of insolvency. Companies that are too highly leveraged (that have large amounts of debt as compared to equity) often find it difficult to grow because of the high cost of servicing the debt.
- Cash flow is required for both principal and interest payments and must be budgeted for. Most loans are not repayable in varying amounts over time based on the business cycles of the company.
- Debt instruments often contain restrictions on the company's activities, preventing management from pursuing alternative financing options and non-core business opportunities.
- The larger a company's debt-equity ratio, the more risky the company is considered by lenders and investors. Accordingly, a business is limited as to the amount of debt it can carry.
- The company is usually required to pledge assets of the company to the lender as collateral, and owners of the company are in some cases required to personally guarantee repayment of the loans.

4.26.5 Equity Shares

It is defined by Cambridge Business dictionary as "A share that gives the person who owns it the right to receive part of a company's profits and to vote at shareholder meetings"

Equity shares are those shares which are ordinary in the course of company's business. Ordinary shares in the equity capital of a business entitle the holders to all distributed profits after the holders of debentures and preference shares have been paid. This means that the company issues equity shares for a fair price and these shares represent ownership in the company for anyone who purchases the shares.

Salient Features of Equity Shares

(1) Owned Capital

Equity share capital is owned capital because it is the money of the shareholders who are actually the owners of the company.

(2) Fixed Value or Nominal Value

Every share has fixed value or a nominal value. For example, the price of a share is ₹ 10/- which indicates a fixed value or a nominal value.

(3) Distinctive Number

Every share is given a distinct number just like a roll number for the purpose of identification.

(4) Attached Rights

A share gives its owner the right to receive dividend, the right to vote, the right to attend meetings, the right to inspect the books of accounts.

(5) Return on Shares

Every shareholder is entitled to a return on shares which is known as dividend. Dividend depends on the profits made by a company. Higher the profits, higher will be the dividend and vice versa.

(6) Transfer of Shares

Equity shares are easily transferable, that is if a person buys shares of a particular company and he does not want them, he can sell them to any one, thereby transferring the shares in the name of that person.

(7) Benefit of Right Issue

When a company makes fresh issue of shares, the equity shareholders are given certain rights in the company. The company has to offer the new shares first to the equity shareholders in the proportion to their existing share holding. In case they do not take up the shares offered to them, the same can be issued to others. Thus, equity shareholders get the benefits of the right issue.

(8) Benefit of Bonus Shares

Joint stock companies which make huge profits, issue bonus shares to their ordinary shareholders out of the accumulated profits. These shares are issued free of cost in proportion to the number of existing equity share holding. In case they do not take up the shares offered to them, the same can be issued to others. Thus, equity shareholders get the benefits of the right issue.

(9) Irredeemable

Equity shares are always irredeemable. This means equity capital is not returnable during the life time of a company.

(10) Capital Appreciation

The nominal or par value of equity shares is fixed but the market value fluctuates. The market value mainly depends upon profitability and prosperity of the company. High rate of dividend is paid with high rate of profit, the shareholders capital is appreciated through an appreciation in the market value of shares. (i.e. higher the rate of dividend, higher the market value of the shares.)

4.26.6 Debenture Capital

It is the capital borrowed by a company, using its fixed assets as security.

IMPORTANT POINTS

- Important definitions in construction economy.
- Marshall's law of diminishing utility with e.g. and assumptions of the law.
- Law of substitution with its limitations and applications w.r.t. engineering economies.
- Three types of demand with concept of law of demand with exceptions to the law.
- Supply curve with e.g. factors affecting the supply curve.
- Shift in supply curve.
- Concept of indifference curve analysis with properties of indifference curve.
- Concept of elasticity of demand with its five cases.
- Types of elasticity with its types and factors determining the price elasticity of demand.

QUESTIONS

1. What is the importance of Economics in case of Civil Engineering field.
2. Define the term Economics and its relevance to the Engineering by giving suitable examples.
3. What are the demand and supply curves ? Explain how the price equilibrium takes place.
4. What are the types of demand ? Explain each of these by giving examples.

5. What is the elasticity of demand ? Describe each one in detail.
6. What is the indifference curve analysis ?
7. Explain the methods of determining the elasticity of demands. What are the elasticity of demand for necessary good and luxury goods ?
8. What are the income effect, price effect and substitution effect ?
9. What is meant by cost of capital? What are its applications?
10. Explain with the help of suitable example the Time Value of Money.
11. What are the various sources of finance?
12. Differentiate between debt and equity.

UNIVERSITY QUESTIONS

1. Give the definitions of Demand and Supply. Also explain the 'Law of Demand'. **[May 07, 10] [2+3]**
2. Draw the supply curve and explain it. Also describe the elasticity of supply. **[May 07] [5]**
3. Explain with one example, the 'Law of Diminishing Marginal Utility'. **[May 07] [6]**
4. What are the factors that decide the price of a commodity ? **[May 07] [6]**
5. What is the importance of Economics in Civil Engineering Construction Field. **[May 07] [5]**
6. Give definitions of the following : Cost, Price, Value, Goods, Wants. **[May 07] [5]**
7. Explain demand and supply with suitable example. **[Dec. 07] [6]**
8. Discuss the indifference curve technique. **[Dec. 07] [4]**
9. What is meant by equilibrium price and equilibrium quantity ? Explain equilibrium price and equilibrium quantity in relation to demand and supply with example. **[Dec. 07] [8]**
10. State the factors that decide the price of a commodity. Discuss any three factors in detail. **[Dec. 08] [2+6]**
11. Discuss the following in brief : **[2+2=4]**
    (i) Equilibrium price **[Dec. 08]**

  (ii) Equilibrium amount. **[May 10]**

12. Explain the following terms with suitable example. : **[Dec. 08, 10] [6]**

  (i) Law of substitution; (ii) Elasticity of demand.

13. Explain with suitable example, the law of diminishing marginal utility.

  [Dec. 08, May 10, Dec. 10] [6]

14. What are demand and supply curves ? Describe the elasticity of supply.

  [Dec. 08, 10] [2+2=4]

15. Define Engineering Economics and explain the importance of it in Civil Engineering.

  [Dec. 08, May 10] [2+4=6]

17. State and explain law of Diminishing Marginal Utility. **[May 09] [6]**

18. Explain in brief the different types of tools for Engineering Economics. **May 09] [5]**

19. Define Price and explain its relevance to marketing utility. **[May 09] [5]**

20. Explain law of increasing returns. State the factors affecting it. **[May 09] [3+3]**

21. State and explain Law of Supply. **[May 09, 10, Dec. 10] [6]**

22. Explain in brief Elasticity of Demand. **[May 09, 10] [5]**

23. Explain in brief Law of Substitution. **[May 09, 10] [5]**

24. Define : (i) Wealth, (ii) Goods, (iii) Wants, (iv) Cost, (v) Price, (vi) Value (vii) Demand

  [Dec. 07, 08, May, Dec. 10]

25. Discuss Applications of Economics to Civil Engineering. **[Dec. 10] [6]**

26. Write short notes on the following (any four) : **[18]**

  (i) Annuity **[May 07]**

  (ii) Money **[May 07]**

  (iii) Working Capital **[May 07]**

  (iv) Fixed Capital **[Dec. 08]**

27. Define capital. Explain fixed and working capital. **[Dec. 07] [2+4]**

28. Explain the term Annuities. **[Dec. 07, Dec. 10]**

  (a) Differentiate between the following :

    (i) Working Capital and Fixed Capital. **[May 10]**

(b) Write short notes on any two of the following : **[May 11] [8]**
   (i) Time value of money
   (ii) Annuity
   (iii) Net present value.

29. What is time value of money ? **[Dec. 11] [2]**
30. What is time value of money? Explain with an example. **[May 12] [3]**
31. Differentiate between "Working Capital" and "Fixed Capital"? **[May 12] [3]**
32. (a) Define capital. Explain Fixed and Working capital. **[Dec. 12] [6]**
    (b) Differentiate between N.P.V. and I.R.R. **[Dec. 12] [6]**
    (c) Explain "Time Value of Money" with an example. **[Dec. 12] [4]**
33. Define Annuity. What are the different types of annuities. **[Dec. 12] [6]**

UNIT V

PROJECT RESOURCES AND SAFETY ASPECTS

5.1 INTRODUCTION

Management of materials required for any project has always remained perplexing problem to industries. Most of the activities in industries are connected with men, material and machinery and the personnel in industries have to co-ordinate these key factors for progressive planning so as to make use of these resources to produce useful products in most effective way. Though the importance of each of the above factors has been known but very recently the field of study of material management has been recognised. Basically it includes both the technical and economical efficiency which are necessary for the well running of the industry, so to say survival and growth. It is concerned with planning and programming of materials, predesign, value analysis and market research of purchase, procurement of all the necessary materials including raw materials, components, subassemblies, assemblies, finished goods, packing material and any other necessary things and transportation cost etc.

In any civil engineering project the material is very important part as it constitutes 40% to 60% of the project cost and hence the success of the project depends upon the materials management. It is very necessary to have proper planning for the materials management before and during the project work. If required materials, in quality and quantity, are made available at the proper time, there will be substantial saving in cost, time and also there will be improvement in quality of construction or the project. But for this, proper storage arrangements and watchfulness on the use of materials is necessary, also that there is no wastage of materials in any manner.

Uncontrolled supply of materials may result in excessive supply or inadequate supply. The excessive supply may lead to problems of storage and wastage due to improper storage arrangements. It may also block capital unnecessarily and hence proper materials management and planning is absolutely necessary for construction projects and it forms very important aspect of construction management or any other project.

5.1.1 Materials Management [Nov./Dec.-12]

Materials management is a recent field of management and it deals with planning of materials as required for the business before and during the project. It decides scientifically what to purchase, when to purchase, how much to purchase, from where to purchase, where and how to store and general flow of materials for any project and therefore, forms an important part of big projects. The materials management covers all the aspects of materials costs, materials supply and materials utilisation. It is the technique to improve the productivity of the capital by reducing the materials cost, preventing blocking up of large amount of capital in materials for long periods. This improves the capital turnover ratio. There are some important features of materials management in construction industry.

Important features of materials management in construction industry :

- Purchase of goods materials; for quality to be purchased from reliable place.
- Timely purchase of materials to fit in the construction schedule in the required right quantity.
- Purchase of materials at reasonable rate. Bulk purchase of materials may increase profit margin and may contribute to saving in time.
- Proper arrangements for storing of materials and proper inventory control.
- Avoiding wastage of materials.
- Managing perfect and close co-ordination between the various wings of construction from view point of material supply.
- To watch the market conditions and price fluctuations with regards to the materials required for the project and to take proper decisions regarding purchase.
- To safeguard the interests of the organisation in general.

It is further important to note that :

1. Materials are going to represent a larger proportion of total cost involved in any project or business.
2. Problem of material management including procurement of material and its control are going to become more and more difficult and complicated in future.
3. As such scientific methods of material management may provide some solution to above problems.

5.1.2 Objectives [Nov./Dec.-11, May-12]

The objectives of material management can be broadly divided into two groups as detailed below :

1. **Primary Objectives**

    The primary objectives include :

    (a) Provisioning of materials in specified quantity, of specified quality at economical cost and the maintenance of continuity of supply.

    (b) Minimising investments and cost of inventories and assurance of a high inventory turnover.

2. Secondary Objectives

The secondary objectives include :

(a) Locating new sources of supply.

(b) Achieving a reduction in costs through different techniques such as variety reduction, simplification of procedures, standardisation and quality control, value analysis, purchase research, inventory control etc.

(c) Co-ordinating such functions as planning, scheduling, storage, maintenance etc. for smooth flow of material.

(d) Developing skills and personnel under the new concept of material management.

5.2 FUNCTIONS OF MATERIAL MANAGER

The General Electric Company in U.S.A., a pioneer in the field of materials management, has grouped together the following functions under the heading of material management.

- Material planning, programming and budgeting.
- Material Purchasing and Procurement.
- Receiving, Inspection and Storing of materials.
- Inventory control.
- Storekeeping.
- Value analysis and standardisation.
- Material handling and traffic control.
- Dispatching, shipping and disposal of scrap and surplus etc.
- Co-ordination of all above functions and keeping a liason between design, engineering, manufacturing and marketing.

5.2.1 Qualities of a Material Manager [Nov./Dec.-11]

Material manager should possess the following qualities or skills :

- Know the market trends.
- Know newly introduced materials.
- Understand the system in the organisation thoroughly.
- Possess ability in analysis, organisation and communication.
- Possess ability to use computer equipment and softwares.
- Familiar with the supply chain management systems.
- Should have training in project management to support production schedule, to plan requirements for purchasing materials or services and to ensure delivery of required materials to production consistent with established schedules.

5.3 MATERIAL PLANNING AND PROGRAMMING

Whatsoever type of industry may be, effective material management and planning will bring good yield. It will lead to improved productivity. It is a part of material management, the objective being either to save the materials or saving of money spent on materials at different stages of production. The following guidelines may be followed to achieve the objective :

- There should not be any production hold up for want of materials.
- The purchases are to be made in time in order to avoid increased cost of rush orders of materials.
- Inventory holdings be kept at a minimum level in order to avoid higher carrying cost. It involves right purchase quantity to have minimum balance in stock. It leads to optimum use of materials and to follow the guidelines given above one must be clear about the following aspects of material planning to be a success :
    1. Making a purchase decision
    2. Value analysis
    3. Purchase budget
    4. Inventory level and reorder point .

Purchase decisions have to be taken by the planning department keeping an eye on the production schedule, plant capacity, cost involved and the available finances. Some peculiar problems may sometimes be faced such as too much dependence on rare sources of supply such as those requiring import licence for foreign materials in case of production of some commodities etc. or frequent changes in production schedule. In case of all such problems effective decision need to be taken by Materials Manager for which he should be supplied with timely and pertinent information and should have knowledge of risk involved and the consequences in terms of final goal to be achieved. In case of purchase of different components priority should be given to the purchase of raw materials. Though value analysis is a methodical analysis, it is mostly based on common sense in the logical selection in the use of materials and equipment to obtain significant results. It can be effectively applied to predesign stage and in preparation of bill of materials. Application of this concept may lead to reduction in costs.

Purchase budget is financial commitment which must satisfy the following aspects :

- The right quantity of material required.
- The quantity of material in stock at hand.
- The required finance to obtain fresh supplies.
- Variation in market trend.

While budgeting, attention must be paid to the various materials directly related to the product and the project. Knowledge of inventory level and the reorder point is very important. It involves more effective way of controlling the inventory flow through various stages of production of Civil Engineering Construction. This science is known as *Rheochrematics* applied to production engineering. It is the management of flow of materials.

It may be used effectively to gain following advantages :

- Faster turnover of inventories.
- Greater assurance of material availability.
- Reduced material handling cost.
- Improved relations with suppliers.
- Reduced office work and paper work.
- Cheaper and faster communication.

5.3.1 Functions in Material Management

As stated above the functions involved in material management are :

(a) Purchasing (b) Material handling (c) Inventory.

Their inter-relation can be illustrated with the diagram in Fig. 5.1.

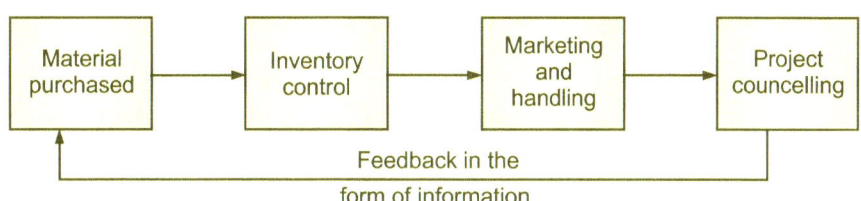

Fig. 5.1

5.3.2 Purchasing

The purchasing function has to be efficient and there should be effective control over the expenditure fund and inventory flow of material. Though purchasing has to be done at a reasonable price, quality of the material has to be maintained and it is not necessary that the purchase be made always from the lowest bidder as it may not maintain the needed quality. For maintaining the quality, the specifications laid down should be in details without any ambiguity. It is necessary that the right quality material should be purchased at right time at reliable right rate. The suppliers from whom the purchase is made should be reliable. Sometimes purchasing of different material is effected through agencies. Such agencies should be reliable. There should be a list of materials necessary for the project with the specifications and the quantity. It is also necessary that a list of reliable suppliers and agencies supplying the various materials be maintained and this list should be modified from time to time to accommodate new reliable suppliers and agencies. It is also responsibility of the purchase department that payments are made within reasonable period after the purchase is effected and found satisfactory.

Purchasing is a service function that supports the activities of other operations. There must be steady and reliable flow of information between concerned departments. The different concerned departments may be :

- Design
- Accounts
- Different suppliers in market
- Stores for receiving the material
- Actual construction or production
- Legal department for disputes.

The structure of purchase department and relationship with other departments is illustrated in Fig. 5.2.

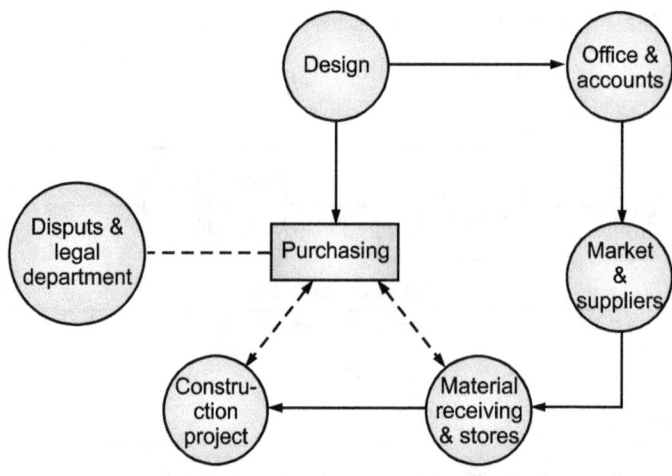

Fig. 5.2

5.3.3 Method of Purchasing

Various methods of purchasing are adopted depending upon the conditions, time and urgency. The two popular methods adopted for market purchasing are :

1. Inviting tenders
2. Rate contract purchase.

In the first method, a list of reliable suppliers is prepared for different materials and tenders are invited from them.

The information about the quality of the material required in the form of specifications and the quantity and the period of supply is given in the tender. The tenders are published in leading newspapers.

The suppliers desirous of accepting the offer for supply of the material are required to quote their rates for the supply.

After receiving the tenders a comparative statement is prepared and order is placed with the firm normally quoting the lowest bid.

However, in some cases lowest bid may be rejected if there are reasons to do so depending upon factors like past experience etc. In rate contract purchase the rates are invited for supply of materials for a specific period and it is a binding on the supplier firm as well as the purchasor to stick to the quoted rates irrespective of the rates in the market.

5.3.4 Procurement of Materials

Materials for construction are procured by direct purchasing or obtained from the stores. For small works and small organisations the materials are purchased directly as and when required keeping particular purchase schedule. However, for big organisations the purchasing etc. is done by the materials management department and is procured for the construction from the stores.

Every organisation, small or big, must have separate purchase department. The purchase department has the following responsibilities and functions :

1. To get the right quantity of materials of the required specifications, at the minimum overall cost including transportation etc.
2. To adopt the proper procedure for the purchase.

In purchases made by Government and Semi-Govt. bodies, public undertakings, proper procedures has to be adopted and rules and regulations have to be followed.

There are following methods of purchases.

(a) **Market Purchasing :** Method adopted for locally available materials by private concerns.

(b) **Centralised Purchasing :** Method adopted by Government bodies and also when the construction organisation has several projects undertaken simultaneously.

(c) **Rate Contract Purchasing :** This is for specific items which are required regularly in large quantities. Normally rate contract is for a period of one year.

A sample purchase order is as shown below :

XYZ CO. LTD.

CONSTRUCTION DEPARTMENT

TEL. : 12345678   FAX : 87654321

PURCHASE ORDER

Supplier's Name	:	_____	**P.O. No.**	:	_____
Address	:	_____	**Date**	:	_____
	:	_____	**Site**	:	_____

Dear Sir,

    We are pleased to place this order for the following material, subject to the terms and conditions printed overleaf.

Sr. No.	Description with sizes	Brand Make	Unit	Qty.	Unit Rate	Amt. (₹)

Supplier's Quotation No. : Date :		Guarantee / Warranty	:
Sales Tax : Extra / Inclusive		Payment Terms	:
Octroi : Extra / Inclusive		Requisition No.	:
Freight : Extra / Inclusive			
Delivery Schedule :			
			Director

*   **Note :** Octroi should be paid in "Octroi Educational Deposit A/c" only, else no reimbursement will be made.

5.3.5 Material Handling and Control

It is the movement of material from receiving to finished goods storage through manufacturing or in process storing. In Civil engineering project, it is the movement of materials to its use as it is as a raw material or after processing if any in actual construction. Timber may be purchased as a raw material and then may be processed at sight for preparation of doors and window frames, shutters or trusses which are used in construction. Material handling, therefore, is the movement from raw material to finished goods ready for dispatch. Material handling also includes the supply of material at the place of use from the stores or the market and involves transportation. The transportation cost of the materials in India is quite high and at times good time is also required for transportation. Material handling system has to be efficient with good control over the same. The following points should be noted for the same.

- There should be perfect co-ordination between the various agencies involved. These agencies includes finance, transport, stores, issue, control, sale etc. A senior person may look after this co-ordination.
- There must be good record keeping so that the position of material required, in stock, that ordered etc. can be known at any instant. Record of receipt, stock and issue is maintained daily and properly and the information may be given to higher authorities.

The entries made in GPR (General Purchase Register) are as follows :

XYZ CO. LTD.

CONSTRUCTION SITE

MATERIAL ISSUE SLIP

No.   : _____
Site   : _____
Date   : _____

To Store   : _____
Issue to Contractor   : _____
Through His Representative : _____

Item with Size	Quantity	Building No. / Location

Issued by : _____   Storekeeper : _____
Recd. by : _____

General Purchase Register (For Aggregates)										
Sr. No.	Date	GPR No.	Challan No.	Truck No.	Bill Qty.	Bill Date	Rate	Amt.	Sign	Remark

- The demand of material is received well in advance and should be communicated to the purchase department immediately so that the needed material is made available at the right time for use.

The material issue slip is shown in the above table

5.4 FUNCTIONS OF MATERIAL MANAGER

In big concerns, therefore, there is a separate materials management department and the top officer incharge of that department is Materials Manager. In small concerns alongwith the planning, this department is looked after by the Planning Manager.

The functions of the Materials Manager can be enlisted as below :

- Planning of required materials and its programming i.e. phasing the supply of different materials required for the project.
- Procuring of materials required for the construction project.
- Arranging for storing the materials needed and purchased.
- To plan the economic use of the materials.
- To keep close watch on the supply and use of materials at every stage of the project.
- To see that unnecessary large supply of materials is not made and unrequired materials is not stored.
- To keep careful watch and to see that proper material is utilised at right place and bad workmanship is eliminated.
- To see that site space for storing material is properly utilised.
- To see that stores are so arranged that the materials are easily accessible and can be easily removed for use for actual construction.
- To see that there is proper transportation arrangements for receiving the material at the site and proper passage for movements of trucks, carts, machinery and the equipment for stocking, utilisation and removal of the materials to and from the storing site.
- To see that capital locking is avoided and unnecessarily large quantity of material is not purchased and stored.
- To have proper accounting of the materials.

- To have proper inventory control of the material stores.
- To have proper value analysis of the stores.
- To see that excess use of materials is avoided and bad workmanship is prevented. Rejection of materials and material product is also avoided.
- To see to the proper disposal of surplus material and also of the scrap and rejected material if any.

5.4.1 Economical Uses of Materials

Economic use of the materials is of prime importance and is one of the most important responsibilities of Materials Manager. The economic use of materials lead to economy in general and reduction in time of completion of the project. To achieve this, the materials manager has to look carefully to the following points.

- Costly material like cement, steel, timber etc. is stored in closed space with lock and key arrangement and they are properly stacked and stored and only the required material is issued.
- Scattering of other materials like sand, coarse aggregate is avoided and they are stocked properly so that loss is avoided.
- If excess material is supplied from the stores, this excess material is recovered and redeposited in the stores.
- All the surplus materials and the scrap should be constantly collected from the worksite and the stores should always be kept clean. The surplus material and the scrap should be disposed off and the value should be recovered.
- The materials used for auxiliary services (e.g. materials used for scaffolding, centering etc.) should be properly and economically used and wastage and wasteful use of such indirect materials (Bamboo, corrugated iron sheets, roaps etc.) is avoided on large constructions.
- The small tools and plants such as ghamelas, pawadas, pickaxes etc. are properly used and they are not misused so that their life is not reduced.
- To study how material can be fruitfully used and economically handled. This is a challenge to the Materials Manager.

5.5 REQUIREMENT OF CONSTRUCTION MATERIALS AND PHASING

In planning of construction projects various schedules prepared are :
- Labour schedule
- Equipment schedule
- Material schedule
- Finance schedule

Before commencement of the work, detailed quantities of various materials required for the different items of work are found out. The material schedule consists of the quantities of different items and their phasing. The material schedule gives the actual quantities of different materials, their specifications and the time by which they should be made available. The materials required should be kept ready at the right time for the use.

Normally for engineering construction projects the following materials are required :

- Sand, rubble, aggregate, bricks, lime etc. which are available in local market or can be manufactured locally.
- Cement, steel, timber etc. which will have to be purchased. The different timber items like door and window frames, shutters etc. can be ordered directly or can be prepared on site from the timer purchased.
- Steel windows, grills, gates etc. to be fabricated according to the specific requirements.
- Water supply and sanitary fittings and pipelines.
- Electrical materials.
- Paints, locks, tiles etc.
- Special materials like special plaster sand, special fittings if any like lifts etc.

5.5.1 Some Important Points Related to Material Management

Most of the above material is available locally whereas special materials will have to be brought from distant places where they are available. Some special fittings will be supplied by special agencies only. For lifts etc. special agencies may take up the work of supplying and fixing the same and in such case there will be no responsibility on the material manager. However, procurement of cement and steel is very important as the construction programme is closely related to these materials.

Normally there is no difficulty in procurement of these materials but sometimes shortage of these materials is felt in the market and therefore, it should be properly visualised and supply of such materials is so arranged that the work is not hampered because of short supply of the materials.

On Government works cement, steel and some other materials may be supplied by the Government and it should be seen that the required material is supplied in time by the Government and for that the indents are placed in right time to the proper authorities. In materials management, the supply of different materials is properly linked to the schedule of construction and accordingly the material schedule is prepared and adhered to. For this, the Material Manager has to adopt proper procedure.

The procedure may include the following stages :

- Registration of reliable suppliers and manufacturers and updating the list from time to time.
- Finding the quantities of different materials with their specifications required for the complete project and the period over which they will be required.
- Preparing the supply schedule and the phasing programme of procurement of the materials. Co-ordination of the supply schedule and the construction schedule is very important so that required material is made available at right time and construction is not delayed for non-supply of material.
- Preparing purchase schedule giving due attention to the priorities.
- Purchase formalities like calling quotations, inviting supply tenders, calling for samples, inspecting samples and fixing the agencies for different supplies. For Government works placing indents for the different materials supplied by the Government right in earnest is important.
- Placing orders as per the purchase schedule with proper quantities, specification, date of supply, rates etc.
- Inspection of materials before supply to see that proper material as per specification is only supplied.
- Making suitable arrangements for storing the materials in the permanent central stores if any or in the temporary stores at the work site. Proper arrangement for storing and stacking of materials like cement is made with lock and key to stores. Arrangement for storing of other material like sand etc. is made prior to receiving of the material.
- Acceptance, storing and issue of material. Proper entries in the relevant stock books are made about storing and issue of material from time to time.
- Keeping watch and vigilance on the stores and making proper arrangements to avoid theft.

5.5.2 Indent, Storing of Material and Issue

5.5.2.1 Indent

For Government works some materials such as cement, steel, G.I. Sheets, asbestos sheets or some tools are supplied by the Government to the contractor, as per the conditions of contract. The materials to be supplied are specified in the contract. For receiving such materials from the Government stores the contractor has to put up a requisition in writing in prescribed form which is called *indent*.

The indent is in prescribed Form No. 7 and is in a booklet form, each page in triplicate. This indent book is machine numbered and consists of indent, counterfoil and invoice. With each subdivision of Government Engineering Department, there is an indent book and for the required materials the indent is prepared by the Sub-divisional Officer or the Deputy Engineer or the Assistant Engineer incharge of the subdivision and sent to the officer incharge of the stores. The indenting officer will fill the details on the indent and the counterfoil and the officer incharge of the stock will issue the materials as per the availability in the stock and will correct the indent according to the actual material issued and accordingly will make the entries in the invoice and will send the indent book back to the indenting officer. After receiving the materials the indenting officer will return the invoice to the stores officer after signing the invoice as acknowledgment of having received the material as per the invoice. The invoice is the voucher for the issue of the materials from the central stores.

If the material is issued to the contractor, the signature of the contractor is taken on the invoice and the cost of such materials issued to the contractor is recovered from his running bills at the issue rate. For such materials unstamped receipt in triplicate is obtained from the contractor, where in all the details of the materials issued are incorporated. A form of indent is given below. System of indents may be followed by very big construction companies which may have central stores and where some works are in progress in nearby areas.

FORM OF INDENT

No. : _____

Site : _____

REQUISITION SLIP

Date : _____

Sr. No.	Description of Material	New Qty. Reqd.	Delivery Reqd. up to Date	Total Received up to Date	Store Regd. Page No.	Remark/ Material for Bldg.	For Purchase Dept. Remark	
							Ordered to	Ordered no. & Date

_____ P.E. _____ Scrolling _____ D & D / Project Coordinator _____

Site Name : _____

Supplier Name : _____

Purchase Order No. : _____

Challan No. and Date : _____

Group

Goods Receipt Note

GRN No. : _____

Date : _____

Truck No. : _____

Time : _____

Sr. No.	Description	Received Qty.	Accepted Qty.	Rejected Qty.	Remarks

Storage Incharge   QA Incharge   Project Manger

5.5.2.2 Storing

On any civil engineering works different types of materials are required simultaneously and hence the storing of materials has to be done systematically so that the materials can be received, stored and issued for use without any difficulty. For such storing a proper layout of the stores is very essential. Proper arrangements are also necessary for security of the materials from theft, and from manhandling. Materials like petrol, diesel etc. have to be stored very carefully and absolute care has to be taken for them. In general, materials are stored as per the nature of the materials and their cost. The stores may consist of sheds and open area with compound wall or barbed wire fencing.

Construction materials are generally stored as below :

- Materials like cement, timber, doors and windows, grills, paints, fuels, small tools are stored in sheds. Proper arrangement is made for stocking cement bags, timber etc. Fuels and any materials which can catch fire easily should be stored separately. Such stores must have locking arrangement.
- Materials like sand, rubble, coarse, aggregate, bricks can be stored in open area without any enclosure.
- Materials like steel, bituman drums, pipes, C.I. and A.C. and their fillings may be stored in open space with enclosures.
- Materials like small parts, pipe fitting, door fittings etc. to be stored in sheds and are properly stored in containers, properly labelled.
- Perishable materials requiring careful handling may be stored in open sheds.

Security measures for the stores may include the following :

(a) Providing chaukidar and/or other security staff.

(b) Adopting gate pass system.

(c) Providing locking arrangement for sheds.

(d) Providing double lock systems for the materials issued by Government to the contractor on Government works.

Proper maintenance of the stores, and also stores account is very important. Annual stock verification, inventory etc. are the routine part of stores management but surprise checks are also carried out. Proper account of receipt, and issue of the materials is maintained and total value of the stock in stores should be known. The stock verification is carried to verify if there are any excesses or shortages and then the responsibility of such has to be fixed. Also some times losses are written off and surplus materials are disposed off after taking due permission with proper procedures. Proper registers are maintained for the stores.

5.5.2.3 Issue of Materials

Any issue of materials from the stores should be against the authorised indent only. If the central stores is very big one, the issue can be systematised by fixing the days/dates of issue of different materials or days/dates for different subdivisions or sections. However, on every day the stock books must be updated and balance of every item and value of stocks must be worked out every day.

5.5.3 Organisation of Purchase Department

Primarily it is connected with material planning. It should be headed by a man of high integrity with wide market knowledge. The purchase statistics and usual purchase organisation chart is given below :

Purchase statistics consists of the following steps :

1. Analysis
2. Interpretation
3. Vendor programmes
4. Safety levels
5. Purchase efficiency

In bigger industrial organisations the amount of purchasing involved is so big that each and every work is assigned to different persons i.e. arrangement for transportation of the different incoming materials and outgoing materials has to be assigned to separate person or separate department. As such the purchase department must have many subdivisions specialising in different lines depending upon the requirements. In case the money involved in purchasing is very high there may be a purchase research department involving continuing research regarding availability of various materials, their costs trend and their substitutes if any. This department may keep a thorough record of market fluctuations and try to make use of it by purchasing inventories at the lowest cost. An additional subdivision may keep all record such as invoice checking, order-writing, record keeping etc. Such systematic up-to-date record keeping will be useful in bringing out any information needed at any time which will be useful to the purchase department in procuring quality materials in required quantity timely at low cost. A sample of the purchase organisation working under Materials Manager may be as under.

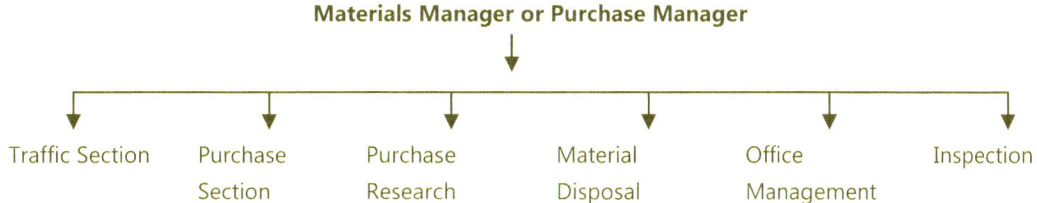

Each section may be headed by Deputy Manager or Assistant Manager.

In general in purchases the types of organisations are :

1. Centralised Purchase Department.
2. Decentralised Purchase Department.

Centralisation is very common in single plant industry while decentralisation is useful where the plants are in different geographical areas. However, the modern trend is that the firms want to switch over decentralisation.

Each of the above methods have their own strength and weakness.

Reasons for Centralisation are

- The firms gain advantage of standardization.
- Paper work is reduced.
- Better control and greater flexibility and thus high economy can be achieved.
- The organisation can purchase large volume of materials for the entire plant resulting in economy.

Reasons for Decentralisation are

- Services and efficiency of purchasing is improved if the enterprise is organised into separate sections.
- There will be better control in purchasing of dissimilar materials required at different plants or at different projects of dissimilar nature.
- It may provide greater flexibility in procurement.

- There will be better direct vendor control.
- Operations of purchase may become easier and in some cases even economical.

But in order to keep up the efficiency in decentralisation the following points should be borne in mind.

- The purchase procedures should be properly organised otherwise it may result in lack of control.
- The organisation has to miss the quantity discount. There will be lot of duplication of paper work and may cause delay in delivery.
- There may be lose control of inventory.
- Stock of basic material plant wise and project wise will be necessary.

5.6 INVENTORY [May-11,12, Nov./Dec.-12]

Inventory is a detailed descriptive list of movable goods which gives the quantity in stock and money value of each item. Inventory includes raw materials, work-in-process inventories, components, finished products etc. held in storage awaiting use. The term inventory excludes the machinery, furniture and other fixtures if they are in use. The inventory term can be classified into two broad classes :

1. **Direct Inventory :** These are the items which are directly used in the manufacturing of product or civil engineering construction and become an integral part of the finished product. Direct inventories are further classified into three groups.
   - **Raw Material Inventory :** These are such items which require further processing before they are ready to be used in the assembly in finished product.
   - **Work-in-Process Inventory :** These are the materials which are handed over to the production department as they are required during the assembly in finishing the product and without which the final assembly or product is not possible.
   - **Finished Goods Inventory :** The finished units, subassemblies, assemblies which are in stock and ready for shipment to consumers, such inventories are called finished inventories.
2. **Indirect Inventories :** It is the supply of those items such as oils, paints, lubricants, office material etc. which are necessary for manufacturing but do not become an integral part of finished product.

Efficient Material Management depends strongly on inventory. In the total project context, the inventory is an idle resource which acts as a cushion between the supply and the demand of the material used for production or construction in Civil Engineering. In industries, the inventory enables the firm to meet the orders and also helps in keeping up the manufacturing cycle. A proper control on inventory increases the profit in industry. Inventory Management, therefore, has two objectives :

- It should be able to provide acceptable consumer service and
- It should have low capital investment in inventory.

It, therefore, means that the inventory management has to maintain a store of goods which provides acceptable service to customers but does not need excessive amount of capital. But this simple statement is very difficult to apply in practical and operating situations. Sometimes inventories are out of stock and the management has to face an odd situation. As against this there may be unnecessary inventory, locking large capital, creating financial burden on the organisation. Hence inventory management is very complex as it is very difficult to decide how big inventory is necessary so that the continuous production or construction in Civil Engineering is not affected and at the same time it will not cost unnecessary financial burden. In Civil Engineering projects many times the works are held due to non-availability of materials. This results in increase in projects duration and unnecessary financial load on idle labour and increase in administrative cost. This either reduces the profit of the contractor or increases the cost of the project.

5.7 INVENTORY MANAGEMENT [May-12]

Consumable articles are continuously required in all industries including Civil Engineering projects and inventory management is carried out to determine the frequency of ordering the consumables and the fast wearing parts. It is necessary to ensure that the consumables and other articles required for the production are always available as and when required. The purpose of preparation of inventory is to ensure this and at the same time to see that the cost of the procurement is kept minimum. This is achieved by making minimum stock of consumables and other articles to such an extent which would be required for continuous production or execution of the project and at the same time the project or the production will not be held up because of non-availability of the materials. Thus, stock holding is an integral part of inventory control and stock control deserves special attention in production planning and control. There are six basic reasons for holding inventories :

1. To create a buffer or safety stock between the input and the output. The output and input rates may vary many times and when the output rate surpasses the input the inventory meets the demand. Because of the inventory the inflow characteristics of the material may not affect the outflow characteristic and the production or the project is not held up.

2. To ensure against the delays in deliveries of the materials. When a fresh order of the stock is made, supply normally is not immediately available and there is always a time gap between the two. This replenishment period or the lead time between the time of placing the order and the time of arrival of stock is often subjected to some variations. The different factors responsible may include non-availability of material, transportation facilities, strikes etc. which are not under the control of purchasing

organisation. Therefore, it is necessary to have a stock so that the output may not be affected because of the non-availability of the materials even after ordering in due time.

3. To allow for possible increase in the output if necessary. Changes are always expected because of market requirements, seasonal changes etc. If the normal production rate cannot cope up to increased demand, the production has to be increased at that time and hence there should be enough stock of materials to face the situation and gain the profit.
4. To take the advantage of quantity discount.
5. To ensure against the scarcity of material in the market.
6. To purchase the material when the prices are low.

5.7.1 The Objectives of Inventory Control

The management of inventory control is very complex as it is affected by different factors such as finance involved and capital locked, credit terms, market fluctuations transportation etc. and hence the management of inventory control should be with the following objectives.

- There should not be excessive inventories which may lead to wastage or unnecessary holding of stock.
- There should neither be shortage of inventory which may lead to stopping of production and delay in project duration.
- There should be acceptable consumer service.

Inventory control functions can be summarised as below :

- It allows for the errors in forecasting the demand.
- It minimises the difference between the scheduled progress and actual progress.
- It permits more economical use of ancillary services such as building and also use of machinery, equipment and manpower during fluctuations in demand.
- It permits the organisation to purchase the material and to manufacture the products in economic lot size.

5.7.2 Steps in Inventory Control

Inventory Control problem is complex. There should neither be a situation of no stock nor excessive stock. Most of the time the Material Manager is busy with the inventory problems such as 'how often should he order', 'how should he coup up with the production when sales are uncertain', 'how can he plan production and procurement for season sales' etc. and hence following steps should be followed for inventory control.

1. Planning the operation for purchase of different material and effective method of acquisition.
2. Physical verification of the material in stock from time to time.
3. Proper arrangement for storing the material.
4. To see that there is no damage to the material during the storage. To take due precautions in the store for the same.
5. To ensure security of stock.
6. Maintenance of proper record of stock-receipt and issue of inventory and posting information regularly and sincerely.
7. Fixing responsibility of performance.

5.8 ECONOMICAL ORDER QUANTITY [Nov./Dec.-11, 12]

The Material Manager has to make better decisions regarding the complex problems about inventories and such decisions can be arrived at, provided the problems are analysed and some scientific technique is applied to approach the problem. If proper system is developed to analyse the various functions of inventory, keep up-to-date measurement of the proper level of stocks and control the sub-systems, then it is always profitable to take quick decisions. In this connection following two aspects are important :

- Framing an analytical approach including the inventory cost analysis.
- Obtaining an optimum lot size including reorder point and lead time.

The inventory analysis starts with the question "how big should inventories be". The inventory cost influences this decision and answer to this cannot be given till the inventory cost is not properly analysed. It is the cost of the inventory which influences the inventory policies.

5.8.1 Inventory Costs (Indirect Cost) [May-12]

Inventory costs can be divided into following three sections :

- Processing or ordering cost
- Inventory carrying cost
- Stock out cost.

The processing or ordering cost consist of expenditure made on inventories till they are stocked in the stores. It, therefore, consists of :

(a) Cost of processing the requisition and any follow up. It is the cost involved in official procedure of ordering for the materials and any follow up.

(b) Cost of receiving the material. This includes the expenditure for inspection and labour for receiving.

(c) Cost involved in processing vendors invoice.

(d) Cost of material delivery to stores and proper arrangement of storing.

Inventory carrying cost consists of the following :

(a) Loss of interest on capital involved in inventory and no return on such investments.

(b) Cost of storing in the form of space requirement.

(c) Handling during storage and issue.

(d) Cost of insurance, deterioration, damages, depreciation, obsolescence and taxes if any.

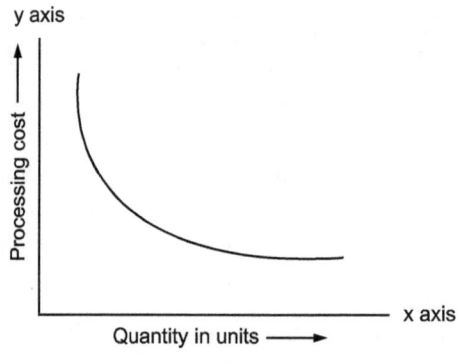

Fig. 5.3

The stock out cost is also a major cost which must be eliminated and if not possible atleast be minimised by logical planning. It is easy to understand that the procurement cost (which is called as Direct cost) includes the cost of the material and acquisition cost which consists of all the expenditure connected with actual procurement such as salaries and wages of personnel in purchase department, official expenditure on calling quotations, inspection, stationary and postage charges and any other expenditure connected with actual procurement.

The acquisition cost is more or less same irrespective of the quantity to be purchased. Hence if the quantity to be purchased is a big lot the acquisition cost will work out to be less per unit of the material purchased. The variation of the processing cost with reference to quantity ordered is shown in Fig. 5.3. It is quite clear that the processing cost will be inversely proportional to the quantity ordered and purchased.

As far the inventory carrying cost is concerned it will be directly proportional to the quantity of the material and hence the variation of the inventory carrying cost with reference to the quantity is as shown in Fig. 5.4.

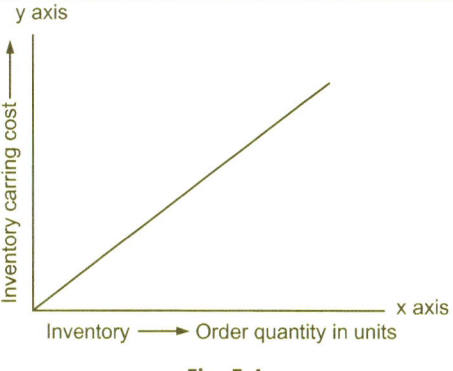

Fig. 5.4

The total inventory cost is therefore the sum of the processing cost and the inventory carrying cost and hence the variation of the total cost with reference to the quantity is as shown in Fig. 5.5.

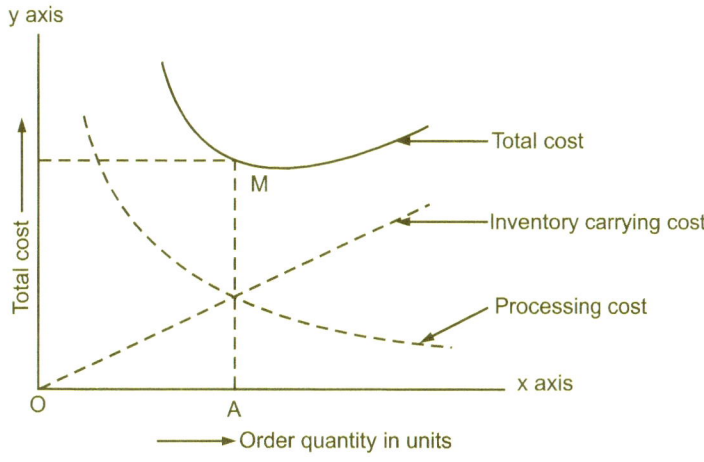

Fig. 5.5

At some point A for the quantity ordered the processing cost and the inventory carrying cost are balanced and are equal. The total inventory cost curve as shown in the figure is drawn by adding the inventory carrying cost and the processing cost i.e. adding the ordinates of the two graphs. It is found from the total cost curve that at point A where the processing cost and the inventory carrying costs are balanced, the total cost is minimum as represented by the point M on the total cost curve. This unit of quantity represented by the point A is, therefore, the quantity lot size for which the total cost is minimum and hence this quantity is called **Economic Order Quantity**. The Economic Order Quantity is, therefore, one for which the processing cost and the inventory carrying costs are equal and the total cost is minimum as represented by point M on the total cost curve and point A on the abssise. The economic order quantity will depend upon unit cost of the material, acquisition cost per order and the carrying cost. The mathematical expression for the Economic Order Quantity can be derived as below. Inventory model in general situation is with the assumption that the demand rate is uniform and the production rate or the rate of usage is infinite. The model is as shown in the Fig. 5.6.

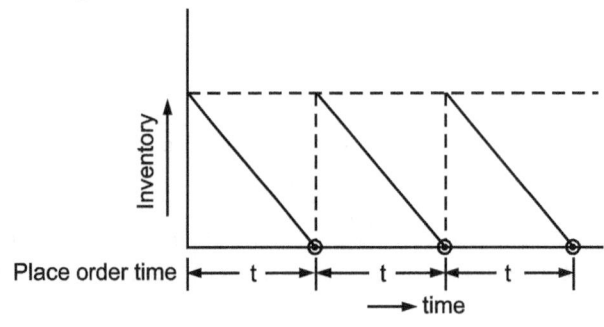

Fig. 5.6

For a particular project or production a particular material is required. The monthly demand of the material is fixed and as soon as the stock of the material is used up a new lot is immediately supplied or refilled. The cost of inventory is proportional to the amount of inventory as well as the time the inventory is held. The Material Manager has to decide :

- How many units of the material be ordered ?
- How frequently the material be reordered ?

As discussed earlier, the economic order quantity will be one for which the inventory cost and the processing cost will balance so that the total cost is minimum.

Let C_o = Ordering or Processing cost of the commodity per order in ₹

= Procurement cost – Actual cost of material.

C_u = Unit cost of commodity i.e. Cost per unit in ₹.

S = Annual requirement of commodity in number of lots.

Q = Economical Order Quantity in units or lots per order.

I = Inventory carrying cost percentage.

It is percentage of cost of inventory.

C_T = Total Inventory Cost.

Since the demand rate i.e. consumption rate is uniform the complete stock is used in the time specified and as such to start with the inventory is Q and at the end it reduces to zero.

Hence, Average inventory = $\dfrac{Q + 0}{2} = \dfrac{Q}{2}$

∴ Total Yearly requirement = S units

and each lot ordered is Q.

Hence, Number of orders placed per year = $\dfrac{S}{Q}$

∴ [Ordering Cost or Processing Cost per year] = [Cost per order × Number of orders placed per year]

∴ $C_p = C_o \times \dfrac{S}{Q}$ ... (5.1)

Annual Carrying Cost = Total inventory cost × Inventory carrying cost percentage

= (Average inventory × Purchase cost per unit × Carrying cost percentage infraction)

$C_I = \left(\dfrac{Q}{2} \times C_u\right) \times I = \dfrac{Q C_u I}{2}$ ... (5.2)

Hence, Total Cost per year = Annual Procuring Cost + Inventory Cost

$C_T = \dfrac{C_o S}{Q} + \dfrac{Q C_u I}{2}$ ... (5.3)

The graphical representation of the equation (5.1), (5.2) and (5.3) are shown in Fig. 5.7.

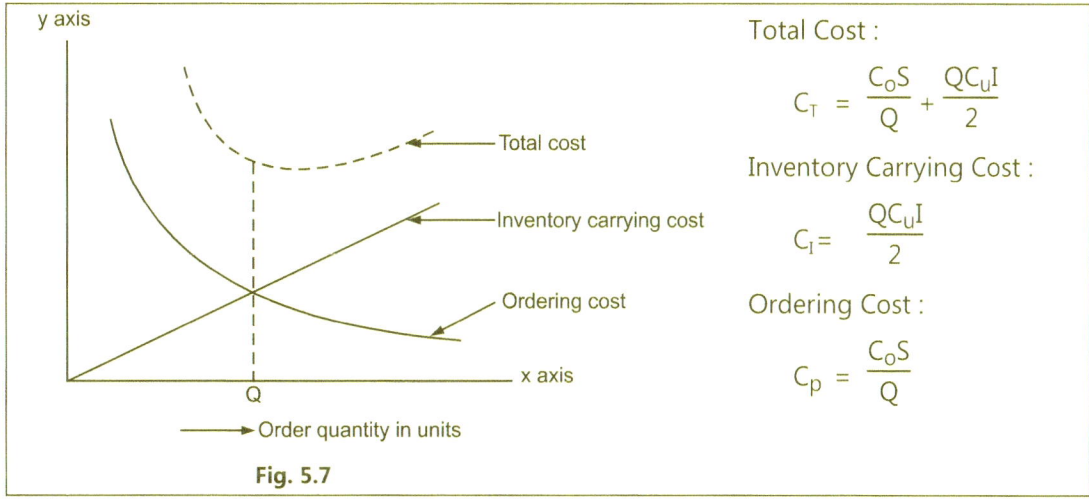

Fig. 5.7

Total Cost:

$C_T = \dfrac{C_o S}{Q} + \dfrac{Q C_u I}{2}$

Inventory Carrying Cost:

$C_I = \dfrac{Q C_u I}{2}$

Ordering Cost:

$C_p = \dfrac{C_o S}{Q}$

For a particular optimum value Q the total cost C_T is minimum which is 'Economical Ordering Quantity'.

$C_T = \dfrac{C_o S}{Q} + \dfrac{Q C_u I}{2}$

For C_T to be minimum,

$$\frac{dC_T}{dQ} = 0 \text{ and } \frac{d^2C_T}{dQ^2} = +ve$$

$$C_T = \frac{C_o S}{Q} + \frac{Q C_u I}{2}$$

∴ $$\frac{dC_T}{dQ} = \frac{-C_o S}{Q^2} + \frac{C_u I}{2}$$

$$= 0$$

i.e. $$\frac{C_o S}{Q^2} = \frac{C_u I}{2}$$

i.e. $$Q^2 = \frac{2 C_o S}{C_u I}$$

$$Q = \sqrt{\frac{2 C_o S}{C_u I}}$$

∴ Economical Order Quantity

$$Q_{optimum} = \sqrt{\frac{2 C_o S}{C_u I}}$$

Also, $$\frac{d^2 C_T}{dQ^2} = \frac{2 C_o S}{Q^3} + 0$$

$$= +ve \text{ Quantity}$$

Hence, $$Q_{optimum} = \sqrt{\frac{2 C_o S}{C_u I}}$$

Example 5.1 : Yearly requirement of cement by a large firm is 240 bags. The cost of a bag of cement is ₹ 200/-, Lead time is one month and the ordering cost per order is ₹ 120/-. Assume Annual Carrying Cost for inventory 20% of Average Inventory Management. Find out the Economical Order Quantity and the Total Inventory Cost.

Solution :

1. Yearly Total Requirement of Cement = 240 bags

   Cost of one bag = ₹ 200

   Annual cost = 200 × 240

   = 48,000 ₹

2.   Lead time = 1 month
Number of orders = 12

3.   Number of bags per month = $\dfrac{240}{12}$
= 20

4.   Ordering Cost = No. of orders × 20
= 12 × 20 = ₹ 240

5.   Order Quantity in ₹ = Cost of 1 bag × No. of bags
= 20 × 200 = 4000 ₹

6.   Average inventory usage = $\dfrac{0 + 4000}{2}$
= ₹ 2000/-

7.   Inventory Carrying Cost = Usage in ₹ × 0.2
= ₹ 2000 × 0.2 = ₹ 400

8.   Total Cost = Ordering Cost + Carrying Cost
= ₹ 240 + ₹ 400 = ₹ 640

Varying the number of orders the total inventory cost is calculated as per example given and is tabulated as below :

Annual No. of Orders (a)	Ordering Cost b = a × 20	No. of Boys Per Order c = $\dfrac{240}{a}$	Cost Account in ₹ Per Order d = c × 200	Inventory Usage e = $\dfrac{0 + d}{2}$	Inventory Carrying Cost f = e × 0.2	Total Cost g = b + g	Remark for Ordering
1	20	240	48,000	24,000	4,800	4,820	Once in year
2	40	120	24,000	12,000	2,400	2,440	Six Monthly
4	80	60	12,000	6,000	1,200	1,280	Quarterly
8	160	30	6,000	3,000	600	760	After $1^1/2$ month
12	240	20	4,000	2,000	400	640	Monthly
16	320	15	3,000	1,500	300	620	Every 3 weeks
24	480	10	2,000	1,000	200	680	Fortnightly
48	960	5	1,000	500	100	1,060	Weekly
60	1200	4	800	400	80	1,280	–

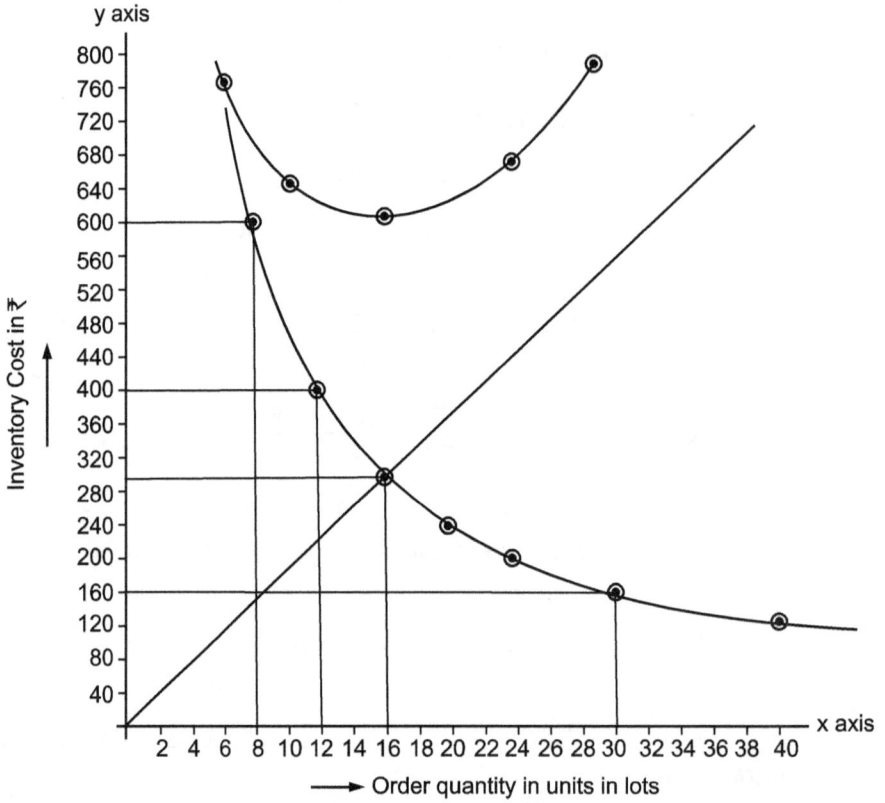

Fig. 5.8

Mathematically,

EOQ $\quad Q = \sqrt{\dfrac{2 C_o S}{C_u I}}$

Where, $\quad C_o$ = Ordering Cost = ₹ 20

S = Total annual demand item in number = 240

I = Annual Carrying Cost for inventory = 0.2

C_u = Unit Cost of item = ₹ 200/- per bag

∴ $\quad Q = \sqrt{\dfrac{2 \times 20 \times 240}{200 \times 0.2}}$

$\quad = 15.49$ say 16

No. of orders = $\dfrac{\text{Annual usage}}{Q}$

$$= \frac{240}{15.49}$$

$$= 15.49 \text{ say } 16$$

No. of bags per order $= \frac{240}{16} = 15$

For this, Ordering cost $= 16 \times 20 = 320$

Inventory usage $= \frac{200 \times 15 + 0}{2}$

$$= ₹ 1500$$

Annual Inventory Carrying Cost

$$= 1500 \times 0.2$$

$$= ₹ 300/-$$

∴ Total Inventory Cost $= ₹ 320 + ₹ 300$

$$= ₹ 620/-$$

From the total cost curve it can be seen that if 16 orders are placed in an year the total inventory cost is minimum.

Frequency of ordering $= \frac{365}{16}$

$$= 23 \text{ days}$$

Example 5.2 : A stockist has to supply 200 units of a commodity to his customer every week. The cost rate is ₹ 100/- per unit from the manufacturer and the ordering cost is ₹ 200/- per order. The carrying cost of invention is 20% per year of the cost of inventory. Find the economical order quantity and yearly expense over the commodity.

Solution :

C_o = Ordering Cost per lot ₹ 200/-

S = Total annual requirement of item

$= 200 \times 52 = 10400$ units

I = Annual Carrying Cost

$= 20\%$

$= 0.2$

C_u = Unit Cost of item

$= ₹ 100/-$ unit

$$\therefore \quad Q = \sqrt{\frac{2\,C_o\,S}{C_u\,I}}$$

$$= \sqrt{\frac{2 \times 200 \times (200 \times 52)}{100 \times 0.2}}$$

$$= 456.07 \text{ units}$$

$$\therefore \quad \text{No. of orders} = \frac{200 \times 52}{456}$$

$$= 22.8 \text{ say } 23$$

$$\text{Frequency of order} = \frac{365}{23} = 15.8 \text{ days}$$

Hence, order will have to be placed after every 16th day.

$$\text{Total cost of inventory} = \text{Processing Cost} + \text{Carrying Cost}$$

$$= 23 \times 200 + \frac{456 \times 100}{2} \times 0.2$$

$$= 4600 + 4560$$

$$= ₹9160$$

$$\therefore \quad \text{Total Expenses yearly} = (200 \times 52) \times 100 + 9610$$

$$= 10{,}40{,}000 + 9{,}610$$

$$= ₹10{,}49{,}610 \text{ year.}$$

Example 5.3 : A construction company requires 1500 door frames per year. Cost of each door frame is ₹ 1800 per frame. Ordering Cost is ₹ 2000 per order and holding cost is 18%. Calculate EOQ. **[May 11] [4]**

Solution :

$$EOQ = \sqrt{\frac{2 \times C_o S}{C_u}}$$

C_u = Unit cost = ₹ 1,800/- per frame
S = Annual requirement = 1500
I = Inventory carrying cost = 18%
C_o = Order cost = ₹ 2000 per order

$$EOQ = \sqrt{\frac{2 \times 2000 \times 1500}{1800 \times 0.18}}$$

$$= 136 \text{ units}$$

$$\therefore \quad \text{No. of orders} = \frac{1500}{136} \doteq 11$$

Example 5.4 : A construction company purchases 10,000 bags of cement annually. Each bag of cement cost ₹ 300/- and cost incurred in procurring each lot is ₹ 150/-. The cost of carrying is 25%. What is the most Economic Order Quantity? What is the average inventory level? **[May 11] [6]**

Solution :

C_u = Unit cost = 300

S = Annual requirement = 10,000

I = Inventory carrying cost = 25%

C_o = ₹ 150

$$E.O.Q = \sqrt{\frac{2 \times C_o S}{C_u I}}$$

$$= \sqrt{\frac{2 \times 150 \times 10000}{300 \times 0.25}}$$

$$= 40$$

∴ No. of orders = $\frac{10000}{40}$ = 250

Average inventory = $\frac{40 + 0}{2}$ = 20

Example 5.5 : A supplier has to supply 400 units of a commodity to his customer every week. The cost rate is ₹ 200 per unit and ordering cost is ₹ 200 per order. The carrying cost of inventory is 20% per year of the cost of inventory. Find Economical Order Quantity.

[Dec. 12] [4]

Solution :

$$EOQ = \sqrt{\frac{2 \times C_o S}{C_u I}}$$

C_u = Unit cost = ₹ 200/- per unit

S = Annual requirement = 400 × 52 weeks

I = Inventory carrying cost = 0.2

C_o = ₹ 200 per order

∴ $$EOQ = \sqrt{\frac{2 \times 200 \times 20800}{200 \times 0.2}}$$

= 456 per order

∴ No. of orders = $\frac{20800}{456}$ = 45.6 = 46 orders

5.9 SAFETY STOCK

There may be certain uncertainties in the demand and delay in supply and to take the account of such uncertainties some stock of material is necessary over and above the usual demand. This stock is called *safety stock*.

The uncertainties may be due to any of the following reasons :

- Fluctuations in rate of consumption or demand,
- Production or Utilisation delay,
- Variation in lead time.

If safetystock is not maintained it may lead to stockout. This situation may create undesirable situation such as :

(a) Loss of customer service in case of finished goods. This will lead to indirect cost. This may occur in case of sale in shops.

(b) In case of production unit not having the material when needed will result in shortfall or delay in production.

It is, therefore, essential that some buffer stock or safety stock be maintained and there should be positive minimum inventory. At the time of placing an order the following condition should exist :

Inventory at hand + Quantity ordered = Safety stock + Forecasted demand over the lead time

Hence, Safety stock = Inventory at hand + Ordered quantity − Forecasted demand over lead time

Thus, the amount of buffer stock depends upon the lead time and accuracy of forecast of demand. Some buffer stock has to be maintained but it should be borne in mind that the policy of never missing out of stock will demand over stock and will prove to be very costly. To strike a golden mean between no stock and overstock, it is essential to set some level of assurance and decide the safety stock accordingly. Higher the level of assurance, high will be buffer stock and will run into higher inventory cost.

5.10 LEAD TIME [May-11, Nov./Dec.-11,12]

It is the period lapsed between the time of material ordered and the time the material is received. Material cannot be received instantaneously and sometimes is lapsed for the necessary operations for effecting the order by the supplier and this is why it is necessary to keep inventories in stock. The concepts of replenishment period, reorder point and the lead time is almost the same. Lead time determines the amount of material to be kept in reserve.

As the lead time increases the required stock also increases. Hence attempt should be made to reduce the lead period.

Lead time consists of :

- Time to process the demand and place the order.
- Time to deliver the order to the supplier.
- Time for the supplier to fill the order.
- Time for the order to be shipped by the vendor and material to be received.

Approximate Lead time for different building materials :

Sr. No.	Type of Material	Lead Time
1.	Cement	1 week
2.	Steel	2 weeks
3.	Door frames wood / M.S.	2 weeks
4.	Sanla, P.O.P	1 week
5.	Gypsum	2 weeks
6.	Granite, Kudappah	1 week
7.	Flooring tiles, Wall tiles	2 months
8.	C.P. and Sanitary wares	2 months
9.	Plumbing materials	2 weeks
10.	Door shutters	2 weeks
11.	Door fittings	1 week
12	Electrical wires, Switches	1 month

5.10.1 Parts of Lead Time

Lead time consist of 2 parts :

Administrative lead time

Suppliers lead time

1. **Administrative Lead Time :**

   This is the time elapsed between need of inventory and fulfillment of the need. So following activities are involved that decides administrative lead time.

   - Ordering/Procurement procedure : If the procedure is well defined, lead time decreases.

- Approvals for purchase.
- Communicating the requirement to the supplier.
- Reminders sent to supplier.

2. **Suppliers Lead Time :**

This is the time elapsed between supplier receiving the order and the inventory is received on site. Suppliers lead time consists of the following activities :

- Type of material : For normal material, stock may be available but for special materials, more time is required.
- Stock in hand with supplier.
- Distance between warehouse and the site.

5.11 INVENTORY MODELS

5.11.1 Introduction

It is the representation of variation of stock level of items against time. It represents the behaviour of an item during the period of its issue from the stock and replenishment. Design of the inventory made is based upon the data received from the use of the item earlier. A well designed model works out successfully in practice and is also effective in keeping the inventory cost minimum and also avoiding the stock out or atleast reducing it to minimum. Three types of models are generally used. They are :

1. The Wilson's Model.
2. Replenishment Model.
3. The Two Bin Model.

In all the above models a uniform rate of consumption and instantaneous replenishment is assumed and in general, therefore, inventory consumption forms a saw-tooth figure.

5.11.2 Willson's Model

It is also called Fixed Reorder Point Model. It is represented by Fig. 5.9. In this, there is an inventory cycle which repeats itself, the dimensions of the cycle remaining constant. The demand is assumed to be constant and lead time for each cycle is same.

The replenishment order is placed for Economical Order Quantity. An order is placed in such a manner that the material from the supplier reaches exactly when the stock of the inventory reduces to zero level.

In the figure A, B, C are the reorder points and L is the lead time. The reorder is placed at a fixed inventory level and hence this model is called *Fixed Reorder Point Model*.

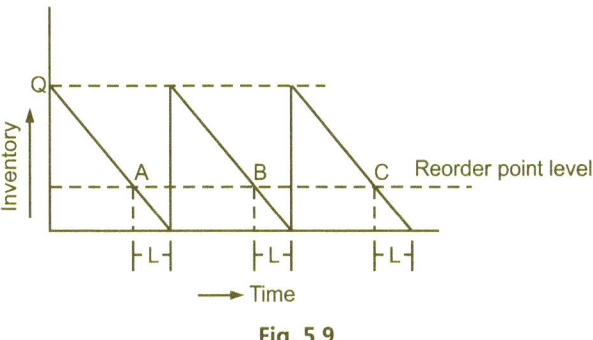

Fig. 5.9

This model is useful but has following drawbacks :

1. If due to any reason demand is increased above average assumed, particularly in lead time, stock out may occur.
2. Lead time has been assumed to be constant. If lead time due to some reason in a cycle extends and becomes more than average, stock out is imminent.

To modify this model a buffer stock or safety stock is introduced. This model is represented in Fig. 5.10. This may eliminate the condition of stock out or occurrence of such conditions will get reduced depending upon the size of buffer stock. This model works in somewhat realistic way and works successfully. This model is extensively used in practice for regularly issued item of class A or class B.

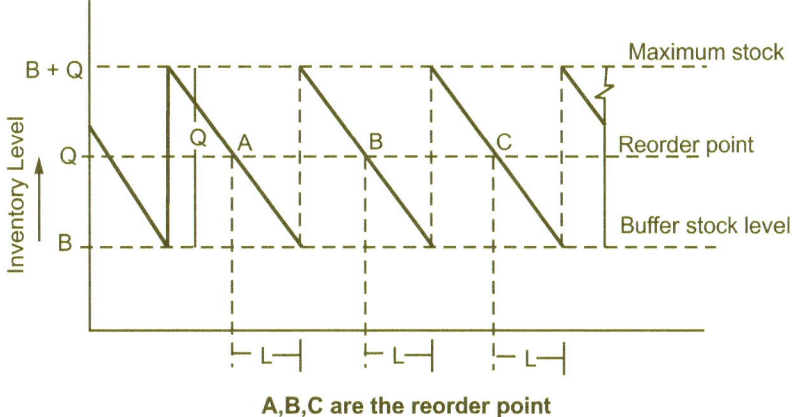

A, B, C are the reorder point

Fig. 5.10

The buffer stock level is B and if L is the lead time and s_d is the average demand the Reorder point level of inventory would be $B + Ls_d$.

When the inventory is replenished the level will be $B + Q$ where Q is the Economic Order Quantity.

5.11.3 Replenishment Model

In this model, review is taken at intervals and the reorder quantity changes at each review. However, the maximum inventory level is fixed on the basis of the previous data of demand and the order is placed for the quantity equal to (Maximum Inventory − Inventory at hand) at each review. This model is generally used for B class items and also for lower A class items.

This model is illustrated in Fig. 5.11.

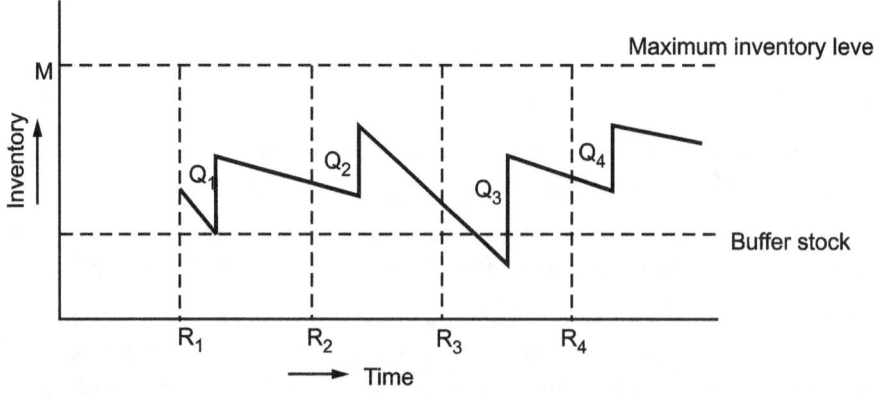

Fig. 5.11

In this model, the demand rate is not uniform and the actual demand rate is taken into consideration.

5.11.4 Two Bin Model

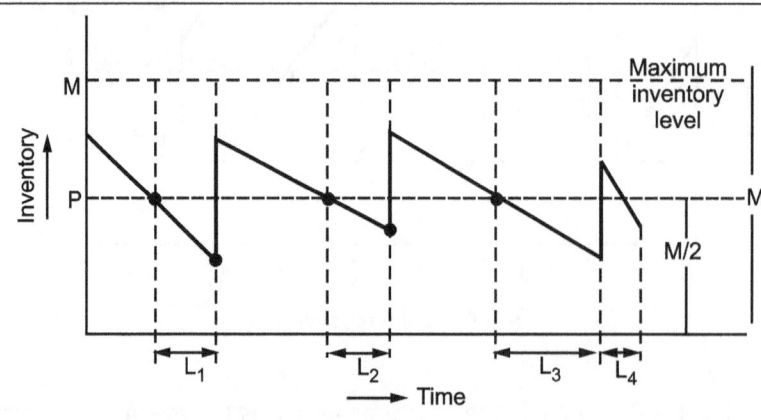

Fig. 5.12

Here, $$Q = \frac{M}{2} = I = P = \frac{M}{2}$$

The simplest of all the models is the two bin model. In this method of reordering the demand rate is not uniform and the lead time also may not be constant. An order is placed when inventory at hand falls to the half of the maximum inventory and hence the order quantity will be $\frac{M}{2}$ every time. Inventory at hand is always more than half the maximum inventory and hence the inventory cost is high as the inventory is quite large. Hence, this is used for C class items where there is low investment and severe control is not necessary. This is used for items like screws, nut bolts etc.

5.12 ABC ANALYSIS [Nov./Dec.-11]

It is one of the methods used effectively to control the inventory. It has been generally found that a small percentage of the total number of items carried in inventory constitutes the bulk of the inventory investments.

If an analysis is carried out in terms of yearly consumption in value, it is found that 10 per cent of the items which are repeatedly used are costing 70 per cent of annual consumptive cost, 20 per cent of the items may account for 20 per cent of the annual consumptive cost and the remaining 70 per cent of the items amount for costing roughly only 10 per cent of the total annual cost.

The 10 per cent of the item costing 70 per cent of the annual expenditure are vital items and are classified as A items and they need careful and full record keeping. The medium consumption items with 20 per cent consumption costing 20 per cent of expenditure are grouped under B class items and all the remaining 70 per cent of the items costing only 10 per cent expenditure are classified as C class items. The items in C class are many in numbers and for such items inventory may be kept as low as possible and least expenditure may be made on their inventory.

Items under group B are less important than items in group A but are more important than those in group C. They should be given medium inventory treatment and they need standard record keeping and maximum stock limits.

For items in group C standard formalities may not be observed and a watch kept at the level of such items is enough. It is also generally recommended that all A items should be reviewed every month, B items every three months and C items every six months.

It should be emphasized, however, that the use and employment of A – B – C analysis greatly reduces the possibility of error in such judgement by clearly pointing out the specific items on which management can profitably concentrate its efforts.

It is important to note that A – B – C analysis does not depend on the unit cost of the items but it is the annual cost consumption which is important. The A – B – C analysis can be represented by graphs as shown in Fig. 5.13 and Fig. 5.14.

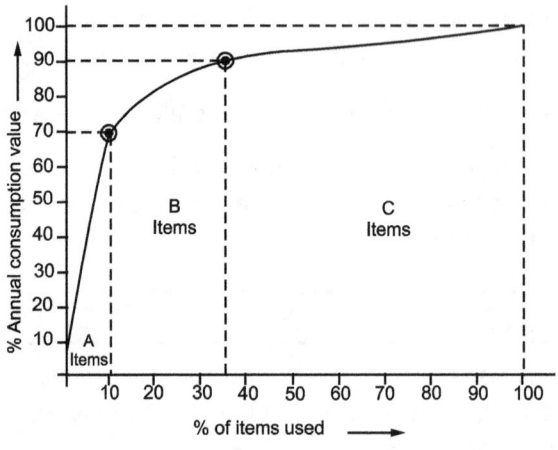

Fig. 5.13

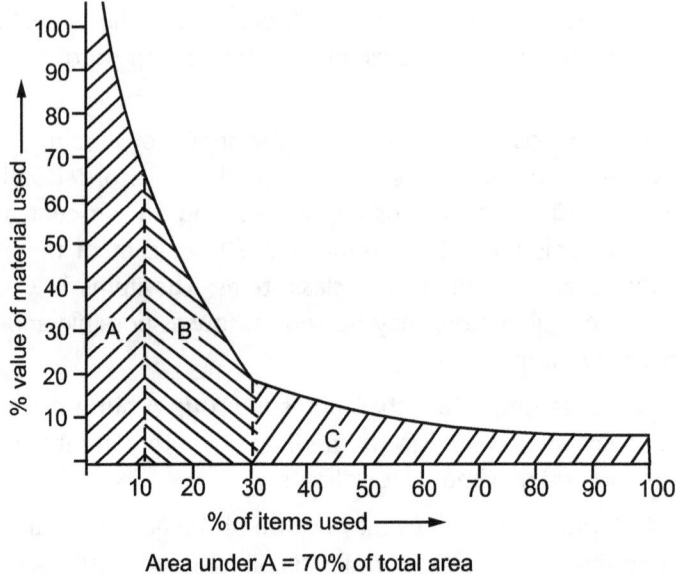

Area under A = 70% of total area
Area under B = 30% of total area
Area under C = 10% of total area

Fig. 5.14

Example 5.6 : Prepare A, B, C ranking of the different items for the data given below from a store :

Item No.	Annual Consumption in unit	Unit Cost	Annual Consumption Value in ₹	Rank
101	14,000	2.00	28,000	V
102	1,50,000	2.40	3,60,000	I
103	1,500	1.80	2,700	VIII
104	52,500	2.80	1,47,000	II
105	2,500	1.60	4,000	VII
106	80,000	1.40	1,12,000	III
107	7,500	3.0	22,500	VI
108	35,000	2.20	77,000	IV

Solution :

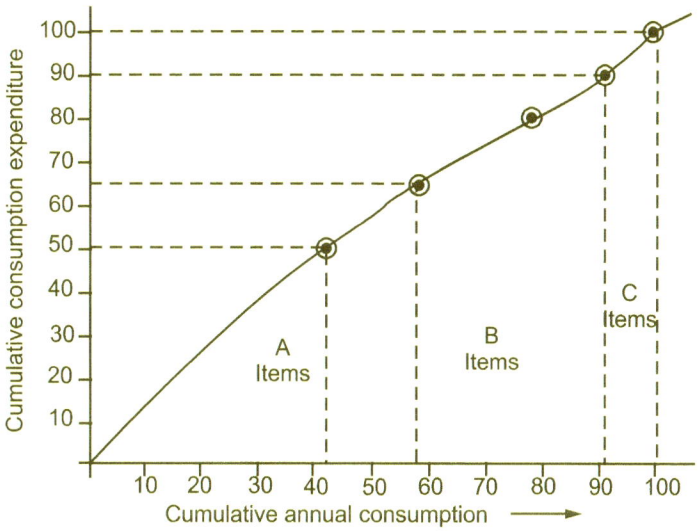

Fig. 5.15

Item No.	Actual Expenditure	Cumulative Expenditure	Expenditure	Class
102	3,60,000	3,60,000	47.8	A
104	1,47,000	5,07,000	67.3	A
106	1,12,000	6,19,000	82.2	B
108	77,000	6,96,000	92.4	B
101	28,000	7,24,000	96.1	C
107	22,500	7,46,500	99.1	C
105	4,000	7,50,000	99.6	C
103	2,700	7,53,200	100	C

Example 5.7 : Following table shows the annual consumption of the items used in a project and their unit cost. Classify them in A, B, C classes and plot the ABC analysis curve.

Sr. No.	Describing Item	Annual Consumption	Unit Cost (₹)
1	Cement	1000 bags	150/bag
2	Sand	3000 m³	15/m³
3	Tor steel	2000 kg	27/kg
4	Mild steel	3000 kg	24/kg
5	10 mm aggregate	3000 m³	18.5/m³
6	20 mm aggregate	3000 m³	15/m³
7	Formwork Plywood	100 m²	150/m²
8	Nails	100 kg	15/kg
9	Oil for cleaning	20 litres	80/litre
10	Water	40 litres	70/litre

Solution :

Following tables are prepared and class is decided :

Sr. No.	Description	Annual Consumption	Unit Costs	Annual Expenditure	Rank
1	Cement	1000 bags	150/bag	1,50,000	1
2	Sand	3000 m^3	15/m^3	45,000	6
3	Tor Steel	2000 kg	27/kg	54,000	4
4	Mild Steel	3000 kg	24/kg	86,400	2
5	10 mm aggregate	3000 m^3	18.5/m^3	55,500	3
6	20 mm aggregate	3000 m^3	15/m^3	45,000	5
7	Form work plywood	100 m^2	150/m^2	15,000	7
8	Nails	100 kg	15/kg	1,500	10
9	Oil for cleaning	20 litres	80/litre	1,600	9
10	Water	40 litres	70/litre	2,800	8

Sr. No. of Rank	Description	Annual Consumption	Annual Expenditure ₹	Cumulative Annual Exp. ₹	% Cumulative Annual Exp.	Class
1	Cement	1,000	1,50,000	1,50,000	32.8	A
2	Mild Steel	3,000	86,400	2,36,400	51.6	A
3	Tor Steel	2,000	54,000	2,90,400	63.60	A
4	10 mm aggregate	3,000	55,500	3,45,900	75.7	B
5	20 mm aggregate	3,000	45,000	3,90,900	85.6	B
6	Sand	3,000	45,000	4,35,000	95.4	C
7	Formwork Plywood	100	15,000	4,50,900	98.7	C
8	Water	40	2,800	4,53,700	99.3	C
9	Oil for cleaning	20	1,600	4,55,300	99.70	C
10	Nails	100	1,500	4,56,800	100	C

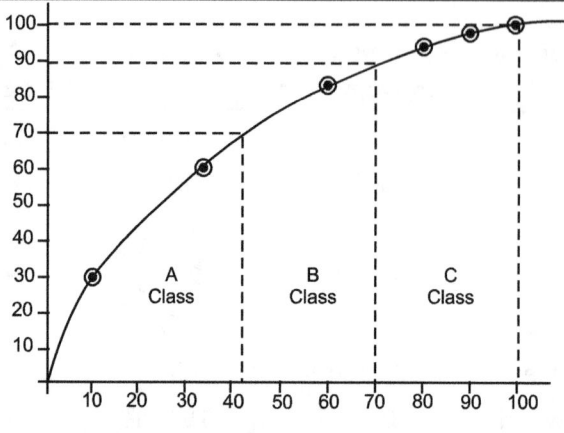

Fig. 5.16

Example 5.8 : Perform ABC Analysis for the following data :

Sr. No.	Item	Annual Expenditure (₹)
1.	Cement	4,90,000
2.	Tiles	90,000
3.	Bricks	95,000
4.	Sand	2,60,000
5.	Steel	1,20,000
6.	Oil	2,000
7.	Timber	30,000
8.	Nails	3,000
9.	Dry distemper	15,000

Categorise the above items and plot ABC curve. **[May 11] [12]**

Solution : Arrange the items as per descending order of their costs.

Sr. No.	Item	Annual Expenditure	Cum. Annual exp.	Cum. % Cost	% Items	A/B/C
1.	Cement	4,90,000	4,90,000	44.3	11.1	A
2.	Sand	2,60,000	7,50,000	67.87	22.2	A
3.	Steel	1,20,000	8,70,000	78.7	33.3	B
4.	Bricks	95,000	9,65,000	87.3	44.4	B
5.	Tiles	90,000	10,55,000	95.47	55.5	C
6.	Timber	30,000	10,85,000	98.19	66.6	C
7.	Dry distemper	15,000	11,00,000	99.55	77.7	C
8.	Nails	3,000	11,03,000	99.82	88.8	C
9.	Oil	2,000	11,05,000	100	100	C

Example 5.9 : Carry out A-B-C analysis for the following construction items. The estimated annual consumption of each item in terms of its cost is given below. Represent the results in a graphical form also. **[Dec. 11] [10]**

Sr. No.	Item Description	Amount (₹)
1.	Cement	3,89,800
2.	Sand	80,000
3.	Aggregate (course)	1,10,000
4.	Steel reinforcement	1,50,000
5.	Bricks	1,40,000
6.	Timber	60,000
7.	Mosaic Tiles	85,000
8.	PVC fittings	25,000
9.	Wash basin	16,000
10.	Stoppers for door	1,000
11.	Electrical items	3,000
12.	Admixtures	10,000

Solution : Arranging the materials in descending order of their costs.

Sr. No.	Item	Cost	Cum. Cost	% Cum. Cost	% Items	A/B/C
1.	Cement	3,89,800	3,89,800	36.4	8.33	A
2.	Steel Reinforcement	1,50,000	5,39,800	50.46	16.67	A
3.	Bricks	1,40,000	6,79,800	63.54	25	A
4.	Aggregate	1,10,000	7,89,800	73.83	33.33	A
5.	Mosaic tiles	85,000	8,74,800	81.77	41.67	B
6.	Sand	80,000	9,54,800	89.25	50	B
7.	Timber	60,000	10,14,800	94.86	58.33	C
8.	PVC fitting	25,000	10,39,800	97.2	66.67	C
9.	Wash basin	16,000	10,55,800	98.69	75	C
10.	Admixtures	10,000	10,65,800	99.63	83.33	C
11.	Electrical items	3,000	10,68,800	99.90	91.67	C
12.	Stoppers for door	1,000	10,69,800	100.00	100	C

Students should plot the graph of % items Vs % cumulative cost and show A, B and C type of materials.

Example 5.10 : Carry out ABC analysis for the following items and plot ABC curve.

[May 12] [10]

Item No.	Item	Annual Expenditure (₹)
1.	Cement	5,00,000
2.	Sand	3,00,000
3.	Bricks	1,00,000
4.	Siporex Blocks	2,50,000
5.	Paint	60,000
6.	Steel	4,50,000
7.	Tiles	70,000
8.	Oil	2,000
9.	Course Aggregate	95,000
10.	Electrical fitting	50,000
11.	Nails	1,500
12.	Timber	42,000

Solution : Arrange all the materials in descending order of their annual expenditure.

	Item	Annual Expenditure	Cu. Annual Exp.	% Cu. Exp.	A/B/C	% Items
1.	Cement	5,00,000	5,00,000	26.00	A	8.33
2.	Steel	4,50,000	9,50,000	49.5	A	16.67
3.	Sand	3,00,000	12,50,000	65.1	A	25
4.	Siporex blocks	2,50,000	15,00,000	78.0	B	33.33
5.	Bricks	1,00,000	16,00,000	83.0	B	41.67
6.	Coarse aggregate	95,000	16,95,000	88.3	B	50
7.	Tiles	70,000	17,65,000	92	B	58.33
8.	Paint	60,000	18,25,000	95	C	66.67
9.	Electrical fitting	50,000	18,75,000	97.6	C	75
10.	Timber	42,000	19,17,000	99.8	C	83.33
11.	Oil	2,000	19,19,000	99.9	C	91.67
12.	Nails	1,500	19,20,500	100	C	100

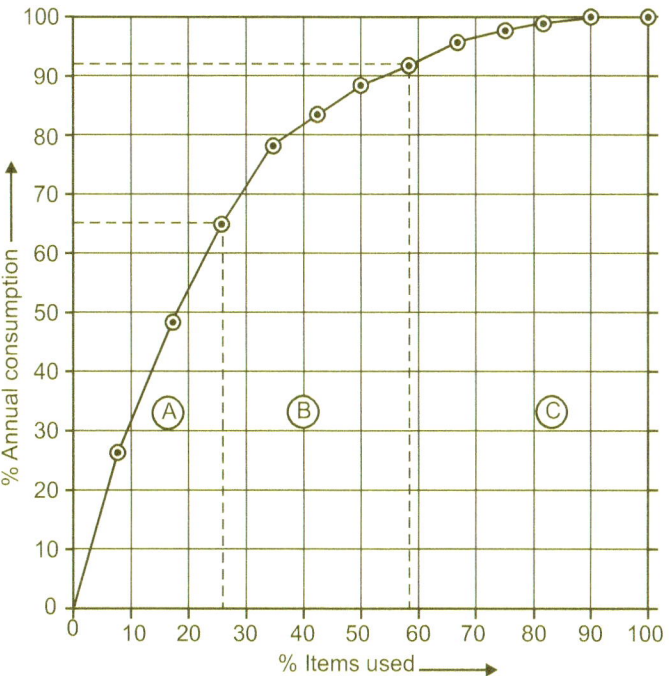

Fig. 5.17 : ABC curve

Example 5.11 : Following table shows the annual consumption of the items used in a project and their unit cost. Classify them in A, B, C classes and plot ABC curve.

[Dec. 12] [12]

Sr. No.	Item	Annual Consumption	Unit cost in ₹
1.	Water	80 litres	20/litre
2.	Cement	2000 bags	300/bag
3.	Fly ash	50 kg	150/kg
4.	Tor steel	4000 kg	50/kg
5.	Mild steel	2000 kg	38/kg
6.	Nails	100 kg	15/kg
7.	12 mm Aggregate	3000 m³	20/m³
8.	20 mm Aggregate	3000 m³	19/m³
9.	Oil	10 litres	100/litre
10.	Sand	3000 m³	20/m³

Solution : The cost of each item is as follows :

Sr. No.	Item	Annual Consumption	Number as Per Descending Order
		(₹)	
1.	Water	1,600	⑧
2.	Cement	6,00,000	①
3	Fly ash	7,500	⑦
4.	Tor steel	2,00,000	②
5.	Mild steel	76,000	③
6.	Nails	1,500	⑨
7.	12 mm Aggregates	60,000	④
8.	20 mm Aggregates	57,000	⑥
9.	Oil	1,000	⑩
10.	Sand	60,000	⑤

Rewrite all the materials alongwith their costs in descending order of costs.

Sr. No.	Item	Cost	Cumulative Cost	% Cu. Cost.		% Items
1.	Cement	6,00,000	6,00,000	56.35	A items	10
2.	TOR steel	2,00,000	8,00,000	75.14		20
3.	Mild steel	76,000	8,76,000	82.28	B items	30
4.	12 mm aggregate	60,000	9,36,000	87.92		40
5.	Sand	60,000	9,96,000	93.55		50
6.	20 mm aggregate	57,000	10,53,000	98.91	C items	60
7.	Fly ash	7,500	10,60,500	99.61		70
8.	Water	1,600	10,62,100	99.76		80
9.	Nails	1,500	10,63,600	99.91		90
10.	Oil	1,000	10,64,600	100		100

Students should draw graph of % items Vs % cumulative cost and show A, B and C materials on it.

Advantages of ABC Analysis

- Helps to exercise selective control.
- Gives result quickly, easy to understand.
- Helps to point out absolute stocks easily.
- Helps better planning of inventory control.
- Provides sound basis for allocation of funds and human resources.

Disadvantages of ABC Analysis

- Considers only money value of items and neglects the importance of items for the production process or functioning.
- Periodic review becomes difficult if any ABC analysis is used.
- Proper standardization and codification of inventory items are needed.
- When other important factors make it obligatory to concentrate on "C" items more, the purpose of ABC analysis is defeated.

5.13 AVOIDING MISUSE AND WASTAGE

The wastage of material varies from 2% to 10% depending upon construction activity. Also, sometimes materials are misused on site.

Misuse of the material may be due to the following :

1. Thefts.
2. Negligence.
3. Careless work.
4. Improper handling.
5. No or improper record keeping.
6. Storing in excess of the requirements.
7. Wastage.

Proper precautions may be taken to avoid misuse.

The wastage in general is again due to following reason.

1. Careless work : Wastage in consumption
2. Absence of planning : (a) Excess purchase and inventory
                                      (b) Wrong purchase

(c) Obsolescence

(d) Deterioration due to no use for long time.

3. Improper handling : (a) Improper storage

(b) Faulty storage

(c) Improper arrangement for transportation from store to the actual work site.

All the above causes of misuse and wastage can be avoided by adopting new techniques of materials management and proper procedures of purchasing, storing and handling. Capital cost locked in the purchase of materials can be reduced and in turn profits be increased.

5.14 FLEET MANAGEMENT

5.14.1 Introduction

Fleet management is the function that oversees, coordinates and facilitates various transport and transport related activities. It covers vehicles involved in the movement of goods; the management of light vehicle; fleets used in the transportation of people and light cargo. Vehicles are valuable assets and critical for business continuity. Especially, in construction field, very heavy vehicles are used. Around 10-20% of the total cost is contributed by vehicles and its operating cost. Proper fleet management will ensure optimizing this cost thus benefitting the organization. They therefore require adequate attention.

Effective fleet management aims at reducing and minimizing overall costs through maximum, cost effective utilization of resources such as vehicles, fuel, spare parts, etc.

The administration and financial management of fleet is very organisational specific. At a glance, some vehicles are restricted to specific projects, others are utilised in pools to serve all projects, some are strictly organisational driver driven and others self-staff driven and coordinated in pools.

5.14.2 Aspects of Fleet Management

- Identifying needs
- Acquisition Process
- Insurance
- Vehicle leasing (Internal and external)
- Vehicle Management
  - Fleet management systems
  - Vehicle maintenance and up-keep

- Vehicle usage
  - Vehicle disposal
- Health, Safety and Security
  - Complying with Legislature and security requirements
  - Drivers

- **Identifying Needs**

Identification of fleet needs is dependent on the nature of emergency and operations, and the size and area of operation. Vehicle selection criteria are guided by :

- uniformity of fleet;
- the appropriate vehicle type for local fuel availability;
- the purpose of the vehicle (type of material handled);
- the terrain in which the vehicle will operate;
- global acquisition cost;
- availability of local dealers;
- local availability of spare parts for the intended vehicle;
- warranties; and
- local availability of competent mechanics.

Depending on the level of emergency the criteria may vary.

- **Acquisition Process**
  - The general criteria for selection of a vehicle would be in conformity with the standard recommended vehicles.
  - The standard tender process is adopted for vehicles, as for all other goods and services, bulk items and items bought on a regular basis. In some cases, the process may result in outsourcing of some aspects of the vehicle management or leasing of vehicles.

- **Insurance**
  - Careful consideration should be given to the form of insurance selected for the vehicles belonging to the organisation. The minimum requirements of the law must always be complied with; this is usually at least third party cover.
  - To ensure compliance with the vehicle insurance requirements, all personnel using operation vehicles under the responsibility of the organisation must be fully conversant with accident and incident reporting procedures for vehicles and personal injury.

- Personnel requirements : the insurance cover for personnel will depend on the type of policy the organisation takes to cover its vehicles : third party, third party fire and theft, comprehensive or liability insurance.
- Rent or outsource : insurance coverage for leased or outsourced vehicles will be dependent upon what the organisation negotiates with the service provider. The organisation will either adopt the service providers insurance as-is or adopt it with amendments. An alternative is to completely outsource the fleet management, but again the type of insurance will be dependent upon what is negotiated with the service provider.

- **Vehicle leasing (internal and external)**

"A vehicle or asset lease is a contract by which one party lets vehicles or assets to another party for a specified period of time".

Or

"A lease is a written agreement by which one party agrees to let another party have the use of specified assets for a period of time for a fixed amount of money".

In an external leasing option, the ownership could :

- remain with the leasing company or entity, but the rights for use are passed on to the lessee for the period of the lease;
- in other cases, at the expiry of the lease, the ownership is transferred to the lessee; and
- The ownership remains with the lessee, but management of some aspects such as maintenance, could remain with the leasing company depending on negotiations.

In Internal leasing, the organisation itself owns the vehicles which are centrally managed and issued to programs on a cost recovery basis. Organisations therefore budget for leasing costs only.

Advantages of Leasing

- Routine repair or maintenance costs are built into leasing costs.
- No overheads in garage set-up and maintenance.
- No high initial purchase items in lessee's books.
- The leassor bears most of the risk.
- The organisation is able to focus on core business.

Disadvantages of leasing

- The organisation losses control of some aspects of its fleet management.
- Discontinuation of services by the service provider can cause huge disruptions in the day-to-day operations.

- If the leasing contract is cancelled for any reason, the organisation may have to make heavy investments in vehicle purchases or temporary hire to ensure business continuity.
- The organisation would not be able to build up any institutional capacity in fleet management.

- **Vehicle Management**
  - The location of the vehicle management function within organizations' structures varies from organisation to organisation. The management may be located within administration, transport function or have an independent fleet manager. For the purpose of the Logistics Operations Guide the manager will be referred to as the fleet manager (FM).
  - Vehicles are expensive but critical to an organisations' operation. They facilitate the movement of personnel and the delivery of relief supplies to beneficiaries. Vehicle management is also one of the aspects of supply management that can be easily abused if not properly managed. If properly managed this aspect would ensure :
    - availability of vehicles as and when required;
    - cost efficiency;
    - programme or response continuity;
    - staff safety;
    - safety on the roads;
    - vehicle safety;
    - vehicle security; and
    - performance management.

To achieve the above, some of the measures taken by the FM are :
- every vehicle carries a logbook;
- logbooks are checked on a weekly basis;
- vehicles are logged out and signed for before every trip. A vehicle allocation chart is recommended;
- the driver records all fuel and maintenance costs in the log book or fuel request and purchase voucher, indicating the reading on the odometer at the time of the expense;
- fuel can be purchased from a central petrol station and a receipt issued. Where there is no appointed petrol station, the vehicle fuel request form is completed and approved before funds are released for fuelling. Should the driver have to purchase fuel from their own funds or petty cash, the amount spent on the purchase will be reimbursed;

- all vehicle keys are surrendered at the end of the day;
- drivers adhere to the carrying capacity as provided by the traffic law;
- no unauthorized staff member is allowed to drive vehicles. Vehicles will be assigned at the discretion of the approving officer; and
- All new staff (those who have a driving license but have not driven for a specified period), will not be allowed to drive the organisation's vehicles unless accompanied by a qualified driver or have been re-tested by the registered automobile association and authorized to drive.

Fleet Management Systems

In recent times, to address problems in fleet management and the ever expanding need to monitor usage of vehicles, commercial organisations have designed automated control systems and other approaches to vehicle management. Simple management systems can be designed in-house for internal use to provide a good analysis of the vehicles and driver performance. Vehicle management systems are structured in a way that enables the capturing of information on various aspects of fleet usage, maintenance and operations. For example :

- distances travelled;
- destinations reached;
- distance travelled by vehicle showing official and private mileage;
- fuel consumption;
- repair and maintenance per vehicle;
- rate of consumption of spare parts; and
- servicing planned and completed.

The reports can be produced on a weekly, monthly or bi-monthly basis, depending on the needs of the organisation. Weekly reports may comprise a summary weekly refuelling by vehicle – which may highlight any exceptions to targets set per vehicle, whereas monthly reports may comprise :

- summary refuelling by vehicle and average fuel consumption;
- summary mileage per vehicle;
- repairs or maintenance; and
- any accidents.

Vehicle Maintenance and Up-Keep
Maintenance

Vehicles are regularly maintained for optimum performance, and kept in good repair. In emergency situations the Logistician is sometimes tasked with the responsibility of managing the vehicle fleet. To streamline vehicle management the FM should put in place a simple process. Such a process could entail the following :

Maintenance Options

There are three main options;

1. "In house maintenance" : performed using the facilities and staff of the organisation.
2. "Outsourced maintenance" : under taken by an outside contractor.
3. "Contract hire" : undertaken by an outside contractor as part of a vehicle operating system.

It will be necessary to review the operational requirements and match the most suitable form of maintenance to the individual operation. Whichever mix is selected, it must be preventative and must be under the control of a competent manager; if it is not, the condition of the vehicles may quickly decline and running costs may increase.

Maintenance Planning

Whichever maintenance options is followed, vehicle maintenance schedules must be drawn up together with, and published by the FM as part of the vehicle planning. All members of the management team must make a commitment to respecting the scheduled dates for maintenance.

A master vehicle inspection and servicing schedule should be drawn up for one year – a wall chart is recommended. This chart can also be used to show road tax renewal, annual inspection dates, etc.

The person responsible for the condition of the vehicles must decide the scope of the servicing work required and how often this should be carried out; taking into account the manufacturer's guidelines and kilometres travelled and in which type of environment the vehicle has been used.

Preventative Maintenance

This is done on a ongoing basis. This type of maintenance addresses the basic things that could cause a problem in vehicles if they are not properly maintained. The Logistician or FM develops an inspection check-list to be used by all drivers as a guide.

Each day, the first driver to use a vehicle will inspect the vehicle using the check-list.

Routine Maintenance

This type of maintenance is done on a monthly basis. It may cover the following :

- the vehicle supervisor should periodically organise a test drive each vehicle and report on its condition and also ensure that normal/regular service has been done for all vehicles;
- tyres : any abnormal wearing should be reported to the FM; and
- cleaning of the engine at least once a month.

In emergency situations, in the absence of local facilities, the organisation would have to undertake its own maintenance and ensure that :

- an experienced mechanic is hired;
- a secure workshop area is identified or set up;
- the necessary tool and equipment are available;
- there is continuous performance monitoring and a system for measuring and monitoring :
  - fleet performance;
  - costs and performance.

Selection of Garage

Based on the organization's needs, the criteria for selection of the right garage is set with the input of the Logistics officer and the FM, keeping in mind the organizations approved procurement procedures.

Basic Spare Parts in a Workshop

Should the organisation decide to manage its vehicle maintenance in-house, certain fast moving spares are recommended for stocking. This reduces vehicle down-time. The number of vehicles owned by the organisation will determine the purchase of these parts and equipment.

Maintenance Documentation

- Vehicle maintenance summary : whoever maintains the vehicles must make a detailed written servicing record report, listing the work done, parts and fluids used and costs incurred on each job. The FM must keep this on the individual vehicle file.
- Workshop job cards : when the written order is received, the workshop raises a workshop 'job card' for each vehicle entering for inspection, service or defect rectification. Work should not be carried out without a job card; each card should include the following information :
  - details of all work required to be carried out;
  - actual work carried out;
  - name of staff and hours worked;
  - details of spare parts and materials used; and
  - space for the cost of the work.

Once all relevant information has been taken from the job cards they should then be filed with the vehicle files.

- Vehicle Files and documentation : general vehicle correspondence files should be maintained for each vehicle. This file should contain the following documents to facilitate tracking of expenditure and maintenance :
    - copies of purchase request;
    - copy of internal service request;
    - copy of local purchase order;
    - invoice;
    - all important documentations (bill of lading, etc);
    - insurance papers;
    - copies of all repair bills;
    - job order;
    - accident report; and
    - fuel log-in sheets.
- **Vehicle Usage**

It is necessary to have a clearly defined policy regarding vehicle usage and staff benefits. Most organisations do not have the capacity to assign a driver for each vehicle that they own.

Under these circumstances, staff may be authorised to self drive, after testing. The vehicles would in most cases be pooled and rotated based on needs, except where a specific donor requirement conditions ties a vehicle to a specific project. For practical reasons, light vehicles are utilised for office operations and within urban settings and heavy vehicles for field based operations.

Vehicle Disposal

Running old vehicles may lead to high costs of maintenance and uneconomical fuel consumption. To avoid this, organisations should have approved and clearly stipulated policies and procedures on how and when to replace and dispose of vehicles/assets. The need to dispose may arise due to any of the following reasons :

- as a result of extensive unrepairable damage, or cost-prohibitive repairs;
- when the vehicle attains the stipulated mileage or years for disposal;
- when the vehicle is no longer economically sustainable;
- when the vehicle is no-longer required; and
- when programs downscale or shut down.

- **Health, Safety and Security**

Vehicle safety is one of the key roles of the FM. It leads to staff safety and enhances road safety. Legislature and security requirements are country specific and may relate to :
- driving authorisation documents;
- type of vehicle allowed;
- size of vehicles;
- communication equipments fitted into vehicles;
- duties and taxes;
- return of vehicles - some countries do not allow the re-export of vehicles;
- safety requirements; and
- vehicle jurisdiction - some vehicle cannot operate outside a specified area.

The key to successful observance of health and safety is the development of an organisational culture of awareness of, and compliance with health and safety issues. To ensure that this is possible the Health and Safety policy document must be practical and be incorporated within day to day tasks. Some organisations manage their own routine minor repairs and service workshops. Some basic health and safety measures for workshops would be :
- clear environments around work stations;
- completed risk assessments and action taken where risks are highlighted, i.e. warning tape on raised flooring;
- inductions;
- practice drills for fire evacuation; and
- availability of and mandatory use of safety equipment such a goggles, boots, gloves, etc.

Drivers

As part of fleet management it is necessary to divide drivers into categories based on skills and competence. Constant evaluation of their skills, regular training and refresher courses will improve driver and vehicle performance, reduce number of accidents and reduce maintenance costs. Each organization has the responsibility of identifying relevant training and courses available. These could be included in organizational capacity building programs for drivers.

5.15 PRODUCTIVITY STUDIES

The productivity of any construction equipment is a term that indicates how many units of output the equipment produces in an hour depending on the job conditions and management as well as the operators' skill, persistence and co-ordination with other construction forces. In simple terms, productivity refers to the ratio of output versus input.

Output here has to be of specified quality produced within scheduled time. Input are the resources deployed for achieving the desired output.

Productivity is useful as a relative measure of actual output of production compared to the actual input of resources, measured across time or against common entities. As output increases for a level of input, or as the amount of input decreases for a constant level of output, an increase in productivity occurs. Therefore, a "productivity measure" describes how well the resources of an organization are being used to produce input.

5.15.1 Types of Productivity

productivity can be More specifically classified depending upon its applications and degree as follows :

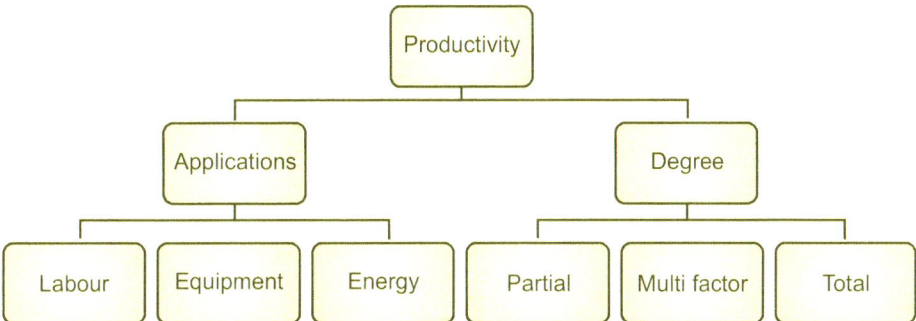

These types are briefly explained as below :

- **Labour Productivity** : Units of output per labor hour or Units of output per shift.
- **Equipment Productivity** : Units of output per machine hour or Output per unit machine.
- **Energy Productivity** : Units of output per kilowatt- hour or Rupee value of output per kilowatt-hour.
- **Partial Productivity** : It measures output against a specific input e.g. items made/employee. It is concerned with efficiency of one particular characteristic.
- **Multifactor Productivity** : It is ratio of output to a group of inputs such as labor and material. Hence, it is an index of output obtained from more than one of the resources used in production or service.

$$\text{Multifactor productivity} = \frac{\text{output}}{\text{labour + machine}} + \frac{\text{output}}{\text{labour + energy}}$$

- **Total Productivity** : It includes all inputs in an organization i.e. labor, materials, overheads, capital. Hence, it is the broadest measure of production and is concerned with the performance of entire plant/ organization.

    Total Productivity = Revenues, Profits/All inputs

Examples 5.12 : Determine the MFP for the combined input of labor and machine time using the following data :

Output : 7040 units @ ₹ 10 each

Input :
- Labor : ₹ 1000
- Materials : ₹ 520
- Overhead : ₹ 2000

Solution :

$$\text{Multifactor productivity} = \frac{\text{output}}{\text{Labour + Materials + Overhead}} = \frac{7040 \text{ units} \times ₹ 10}{1000 + 520 + 2000}$$

$$= 20 \text{ units output / ₹ input}$$

Example 5.13 : A team of workers make 500 units of a product having cost of ₹ 10 each. Actual cost is ₹ 400 for labor and ₹ 2000 for material and ₹ 500 for overheads, calculate the productivity

Solution :

$$\text{Multifactor productivity} = \frac{(500 \text{ units})(10/\text{unit})}{400 + 2000 + 500} = \frac{5000}{2900} = 1.72$$

5.15.2 Overall Equipment Effectiveness (OEE)

Another measure of productivity is defined as Overall equipment effectiveness (OEE) which reports the overall utilization of facilities, time and material for manufacturing operations. It quantifies how well a manufacturing unit performs relative to its designed capacity, during the periods when it is scheduled to run. OEE breaks the performance of a manufacturing unit into three separate but measurable components : Availability, Performance, and Quality.

Availability

Availability takes into account **Down Time Loss**, which includes all events that stop planned production for an appreciable length of time (typically several minutes or longer).

It is calculated as the ratio of Operating Time to Planned Production Time, where Operating Time is simply Planned Production Time less Down Time :

Performance

Performance takes into account **Speed Loss**, which includes all factors that cause the production asset to operate at less than the maximum possible speed when running.

It is calculated as the ratio of Net Operating Time to Operating Time. In practice, it is calculated as :

(Ideal Cycle Time × Total Pieces) / Operating Time

Ideal Cycle Time is the theoretical fastest possible time to manufacture one piece. Therefore, when it is multiplied by Total Pieces the result is Net Operating Time – the theoretical fastest possible time to manufacture the total quantity of pieces.

Quality

Quality takes into account **Quality Loss**, which factors out manufactured pieces that do not meet quality standards, including pieces that require rework.

It is calculated as the ratio of Fully Productive Time (fastest possible time for Good Pieces) to Net Operating Time (fastest possible time for Total Pieces). In practice it is calculated as : Good Pieces / Total Pieces

Each component points to an aspect of the process that can be targeted for improvement. It is unlikely that any manufacturing process can run at 100% OEE. Many manufacturers benchmark their industry to set a challenging target; 85% is not uncommon.

- OEE is calculated with the formula (Availability)*(Performance)*(Quality)
- E.g. OEE = (Availability= 84.6%)*(Performance=92%)*(Quality=92.8%) = (72.23%)

5.16 DOWN TIME

It the hours when the equipment is not in a condition or is not available to perform its intended function. It does not include any portion of nonscheduled time. Downtime management refers to the ability to collect and classify downtime data from the shop floor into meaningful information that can help managers understand the root causes of production inefficiency.

Downtime is dangerous to any manufacturing group. After all, the old saying that compares time to money is true. If people or machines are idle, then products are not being made, which certainly affects the business's bottom line - minimizing manufacturing downtime makes money for a company. Understanding how to communicate with and evaluate employees, providing regular equipment maintenance, increasing incentives to produce and establishing production goals are effective ways to minimize manufacturing downtime. There are five ways to reduce the down time.

1. **Update or Service the Machinery**

Minimizing manufacturing downtime means preventing machinery malfunctions. Outdated machines slow down the manufacturing process. Similarly, any machinery that continuously jams or breaks down has a huge negative impact on outcomes. Regular maintenance is important, as is installing new equipment.

Managers should stay up-to-date on the latest technology and suggest updates to improve productivity.

2. Explain Downtime to Employees

The best managers are clear and honest with employees so that they feel appreciated and understood. Research has shown clear communication between managers and employees is crucial in terms of boosting efficiency. If a supervisor explains the relationship between downtime and business profits, then employees feel part of the team, included in decisions, and important — all of which are key to increasing productivity. Employees may also have suggestions about how to limit downtime, increase morale, better service machines and produce more goods. Educating employees about each part of the manufacturing process may help them better understand their specific role and job.

3. Regular Evaluations

Regular employee evaluations are standard, but the key is in how they are administered. Evaluations of new and current employees need to be honest and straightforward. Despite management's request that the employee keep his or her evaluation confidential, in the real world it doesn't work that way :

Employees talk to fellow employees about their evaluation sessions, so being straightforward with each individual is crucial. Likewise, evaluations should focus on what management views as areas of excellence and areas needing improvement.

4. Monitor the Efficiency of Manufacturing Processes

Sometimes, departments are affected by other groups or rules. For example, a specific part of the production process may be delayed if another department is experiencing issues or if red tape and paperwork abound. Smart supervisors evaluate all parts of the manufacturing process to ensure that items are efficiently made, reviewed, and distributed.

5. Establish Specific Incentives and Goals

Penalizing employees for causing excessive downtime is the natural response of many companies when an employee or group of employees doesn't perform. Praising departments when they reach certain goals and keeping employees updated on productivity numbers help minimize downtime. When goals are met, gift cards, paid lunch and small get-togethers can motivate staff to do their best. Smart managers post status reports each day or even provide updates via real-time displays, or over the loudspeaker. Everyone feels valued if he or she is part of achieving specific daily and quarterly goals. Managers must follow through on incentives and promises to build trust and limit the amount of downtime. Happy and motivated staff do a better job than employees who are clocking in hours only to earn a paycheck. Employees need to understand the role they play in the manufacturing process, and understand that their supervisor cares about them as well as the manufacturing goals. Proper communication means talking to staff about business goals, as well as providing regular evaluations. Smart managers make sure that all employees have incentives to excel and that their suggestions are considered.

5.17 SELECTION OF EQUIPMENTS

For speedy and economic construction of a project, proper choice of equipment is of preliminary importance for civil engineers. The versatile range of equipment available commercially involves the decision of people. There are few basic things that are considered in selection of suitable equipment.

They are as follows :

Use of Available Construction Equipment :

Where the full utilization of new equipment for its entire working life is not foreseen, or its utilization on further projects is uncertain, it may be desirable to use existing old equipment even if its operation is some what more expensive. The depreciation cost of the new machine is likely to be high, and this would raise the owning cost of the equipment and thus the unit cost of work.

Suitability for Job Conditions :

The equipment chosen should suit the conditions of the job, soil, valley, working conditions and climate of the region.

Uniformity in Type :

A minimum number of types should be acquired so that there is uniformity in the type of equipment on a job. A common type of engine should be selected for the different types machines such as excavators, dump trucks, tractors and scrapers that are on the project.

Size of Construction Equipment :

Larger equipment gives higher output on full load, but its cost of production on part load is usually greater than that of smaller units working on full load. Larger equipment needs correspondingly larger size of matching units, and shutting down of one primary unit may render several other large units idle.

Transportation to works is generally difficult and costly. Servicing, maintenance and repair facilities have to be greater for larger units. However, larger machines are usually more sturdy and suitable for tough working conditions. It is desirable to have equipment of same size on the project. With standbys, the cost of larger size standby equipment is more than that of smaller size.

Use of Standard Construction Equipment :

Standard equipment is commonly manufactured and is available. Such equipment is manufactured in large numbers and so readily available and moderately priced. Spare parts of standard equipment are easily available and are less costly. After the work is over, disposing off standard equipment and its spare parts is generally easier than disposing off non-standard or specialized equipment.

Unit Cost of Production :

The economics of equipment is one of the most important considerations in the selection of equipment. When calculating owning cost, all items of expenses, like freight, packing and forwarding, insurance, erection, commissioning, etc. should be included with the price paid to the supplier.

Country of Origin :

For imported equipment, it is preferable to import from a soft currency rather from a hard currency area, to save foreign currency reserves.

Availability of Spare Parts :

The availability of spare parts at reasonable costs during the entire working life of the equipment should be ensured while selecting a particular type or make of equipment, especially of imported equipment. Downtime due to shortage of spare parts commonly accounts for long idle periods during the working life of equipment. If specialists are needed, their availability should also kept in mind.

Versatility :

The machine selected should, if possible, be able to do more than one function and should be inter-convertible wherever possible.

Selection of Manufacturer :

It is good to have equipment of the same manufacturer on a project as far as possible and to have minimum number of different makes of equipment. The quality and commitment of local dealers is important. They should be sincere and capable of extending prompt after sales service.

Suitability of Local Labour :

The locally available operators and technicians should be able to handle the equipment selected. A special equipment may have excellent performance but it may be difficult to handle it through available know-how.

Adaptability for Future Use :

If the machine is required to work for only a part of its useful life then possibility on of disposing it off or its employment some other job should be considered. Obsolescence of the machine should not be overlooked.

5.18 SIZING AND MATCHING OF EQUIPMENT

What size machine does it take to get the job done? It's a question with varied answers dependent on the type of equipment, the application, methods of transportation and the environment. Also, too small of a machine could leave you short of your production needs, and too large of a machine could prove inefficient and costly related to owning and operating costs. Following factors related to size will guide for renting or purchasing a new piece of equipment.

- The bucket capacity of excavator and carrying capacity of the hauling equipments should match. It means, dumpers should get completely filled by the soil within 3-4 cycles of excavators. More number of cycles indicates that, the excavator bucket capacity is not matching with the dumper capacity as it is too less. This increases the cycle time and affects the production. Lesser number of cycles indicates that the capacity of excavator bucket is large and soil is spilling over the dumper at each cycle, thus reducing the productivity.
- Large size excavators or dumpers require more are area to maneuver and to be selected depending upon the site conditions. Small size equipments are having lesser turning radius and hence can be easily turned. However, too small size increases number of equipment required.
- Large size equipments are difficult to dispose as that size may not be suitable for all the sites. Also, as the size increases, it is difficult to transport the vehicles from one site to another.

5.19 SAFETY CONSCIOUSNESS

This refers educating the employees towards safety awareness and safe work practices. A worker will accept the use of safety measures if he is convinced of its necessity.

Therefore, suitable measure should be adopted to increase the awareness of a need for safety in the work environment.

Measures to develop safety consciousness among employees are :
- Display of safety posters and slogans.
- Providing simple and convenient safety devices.
- Allowance to workers for setting, removing and replacing any necessary safety devices.
- Hold safety competition and award prizes for the safe practices.
- Give the identity, and recognition to safe workers.
- Hold regular safety meetings.
- Report safety activities to all employees.
- Cross mark all accident prone areas.
- Conduct safety training programmes at regular intervals.

Definition of Safety : "Industrial safety is that condition of enterprise operations in which, by controlling hazards, accident free production is achieved".

5.20 ACCIDENTS

Accidents are readily recognized when there is a damage to properties and someone is injured. It is not necessary that all accidents should result in personal injury. Generally an accident is defined as "an event which is unexpected or the cause of which is unforeseen" but this definition does not gives scope for accident prevention. Thus, a definition which provides the basis for industrial accident prevention is as follows, "An **accident** is any occurrence that interrupts or the cause of which is unforeseen, but this definition does not gives scope for accident prevention". Thus, a definition which provides the basis for industrial accident prevention is as follows, "An accident is any occurrence that interrupts or interferes with, the orderly progress of the activity in question".

5.20.1 Accident Control

Industrial accidents cause personal suffering and also cause significant economic loss to the whole community and hence demands a determined and sustained efforts by all concerned to reduce the accident rate and frequency. Safety at work is a direct responsibility of top management. It should provide adequate safety arrangements and in consultation with trade unions take corrective and prompt measures to provide the highest degree of safety to work. The management responsibility and duties with respect to accident control are categorized into four heads;

- Employer must take reasonable care in selecting competent and adequate staff.
- The employer should ensure that the place of work is safe and also he must take reasonable steps to remedy dangers he knows or ought to know.
- Plant and appliances must be safe.
- Employer should provide for a safe system of work. It involves the matter like plant layout, sequence of operations, safety training etc.

The safety control measures would be more effective, if the management has the support of employees, with trade unions encouraging this in every possible way. Some conceptions regarding accidents are given here.

5.20.2 Conceptions Regarding Accident

- An accident is an effect and as all effects have causes, thus accidents are caused. They do not just happen.
- An accident is a part of process.
- An accident is an unplanned event and therefore the emphasis must be on the planned behaviour and control of conditions.
- Each accident is one of the sequence of events which can be controlled upto certain time. If proper adjustments were made at that point, the unplanned incident can be controlled.

- Accident appears as a link of long chain of inconsequential events and a cause of accident is associated with these events.

5.20.3 Basic Factors for Occurrence of Accidents

- Accidents are caused and not just happen.
- Unsafe conditions or unsafe acts cause occurrence of accidents.
- Human faults can cause unsafe conditions of work and unsafe act.
- Faults are due to unsuitability of workers, mismatch between job and worker, physical environment, improper work attitudes, lack of job knowledge and poor supervision.

An accident is caused by the material handling system, falling objects, fall of persons etc. An accident can be the reason for poor morale and in turn, low morale can cause accidents. Industrial accidents apart from causing human sufferings, are the major factor in loss of production. Accidents lead to less turnover and absenteeism of workers, and machine idleness will increase. These cause a substantial burden to direct and indirect cost of production. The loss of production may cause the missed delivery to customers which in turn result in loss of customers. The Various direct and indirect costs are associated with accidents.

5.20.4 Causes of Accidents

1. **Technical causes reflect deficiencies in plant, equipment etc. and general work environment.**

    (a) **Mechanical Causes :**
    - Unsafe design and / or construction.
    - Improper machine guarding.
    - Improper loading of the machine.
    - Unsafe and improper material handling system.
    - Leakages of valves of dangerous liquids and gases.
    - Broken safety guards.

    (b) **Environmental Factors :**
    - These refer to improper conditions of work :
    - Too high or too low temperature.
    - High humidity causing excessive fatigue.
    - Defective and in appropriate illumination.

- Presence of dust, fumes and smokes.
- Poor house keeping.

2. **Human causes or unsafe acts by the person concerned are due to his ignorance or carelessness etc.**

The human causes include :

- Age, health and mental condition.
- Financial position and number of dependents.
- Lack of job knowledge and skill.
- Improper attitude towards the work.
- Incorrect machine habits.
- High anxiety level.
- No use of safety devices.
- Working at unsafe speeds.
- Improper handling of tools.

Normally,

- 88% injuries are due to personal unsafe acts.
- 10% injuries are due to dangerous physical and mechanical conditions.
- 2% injuries are due to unavoidable reasons.

5.20.5 Types of Accidents

1. Near accident - An accident with no damage or injury.
2. Trivial
3. Minor
4. Serious
5. Fatal.

5.21 ECONOMIC ASPECTS OF ACCIDENTS

5.21.1 Costs Associated with Accidents

An accident can be very costly to the injured employee as well as to the employer or the concern. It may bring losses in the form of sacrifice of human life, loss of materials or equipment, injuries to workers, damages to other properties, loss of time and ultimately loss of credibility of the management. It results, thus, in increase in the cost of construction and decreases the profit of the contractor.

There are definite costs associated with accidents as given below :

- Direct and measurable costs.
- Indirect – Somewhat intangible but nevertheless real costs.

5.21.2 Direct Costs of an Accidents

These costs can be easily evaluated and hence known as direct costs. They include :

- Payment to the worker for the temporary or permanent injury or to his family in case of death in the form of compensation.
- Overhead cost.

The above two can be reduced by taking insurance policy.

- Uncompensated wage loss of the injured employee.
- Cost of medical care and hospitalization.

5.21.3 Indirect Costs of an Accidents

These are the costs which cannot be easily evaluated and hence are known as indirect costs. They include the following :

- Cost of damage to equipment and material.
- Cost of wages paid for the time lost by the other workers not injured as the work is stopped due to accident.
- Cost of wages paid to injured workers.
- Cost of loss in production because of accident.
- Cost of time lost and of wages lost of the supervisors in dealing work related to the accident. e.g. reporting, inquiry, cause finding, alternate arrangement etc.
- Cost of replacing injured employee.
- Cost of lowered production and efficiency by the substitute employee.
- Cost of reduction in efficiency of the injured worker when he joins his duties again after he is recovered.
- Influence of accident on the moral of the employee.

The survey has as indicated that the indirect costs are four time the direct costs.

5.22 NATURE AND EXTENT OF ACCIDENTS [May-11]

The following factors are used to judge the nature and extent of accidents.

- Injury frequency rate
- Injury severity rate.

The injury frequency rate (I.F. rate) is defined as 'the number of disabling injuries per 10,00,000 man-hours worked'.

$$\text{I.F. Rate} = \frac{\text{No. of disabling injuries} \times 10{,}00{,}000}{\text{No. of man-hours worked}}$$

The relationship does not take into account the time lost due to an injury.

Injury severity rate (I.S. Rate) is defined as 'the number of days of lost time because of injuries per 1000 man-hours worked'.

$$\text{I.S. Rate} = \frac{\text{No. of days lost} \times 1000}{\text{No. of man-hours worked}}$$

5.23 CAUSES AND PRECAUTIONS [May-12, Nov./Dec.-12]

The different common causes of accidents in construction industry and precautions and safety measures to avoid the same are detailed below :

Cause of Accident	Safety Measures and Procedure
(A) Personal lacking 1. Lack of ability and knowledge 2. Lack of interest in work 3. Deliberate risk 4. Fatigue 5. Other personal factors	Education of workers by giving training for proper handling of tools, machinery, display of posters, film shows on safety precautions and measures. Avoiding fatigue by not enforcing overtime. Arranging training for use of new and complicated machines and new processes. Maintaining good labour management relations.
(B) Faulty working methods 1. Striking against objects	1. Provision of good layout and sufficient working space. 2. Removal of obstruction in working space if any.
2. Falling objects	1. Careful handling of tools and materials while working at higher level. 2. Use of protective devices, use helmets.
3. Person falling	1. Proper construction of working platforms. 2. Provision of guards and rails while working above ground level.
4. Failures of forms, scaffolding and ladders etc. (A most common cause of accidents in construction industry)	1. Use of strong material. 2. Proper method of erection especially for high scaffolds. 3. Checking the strength from time to time before reuse. 4. Checking condition of high scaffolds etc. during construction.

Contd...

Cause of Accident	Safety Measures and Procedure
5. Hazards in use of explosives	1. Careful storage, handling and use. 2. Clearing, vacating explosion area. 3. Counting the number of explosions. 4. Checking misfires and dealing it very carefully.
6. Presence of injurious gases, toxic dusts etc. (likely to be encounted in tunneling)	1. Ready medical aid. 2. Use of masks, hoods and other protective devices. 3. Proper ventilation.
7. Unforeseen causes	1. Rescue measures and devices. 2. Immediate first aid provision. 3. Ready medical aid.
(C) Structural failures	
1. Failure of substratum	1. Careful subsurface investigations. 2. Providing suitable type of foundation. 3. Preventing excavation in the loaded substratum.
2. Failure of excavation	1. Careful stability investigations. 2. Providing slopes or supporting sides properly. 3. Quick completion of foundation and refilling.
3. Use of substandard materials	1. Proper testing of materials (Testing cement, concrete, bricks, steel bars, road metal, soil etc.). 2. Sorting out good material and rejecting the other (washing of sand, rejecting bad bricks using good rubble etc.) 3. Using proper proportions for morter, concrete etc. 4. Using proper water cement ratio etc.
4. Faulty implementation of the design	1. Proper checking by competent authority. 2. Competent and complete supervision.
5. Faulty construction practices	1. Competent and proper supervision. 2. Employment of able trade workers. 3. Providing proper training for good job practice.

Cause of Accident	Safety Measures and Procedure
6. Unauthorised changes	1. Only competent authorities be allowed to make proper changes after due consideration. 2. Changes to be made only on written orders from competent authorities.
7. Carelessness in supervision	1. Fixing responsibility of the supervisors. 2. Supervise supervisors by higher competent authorities. 3. Written certificate from the competent authority at every important stage e.g. passing of foundation bed before concreting, passing of reinforcement and form work before casting R.C.C. units etc.
8. Natural causes like earthquake	1. Assessment of the magnitude and effects and suitable provisions in the design for the same.

5.24 ACCIDENT PRONENESS

Accident proneness may be defined as 'the continuous tendency of a person to have more accidents as a result of his persisting characteristics'. Accident proneness is because of peculiar psychological and physiological make up of certain person. Some workers who are consistently found to experience more accidents than the other workers are classified as accident prone employees.

Causes of Accident Proneness
1. Lack of attention towards the work and day dreaming.
2. Poor eye sight and hearing problems.
3. To much sensitive to disturbance.
4. Lack of emotional stability.
5. Unsafe behaviour like intentionally not using protective devices etc. and violating safety practices.

Methods to Reduce Accident Proneness
- Proper selection of person who possess required standards of physical and mental ability to match the requirements of jobs.
- Transfer accident prone workers to less hazardous job situations.
- Impart adequate training and inculcate safety mindedness.
- Keep the-morale of the workers high.

5.25 PREVENTION OF ACCIDENT

Clients, project supervisors, employers, individual contractors and self-employed persons all have responsibilities to ensure safety. Relevant requirements set by various Directives include :

1. Considering occupational safety and health from the planning stage onwards in all construction work. Work has to be co-ordinated between all parties involved in planning and doing the work.

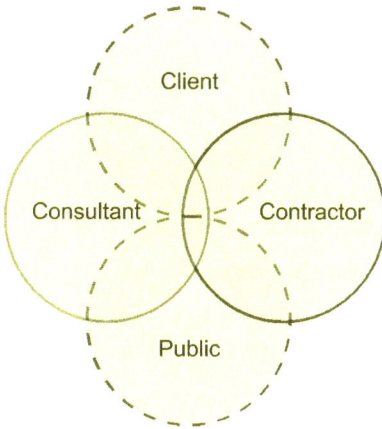

Fig. 5.18

2. Ensuring safe work equipment (covers suitability, selection, safety features, safe use, training and information, inspection and maintenance).

3. Providing safety and/or health signs where hazards cannot be avoided or adequately reduced by preventive measures.

Fig. 5.19 : Safety signs

4. Providing personal protective equipment (hard helmets, safety harnesses, eye and respiratory protection, safety footwear etc.) appropriate for the risks involved and where they can not be prevented by other means.

5. Ensuring a safe working environment and welfare facilities for construction workers, e.g. access, safe traffic routes.

6. Following a general Framework to manage health and safety, including : assessment and prevention of risks; giving priority to collective measures to eliminate risks; consulting employees, providing information and training; and co-ordination on safety with contractors.

The minimum requirements set by Directives have been implemented in national legislation that may include additional requirements. Employees have duties to co-operate actively with employers preventive measures, following instructions in accordance with training given. Consulting the workforce is a requirement. Using their knowledge helps to ensure hazards are correctly spotted and workable solutions implemented.

Preventing Accidents - Assessing the Risks

There are many hazards in construction work. However, there is much "good practice" that can be easily applied to prevent accidents.

Some good practices are as follows :

- The first step is to carry out a suitable and sufficient risk assessment.
- To ensure a real reduction in the exposure of workers and others (including site visitors, passing members of the public) to harm.
- The risk assessment should consider all the risks and hazards on. Ensure reduction of one risk does not increase another.
- All the hazards should be identified, including those arising from work activities and from other factors, e.g. site layout. This is followed by evaluating the extent of risks involved, taking account of existing precautions. The risk assessment results will help in selecting the most appropriate good practice measures to use.

5.26 IMPORTANCE OF SAFETY TRAINING ON CONSTRUCTION SITE [May-12, Nov./Dec.-12]

Construction sites are full of hazards and risks. It is one of the most dangerous sectors to work in with high injury and fatality rates around the world viz. accidents due to heavy machineries, electrocution in the vicinity of electrical cables, falling from height and many more. Training staff in identifying and avoiding such hazards is a vitally important way of reducing the number of incidents in construction. Training should be updated regularly to ensure that all workers are fully knowledgeable on the risks posed on a daily basis.

The importance of training is as stated below :

- To make employees aware of the workplace hazards so that they may identify the risks at their workplaces and take sufficient steps to minimize or overcome.
- To fulfill legal obligations, because attendance can be taken at a training course, and therefore the company can prove that they have taken adequate steps to prevent accidents or injuries.
- To give confidence to the employees that they are working in safe environment thus indirectly increasing productivity and loyalty.

5.27 SAFETY PROGRAMME [May-11, Nov./Dec.-12]

There is a general practice to prepare safety programmes on particular sites for various construction activities. Different guidelines given by OSHA and CIDC are to be followed depending upon type of work.

Example, tunneling and pilling, machinery and materials, roads and bridges, building and structures, oil and gas sector and many more.

5.27.1 Guidelines Related to Building Construction

A few guidelines related to building construction are as given below.

A safety programme is introduced to reduce and avoid accidents. The main aims of the safety programmes are as below.

- It tends to discover when, where and why accidents occur.
- It aims at reducing accidents and losses associated with it.
- It begins with the assumption that most work connected accidents can be prevented.
- It does not have an end, rather it is a continuous process to achieve adequate safety.
- It tries to reduce the influence of personal and environmental factors that cause accidents.
- It involves providing safety equipments and special training to employees.
- It is composed of one or more of the following elements :
    (a) Support by top Management.
    (b) Appointing a Safety Director/Officer.
    (c) Engineering a safe plant, processes and operations.
    (d) Studying and analysing the accidents prevents their occurrence in future.
    (e) Educating all the employees to work safely.
    (f) Holding safety contests, safety weeks etc. and giving incentives to divisions/sections/ projects having least number of accidents.

A safety programme includes the following four E's.

1. Engineering : Safety at the design and equipment.
2. Education : Education of employees in safe practices.
3. Enlistment : It concerns the attitude of employees and management towards the safety programme and its purpose.
4. Enforcement : Enforcing adherence to safety rules and safe practices.

5.27.2 The Principle Hazards

Ladders
- Workers falling from ladders.
- Ladders slipping outwards at the base or falling away at the top (the 1 out 4 up rule should always be used).
- Use of defective ladder.
- Over-reaching situations.

Falls from Working Platforms
- Unfenced or inadequately fenced working platforms.
- Inadequate boarding to scaffolds.
- Defective boarding.
- Absence of toe boards.

Falls of Materials
- Small objects, such as bricks or hand tools, dropped from a height.
- Poor standards of housekeeping on working platforms.
- Inadequate or absent toe boards and barriers.
- Incorrect assembly of gin wheels for raising and lowering materials.
- Incorrect or careless hooking and slinging of loads.
- Failure to install catching platforms(fans) for failing debris.
- Demolition materials being thrown to the ground.

Falls from Pitched Roofs and Through Fragile Roofs
- Unsafe working practices.
- Inappropriate footwear.
- Failure to provide eaves protection and verge protection.
- Failure to use crawl boards.
- Stacking of materials on fragile roofs.

Falls through Openings in Flat Roofs and Floors

- Failure to cover openings or provide edge protection.
- Failure to replace after use.
- Covers not clearly marked to show their presence.

Collapses of Excavations

- Failure to support trench excavations.
- Inadequate timbering and shoring.
- Shifting sand situations.
- Presence of water in large quantities e.g. flash floods.
- Timbering collapses due to material stacked to close to the edge of the excavation.
- Defective and inadequate shoring materials.
- Failure to reinstate shoring after damage.

Transport

- Men falling off vehicles not designed to carry passengers, e.g. dumper trucks.
- Men being run over or crushed by reversing lorries and trucks.
- Poor maintenance of site vehicles, e.g. braking and reversing systems.
- Operation of vehicles and equipment, particularly lifting appliances, such as cranes, hoists and winches, by in-experienced and incompetent persons.
- Overloading of passenger carrying vehicles.
- Poor standards of driving onsite roads.
- Mud or loose soil on the roads.
- Poor housekeeping on roads can cause skidding and obstruction.

Machinery and Powered Hand Tools

- Failure to adequately guard all moving parts of machinery, e.g. power take-offs, cooling fans and belt drives.
- Dangerous wood working machines particularly circular saws.
- Portable hand powered tools with exposed rotating heads.
- Defective or un-insulated electric hand tools.

Housekeeping

- Poor housekeeping standards.
- Trips and falls over debris that can accumulate during construction.

Fire
- Poor fire protection measures, often associated with poor site supervision.

Personal Protective Equipment
- Failure to provide and to enforce the wearing and use of personal protective equipment, e.g., safety helmets, safety boots, gloves, overalls, full-face protection, goggles etc.

Safety Measures Ignored
   (a) People standing on scaffolding without using helmet or a safety belt.
   (b) No cross bracing used.

5.27.3 Competent Person [Nov./Dec.-12]

The word competent person occurs frequently in safety legislation, certain inspections, examinations, and supervisory duties must be undertaken by competent persons. Broadly, a competent person should have practical and theoretical knowledge as well as sufficient experience of the particular machinery, plant or procedure involved to enable him to identify defects or weaknesses during plant and machinery examinations, and to asses their importance in relation to the strength and function of that plant and machinery. Competent persons are used in the following construction related activities.

- Supervision of demolition work.
- Supervision of handling and use of explosives.
- Inspection of scaffolding materials prior to erection of scaffolding.
- Supervision and erection of, substantial alteration, or additions to, and dismantling of scaffolds.
- Inspection of scaffolds after seven days and after adverse weather conditions which could affect the strength and stability of a scaffold or cause displacement of any part.
- Inspections of excavation on daily basis.
- Supervision of the erection cranes.
- Testing of cranes after erection, re-erection and any removal or adjustment involving changes of anchorage or ballasting.
- Examination of appliances for anchorage or ballasting prior to crane erection.

5.27.4 Safe Working Conditions

- Areas where people work must be covered so that they are protected from any failing materials.
- Temporary structures must be of good construction, sound material, adequate strength and stability, free from patent defect and adequately maintained.

- Suitable and sufficient safe access and egress must be maintained for every working position.
- All work areas must be made and kept safe for all persons working there.
- Scaffolds or if appropriate ladders or other suitable means of support must be provided and properly maintained where work cannot be done safely on or from the ground or from part of building or other permanent structure.
- Any openings, corners, breaks or edges in floors wall and roofs must be fenced or barricaded.
- Safety sheets, or nets or safety belts, must be used when other legal requirements designed to prevent falls cannot be complied with.
- All practicable steps must be taken to prevent danger from live electric cables or apparatus.

5.27.5 Scaffolding [May-12]

1. Erection of scaffolds : a competent person must inspect the scaffolding materials before each occasion on which they are put into use.
2. Any erection, substantial alterations or additions to, and dismantling of scaffolding must be under the immediate supervision of a competent person. Competent and experienced workmen must be employed, so as far as possible for the erection substantial alterations or additions to and dismantling of scaffolds.
3. Every part of a scaffold must be fixed, secured or placed as to prevent accidental displacement as far as is practicable.
4. Scaffolds must be constructed of suitable and sound material and of adequate strength.
5. They must be rigidly connected to the building or other structure unless designed and constructed as an independent scaffold. Scaffolds must be securely supported or suspended and strutted, or braced where necessary.
6. Parts of building or other structures must not be used to support scaffolds unless they are of sound material and sufficiently strong and stable.
7. Gutters must not be used as support unless they are suitable for the purpose and of adequate strength. Overhanging eaves gutters must not be so used unless designed as walkways.

    Loose bricks and other rubble must not be used as support except for certain low platforms.

5.27.6 Inspections and Maintenance of Scaffolds

1. All scaffolds used must have been inspected by a competent person within the preceding seven days unless no part has been erected for over seven days.
2. Scaffolds must be inspected after being exposed to weather conditions likely to affect the strength or stability of the scaffolds or to have displaced any part.
3. The results of inspections of scaffolds must be entered in or attached to the prescribed register (except for ladder scaffolds, trestle scaffolds and scaffolds from which persons cannot fall more than two metres).
4. Each employer whose men use a scaffold must satisfy himself that it complies with regulations whether or not his own men have erected it.
5. All scaffolds must be properly maintained. Platforms, gangways, runs and stairs must be kept clear of unnecessary obstructions materials or rubbish and from projecting nails. Slippery platforms, gangways, runs, and stairs must be sanded, cleaned or otherwise remedied as soon as practicable.
6. Scaffolds must never overloaded. Materials must not be kept on scaffolds unless needed within reasonable time. Movement of materials on or on to scaffolds must be carried out without causing any violent shock. Loads on scaffolds must be evenly distributed as far as practicable.
7. Partly erected or dismantled scaffolds must either comply with the regulations even in their incomplete state, or else have prominent warning notices to indicate that they must not be used or have access to them blocked as far as reasonably practicable.

5.27.7 Excavations [May-11]

Materials and Equipments :

An adequate supply of timber or other suitable materials must be provided. Any machinery in use must have any dangerous parts securely fenced or guarded (unless safe by position or construction).

Fencing

Barriers must be provided around excavation, shafts, pits and openings into which persons can fall a vertical distance of more than 1.98 m and such barriers must be as close as practicable to the edge of the excavation etc. Barriers must be maintained in position except when necessarily removed for the access of persons or materials.

Timbering

- Adequate and suitable materials must be used to prevent danger from falls or dislodgement of the sides of any excavation etc. or materials adjacent to it.

- Timbering must be undertaken as early as practicable in the course of work, and persons engaged in timbering must be protected as far as possible from danger.
- Timbering or other supports must be of good construction, sound material, free from patent defect and of adequate strength for the purpose. Struts and braces must be properly and adequately secured to prevent accidental displacement or fall.
- A competent person must be employed to direct the erection and dismantling of all timbering and other supports, as well as any subsequent alterations or additions to it. Workmen must further be employed, as far as possible, for the erection, dismantling etc. of timbering and other supports.

Inspections and Examinations

Material for timbering and other supports must be inspected by a competent person before being taken into use. Every part of any excavation, shaft, earthwork or tunnel must be inspected by a competent person at least once during every day that persons are employed there. The face of every tunnel and base or crown of every shaft must be inspected by a competent person at the beginning of each shift. The working end of every trench more than 2.0 m must be inspected by a competent person before beginning of every shift. No person must work in any excavation etc. after explosives have been used in or near it, in a manner likely to affect stability, until a thorough examination by a competent person has been made. No person must work in any excavation etc. unless it has been thoroughly examined by a competent person within previous seven days.

No person must work in any excavation etc. after an unexpected fall of rocks, earth, or other material, or after substantial damage to timber or other supports, unless the concerned part has been thoroughly examined by a competent person.

5.27.8 Other Precautions

- Excavations and the approaches to the same must be well lit.
- Materials must not be placed near the edge of any excavation etc. so as to endanger persons below.
- If the excavation is likely to affect the security of another structure (permanent or temporary) steps must be taken to safeguard the persons employed from possible collapse of that structure.
- Means of reaching place of safety must be provided, as far as practicable, when there may be danger from rising water or eruption of water or material.
- Means to prevent overrunning must be provided when a vehicle is used to tip material into a pit or excavation or over the edge of any embankment or earthwork.

The atmosphere in an excavation must be well ventilated and free from dust and fumes.

5.27.9 Lifting Appliances and Lifting Gear

- Packing or other means must be used to prevent the edges of a load from coming into contact with slings, ropes or chains, if this could cause danger.
- The angle between the legs of multiple slings must not be so great that the safe working load is exceeded.
- Every part of the load must be securely suspended and supported and secured to prevent displacement or slipping. Slings must be securely attached to the appliance and in a way not likely to damage the slings of any lifting gear.
- The hoisting mechanism of a crane must be used only for vertical raising or lowering, unless it can be used otherwise without imposing undue stress or endangering stability and is so used under supervision of a competent person. The safe working load of the appliance must not be exceeded.
- The radius of the load must not exceed the maximum working radius of the jib.
- Where a load is equal to, or nearly equal to the safe working load lifting must be halted for a moment after the load has been raised for a short distance.
- All practicable measures must be taken to prevent a load coming into contact with, and displacing, any other object.
- No load must be left suspended unless a competent person is actually in charge of the lifting appliance.
- Loads being lowered onto a scaffold must be deposited without causing any violent shock to the scaffold.
- Where more than one appliance is used for a lift, work must be so arranged that no appliance is overloaded or rendered unstable, and the operation must be supervised by a competent person.
- Lifting appliances must not be used on soft or uneven surfaces nor on a slope unless precautions are taken to ensure stability.
- No crane must be used for raising or lowering unless it is either securely anchored or adequately weighted with ballast properly placed and secured.
- Rails on which cranes are mounted must not be used as anchorages.
- Only trained and competent persons must operate a lifting appliance. No person under the age of 18 years must operate any lifting appliance driven by mechanical power, or give signals to a driver of a power operated lifting appliance.

5.27.10 Roof Work and Working at Heights [May-11]

General requirements for safe working :
- A safe system of work should be established e.g. method statement before work commences. This should include all contractors, sub-contractors involved and should incorporate the provision of scaffolding, barriers, gin wheels, hoists etc., the maintenance of a safe place of work and records of inspection of plant, equipment, access arrangements and working positions.
- Roofing : Where a properly erected scaffold is not used, a rigid roof edge barrier, incorporating a guard rail and toe boards, must be provided before work commences. This arrangement may stay in position until work is completed.
- Any roof opening left open as work progresses must be suitably guarded or secured and marked "Hole Below".
- Suitable crawling boards must be used for access and working areas on pitched roofs, while working on fragile roofs or roofs which may become slippery and in every case where roofs have a pitch greater than 30°.
- Precautions must be taken against adverse weather conditions, including the arrangements for storage of equipment and materials on the roof.
- Dry powder appliances must be provided when fires are used to heat mastics. Distances between boilers not being heated and the fires in use must be not less than 10 feet (3.3 m).
- Care must be taken not to overload partially completed roofs or roof trusses.
- Where excessive loading is anticipated, purpose-designed loading towers should be used.
- Satisfactory access must be provided to the working areas.
- The method of lifting or storage of materials must be established with a safe place of work to operate from.
- The collection of all roof material off-cuts must be closely monitored.

Cladding
- The method of lifting or storage of materials must be established with a safe place of work to operate from.
- A suitable scaffold-working platform may be required.
- The method of tying in the scaffold must be satisfactory.
- Mobile access towers must have appropriate base dimensions and good ground conditions.
- Satisfactory access and means of lifting materials must be provided.

5.27.11 Work Above Ground

Work above ground generally entails the use of scaffolds, mobile access equipment and/or ladders. The following factors need consideration to ensure safe working practices for this type of work.

Basic Scaffolding Requirements :

- Suitable and sufficient means of access to the working platform and egress from it must be provided.
- As far as practicable, all working platforms must be made safe.
- Scaffolds must be provided at working heights exceeding two metres above ground/floor level.
- Toe boards and handrails must be fitted on scaffolds exceeding two metres above ground/floor level.
- Scaffolds must be adequately lit.
- Materials must not be thrown or tipped from working platforms.
- Scaffolds must be constructed using approved materials, in sound condition, and free from excessive rust etc.
- Scaffolds must be rigid, every part so fixed, secured or placed as to prevent accidental displacement, and erected on sound foundation.
- Standards must be vertical, or lean towards the structure, and be securely fixed and braced.
- Ledgers and transoms must be horizontal and securely fixed so as to prevent movement.
- Putlogs must be straight, provided with flat ends, securely fixed into the structure.
- A scaffold board must not project beyond its support more than four times its thickness.
- The minimum width for gangways provided at heights exceeding two metres above floor /ground level is 0.44 m (17").
- Stairs must be provided throughout their lengths with handrails and other accepted safety measures in order to prevent the fall of workmen and materials. The fitting of toeboards is necessary on landings but not on stairs.
- Minimum permitted widths for scaffolds are :
    - General – 0.64 m (25") except where used for special tasks.
    - For men and materials – 0.87 m (34").

- For supporting another platform – 1.07 m (42").
- For the side of a sloping roof – 0.
- Partly erected/dismantled scaffolds must display appropriate warning notices and access blocked.
- When dismantling scaffolds tubes and fittings must be lowered to the ground, not thrown.
- Competent person to inspect a scaffold materials before each occasion on which they are put into use.
- Erection, substantial alterations or addition to and dismantling of scaffolds to be carried under the immediate supervision of a competent person.
- Competent and experienced workmen to be employed, so far as is practicable, for the erection, substantial alterations or additions to and dismantling of scaffolds.
- Scaffolds to be rigidly connected to the building or other structures unless designed and constructed as an independent scaffold.
- Scaffolds to be securely supported or suspended and strutted or braced where necessary.
- Parts of a building or other structures not to be used to support scaffolds until they are of sound material and sufficiently strong and stable.
- Gutters not to be used as supports, unless they are suitable for the purpose and, adequate strength.
- Overhanging eaves, gutters not to be used so, unless designed as walkways.

5.27.12 Inspection and Maintenance

1. All scaffolds in use must have been inspected by a competent person within the preceding seven days unless no part has been erected for over seven days.
2. Scaffolds must be inspected after being exposed to adverse weather conditions likely to affect the strength or stability or displacement of any part.
3. Results of inspections to be entered in or attached to the prescribed register (except for ladder scaffolds, trestle scaffolds, and scaffolds from which persons cannot fall more than 6'6"(2.0 m)).
4. All scaffolds must be properly maintained.
5. Platforms, gangways, runs and stairs to be kept clear of unnecessary material or rubbish and from projecting nails.
6. Slippery platforms, gangways, runs and stairs to be sanded, cleaned or otherwise remedied as soon as practicable.

7. Movement of materials on or onto scaffolds to be done without causing any violent shock.
8. Loads on scaffolds to be evenly distributed as far as practicable.

5.27.13 Moveable Access Equipment

This type of equipment, which takes the form of an access tower, may take several forms.

- A moveable tower formed from scaffold tubes.
- A similar moveable tower but constructed from pre-formed frames, which interlock together.

In each case, the tower incorporates a working platform, access by means of an externally fixed ladder or a series of internally placed raking ladders, and castor wheels at the base which permit the tower to be moved with ease as such this form of equipment is very adaptable, being used for a wide range of activities of both construction sites or in routine maintenance tasks in all types of premises. They are commonly used for :

- High level maintenance work,
- Painting inner roof surfaces and walls, and
- Small scale building operations.

The following precautions should be taken in their use :

- Working platforms should be fitted with guard rails and toe boards.
- The platform should be secure and completely boarded.
- The height of the working platform must not exceed three times the smaller base dimensions, and no tower should have a base dimension of less than four feet.
- In certain cases, e.g. when working in windy conditions outriggers should be fitted to increase stability.
- Rigidity of the tower should be increased by the use of diagonal bracing on all four elevations and horizontally.
- Castors used with the tower should be fixed at the extreme corners of the tower in such a manner that they should not fall out when the tower is moved. Castors should be fitted with an effective wheel brake.
- Towers should be moved with great care, and under no circumstances should they be moved while a person is present on the working platform. All equipments and materials should be removed from the platform prior to moving the tower.
- The tower should be moved by pulling or pushing at the base level.

5.27.14 Ladders [May-12]

Construction :

1. All ladders should be of good construction, suitable and sound material, adequate strength and properly maintained.
2. Ladders with missing or defective rung, split stiles or other forms of defect should not be used.
3. Wooden stiles and rungs should have grain running lengthwise.
4. Wooden ladder should not be painted or treated in such a way that defects in the timber may be concealed. Wooden ladders may however be treated with clear preservative.
5. Wooden ladders should be fitted with reinforcing ties if tenon joints are not secured by wedges.

Use :

6. Ladders not standing on a base should be securely, equally and properly suspended by each stile and secured where necessary to prevent undue swinging or swaying.
7. Ladders standing on a base to be equally and properly supported on each stile.
8. A ladder standing on a base to be securely fixed near its upper resting-place (or its upper end, if vertical). If such fixing is impracticable, the ladder must be fixed at or near its lower end.

Where this is also impracticable, a person must be stationed at the foot of the ladder to prevent it from slipping.

9. Except where there are adequate handholds, ladders must rise to height of at least 3' 6" (1 m) above the landing place or above the highest rung reached by a person using the ladder.
10. The space at each rung must be sufficient to provide an adequate foothold.
11. Landing places of adequate size to be provided if practicable every 30'. 0' (9.14 m) of vertical distance, or more frequently.
12. Landing place from which persons are liable to fall more than 6"6" (1.98 m) to have hand rails to a height of between 3"0" (0.92 m) and 3'. 9"(1.15 m) and also toe boards or other barriers to a height of at least 6" (0.155 m). The space between the toe board and the nearest guard-rail must not be more than 2'. 6" (0.76 m).
13. Openings in landings through which ladders pass must b as small as practicable.
14. Folding stepladders must have a level and firm footing and must not be on loose bricks or other packing.

5.28 WORK BELOW GROUND

Excavation work and other forms of work below ground can be particularly dangerous due to the risk of collapse of such excavations, flooding of same or people, materials, and vehicles falling into it.

General Safety Requirements

The methods of supporting the sides of excavation vary widely in design, the method of placing materials and the materials used.

For larger excavations the support will be based on the anticipated soil and structural pressures, taking into account the various stages during construction when the support will be installed and subsequently dismantled.

For smaller excavations, one of the three systems is generally used. Where timber runners or boards are used these could equally well be replaced by steel trench sheeting. Similarly, timber struts could be replaced by adjustable steel struts or hand operated hydraulic shoring depending upon :

- The nature of subsoil.
- Projected life of the excavation.
- Work to be undertaken, including equipment used.
- The possibility of flooding from ground water and heavy rains.
- The depth of excavation, and
- The number of people using the excavation at any one time.

In addition to these hazards, the ever-present risk of asbestos inhalation must be considered. The presence or otherwise of asbestos should be assessed in any pre-demolition survey undertaken.

5.29 CONSTRUCTION OF TUNNELS [Nov./Dec.-11]

The safety measures to be adopted are :
1. Store explosives away from work area and safeguard properly.
2. Provide adequate ventilation and illumination inside tunnel.
3. Take measures to control flooding.
4. Make compulsion for using PPE.
5. Keep good communication network.
6. Prepare emergency procedures such as evacuation plans ready.

5.30 SAFETY PROGRAMME FOR A NATIONAL HIGHWAY PROJECT

Consider following Points

1. **Excavation :** Fencing, shoring, plant and machinery, access, common hazards, responsibilities of supervisor.
2. **Drilling and Blasting :** Storage, transportation and handling of explosives, use of explosives.
3. **Handling Machinery :** Fencing, operational guidelines for various earthmoving, excavating equipments, cranes, mixing plants (RMC and hot mix plant).
4. Important instructions to drivers.
5. **Handling of Materials :** Types of storage of different materials.
6. Special considerations for HOT mix plant.
7. Traffic management during road construction.
8. If construction of bridges, culverts are involved, then safety measures are to be considered separately w.r.t. RCC work, structural steel work, use of compressed air.
9. Other safety measures such as electrical installations, handling of pneumatic tools.
10. Use of personal protective equipments / life saving equipments.

5.31 MANAGEMENT OF THE DEMOLITION PROCESS

Principal features of this process includes pre-demolition survey, the action necessary prior to demolition, the action while demolition is in progress and the procedures to ensure close supervision of demolition sites.

5.31.1 Pre-Demolition Survey

Prior to demolition commencing, a safe system of work must be established. In most cases, this would be done through a written method statement. Such a system will be determined following a pre-demolition survey undertaken by a competent person and, where possible, perusal of plans of building should be done.

The pre-demolition survey should identify :
- The nature and method of construction of the building or structure.
- The arrangement of buildings adjacent to that for demolition and the condition of such adjoining property.
- The location of underground services e.g. water mains, electricity cables, gaspipes, drains, sewers and telephone cables.

- The previous use of the premises, which could be significant.
- The presence of dangerous substances inherent in the structure, e.g. asbestos or stored internally.
- The method of bonding of the main load bearing walls.
- The system of shoring or the provision of other support necessary during demolition.

5.32 PERSONAL PROTECTIVE EQUIPMENTS [Nov./Dec.-11, 12, May-11]

Prevention of accidents should be done by applying engineering methods rather than any protective equipments. Engineering methods could include design change, substitution, ventilation, mechanical handling, automation etc. But in many cases, we have to use the personal protective equipments to prevent accidents. For example, in construction work there is the possibility of a hand tool, a bolt, or some loose material to fall from an elevated level and strike the head of workman below. It is therefore necessary that the construction worker wears a safety helmet. It is for such situations, Factories Act, 1948 have provisions for use of appropriate type of PPE. Use of PPE is an important and necessary consideration in the development of a safety programme.

Quality of PPE

PPE must meet the following criteria with regard to its quality :

- Provide absolute and full protection against possible hazard; and
- It is so designed and manufactured out of such material that it can withstand the hazard against which it is intended to be used.

Selection of PPE

Selection of the right type of PPE requires consideration of the following factors :

- Nature and severity of the hazard,
- Type of contaminant, its concentration and location of contaminated area with respect to the source of respirable air,
- Expected activity of workman and duration of work,
- Comfort of workman while using PPE,
- Operating characteristics and limitations of PPE,
- Ease of maintenance and cleaning, and
- Conformity to Indian/International standards and availability of test.

Proper Use of PPE

Though PPE are absolutely necessary for safety of workers, they dislike to use them for following reasons :

1. The workers may not understand the severity of situations and necessity.
2. Wearing PPE may not be comfortable to them as it is creating hindrance to the progress of work. Especially in summer season, workers do not use helmets because of excessive sweating. Lady workers find it difficult to carry things on their heads as it increases the height. Now-a-days new helmets have small opening in it for air to pass.

To avoid these resistances, organisations should provide extensive training, education and supervision. When a group of workmen are issued PPE for the first time, clear and reasonable instructions shall be given to them as to why PPE must be worn. Some added advantages as 'Recognition Award', 'Safety Weeks', 'Safety Awards' may be given to the workers.

5.32.1 Categories of PPE

Depending upon the nature of hazard, the PPE is broadly divided into the following two categories:

- **Non-Respiratory:** Those used for protection against injury from outside the body, i.e. for protecting the head, eye, face, hand, arm, foot, leg and other body parts.
- **Respiratory:** Those used for protection from harm due to inhalation of contaminated air.

5.32.2 PPE for Head Protection

Workers working in the areas of risk where the possibility of falling objects from a height must be provided with head protection. Broadly this protection consists of safety helmets, caps, hairnets, turbans etc. Hairnets, turbans etc. are used to protect women and men with long hair to prevent their hair from getting entangled in moving parts.

Helmets are classified into the following two types:

1. Full brimmed type helmet. For added protection to the neck, face and head.
2. Brimless with peak.

IS : 2925-1984, 2745-1983 specifies various requirements of helmets for different work conditions.

5.32.3 PPE for Eye Protection

In some operations it is necessary to choose PPE that will cover the entire face to protect against mechanical injury, chemicals, rays etc. Eyes can be injured from dust, flying particles, harmful radiation, handling, splashing of molten metals while welding, fine particles while cutting, and in some cases harmful radiations.

The following types of PPE provide eye protection:

1. Safety goggles,
2. Safety spectacles, and
3. Safety clip-ons.

The following types of PPE provide protection to both eyes and face :
1. Eye shield,
2. Face shield, and
3. Wire mesh screen guard.

5.32.4 PPE for Hand and Arm Protection

About one-third of the injuries that occur involve hand and arms. Such injuries occur when the workman has to handle materials with sharp ends, hot metals, chemicals, corrosive substances, electrical works etc. In case of workers continuously in contact with concrete and cement, skin diseases develop after some years. In such situations use of PPE to protect hands and arms are absolutely necessary. The portion of hand and arm exposed to the hazard is to be fully covered with suitable material that provides adequate protection against the hazard. The types of Hand and Arm type of PPE are as follows :

- Gloves
- Wrist gloves
- Hand pads
- Thumb and finger and sleeve guards

Normally the most common PPE for hand and arm protection is the gloves which are made up of rubber (natural or synthetic). Particularly care is to be taken when workers are in contact with concrete. If concrete particles go in the sleeves of gloves, it get hardened and the gloves will be useless in short time. IS : 4770-1991 gives specifications for Rubber Gloves for Electrical Purposes. IS : 6994 (Part 1)-1973 gives specifications of Leather and Cotton Gloves.

5.32.5 PPE for Foot and Legs Protection

Protection to foot and leg is required while handling material like cement and concrete and to protect them from nails and other pointed things. Commonly used foot and leg PPE are safety shoes, foot guards, kneepads, leggings and leg guards depending upon nature of hazards. In case of tunneling work where explosions are involved, shoes protect legs from possible injuries. Depending upon the nature of hazards, safety shoes are classified into following six principal types :

- Safety-toe shoes,
- Explosives-operations (non-sparking) shoes,
- Electrical hazard shoes, and
- Shoes suitable for mining operations.

IS : 1989 (Part 1 and 2) - 1986 gives specifications for Leather Safety Boots and Shoes.

5.32.6 Safety Belts and Harness

Safety belts and harness are required to be used by workers who have to work at heights, where a fall may result in serious injury or death. These can be of following types :

- **Body Belt**
  - To limit movement and positioning.
  - To restrict the worker to a safe area.
  - To help prevent a fall.

Body belts allow freedom of body movements. So it can be used where limited fall hazards exist.

- **Body Harness**
  - This is used when the worker must move at dangerous heights.
  - In a fall, the harness distributes impact force over a wider body area than does a belt, reducing the possibility of injury to the wearer.
- **Suspension Belt**
  - This is used at those work situations where it is not possible to work from a fixed surface and the worker must be totally supported by a suspension harness, as in the case of work for suspension bridges or cable stayed bridge, etc.

Lifelines of safety belts and harness are usually nylon ropes of 12 mm diameter or manila ropes of 19 mm diameter. The lifeline should be spliced into snaps and D-rings instead of being knotted.

5.32.7 PPE for Ear Protection

Ear protection is required while working in the close vicinity of high noise which may damage the workers physiologically and psychologically. Ear protectors are of following types :

1. Plug or insert type,
2. Cup or muff type, and
3. Helmet type, which completely surrounds the head

5.32.8 PPE for Respiratory Protection

While working in wells or tunnels, workers may come across toxic gases. To protect them, respiratory protection devices are used which are of following types :

1. **Emergency Type :** Situations where rapid and dangerous effect on life or health even when exposed for short duration.
2. **Non Emergency Type :** Situations where no rapid and dangerous effect on life or health.

The devices like chemical cartridge respirator, canister type gas masks (in case of oxygen deficiency) are most commonly used. Following figure shows some of the personal protective equipments.

Helmet

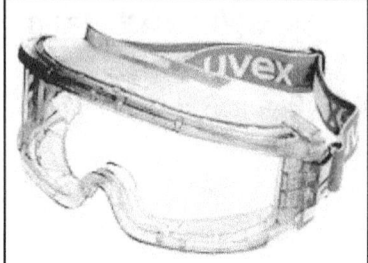
Googles

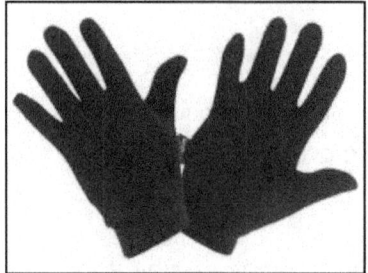
Hand gloves

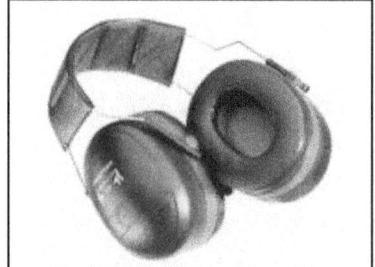
Ear protectors

Safety shoes

Safety belts and life line

Respiratory device

Fig. 5.20 : Personal protective equipments

IMPORTANT POINTS

- Points for educating employees towards safety awareness.
- Causes of accidents and its types :

    Technical causes

    Human causes due to his ignorance
- Costs associated with accidents :

    (a) Direct costs

    (b) Indirect costs
- Common causes leading to accidents on sites and precautions taken to avoid it with their types.
- Safety programme related to building construction.
- Different types of principal Hazards in construction industry.
- Importance of site layout w.r.t. access to site and positioning of different activities on ground.
- Need of PPE, w.r.t. quality, selection and its use.
- Types of PPE while working on construction sites of different activities.

QUESTIONS

1. Bring out importance of materials management in construction industry.
2. Write in details about the functions of the Materials Manager.
3. How economic use of materials can be effected ?
4. Write in details about the Inventory and Inventory control.
5. What are the important aspects of storing of materials ? Bring out all details.
6. What is Economic Order Quantity ? Explain in details. Derive the expression for EOQ.
7. What is A-B-C Analysis? Write in details about the same giving examples.
8. Write short notes about the following :

    (a) Phasing of construction material purchase.

    (b) Inventory cost and procurement cost.

    (c) Issue of materials on indent.

    (d) Procurement of materials.

    (e) Economic use of materials.

(f) Duties of storekeeper.

(g) Lead time.

(h) MRP system.

(i) Buffer stock.

9. What are various inventory models ? Explain them briefly.

10. What are various methods of purchasing ? Explain them briefly.

11. A company uses 3000 units of some material costing ` 1.50 per unit, ordering cost is ` 30/- per order and holding cost is about 20% per year of average inventory.

  (i) Find EOQ

  (ii) If safety stock is 4,500 units and lead time is 14 days find the reorder point and maximum inventory.

12. Enlist four reasons as to why we carry inventories. Explain atleast two of these. [4]

13. 'ABC analysis is for selective control'. Explain with suitable example. [5]

14. What do you mean by : [6]

  (i) Lead time and factors affecting lead time.

  (ii) Economic lot size.

  (iii) Safety stock

15. What are the qualities required for Material Manager ? [4]

16. Explain the mechanics of classifying A, B, C items in case of Material Management. [4]

17. Draw an inventory model showing lead time, safety stock, minimum stock level, maximum stock and rate of consumption. [4]

18. What is stockout ? What are the effects of stockouts ? [3]

19. Explain lead time. What are the factors on which lead time depends ? [3]

20. State and explain any four functions of a Project Manager on a construction site. [4]

21. What do you mean by : [5]

  (i) Economic lot size (ii) Lead time (iii) Safety stock

22. Explain fleet management.

23. Explain aspect of fleet management.

24. Explain productivity studies.

25. Explain safety consciousness and accident control.

26. Write in details about safety programmes.

UNIVERSITY QUESTIONS

1. Describe briefly how ABC Analysis can be applied to : **[Dec. 02] [5]**
   (i) Purchase policy (ii) Marketing (iii) Inventory Control

2. Write short notes on :
   (i) Purchase order
   (ii) Inventory and Inventory control
   (iii) EOQ, BOQ and AOQ
   (iv) Advantages of centralisation of stores and purchasing.
   (v) Objectives of Material Management. **[Dec. 02]**
   (vi) Fixed and Variable cost. **[Dec. 02]**
   (vii) Procurement cost and Inventory Carrying Cost. **[May 04]**

3. Explain centralisation and decentralisation of stores and purchasing. **[May 05] [5]**

4. What is ABC Analysis ? Explain how it is carried out and state its applications. **[May 05] [5]**

5. What is ABC Analysis ? How is it useful in Construction Industry ? **[Dec. 08] [6]**

6. What is the importance of material management. **[May 09] [6]**

7. Explain various activities carried out under stores department. **[May 09] [4]**

8. What are the objectives of Materials Management ? **[Dec. 09] [5]**

9. Discuss the procedure for generation of a purchase order. **[Dec. 09] [6]**

10. With the help of appropriate format explain how an indent order is made. **[Dec. 09] [6]**

11. Explain the procedure of A-B-C analysis. Plot the typical A-B-C curve. Give examples of material being classified as A-B-C materials. **[Dec. 09] [6]**

12. What is inventory ? Explain significance of inventory. What are the different types of inventories ? **[Dec. 09] [5]**

13. Explain the term project updating. Under what circumstances do we need to update a project ? **[Dec. 09] [5]**

14. What do you mean by inventory ? Name the list of inventory used in construction of residential building. **[Dec. 10] [6]**

15. Differentiate between Economic Order Quantity and arbitrary order quantity. **[Dec. 10] [6]**

16. State any 4 functions of materials manager. **[Dec. 10] [4]**
17. Enlist any four functions of materials management and explain inventory control.
    [May 11] [4]
18. What are the objectives of material management ? **[Dec. 11] [6]**
19. Explain in brief (any 4) : **[Dec. 11] [16]**
    (a) Factors affecting EOQ.
    (b) Lead time, safety stock
    (c) Advantage of A-B-C analysis
    (d) Advantages of centralisation of stores and purchasing.
    (e) Qualities of a materials manager.
20. (a) What are the objectives of materials management? **[May 12] [6]**
    (b) Define "Inventory" and "Inventory Management". What are the different methods of inventory control? **[May 12] [2 + 2]**
21. (a) Define the terms: **[Dec. 12] [8]**
    (i) Safety stock
    (ii) Lead time
    (iii) Inventory
    (iv) EOQ
    (b) Explain the importance of materials management in construction industry.
    [Dec. 12] [4]
22. What kind of safety measures are to be adopted on a tunnel construction site ?
    [Dec. 08] [6]
23. What are the various causes of accidents on any building site ? **[Dec. 08] [6]**
24. Define the following : **[Dec. 08] [6]**
    (i) Injury frequency rate
    (ii) Injury severity rate
    (iii) Injury index.
25. A tunnel of length 1.0 km is to be constructed across a hill. Draw a good site layout to facilitate various operations such as blasting, muck removal, ventilation etc., during the construction of the tunnel. **[Dec. 08] [8]**
26. Write short notes on :
    (i) Functions of material manager **[Dec. 08]**

(ii) Inventory control. **[Dec. 08]**

27. Write the important functions of Safety Manager on a construction site.

[May 09] [6]

28. Explain, how the following materials are stored on construction site ? Cement, Aggregates, Steel, Bricks, Paints, Plumbing materials. **[May 09] [6]**

29. How can you achieve quality control for brickwork and plastering on a residential site ? **[May 09] [6]**

30. Write the safety instructions to be followed for a Precast Girder bridge at launching state. **[May 09] [6]**

31. What are the effects of accident on site ? **[May 09] [6]**

32. What are the responsibilities of a project manager with respect to safety management on construction sites ? **[Dec. 09] [5]**

33. Design a safety guideline/checklist of High Rise Building Construction. **[Dec. 09] [6]**

34. Discuss various causes of accidents related to construction cranes. **[Dec. 09] [5]**

35. Write a detail note on occupational Health Hazards. **[Dec. 10] [9]**

36. Write a safety programme for a Road project. **[Dec. 10] [9]**

37. What are the causes and types of accidents ? **[Dec. 10] [9]**

38. Define Injury Frequency Rate and Injury Severity rate. **[May 11] [4]**

(a) As a project manager on site, mention the safety precautions you will take for the labours working at height. **[May 11] [6]**

39. (a) For the site you have visited, write a report on the safety policy adopted on site. Mention the safety gadgets used. **[May 11] [6]**

(b) What are the common accidents that may take place at the time of excavation ? Write the measures to be taken on site to avoid them. **[May 11] [6]**

40. (a) A highway of length 7.5 km is to be constructed. Draw a site layout to facilitate various operations. **[Dec. 11] [8]**

Hint : Students should assume either concrete or bituminous road, considering the requirements and plan the site layout.

(b) What safety measures will you adopt during the construction of a tunnel ?

[Dec. 11] [8]

41. (a) What are the factors affecting the selection of a site layout ? **[Dec. 11] [6]**

(b) What are the causes of accidents on a dam site ? **[Dec. 11] [6]**

(c) What are the various personal protective equipment ? **[Dec. 11] [4]**

43. Explain various precautions required to be adopted for scaffolding, ladders and formwork. **[May 12] [3 + 3 + 3]**
44. Why is safety training required? Write a safety programme for a National Highway project. **[May 12] [2 + 4]**
45. What are the different causes of accident at a tunnel site? **[May 12] [6]**
46. What are the various causes of accidents on any multistoreyed building site? **[Dec. 12] [5]**
47. What are the responsibilities of a safety manager on construction sites? **[Dec. 12] [5]**
48. Explain the significance of "Safety Programme" and "Safety Training". **[Dec. 12] [6]**

UNIT VI

PROJECT APPRAISAL

6.1 PHASES IN DEVELOPMENT OF PROJECT

Phases in Development of Project

- Identification of suitable project.
- Preparation of technical, organisational, economical and financial reports.
- Financial Institutions do field investigations and carry out benefit/cost analysis.
- Negotiations takes place between financial institutions and borrower.
- Implementation and supervision of the project.
- Financial Institutions evaluate the project and prepare performance audit.

Steps before implementing of project.

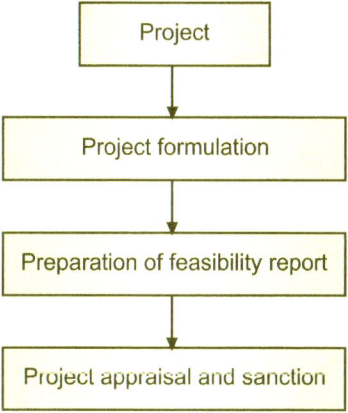

Fig. 6.1

Following are the steps involved in preparing feasibility study report of a project.

- General Information about the industry :
    - Analysis of the industry.
    - Past performance.
    - Type of industry.
- Preliminary analysis of alternatives : contains -
    - Present data on gap between demand and supply.
    - Present data on the capacity of production.
    - List of existing plants, capacity, level of production, list of proposed projects.

- Location of project and its implication.
- Foreign exchange requirement.
- Profitability of different options.
- Calculation of rate of return for different options.

Steps involved in doing preliminary study of a project :

- Product Description : contains –
    - Technology/process chosen for the project.
    - Information on optimality of location.
    - Environmental effects on population, air, water, land, flora and fauna.
    - Information on plant and equipment requirement, water, labour, transport, activity wise phasing of construction.
- Marketing Plan : should contain :
    - Market data, demand and supply.
    - Methods for making estimates.
    - Market areas.
    - Degree of price sensitivity.
    - Past trends in prices.
- Capital Requirement and Costs.
- Operating Cost Requirement.

6.2 PROJECT APPRAISAL

Appraisal is an evaluation or estimation of value. Normally, when a business entrepreneur undertakes a project it is with the objective of profiteering. Business organisation have to survive and grow, however it is necessary for them to undertake different projects as per the present needs or future needs of the society and to complete the same for the benefit of the society in general and to gain the profit for the organisation in particular. It is, therefore, necessary for the organisation to have project appraisal prior to the commencement of the project, so that after the project work is started there should not be any difficulty which may be detrimental to the working of the project and in some cases may terminate into closer. This will put the organisation in financial crises and hence preappraisal of the project before commencement is absolutely essential.

Any project undertaken should be for the benefit of the society in general, and for the benefit of the local population in particular. No project should be undertaken which may pollute the environment, may need large deforestation, may be detrimental to the fertility of the adjoining land, may need dislocation of the public on large scale and many other similar reasons. Non-destruction of natural resources and non-pollution of the atmosphere and environment are the major criteria which should be fulfilled by any big projects. The project should not disturb the ecology of the present system and should not disturb the rights and benefits enjoyed by the nearing population regarding drinking water, irrigation water, transportation system and the like. It is also necessary for the organisation undertaking the project that they have the necessary resources with them or such resources could be procured by them. In these resources the important are men consisting of technical personal and the labour and the necessary machinery. In addition to this required is the raw materials for the project. The organisation may not be able to carry out all the necessary activities and hence there may be need of subcontracting. For all above, MONEY is needed and final goal is 'making the estimated profit for the organisation' should be kept in mind. For all above, it is very necessary that there should be appraisal of the project before it is undertaken. The appraisal of any project is counted on the following criteria on which it should stand firmly :

1. Social Appraisal
2. Environmental Appraisal
3. Technical Appraisal
4. Financial Appraisal
5. Economical Appraisal
6. Technical Appraisal
7. Technolegal Appraisal

6.2.1 Social Appraisal

The project undertaken should be in general for the social benefits and in no case should be detrimental to society in general. A project can create employment opportunities to the exceeding population and can provide better transportation facilities and in general may become a source of uplift for the area and can raise standard of living of the nearby population. In such a case the project is accepted by the people of the area. However, if the project in any way creating difficulties in any manner to the population in adjoining area it is not only accepted by the people but there is adverse reaction of the people in the area. As such, it is necessary that information of the proposed project should be given wide publicity through advertisement in newspaper and other information media, and objection if any from the public be invited; so that they could be considered constructively and changes and amendments, if any may be made in the project; so that the project is accepted by the people.

6.2.2 Environmental Appraisal

Environmental aspects consist of air, water and soil pollution, list of pollutants/hazardous substances, their safety, handling and disposal arrangements, compliance with national and international standards, clearances and no objection certificates required and obtained etc.

The goods and services provided by natural resources play an important role in the economy of any country or region. Environmental appraisal is the term used to describe the assessment of the environmental effects of proposed land-use policies, plans or programme and to evaluate the likely significant environmental consequences of it.

Need for Environmental Appraisal

- All biological resources including their interrelationships, are natural assets. Human beings are benefited from those in the form of goods and services for current and future generations. However, world is facing increasing degradation and depletion of biological resources and bio-diversity.

- The deterioration of natural resources has generated many environmental problems that have spread from local origins to a much wider areas.

- Therefore, the economic value of natural resources is a key element for their effective management. Knowledge of their real value would allow different resources to be ranked in order of importance to define priorities of their optimum current and future use in society.

- Many countries have started indicating environmental sustainability based on GNP value to which certain numerical adjustments are applied to produce environmental values.

- In order to calculate the impacts of these indicators, economic values of natural resources are established. Thus, amortisation of natural asses and the loss of bio-diversity among other values can be deducted.

- Economic appraisal of natural resources and environmental services are based on market prices. For those goods (E.g. water, biological diversity, genetic resources etc) and services (environmental purification, soil fertility, capacity for assimiliation of waste, etc) for which a market does not exist, the methods focus on changes in environmental quality that affect human well being. Thus, quality will increase in the case of positive external action e.g. recreation, beauty of landscape etc. Quality will decrease in case of negative external action like noise, smoke, water pollution etc.

Stages of Environmental Assessment

- Defining the boundaries of investigation, assessment and assumptions needed.
- Documentation of the state of the environment.
- Determination of likely environmental impacts, to focus on direction of change rather than Fig.
- Informing and consulting the public.
- Giving decisions based on the assessment.
- Monitoring of the effects of plans and programmes after their implementation.

Aims of Environmental Appraisal

- Promotion of sustainable and equitable system.
- Encouragement of energy efficiency.
- Promotion of renewable resources.
- Enhancement and protection of built, physical, environmental including quality, character and distinctiveness.
- Overall effect on human well being and health.

Criteria of Appraisal

The criteria for carrying on the appraisal have been based on following :

- Physical environment on existing and proposed changes.
- Biodiveristy impacts.
- Social requirements and general well being.
- Economic considerations.
- Resource requirement and alternatives.
- Sustainability assessment.

Let us, consider a local area plan which is under development. It is to be reviewed and monitored which include the on-going appraisal of policies and proposals as well as the refinement of measurable indicators of environmental changes and actual scope of monitoring. Various units of the local area plan are judged for some criterions and its impact is given as √ for positive, * for negative, O for neutral and ? for uncertain.

The results are tabulated as under :

Units	Biodiversity	Population	Human Health	Flood/ Fauna	Water	Soil	Air Quality	Climate Factor	Material Heritage	Cultural Heritage	Landsacpe
Mixed Use	O	√	√	?	O	O	O	*	O	√	O
Retail Development	O	√	√	O	O	O	O	*	O	√	O
Exhibition Centre	O	√	√	?	O	O	O	*	O	√	√
Two Way Routing	O	√	√	?	O	O	*	*	O	O	O
Public open spaces	√	√	√	√	√	√	√	√	O	√	√
Public lighting	O	√	√	O	O	O	O	O	O	√	√
Surveying & monitoring	O	O	O	O	O	O	O	O	O	√	√
Archaelogical Interest	O	O	O	O	O	√	O	O	O	√	√
Conservation	O	O	O	?	O	√	O	O	O	√	√
Refurbishment	?	O	O	?	O	√	O	O	O	√	√
Infrastructure	O	*	O	?	O	*	*	O	O	O	√
Sustainable Building Practice	√	√	√	√	√	√	√	√	O	O	O

6.2.3 Technical Appraisal

The project is amalgamation of different activities, may be interdependent or independent. Each activity is a process for completion of which different technical and engineering operations are performed. The activities therefore, need material, man and machinery. The project is therefore broken into different activities and techniques like CANT, Chart, CPM or PERT or any recent technique is used to analyse the process and find out the requirements of the designers, engineers and other technical staff, labour and required machinery and material. After knowing all such requirements the entrepreneur is in a position to decide how these requirements can be met with either by employing the needed technical manpower or subletting some of the processes or activities in the project of different organizations working in these areas. Similarly, the requirement of needed machinery can be met with either machinery owned by the organisation or by hiring the same or again subletting a particular part or activity to organisations which are expert in particular process. Same thing can be said about the materials. Procurement of needed materials will consist of the location where materials are available, transportation storing and inventory. Sometimes, special materials may have to be imported to which government permission may be necessary. In simple language, this has been put up but the whole exercise requires knowledge of all the project and may be little complicated and may require sufficient time to come to proper conclusion. All this is the technical appraisal of the project which consist of knowing the complete requirement of technical staff required, technical work to be carried out, requirement of needed machinery and materials and the method of procurement of the same before commencement of the project.

6.2.4 Financial Appraisal

Ones the total requirement of man, material and machinery is known the organisation is in a position to come to a conclusion as to what would be financial requirement. The project may be spread over for a long period may be from 6 months for small project to 5-10 years for a big project. With the help of techniques like CPM, Gantt chart or any other recent techniques exact spread area of all the resources over the completion period of the project can be estimated and financial requirement can be contemplated. Depending upon the duration of the project proper escalation in the prices of material increase in the salary of technical and non-technical manpower has to be given proper consideration and financial requirement along the CPM line can be calculated. The organisation is then aware of the financial outlay needed for completion of the project. Provisions has also to be made for uncertainties and unforeseen expenditure. Thus, financial appraisal consists of completely knowing the periodical supply of money needed for the project from start to end without any kind of interception. It may be necessary to raise the capital by way of borrowing money from the banks or financial institution and hence the capital and interest to be paid will have to be considered in addition to the cost of other resources cited above. While giving considerations to all above, escalation to the prices should also be considered while calculating the total area of finance required from start to end and also to cash flow required for the total period of completion of the project. Taxes, duties, depreciation should also be considered while calculating the total cost of the project.

The organisation is receiving a business for gain of profit. Any project knowing the total cost of the project, therefore should finally be profitable. A fair percentage of profit is considered and that the final cost of the finished product has to be decided. This final cost of sale of finished product should be in comparison like the similar products of other entrepreneurs. Then only the project can be said successful. As such the financial appraisal is the approximate estimate of the expenditure required for the completion of the project and the final sale price of the project considering, the predecided percentage of the profit. If this sale price is acceptable to the consumers the project will be successful. Thus, the financial appraisal is the approximate estimate of the expenditure on the project and the income receivable from the sale of the finished product of the project which will give predetermined percentage of profit to the organisation.

6.2.5 Economical Analysis

Economical analysis consist of the provision of the finances required for the project. The total finance required has been worked out along with the cash flow necessary during the period of completion of the project. The organisation in most of the cases will not be able to invert all the finance necessary and hence it will be necessary to raise the necessary finance by way of raising loan or other present measures form the capital market. The ways and means for the same will have to be considered and decided. So that needed cash flow is available along the high period of the project. It will also be necessary to decide the methodology of sale of finished product keeping in mind the desirable percentage of profit and the benefit cost ratio. Considering all the variables the break even period to the product will have to be decided in economical appraisal.

Economics is optimum or best possible use of resources. The economical appraisal includes all the applied economics which relates the industry e.g. production, distribution, exchange and public finance. Industrialist have to read thoroughly consumers' behaviour for creating demands for their goods and for expanding their markets. Thus, economical analysis includes a study of industry, money, banking, trade, taxation and other fiscal matters, consumption pattern, demand and supply, factors of production, law of production and industrial management, labour problem, problem of accounting and costing etc. It is therefore, necessary to combine technical and economical knowledge. However, growth and application of mathematical tools, statistics and computer techniques have permitted the quantitative handling of economical problems and in economical analysis above techniques are used. Thus, considering the different variables in the project and using all modern techniques, economical appraisal is performed. However, it should be borne in mind that the ultimate aim of all engineering pursuits is nothing but to do maximum good for the maximum number of persons so that the nation is benefited.

6.2.6 Technolegal Appraisal

This is an upcoming area which is gaining popularity in all fields. Construction work involves large volume of finance, human resources, materials and is directly related with safety issues of labours and common man. Hence, technolegal consultancy is very important especially at tender stage and prebid stage. So that legal complications are minimized. Technolegal consultants play a vital role in tender submission, to frame condition of contract, special condition of contract to finalise arbitration clauses, to decide jurisdiction of disputes, etc., technolegal consultants also keenly frame the clauses related to quality of work, time of completion and specifications to remove any ambiguities. Thus looking at the vast scope of construction, there is equally vast scope of technolegal consultants in India.

6.3 METHODS OF FRAMING APPRAISALS

6.3.1 Technical Appraisal

The technical appraisal will consists of following steps :

1. Dividing the project is different activities and preparing a CPM net wise.
2. Finalising the requirements of administrative, technical and engineering personnel for each activity along the line of CPM.
3. Frame above deciding the technical manpower necessary for the project and the particular period if any for which the man power is needed.
4. Different types of technical personnel needed may be architects, engineering, designers, administrative officers, accounts officers, legal experts.
5. Deciding the requirements of skilled workers throughout the project. These skilled workers may consists of operations operating earth moving machinery, other drivers, masons, carpenters, concreters, painters, clerks, computer operators etc. This will also depend upon whether the actual construction work is carried by the organisation departmentally or by subletting to different organisations or contractors.
6. Deciding the requirements of unskilled labour.
7. Appraisal of the different types of machinery needed for the project including earthmoving machinery, road construction machinery, concreting machinery including mixers, compacter survey equipment etc. under the complete period of the project.

Thus, technical appraisal for any project is to have a total know how of the technical requirements which includes :

- Technical and engineering personnel and other administrative staff requirement.
- Requirement of skilled labour and semiskilled labour.
- Requirement of unskilled labour.
- Requirement of different machinery.
- Requirement of different kinds of material needed.

All these requirements along the CPM line should be completely known and plan how these requirements could be met with and should be ready.

6.3.2 Financial and Economical Appraisal

The financial and economical appraisal will consist of the following :

- Following the technical appraisal and knowning all these requirements. What will be the total cost of the project and how cash flow will have to be provided along the life of the project. While considering the total cost, the different taxes to be paid, fees to be paid for obtaining different permissions, legal expenditure for different contacts, escalation percentage over the period of the project, depreciation, maintenance cost of the machinery, running cost etc. has to be considered and provisions has to be made for unforeseen expenditure. In economical appraisal the organisation has to work as the ways and means of providing the necessary finance as and when required by way of finance which could be provided by the organisation and deciding different other ways of raising the necessary finance from capital market. It will also be necessary to decide about the methodology of sale of finished product, so that all the necessary cost of the project including the interest to be paid to raising the capital and other unproductive expenditure alongwith the predetermined percentage of project is recovered.

Following factors are considered in financial and economical analysis :

- Financial Analysis
  - To assess financial viability.
  - Consider depreciation, foreign exchange requirement, income tax rebate, incentive from backward area.
  - Carry out sensitivity analysis.
- Economic analysis
  - Impact of enterprise' operations on foreign trade.
  - Correction in input and costs.

Difference between Financial and Economical Analysis :

Sr. No.	Financial Analysis	Economical Analysis
1.	Costs and benefits of the project are considered from project entity point of view.	Costs and benefits are considered from society point of view.
2.	Costs and benefits are quantified.	Costs and benefits are quantified but sometimes qualitative study is also done.
3.	Taxes, duties, fees, local taxes, excise duties etc. are considered on cost side while subsidy on benefit side.	Taxes, duties, fees, local taxes, excise duties etc. are not considered on cost side at the same time, subsidy is also excluded from benefit side.
4.	Costs and benefits are measured at market prices.	Market process may be modified as shadow prices or world prices to calculate costs and benefits. These ensures efficient use of resources
5.	The objective of the analysis is to analyze / calculate profit of the project.	Objective of the analysis is to study contribution of the project towards development of nation

Interest and depreciation both are excluded from the total costs in both analyses. Interest is taken care of in discounting and as depreciation is neither a financial cost nor an economic one, rate of return takes care of depreciation.

6.4 CRITERIA FOR PROJECT SELECTION CAPITAL BUDGETING

As defined by - Charles T Horngren, "Capital budgeting is the long term planning to make and finance proposed capital outlays".

Capital budgeting is used :

- For long term planning for selection and financial investment proposals.
- Process of evaluating relative worth of long term investment proposals on the basis of their respective profitability.

Steps in Evaluating Capital Budgeting

- Generating investment proposals.
- Estimating cash flows for the proposals.

- Evaluating cash flow.
- Selection of projects on the acceptance criterion.
- Monitoring and reevaluating on a continuous basis, the investment projects, once they are accepted.

Characteristics of Capital Budgeting
- Involves substantial capital outlay.
- Long term implications.
- Can affect the future of the company.
- Once the funds are invested in one of the option, it is irreversible.
- Involves varying cash flows at different points of time.
- Considers Time Value of Money.

Kinds of Capital Budgeting Decisions

As discussed earlier, decisions are to be taken by an organisation for various reasons. They are :
- Replacement of old machinery / technique.
- Expansion of existing business.
- Diversification of products.
- Research and Development.
- Abandon the product / project.

For any of the above reason, one has to be very careful in forecasting and accordingly analyzing the present. Various methods are adopted for the same. Some of them are as follows :

Methods of Capital Budgeting
- Traditional methods :
    - Payback Period.
    - Accounting Rate of Returns.
- Discounted cash flow method :
    - Internal Rate of Return Method (IRR).
    - Net Present Worth Method (NPV).

6.4.1 Payback Period

- It is period within which original cost of project is recovered.
- Payback period = $\dfrac{\text{Cost of the project}}{\text{Annual cash inflows}}$

- If cash inflows are uneven, take cumulative cash inflows and find time to recover original cost.
- Where the cash inflows are same but timing is different, choose the project which has higher cash inflows in the initial years.

Advantages of Pay Back Period
- Easy to calculate and understand.
- Emphasis on the earlier cash flows are more likely to be accurate than later cash flow.
- Reliable technique for volatile business conditions such as change in technology, changing fashions or customer's taste/ preferences.

Disadvantages of Pay Back Period
- Ignores earnings after pay back period, total life of project and total profitability.
- All cash flows are given equal weightages.
- Liquidity of the proposal is over emphasized by choosing only cash inflows.

Example 6.1 : The cost of a project is ₹ 50,000. Annual cash inflow for the next 4 years is ₹ 25,000 per year. What is the payback period for the project at discount rate of 8% ?

Solution : Method 1 : If the above example is to be solved by traditional method, i.e. without considering discounted returns, the payback period is 2 years since after two years, total cash inflow is ₹ 50,000 which is equal to the cost of project.

Following table shows the present worth of cash inflow for 4 years

Year	Cash Inflow	Present Worth	Cumulative Returns
1	25,000	$25000/(1 + 0.8) = 23148$	23148
2	25,000	$25000/(1 + 0.8)^2 = 21433$	44581
3	25,000	$25000/(1 + 0.8)^3 = 19845$	64426
4	25,000	$25000/(1 + 0.8)^4 = 18375$	82801

As calculated above, payback period is between year 2 and 3. If calculated by the method of interpolation, payback period comes out to be 2.273 years.

Remember

If payback period and cost of both projects are same, the one is chosen which gives more returns initially.

6.4.2 Accounting Rate of Return (ARR) Method

- ARR = $\dfrac{\text{Average annual profits after taxes}}{\text{Average Investment}}$

- Average investment = half of original investment.
- Higher ARR, better is the profitability.
- If working capital and scrap is added,
  - Average investment = (Cost − Scrap)/2 + Scrap of old asset + Working Capital.

Advantages of ARR Method
- Easy to calculate, understand.
- Can be compared with the cut-off point of return and hence decision is easy.
- Considers all cash inflows.
- Reliable as it considers earnings, depreciation, interest and taxes.

Disadvantages of ARR Method
- Time value of money not considered.
- Unless a cut-off point of return, rate of return is meaningless.
- Method is not standardized.
- Concept is not reliable.

Discounted Cash Flow Methods
- Discounted cash flows are the future cash inflows reduced to their present value based on a discounting factor.
- The process of reducing the future cash inflows to their present value based on a discounting factor or cut-off return is called discounting.
- Considers time value of money.

6.4.3 Net Present Value Method (May 11, 12, Nov./Dec. 12)

Net Present Value refers to the excess of present value of future cash inflows over and above the cost of original investment :

$$NPV = (PVCFAT) - (PVC)$$

PVCFAT = Present value of future cash inflows after taxes.

PVC = Present value of original investment or capital.

NPV of a project is the sum of present values of all cash flows (positive as well as negative) that are expected to occur over the life of the project.

$$NPV = \sum_{t=1}^{n} \frac{C_t}{(1+i)^t} - \text{Initial investment}$$

Where,
C_t = Cash flow at the end of year t

n = Life of project

i = Discount rate

Criteria for Selection of Project
If NPV > 0; project is accepted
If NPV < 0; project is rejected
If NPV = 0; indifferent (risky situation)

Procedure of Calculating NPV
- From PV factor table, identify PV factor for the given discount rate.
- Multiply cash flows with the corresponding PV factor to find
  DCF = (PV) × (CFAT)
- Find sum of products.
- If sum is positive, project is profitable.
- In case of projects with different NPVs, choose the project with highest NPV.

Example 6.2 : Cost of a project is ₹ 50,000 has cash flow of ₹ 22,000 for a period of 5 years. What is the NPV if the firm expects 14% per annum ? Also state whether the project is feasible or not.

Solution :

$$NPV = \sum_{t=1}^{n} \frac{C_t}{(1+i)^t} - \text{Initial investment}$$

$$= \frac{22000}{(1+0.14)} + \frac{22000}{(1+0.14)^2} + \frac{22000}{(1+0.14)^3} + \frac{22000}{(1+0.14)^4} + \frac{22000}{(1+0.14)^5} - 50,000$$

$$= 75527 - 50000$$

$$= ₹ 25527$$

As NPV > 0, the project may be accepted.

Example 6.3 : From the following details relating to two projects A and B, suggest which one is to be accepted using NPV method.

	Project A	Project B
Estimated cost (in ₹)	350000	415000
Estimated life (in years)	6	7
Annual income (in ₹)		
Year 1	1,50,000	1,70,000
2	1,50,000	1,60,000
3	76,000	1,00,000
4	70,000	75,000
5	65,000	60,000
6	50,000	60,000
7	Nil	50,000

The company expects a return of 10%.

Solution : Project A :

$$NPV = \frac{150000}{(1+0.1)^1} + \frac{150000}{(1+0.1)^2} + \frac{76000}{(1+0.1)^3} + \frac{70000}{(1+0.1)^4} + \frac{65000}{(1+0.1)^5}$$

$$+ \frac{50000}{(1+0.1)^6} - 350000$$

$$= 83,825$$

Project B :

$$NPV = \frac{170000}{(1+0.1)} + \frac{160000}{(1+0.1)^2} + \frac{100000}{(1+0.1)^3} + \frac{75000}{(1+0.1)^4} + \frac{60000}{(1+0.1)^5}$$

$$+ \frac{60000}{(1+0.1)^6} + \frac{50000}{(1+0.1)^7} - 415000$$

$$= 94,915$$

As NPV for project B > NPV for project A, Project B is selected.

Example 6.4 : A company is thinking about investing ₹ 10 lakhs in a new project. According to budget analysis the company will generate the following cash flows. The rate of interest is 12%. Should the company invest in the new project? **[May 12] [8]**

Year	Cash flow in ₹
1	2 lakhs
2	6 lakhs
3	8 lakhs
4	2 lakhs

Solution :

$$NPV = \left(\frac{2}{1.12} + \frac{6}{1.12^2} + \frac{8}{1.12^3} + \frac{2}{1.12^4}\right) - 10 \text{ lakhs}$$

$$= ₹ 3.53 \text{ lakhs}$$

as NPV is positive, the company may invest in the new project.

Example 6.5 : A company wishes to invest in a new project. It has two alternatives A and B. Following data pertains to the two alternatives. **[May 12] [10]**

Particulars	Project A	Project B
Initial investment	1,00,000	1,50,000
Cash inflows		
Year 1	70,000	90,000
2	50,000	85,000
Interest Rate	10%	10%

Which project will the company select based on N.P.V. and I.R.R.?

Solution :

	Project A	**Project B**
NPV	$\left(\dfrac{70000}{1.1} + \dfrac{50000}{1.1^2}\right) - 1,00,000$ = ₹ 4956.7	$\left(\dfrac{90000}{1.1} + \dfrac{85000}{1.1^2}\right) - 1,50,000$ = ₹ 2066.11
	∴ Select Project A	
IRR	$\dfrac{70000}{(1+i)} + \dfrac{50000}{(1+i)^2} = 1,00,000$ By trial and error method, $i \doteq 14\%$	$\dfrac{90000}{(1+i)} + \dfrac{85000}{(1+i)^2} = 1,50,000$ By trial and error method, $i \doteq 11\%$
	∴ Select Project A	

6.4.4 Internal Rate of Return Method (May 12, Nov./Dec. 12)

It is that rate of return at which the present value of expected cash flows of a project exactly equals the original investment. In other words, IRR of a project is the discount rate which makes its NPV = 0. It is a trial and error method.

- It equates the present value of a given project with its outlay.
- This is the cut-off point at which the income equals the expenditure or the investment breaks even.
- It is the rate at which the difference between the present value of cash inflows and the original cost is equal to zero.
- Higher the IRR, better is the profitability.

Advantages

- Based on time value of money.
- Based on inflows of all years.
- Compares projects with different cash inflows and life span.
- Independent of cost of capital.
- Contributes to "wealth maximisation goal" of the finance manager.

Disadvantages

- Difficult to understand.
- There could be non-conventional projects with multiple IRR where this method is hard to apply.

Putting the value of NPV = 0; following is the formula for IRR

$$0 = \sum_{t=1}^{n} \frac{C_t}{(1+i)^t} - \text{Initial investment}$$

Number of periods i.e. t is known, also C_t is known. By trial and error method, i is calculated.

Example 6.6 : A project cost ₹ 1,00,000. Its estimated life is 6 years with an average annual cash flow of ₹ 40,000. Calculate IRR for the same.

Solution : Putting these values in the formula above,

$$0 = \frac{40000}{(1+i)} + \frac{40000}{(1+i)^2} + \frac{40000}{(1+i)^3} + \frac{40000}{(1+i)^4} + \frac{40000}{(1+i)^5} - 100000$$

Trial 1; consider i = 10%; RHS = 75210

Trial 2; consider i = 20%; RHS = 34086

Trial 3; consider i = 30%; RHS = 8195

Trial 4; consider i = 40%; RHS = – 18,593

For i = 33.7%, RHS equals 0.

∴ IRR = 33.7%

Example 6.7 : For the example 6.3 given for NPV, find the IRR for both methods. Which project is to be selected based on IRR?

Solution : For Project A :

$$0 = \frac{150000}{(1+i)} + \frac{150000}{(1+i)^2} + \frac{76000}{(1+i)^3} + \frac{70000}{(1+i)^4} + \frac{65000}{(1+i)^5} + \frac{50000}{(1+i)^6} - 350000$$

Trial 1; i = 20%; RHS = 228

Trial 2; i = 19%; RHS = -6826

For i = 19.98 %, RHS equals 0.

∴ IRR = 19.98%

For Project B :

$$0 = \frac{170000}{(1+i)} + \frac{160000}{(1+i)^2} + \frac{100000}{(1+i)^3} + \frac{75000}{(1+i)^4} + \frac{60000}{(1+i)^5} + \frac{60000}{(1+i)^6} + \frac{50000}{(1+i)^7} - 415000$$

Trial 1; i = 20%; RHS = –10022

Trial 2; i = 17%; RHS = 16228

For i = 18.83 %, RHS equals 0.

∴ IRR = 18.83%

As IRR for Project A > IRR for project B, Project A is selected.

Example 6.8 : Find IRR for the project with following details :

(i) Duration of project – 5 years

(ii) Initial investment – ₹ 10,000/-

(iii) Periodic return – ₹ 5,000 per year

Solution :

Duration = 5 years

Initial investment = Rs. 10,000/-

Periodic return = Rs. 5,000/- per year

Let IRR = i%

$$\therefore \frac{5000}{(1+i)} + \frac{5000}{(1+i)^2} + \frac{5000}{(1+i)^3} + \frac{5000}{(1+i)^4} + \frac{5000}{(1+i)^5} - 10{,}000 = 0$$

To start with, assume i = 20%

Using trial and error method, I = 41%.

Difference between NPV and IRR

- In IRR, we assume that the cash inflows during life of the project are reinvested at the same IRR.
- In NPV, it is assumed that it is reinvested as per the opportunity available.

6.4.5 Benefit Cost Ratio

It is simply the division of benefits from a project (cash inflows) to cost involved (cash outflow). The project that gives maximum benefit to cost ratio is selected.

6.4.6 Break Even Analysis

One of the important indicators of success of the start-up company is the time from starting the business till the moment when revenues of product sales equals the total costs associated with the sale of product – it is also called break-even point. In other words *profit = 0*. Breakeven analysis is accounting tool to help plan and control the business operations. Break-even point represents the volume of business, where company's total revenues (money coming into a business) are equal to its total expenses (total costs).

Total Revenue = Total cost

Break-even analysis is based on categorizing production costs between those which are :

- VARIABLE cost that do vary with the number of units produced and sold (raw materials, fuel, direct labor, revenue-related costs), and those that are
- FIXED costs that don't vary with the number of units produced and sold (salaries, rent and rates, depreciation, marketing costs, administration costs, R and R, insurance)

Calculating Break-even Point

To calculate break-even point we need to know following information :

- The price that the company is charging,
- variable costs (direct costs) of each unit and
- fixed costs (or indirect costs/overheads).

$$TR = \text{Total Revenue}$$
$$P = \text{Selling Price}$$
$$Q = \text{Number of Units Sold}$$
$$TC = \text{Total Costs}$$
$$F = \text{Fixed Costs}$$
$$V = \text{Variable Costs}$$
$$FC = \text{Total fixed Costs}$$
$$VC = \text{Total variable Costs}$$
$$TR = P \times Q$$
$$VC = C \times Q$$
$$TC = FC + VC$$
$$TR - TC = \text{profit}$$

Because there is no profit

$$TR - TC = 0$$
$$P \times Q - (F + V \times Q) = 0$$
$$Q = F \times (P - V)$$

It is quicker to use the following formula :

$$\text{Break Even Point} = FC / (P - VC)$$

Note : the higher the fixed costs are the higher is the break-even point!

Example of Break-even analysis diagram

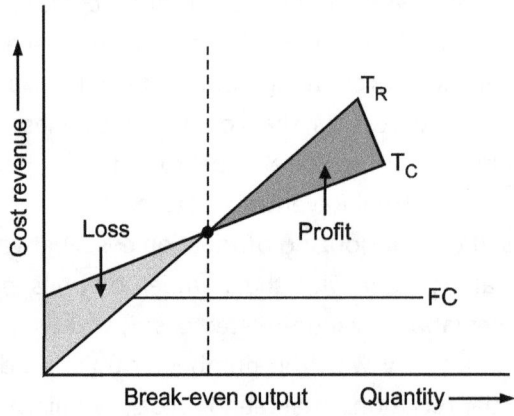

Fig. 6.2

Why do companies want (and need) to know the break-even point?

- First, in order to even know what volume of operations allows them to operate without loss, or, what is the volume of business in which the loss breaks in the profits;
- further in order to determine, if they sufficient capacity for this volume of business and ultimately therefore, to find out if there is sufficient market for such volume of operations

6.5 DETAILED PROJECT REPORT (DPR)

Detailed project report (DPR) is a complete document for investment decision-making, approval, planning. DPR is base document for planning and implementing the project. Preparation of DPR is a step in building up the proposal. When a major investment proposal has been approved on the basis of functional report, it would be necessary for DPR to firm up the proposal for the capital cost as well as the various facilities.

6.5.1 Contents of DPR

There is no set pattern for the DPR. However, the contents may include following points and varies from project to project.

General Information

- The general information provided could be as follows :
- Name of the project
- Name of client and consultant
- Constitution of the proposed company (for e.g. whether it is public or private limited) and sector
- Nature of industry and product
- Cost of the project

Means of finance

Contractor's Details

The business and family background of the contractors are mainly discussed under this heading. Their previous business experience and performance, if any, will be explained here.

Particulars of the Project

It includes

- Specifications of the project
- Location and site
- Plant and machinery
- Inventory required
- Utilities

Technical Arrangements

The technical infrastructure required to start the project, and whether the contractor have any foreign collaboration(s) for the project will be explained here. The cost of buying or installing technical infrastructure and whether it is cost effective, will be clarified under this heading.

Construction Process

The technical process proposed is explained enclosing copy of the activity flow chart with resources.

Environmental Aspects

The impact of discharging effluents of the production process in the environment, as well as, precautions that have to be taken will be dealt with, in this area of the report

- Furnish details of the nature of atmospheric, soil and water pollution. Indicate whether necessary permissions for the disposal of effluents have been obtained.
- Enclose copy of approval from concerned authorities.

Schedule of Implementation

- Describe how design engineering, erection, construction, installation and commissioning of the project will be carried out
- Furnish the schedule of implementation

Cost of the Project

The detailed break up of all costs related with the project, has to be listed, here :

- Land
- Site development
- Buildings and other civil works
- Plant and machinery
- Technical know how fees
- Expenses on technicians
- Miscellaneous Fixed Assets (MFA)
- Preliminary
- Preoperative expenses
- Provision for contingencies
- Margin money for working capital (give details of calculations)

Means of Finance

The break up and sources of funds for the project are discussed :

- Equity- Promoters, Financial Institutions, Public holdings, and others
- Pref. Shares

- Subsidy (if any)
- Term loans
- Debentures
- Unsecured loans and deposits
- Deferred payments
- Internal accruals
- Bank borrowings
- Working capital
- Others

Profitability Estimates

- Assumptions
- Projected income statement
- Projected balance sheet
- Projected cash flow statement

Appraisal Based on Profitability Estimates

- Give estimates of costs of production and working results for the first 10 years in annexure
- Provide a cash flow statement for the company as a whole
- Provide a projected balance sheet for ten operating years
- Give the break even and sensitivity analysis for the project

Economic Considerations

- Give prices of competing import and export products and landed costs and selling prices.
- Provide explanation for differences in prices, between the product and those imported
- Brief write ups on the economic benefits to the region and country due to the proposed project

Appendices

- Estimates of costs of production
- Calculation of depreciation
- Calculation of working capital and margin money for working capital
- Repayment/ Interest schedule of term loan and finance

- Calculation of tax
- Various Coverage ratios
- Various Evaluation technique like NPV, IRR, NBCR, BCR, PI, DPB etc. to evaluate the project and its viability
- Sensitivity analysis

Hence these DPR is to be made before investment in any project. Thus formulation of investment is based on the studies made. These can be considered as pre-investment decision. Detailed project report is prepared not only for the investment decision-making approval, but also execution of the project and preparation of the plan.

6.6 PROJECT FEASIBILITY REPORT

Feasibility study report is prepared to support the investment proposal. Feasibilities for the various aspects related to technical, commercial and financial are examined in detail by the experts and consultants brought in feasibility study report. Feasibility study report is termed as a techno economic feasibility study. It is the primary report for the formulation of the investment proposal. Investment decisions are taken based on the details incorporated in the study. Thus feasibility is prepared only for the formulation and investment decision-making. The first step in feasibility study is the needs analysis in which overall objectives of the system proposed is designed. The second and perhaps the most important thing is system identification.

6.6.1 Feasibility Study Report Contains

- A broad indication of demand and availability of the product.
- Required sources for the development of the project.
- Selection of suitable process and technology.
- Fixation of capacity on the basis of the project.
- Process description and layout plans for the project.
- Available facilities.
- Evaluation of available facilities.
- Capital cost.
- Profitability analysis.
- Project schedule and schedule control.
- Design and flow diagrams.

After the preparation of feasibility study report, it should be submitted to the experts of the concerned departments of operation such as finance, commercial, project etc to examine it. In case of any differences, the feasibility study report is discussed with the experts, consultants and is modified according to it.

6.7 ROLE OF PROJECT MANAGEMENT CONSULTANT

Project Management Consultancy (PMC) is one of the management solutions to improve the efficiency of a project in construction. The use of these services has been increased in construction industry around the world. Many companies have invested in training project managers to employ this approach.

6.7.1 Definition of Project Management Consultant

There is no specific definition of project consultant. In general, it can be defined by giving its roles, responsibilities and services that they provide using tools and skills they have in delivering a task assigned by the client or the owner of the project. Some of the contractors do some consulting, and some of the consultant also acts as contractors. This happens because the roles and responsibilities of consultants are very wide and depends on their skills and experiences. Consultation is happening if the clients seek expert knowledge or some opinions on some engineering problems or anything that involves engineering matters.

PMCs have different roles or scope of works and services depending on whom they represent such as :

(1) PMCs representing the Clients (public/government) and private sectors (developers, investors, landowners)
(2) PMCs representing the Designers (architects, engineer, etc)
(3) PMCs representing the Contractor (traditional, turnkey, design and build)

6.7.2 Preconstruction Stage Responsibilities

- Analyze Client's project related requirements
- Prepare the Design Brief in terms of function ability, cost, time, quality and safety
- Develop project control systems
- Finalization of project organization chart.
- Establishment of project communication and reporting system
- Preparation of works breakdown structure
- Preparation of Project Master Schedule with base line
- Preparation of Design / Drawings deliverables schedule
- Feedback on the Master Budget of the project
- Co-ordination and follow-up with Architect and other design consultants for their inputs
- To identify and suggest consultants/designers for specialized requirements
- Lead project meetings as necessary for review of progress
- To set up, track, monitor a design deliverable schedule
- Checking and verification of designer's submissions (design basis reports, value engineering, cost benefit analysis, drawings etc)

- Cost control during all stages of design and design development
- Preparation of procurement plan
- Review of technical specifications and Bill of Quantities (BOQ)
- Monitoring the statutory approvals process by follow-ups with liaison consultants and reporting the progress.
- Conducting Pre-bid meetings and feedback for completeness of tender specifications and technical parameters.
- Comparative statements & techno-commercial evaluation reports
- Submitting Weekly and Monthly progress reports

6.7.3 Responsibilities in Construction Phase

- Full time supervision of All construction works / activities for the project
- On-site design co-ordination and issue of drawings / clarifications
- Organize approval to contractors shop drawings, product data sheets, samples
- Refinement of works breakdown structure
- Monitoring the progress of work with the Master construction schedule
- Prior flagging of anticipated bottlenecks and analysis of its reasons
- Day to day correspondences including contractual issues
- Change order management for design changes and extra items
- Prepare QA/QC plan and Method Statement
- Quality assurance and control to ensure conformance to drawings and specifications
- Establish EHS plan (Environment, Health and Safety)
- Issue drawings to respective contractors and keep updated record issued.
- Scrutinize and check working drawings received from Architects /designer
- Organize Progress review meetings on weekly basis.
- Collect, review and maintain all the records of contractors' daily progress reports

6.7.4 Post Construction Responsibilities

- Advice about probable date of Substantial Completion
- Preparing and addressing the schedule of defects / punch lists
- Provide assistance in Testing and commissioning of the facility
- Collection and integration of various O and M manuals, commissioning & test certificates
- Reconciliation and Certification of Final bills of contractors, suppliers, vendors and consultants
- Preparation of project close-out report including learning

- Collate and verify all As-built drawings
- Addressing any queries during defects liability period
- Co-ordination with the Contractors to rectify the defects during the defects liability period.

Example 6.9 : Example 6.3 can be solved with method of benefit to cost ratio as :

Solution : Project A :

$$\text{Benefits} = \frac{150000}{(1+0.1)} + \frac{150000}{(1+0.1)^2} + \frac{76000}{(1+0.1)^3} + \frac{70000}{(1+0.1)^4} + \frac{65000}{(1+0.1)^5} + \frac{50000}{(1+0.1)^6}$$

$$= 4,33,825$$

Cost = 3,50,000

Benefit cost ratio = 1.24

Project B :

$$\text{Benefits} = \frac{170000}{(1+i)} + \frac{160000}{(1+i)^2} + \frac{100000}{(1+i)^3} + \frac{75000}{(1+i)^4} + \frac{60000}{(1+i)^5} + \frac{60000}{(1+i)^6} + \frac{50000}{(1+i)^7}$$

$$= 5,09,915$$

Cost = 4,15,000

Benefit cost ratio = 1.23

As B/C ratio for project A > B/C ratio for project B, project A is selected.

Example 6.10 : Following data pertains to two projects. Rank the projects based on B/C ratio and NPV value. **[Dec. 11] [10]**

Particulars	Project X	Project Y
Investment in ₹	1,10,000	1,10,000
Cash inflow in ₹		
Year 1	31,000	71,000
Year 2	40,000	40,000
Year 3	50,000	40,000
Year 4	70,000	20,000
Interest Rate (%)	14	14

Solution : Considering the time value of money.

	Project X	**Project Y**
Benefit/ Cost ratio	Benefits $= \dfrac{31000}{1.14} + \dfrac{40000}{1.14^2} + \dfrac{50000}{1.14^3} + \dfrac{70000}{1.14^4}$ $= ₹\,1,33,165$ Cost $= ₹\,1,10,000$ $\therefore$ B/C ratio $= 1.21$	Benefits $= \dfrac{71000}{1.14} + \dfrac{40000}{1.14^2} + \dfrac{40000}{1.14^3} + \dfrac{20000}{1.14^4}$ $= ₹\,1,31,899$ Cost $= ₹\,1,10,000$ $\therefore$ B/C ratio $= 1.2$
Rank	$\therefore$ I	II
NPV	NPV $= 1,33,165 - 1,10,000$ $= ₹\,23,165$	NPV $= 1,31,899 - 1,10,000$ $= ₹\,21,899$
Rank	$\therefore$ I	II

Example 6.11 : Following data pertains to two projects A and B. Suggest which one is to be selected based on :

   (i) NPV @ 10% interest

  (ii) IRR   **[Dec. 11] [12]**

Particulars	Project A	Project B
Initial investment (₹)	4,00,000	3,50,000
Annual Income (₹)		
Year 1	1,50,000	1,00,000
Year 2	2,00,000	3,00,000
Year 3	80,000	50,000
Year 4	1,00,000	90,000
Year 5	20,000	60,000

Solution :

	Project A	**Project B**
NPV	NPV $= \dfrac{150000}{1.1} + \dfrac{200000}{1.1^2} + \dfrac{80000}{1.1^3} + \dfrac{100000}{1.1^4} + \dfrac{20000}{1.1^5} - 4,00,000$ $= ₹\,42,477$	NPV $= \dfrac{100000}{1.1} + \dfrac{300000}{1.1^2} + \dfrac{50000}{1.1^3} + \dfrac{90000}{1.1^4} + \dfrac{60000}{1.1^5} - 3,50,000$ $= ₹\,1,25,135$

...Cont.

		Select Project B.	
IRR	$IRR = \dfrac{150000}{(1+i)} + \dfrac{200000}{(1+i)^2} + \dfrac{80000}{(1+i)^3}$ $+ \dfrac{100000}{(1+i)^4} + \dfrac{20000}{(1+i)^5}$ $- 4,00,000$ $= 0$ Using trial and error method find i. IRR = 15.18%		$IRR = \dfrac{100000}{(1+i)} + \dfrac{300000}{(1+i)^2} + \dfrac{50000}{(1+i)^3}$ $+ \dfrac{90000}{(1+i)^4} + \dfrac{60000}{(1+i)^5} - 3,50,000$ $= 0$ Using trial and error method find i. IRR = 25.66%
		Select Project B.	

Example 6.12 : The following are the details of a project A and B. **[Dec. 12] [10]**
Suggest which one is to be accepted by using

  (i) NPV

  (ii) BCR [i = 8%]

Years	Project A	Project B
0	4,00,000	4,50,000
1	1,20,000	1,40,000
2	1,25,000	1,45,000
3	78,000	76,000
4	80,000	65,000
5	75,000	60,000
6	–	90,000

Solution : NPV for Project A

$$\dfrac{120000}{1.08} + \dfrac{125000}{1.08^2} + \dfrac{78000}{1.08^3} + \dfrac{80000}{1.08^4} + \dfrac{75000}{1.08^5} - 4,00,000$$

= – 9956.5

NPV for Project B

$$\dfrac{140000}{1.08} + \dfrac{145000}{1.08^2} + \dfrac{76000}{1.08^3} + \dfrac{65000}{1.08^4} + \dfrac{60000}{1.08^5} + \dfrac{90000}{1.08^6} - 4,50,000$$

= ₹ 9602

∴ Choose Project B

Benefit Cost Ratio:

For Project B : $\dfrac{459602}{450000} = 1.02$

For Project A : $\dfrac{390044}{400000} = 0.975$

∴ Select Project B.

IMPORTANT POINTS

- Project appraisal in construction and its various criteria :
  (a) Social appraisal
  (b) Environmental appraisal
  (c) Technical appraisal
  (d) Financial appraisal
  (e) Economical appraisal
- Different steps involved in technical appraisal.
- Difference between financial and economical analysis.
- Concept of annuity and features of annuities.
- Four different types of annuities.
- Concept of capital, types of capital viz.
  (a) Fixed capital
  (b) Working capital
- Methods of capital budgeting :
  (a) Traditional methods with its types
  (b) Discounted cash flow method with its types
- Steps involved in evaluating capital budgeting, characteristics of capital budgeting and kinds of capital budgeting.

UNIVERSITY QUESTIONS

1. Explain Cost Benefit Analysis. **[May 07] [5]**
2. State the steps taken before making decisions. **[Dec. 07] [4]**
3. "Economics is the study of flow of finance". Justify. **[Dec. 07] [6]**
4. State the various types of costs involved in construction projects. Discuss with sketches, the variation of these costs with respect to time. **[Dec. 09] [5]**
5. Explain with neat sketch "Break-even Analysis". **[6]**
6. Explain different types of taxes related to Machinery and material. **[May 10] [6]**
7. Define Project. What are the requirements of a project for its successful completion ? **[May 11] [8]**
8. What are the methods of Project Appraisal ? **[Dec. 11] [6]**
9. State the advantages of N.P.V. method over I.R.R. method. **[May 12] [4]**
10. Explain the principles of Break-Even Analysis. **[Dec. 12] [4]**
11. Explain the role of Project Management consultant at
    (i) Pre tender stage (ii) Post tender stage.
12. Write detailed note on Break Even Points analysis. **[May 11] [6]**
13. Define "Break-Even analysis". Explain the principles and uses of Break-Even Analysis. **[May 12] [2 + 4]**

University Question Papers

May 2011

SECTION – I

1. (a) Write a note on Gantt Chart and its limitations. [5]
   (b) Explain with sketch Matrix Organisation structure. [5]
   (c) Write in brief about the concept of Delegation of Authority. [4]
   (d) Define : to, tm, tp, te, Slack. [4]

   OR

2. (a) A school building project consists of 12 activities. The duration of the activities and their relationship is as under : [18]

Activity	Predecessor	Duration (Days)
A	-	7
B	-	5
C	A	10
D	A	5
E	B	8
F	B	6
G	C	5
H	C	4
I	D & E	10
J	F	5
K	G	8
L	H	9

   Draw a CPM network and calculate project duration and highlight the critical path. Calculate EST, EFT, LST, LFT, TF, FF, INDF, INTF for all the activities.

3. Following table shows the cost duration data for a construction project. Carry out step by step crashing.

   Indirect cost may be taken as ₹ 300/- day.

Activity	Normal Duration (Days)	Normal Cost (₹)	Crash Duration (Days)	Crash Cost (₹)
1-2	6	700	3	1450
1-3	8	400	5	850
2-3	4	600	1	900
2-4	5	800	3	1500
3-4	5	500	3	1100
4-5	2	500	1	400

   (i) Draw a network and highlight the critical path. [4]

(ii) Calculate normal project duration and cost of the project. **[2]**
(iii) Calculate optimum project duration and optimum cost of the project. **[10]**
(iv) Also give all crash solution.

OR

4. The requirement of manpower for ABC construction company is as under :

Activity	Duration (Days)	Men Required Per Day
1-2	7	10
2-3	7	5
2-4	8	10
2-5	7	6
3-5	12	4
4-5	8	10
5-6	9	4

(a) Draw a network and calculate project duration. Show critical path by heavy ruling line. **[6]**
(b) Draw EST squared network, prepare histogram and calculate EFR and IFR. **[5]**
(c) Draw LST squared network, prepare histogram and calculate EFR and IFR. **[5]**

5. (a) Write detailed note on Break Even Point Analysis. **[6]**
(b) Explain the following concepts : Inventory, Lead time, Buffer stock, Stock out, Ordering cost, Inventory carrying cost. **[6]**
(c) A construction company requires 1500 door frames per year. Cost of each door frame is ₹ 1800 per frame. Ordering cost is ₹ 2,000 per order and holding cost is 18%. Calcualte EOQ. **[4]**

OR

6. (a) Perform ABC Analysis for the following data : **[12]**

Sr. No.	Item	Annual Expenditure (₹)
1.	Cement	4,90,000
2.	Tiles	90,000
3.	Bricks	95,000
4.	Sand	2,60,000
5.	Steel	1,20,000
6.	Oil	2,000
7.	Timber	30,000
8.	Nails	3,000
9.	Dry Distemper	15,000

Categorise the above items and plot ABC curve.
(b) Enlist any four functions of materials management and explain inventory control. **[4]**

SECTION – II

7. (a) Give the details of layout for the site you have visited. Mention the stage of work, approximate dimensions of the site, flow of vehicles, flow of materials, labour camp etc. on it. Write the salient features of the site. Also mention your observations. **[8]**

(b) Define Injury Frequency Rate and Injury Severity Rate. **[4]**

(c) As a project manager on site, mention the safety precautions you will take for the labours working at height. **[6]**

OR

8. (a) For the site you have visited, write a report on the safety policy adopted on site. Mention the safety gadgets used. **[6]**

(b) What are the common accidents that may take place at the time of excavation? Write the measures to be taken on site to avoid them. **[6]**

(c) What is the importance of site layout? What are the important points to be followed while planning the site layout? **[6]**

9. (a) Define Economics. State its importance from Civil Engineering point of view. **[8]**

(b) Explain the term Utility. With the help of example, state the law of Diminishing Marginal Utility. **[8] OR**

10. (a) State the Demand and Supply curve with the help of an example. **[8]**

(b) What are the types of demands? Explain them in short. **[8]**

11. (a) Define Project. What are the requirements of a project for its successful completion? **[8]**

(b) Find IRR for the project with the following details: **[8]**

 (i) Duration of project – 5 years.

 (ii) Initial investment – ₹ 10,000/-

 (iii) Periodic return – ₹ 5,000 per year. **OR**

12. (a) What is Cash Flow Diagram? Explain various terms used in it with the help of neat diagram. Draw cash flow diagrams for recurring deposit scheme and housing loan.

[8]

(b) Write short notes on any two of following: **[8]**

 (i) Time value of money.

 (ii) Annuity.

 (iii) Net present value.

PROJECT MGT. & ENGG. ECO. (TE CIVIL SEM. II – PU) UNIVERSITY QUESTION PAPERS

May 2013

SECTION – I

1.
(a) Write a note on project categories. [4]
(b) What do you understand by delegation of authority ? [4]
(c) Explain merits and demerits of Gantt chart. [6]
(d) Define Activity, event and critical event, critical path. [4]

OR

2. Listed below are the activities of a project along their durations.

Activity	1-2	2-3	2-4	2-5	3-10	4-6	4-7	5-10	6-8	7-8	8-9	9-10
Duration (Days)	4	5	7	4	15	7	Dummy	10	6	7	12	10

(i) Draw AOA network and calculate the total project duration. Highlight the critical path. [6]
(ii) Calculate EST, EFT, LST, LFT, Total float, Free float and independent float. Write in tabular form with sample calculation. [12]

3.
(a) Define cost slope and what do you understand by crashing of network ? [4]
(b) Following table shows the cost duration data for a small construction project. Carry out step by step crashing and how much you save crashing network. Indirect cost may be taken as Rs. 300 week.

Activity →		1-2	2-3	2-4	3-5	4-5	5-6
Normal →	Cost	4000	2000	5500	200	2200	4000
	Duration (weeks)	3	6	5	7	4	8
Crash →	Cost	4200	4800	6400	1200	2600	4200
	Duration (weeks)	1	2	2	3	2	4

OR

4. (a) Following table shows the data of small construction project. [16]
(i) Draw the network diagram and update the network by using the following conditions at the end of 10 days.
(ii) What is the change in the project duration ?

Activity	1-2	2-3	2-4	3-5	4-5	5-6	5-7	6-7
Duration (days)	4	6	5	2	1	4	6	6

At the end of 10 days review was taken which indicates :
(a) Actviity1-2 and 2-4 was completed as originally planned.
(b) Activity 2-3 and 3-5 delayed drastically and requires 5 and 6 more days respectively for their completion.
(c) Activity 4-5 and 5-6 is in progress and both require 8 more days for their completion.

(d) Activity 6-7 yet to start and the original time estimate still appear to be accurate.
(e) Activity 5-7 requires 8 days in place of 6 days for its completion.

5. (a) What are the functions of material manager? [4]
(b) Explain the costs associated to inventory problem. [4]
(c) Define (i) Safety stock, (ii) lead time. [2]
(d) Derive expression for EOQ. [6]

OR

6. (a) What are the assumptions made in EOQ. [4]
(b) Segregate the items as per their annual usage and plot ABC curve. [12]

Sr. No.	Item	Annual Usage (Rs.)
1	Cement	170000
2	Sand	41000
3	Wash Basin	65000
4	Steel	155000
5	Aggregate (12 mm)	130000
6	Aggregate (19 mm)	110000
7	Nails	2200
8	Oil	2800
9	Water	1500
10	Grease	1200

SECTION – II

7. (a) What are the points to be considered while preparing the layout? [6]
(b) Write a safety program to be undertaken while working on highway construction. [4]
(c) Draw a site layout for multi-storeyed residential project. [6]

OR

8. (a) What are the various causes of accidents on any building construction site? [6]
(b) How to judge nature and extent of accident? [4]
(c) Draw a site layout of a project you have visited. [6]

9. (a) Explain with one example 'Law of diminishing marginal utility'. [6]
(b) Write a note on :
(i) Demand curve, (ii) Supply curve. [6]
(c) Explain the following terms with suitable examples. [6]
(i) Law of substitution, (ii) Elasticity of demand.

OR

10. (a) What are the income effect, price effect and substitution effect. [6]
(b) Define Engineering Economics. Explain its importance in Civil Engineering. [6]
(c) Explain in brief elasticity of demand. [6]

11. (a) Write a short note on any TWO : [8]
      (i) Annuity.
      (ii) Break even analysis
      (iii) Working capital.
   (b) What do you understand by NPV method ? State the project is feasible or not by NPV method if project cost is Rs. 200000 has cash flow of Rs. 30000 for a period 5 years. Firm expects return at 10% per annum.

OR

12. (a) Write a short note on any FOUR : [16]
      (i) Cash flow diagram.
      (ii) Payback period.
      (iii) Benefit cost ratio.
      (iv) ARR method.
      (v) IRR method.

December 2013

SECTION – I

1. (a) What are the factors affecting on the outcome of any project ? [6]
   (b) What is updating ? When it is required to update the network ? [4]
   (c) Explain with sketch line and staff type of organisation. [4]
   (d) Differentiate between C.P.M. and P.E.R.T. [4]

OR

2. (a) For the work consisting following six activities as shown in table below, work out critical path and days for completion of the work. [6]
   (b) Categorically work out three different floats (TF, FF, IF) and tabulate them. [12]

Activity (i – j)	A	B	C	D	E	F
Activities immediately preceding	None	None	A	A, B	B, C, D	A, D
Activities immediately	C, D, F	D, E	E	E, F	None	None
Duration (Days)	5	3	4	3	2	4

3. (a) What different expenditures can come under direct and indirect cost ? Discuss their relationship with time using graphs. [6]
   (b) Define cost slope with help of graph. [2]
   (c) For the work consisting four activities with given data in table underneath, find out
      (i) normal project period and costs,
      (ii) project cost if project period is to be crashed for two day,
      (iii) Draw CPM and time grid diag for both stages. [8]

Activity	Normal Time (Days)	Normal Cost (Rs.)	Crash Time (Days)	Crash Cost (Rs.)
1-2	4	4,000/-	2	4,200/-
2-3	5	3,000/-	3	7,500/-
2-4	7	3,600/-	2	6,000/-
3-4	4	5,000/-	2	10,000/-

OR

4. Explain the following (Any FOUR) : [16]
   (i) All crash solutions will be uneconomical.
   (ii) Resource smoothening and leveling.
   (iii) PERT analysis.
   (iv) Negative slack and negative float.
   (v) Gantt chart fails in case of large construction project.

5. (a) What are the functions of Material Manager ? [4]
   (b) What are the assumptions made in EOQ ? [4]
   (c) Define safety stock and lead time. Explain factors affecting on it. [6]
   (d) Define EOQ with the help of example. [2]

OR

6. (a) Define inventory. Explain the costs associated with inventory problems with sketch. [6]
   (b) Segregate the items as per their annual usage and plot ABC curve. [10]

Sr. No.	Item	Annual Usage (Rs.)
1	Cemetn	3,00,000
2	Bricks	2,00,000
3	Sand	1,80,000
4	Steel	2,55,000
5	Aggregate (12 mm)	1,40,000
6	Aggregate (19 mm)	1,20,000
7	Nails	3,000
8	Tiles	1,00,000
9	Water	4,000
10	Distemper	5,000

SECTION – II

7. (a) what is site layout ? Explain factors affecting on it. [6]
   (b) What are the personal protective devices used on construction site ? [4]
   (c) Write safety policy's adopted at tunnel construction project. [6]

OR

8. (a) As a Project Manager, list out the safety precautions and personal protective equipment's that you will observe at construction of high rise building. [6]
   (b) "Safety is important but somewhat neglected on construction site" comment. [4]

(c) Define :
(i) I.S.R.
(ii) I.F.R. and
(iii) Injury index. [6]

9. (a) Explain "Law of diminishing marginal utility', with an example. [6]
(b) Explain –
(i) Law of substitution,
(ii) Elasticity of demand. [6]
(c) Write on importance of Economics in Civil Engineering construction industry. [6]

OR

10. (a) Explain with the help of example cost, price and value. [6]
(b) Differentiate between NPV and IRR method. [6]
(c) Explain in brief demand and supply curve. [6]

11. (a) Write a short note on any two : [8]
(i) Annuity and its types.
(ii) Cash flow and its types.
(iii) Capital and types.
(b) What are the different methods of project appraisal ? Explain social and Environmental type of appraisal. [8]

OR

12. (a) List out the different methods used for project selection. Explain any one method. [4]
(b) Following data pertains to two projects A and B. Suggest which one is to be selected ? Consider expected return of 10%. [4]

Particulars	Project A	Project B
Estimated Cost (Rs.)	4,25,000	5,00,000
Estiamted Life (years)	6	6
Annual Income (Rs.)		
Year 1	2,00,000	2,25,000
2	1,75,000	2,00,000
3	1,45,000	1,80,000
4	95,000	1,50,000
5	70,000	1,00,000
6	50,000	80,000

(c) Explain the following with help of suitable example. [8]
(i) Time value of money,
(ii) Benefit cost analysis.

PROJECT MGT. & ENGG. ECO. (TE CIVIL SEM. II – PU) UNIVERSITY QUESTION PAPERS

May 2014

SECTION – I

1. (a) Define organisation and explain the organisation structure mostly suited for construction industry. [4]
   (b) Differentiate between AOA and AON method with help of suitable example. [4]
   (c) The data pertains to small construction firm are as follows : [10]
   (i) Construct the network diagram. (ii) Find expected duration and variance, (iii) What is the probability of completing the project on or before 20 weeks ? Take Probability 93.3 for Z = 1.5 and Probability 94./5 for Z = 1.6, (iv) If the probability of completing project is 0.8, find the expected project completion time. Take Z = –2.4 for probability 0.8.

Activity	A	B	C	D	E	F	G	H
Immed. Predecessors	None	None	A	B	B	C, D	C, D, E	F
a, (weeks)	1	2	6	1	1	1	1	1
m, (weeks)	2	2	7	2	4	5	2	2
b, (weeks)	3	8	8	3	7	9	3	9

2. (a) State the equations showing the relationship between various activity times and floats. [4]
   (b) Listed below are the activities of a project along their durations. [14]

Activity (i – j)	A	B	C	D	E	F	G	H	I	J
Immediately Preceding	None	A	A	A	D	D	E, F	G	C, H	B
Duration (Months)	1	4	2	2	1	3	2	1	3	2

   (i) Draw AOA network and calculate the total project duration. Highlight the critical path.
   (ii) Calculate EST, EFT, LST, LFT find out TF, FF, IF. Write in tabular form with sample calculation.

3. (a) What is Updating of Network ? Explain its necessity. [4]
   (b) The data related to small constructions project is as under [12]

Activity	1-2	2-3	2-4	3-4	4-5	4-6	5-6	5-7	6-7
Normal Time	9	17	10	11	8	8	9	15	10
Minimum Time	7	14	9	8	8	7	9	12	9
Increase in cost for each day less (₹)	10	40	30	20	–	10	–	60	40

   (i) Draw the network diagram and determine minimum normal time for completion of project.
   (ii) Determine minimum crash time for completion of project and additional minimum cost to achieve it.
   (iii) Determine optimum crash time for completion of project and additional minimum cost to achieve it.

OR

4. Consider the project scheduling problem as shown in the following table. **[16]**

Activity	Duration (Weeks)	Mason Requirement
1-2	4	9
1-3	8	5
2-3	10	7
2-4	6	6
3-4	4	8
4-5	2	7

(i) Schedule the activities of the project with maximum limit on man power requirement as 14.
(ii) What would be the increase in project duration?
(iii) Draw histogram and find out EFR before and after levelling.

5. (a) If your are the head of store department How can you purchase and store the material? **[4]**

(b) Define the term EOQ with sketch. "Surya Agrotech, Mayani" monthly demands 1000 bags of Urea. The unit cost of a bag is ₹ 200/- and inventory carrying cost per unit per annum is 20% of average inventory cost. If the cost of procurement is ₹ 70/- determine:
(i) EOQ
(ii) No. order per annum
(iii) Total cost of purchasing. **[8]**

(c) Define safety stock and lead time. Explain factors affecting on it. **[4]**

OR

6. (a) Define inventory. Explain the costs associated with inventory problems with sketch. **[6]**

(b) "Sakshi general stores" carries inventory of 10 items based on the price and usage. Determine which item should be categorized as A, B and C. Plot A-B-C curve. **[10]**

Items	1	2	3	4	5	6	7	8	9	10
Price (₹)	70	45	400	200	40	0.50	18	2.5	5.5	350
Annual Consumption	320	380	500	800	350	4000	200	1600	1000	400

SECTION – II

7. (a) Define site layout. Which factors will you consider in deciding the layout of a typical construction site? **[6]**

(b) On a particular construction project, the contractor on an average employed 100 workers with 60 horus per week. The project lasted for 40 weeks and during this period, 15 disabling injuries occurred. Work out I.F.R. if number of days lost due to injuries is 25 days, work out also I.S.R. and injury index. **[6]**

(c) What are the personal protective devices used on construction site? **[4]**

OR

8. (a) What are the various causes of accidents that may take place during tunnelling operation ? Write down safety measures to avoid it. **[6]**

(b) '"Safety is important but somewhat neglected on construction site", comment. **[4]**

(c) Define : (i) I.S.R., (ii) I.F.R. and (iii) Injury Index.

9. (a) Explain "Law of diminishing marginal utility" and "law of substitution" with an example. **[4]**

(b) Define the following terms with neat sketch w.r.t. break even analysis : **[6]**
   (i) Fixed cost   (ii) Variable cost
   (iii) Total Sales   (iv) Total cost
   (v) Break-even point   (vi) MOS

(c) "Baramati Agro" produces 10,000 units and sells them at ₹ 90/- each. The variable cost per unit is ₹ 20/- and fixed cost amounted to ₹ 3 lakh. Calculate breakeven point in units and sales by graphical representation method. And also calculate margin of safety showing angle of incidence. **[6]**

OR

10. (a) Draw cash flow diagram of equal payment capital recovery amount also state the formula for capital recovery factor. **[8]**

"Mansi Earth Movers" took a loan to purchase an excavator of ₹ 20 lakh at an interest rate of 18% compounded annually. This amount should be repaid in 10 years in equal installments. Find the instalment amount that "Mansi Earth Movers' has to pay to the bank.

(b) Define Engineering Economics. Explain its importance in construction industry. **[4]**

(c) Explain demand and supply curve with suitable sketch. **[4]**

11. (a) Mrs. Shubhangi invests sum of ₹ 50,000 in a bank at nominal interest rate of 18% for 15 years. The compounding is monthly. Find maturity amount after 15 years. **[4]**

(b) Define the terms goods, wants, cost, price, value, capital. **[6]**

(c) Following data pertains to Projects A and B has the net cash flows as follows. Which project is to be selected by using NPV and B/C ratio method ? Consider rate of interest i =10%. **[8]**

Proposal	Initial Investment	End of Years Annual Income (₹)			
		1	2	3	4
A	1,00,000	32,000	76,000	34,000	28,000
B	1,00,000	30,500	25,000	45,000	80,000

OR

12. (a) Mr. Hrishi invests Rs. 10,000 in a bank at nominal interest I = 15% for 12 years. The compounding is quarterly find maturity amount after 12 years. [4]
    (b) What do you mean of project appraisal ? Explain methods of project appraisal. [8]
    (c) The data pertaining to two projects A and B as given below. Suggest which one is to be accepted using NPV method ? Company expects a return of 10%. [6]

Project	Initial Investment (₹)	Annual Benefits (₹)		
		1st year	2nd year	3rd year
A	50,000	35,000	15,000	18,000
B	40,000	23,400	20,600	11,000

November 2014

SECTION – I

1. (a) Define following terms with help of example, associated with network analysis (any 4). [8]
      (i) Event   (ii) Activity
      (iii) Dummy activity (iv) Critical path
      (v) Float.
   (b) Draw network diagram by using the following data. [5]
      (i) Activity A, B, C are starting activity
      (ii) Activity D follows activity C
      (iii) Activity A precedes follows activity F
      (iv) Activity E follows act B and C
      (v) Activity G follows activities E
      (vi) Activity G is terminal activity,
   (c) What do you understand by Gantt chart ? What are its limitations ? [6]

OR

2. (a) Write down advantages of networking methods over bar chart method. [4]
   (b) Define three time estimates used in PERT analysis. How expected duration is found out ? Explain with example. [5]
   (c) PERT calculations yield a project length of 50 weeks with a variance of 16. Within how many weeks would you expect the project to be completed with a probability, of
      (i) 95%. (ii) 75%   (ii) 40%
      Given z values for 95% = + 1.65, 75% = + 0.69, 40% = – 0.25 [9]

3. Data pertains to small construction work is as follows :

Activity	Normal time (Days)	Crash time (Days)	Normal cost (Rs.)	Crash cost (Rs.)
1-2	4	3	3000	3400
2-3	7	5	5000	5200
2-4	5	3	4500	4700
3-5	6	4	4200	4800
4-5	2	1	3600	3900
5-6	3	2	1000	1200

(a) Draw the network diagram find out critical path and project duration. [6]
(b) Crash the network to optimum duration and what will be coat saving after crashing of network ? Assume indirect cost is ₹ 250/- day. [10]

OR

4. A project consists of the following activities with their durations in days.

Activity	10-20	10-30	10-40	20-50	30-60	40-50	40-60	40-70	50-70	60-70
Duration	6	3	4	0	4	12	10	8	5	6

(i) Draw network diagram find out critical path and project duration. [6]
(ii) Is their any change in project duration if following condition state at the end of 10 days.
(a) Activity 10-20, 10-30, 10-40 having completed as per schedule
(b) Activity 40-50, 40-60, 30-60 are in progress and will require 5, 6 mid 1 more days for its completion.
(v) Other activities have not started and their project duration holds good except for activity 50-70 which wilt require only 3 days, instead of 5 days planned originally. [10]

5. (a) What are the functions of material manager ? [4]
(b) What are the assumptions made in EOQ ? [4]
(c) Define safety stock and lead time. Explain factors affecting on it. [4]
(d) Monthly requirement of a cement for a firm 'Swami Samarth Group' is 2000 bags. The cost of a beg of cement is ₹ 300/-. ordering cost of ₹ 110/- per order and annual inventory carrying cost is 20% of average inventory. Find out EOQ. [4]

OR

6. (a) Define inventory. Explain the costs associated with inventory problem with sketch. [6]
(b) Explain method of selective inventory control with help of suitable example. [10]

SECTION -II

7. (a) What is site layout ? Explain factor affecting on it. [6]
(b) What are the personal protective devices used on construction site ? [4]
(c) Draw a site layout for the construction of earthen dam. [6]

OR

8. (a) What are various causes of accidents that may take place during concreting operation at higher level ? Write down safety measures to avoid it. **[6]**
(b) 'Safety is important but some what neglected on construction sine'. Comment. **[4]**
(c) Define : (i) I.S.R. (ii) I.F.R. (iii) Injury index. **[5]**

9. (a) Explain 'Law of diminishing marginal utility' with an example. **[6]**
(b) 'Soury Associates Mayanl' hasfollowing details fixed cost = 20 lakh, variable cost per unit - ₹ 1001- selling price per unit = ₹ 200. Find (i) The break even sales quantity (ii) Break even sales (iii) If the actual production quantity is 60,000 find contribution and margin of safety by all methods. **[12]**

OR

10. (a) Explain with the help of example cost, price and value. **[6]**
(b) Define Engg. economics. Explain its importance in civil Engineering. **[4]**
(c) What are the factors influencing on demand and supply ? Explain in brief demand and supply curve. **[8]**

11. (a) Investments in proposal 'A' and 'B' have the net cash flows as follows : **[8]**

Proposal	End of years				
	0	1	2	3	4
'A' (₹)	−10,000	3,000	3,000	7,000	6,000
'B' (₹)	−10,000	6,000	6,000	3,000	3,000

Compare the present worth of 'A' with that of 'B' at I = 18%. Which proposal should be selected ?

(b) What are the different methods of project appraisal ? Explain social and environmental type of appraisal. **[8]**

OR

12. (a) Draw cash flow diagram of equal payment series sinking fund' and state formula to get Annual amount (A) to be deposited to realize future sum (F). **[4]**
(b) A "Surya Construction Co. Ltd" expects returns of ₹ 5,00,000 after 5 years. It plans to deposit an equal amount at the end of every year at an interest rate of 8% compounded annually. Find the equivalent amount that must be deposited at the end of every year for next 5 years. **[4]**
(c) What are the methods of capital budgeting ? Explain any one method with suitable example ? **[8]**

www.ingramcontent.com/pod-product-compliance
Lightning Source LLC
Chambersburg PA
CBHW080422230426
43662CB00015B/2186